Atlas of Contemporary America

Atlas of Contemporary America

Portrait of a Nation

❏ Politics ❏
❏ Economy ❏
❏ Environment ❏
❏ Ethnic and Religious Diversity ❏
❏ Health Issues ❏
❏ Demographic Patterns ❏
❏ Quality of Life ❏
❏ Crime ❏
❏ Personal Freedoms ❏

RODGER DOYLE

☑
Facts On File®

AN INFOBASE HOLDINGS COMPANY

Atlas of Contemporary America: Portrait of a Nation—Politics, Economy, Environment, Ethnic and Religious Diversity, Health Issues, Demographic Patterns, Quality of Life, Crime, Personal Freedoms

Facts On File, Inc.
460 Park Avenue South
New York NY 10016

Library of Congress Cataloging-in-Publication Data
Doyle, Rodger Pirnie.
The atlas of contemporary America / Rodger Doyle.
p. cm.
Includes bibliographical references and index.
ISBN 0-8160-2545-2 (alk. paper)
1. United States—Maps. 2. United States—Economic
conditions—1981– 3. United States—Social conditions—1980– I. Title.
G1200.D6 1993 <G&M>
912.73—dc20   90-675147

Facts On File books are available at special discounts when purchased in bulk quantities for businesses, associations, institutions or sales promotions. Please call our Special Sales Department in New York at 212/683-2244 or 800/322-8755.

Text and jacket design by Catherine Rincon Hyman
Maps and layout by Sam Moore
Manufactured by Mandarin Offset
Printed in Hong Kong
10 9 8 7 6 5 4 3 2 1
This book is printed on acid-free paper.

For

Rodger, Jr.,

Tallmadge,

and Stephanie

Contents

Preface

Behind every news report are many facts and statistics that you don't hear about. Many are boring and irrelevant, but others are important and fascinating and can provide a deeper understanding of what is happening in America. Take, for example, the two-party system. A dull subject, you may think, but underneath the surface, something important is going on. For the surprising facts, look at Figures 4-1 and 4-2. Another dull subject, taxes, is always in the news, but here again, there are surprises little noticed by the media (see Figure 5-6).

A newspaper article might mention that some nuclear plants are less safe than others. Is one of the less safe near you? To find out, look at Figure 3-10. Again, a newspaper has a story about Americans of German or Italian descent, and you may wonder where such people are most likely to live. To find out, look at Figures 2-10 and 2-21. A TV newscaster may talk of housing segregation as if it were a national phenomenon. In fact, the degree of segregation in housing is highly regional, as Figures 7-8 to 7-11 show. You may hear a radio report about working mothers with young children. For the remarkable facts about these women, see Figure 1-7.

Maps provide a way of comparing some kinds of data to others. Examine, for example, the map on colon cancer (Figure 6-9), and then go to that on toxic waste dumps (Figure 3-6). You will see a striking similarity. Look closely at the other maps and you may find additional suggestive parallels.

The *Atlas of Contemporary America* supplies the all-important background to understanding what is happening in the United States—its politics, economy, quality of life, environmental problems, social problems, its ethnic, religious, and demographic divisions, and the health of its citizens. It shows which areas have the best air quality, the lowest crime rates, and the largest surplus of single men or single women. It tells you which states are hostile to abortion rights and which retain archaic sodomy laws on their books. It shows where social pressures against alcohol are lowest, where hate groups are most prevalent, and where middle-class people can still afford to buy a house. It provides an insight into the great liberal-conservative division in politics and into other less obvious ideological divisions. And it shows which areas are most likely to prosper during the 1990s.

THE SCOPE AND DESIGN OF THE ATLAS

In designing the *Atlas of Contemporary America*, I have tried to cover a wide variety of subjects under the seven chapter headings of "Demographic Patterns," "Ethnic, Linguistic, and Religious Divisions," "The Environment and Quality of Life," "Politics," "The Economy," "Health," and a grab bag of topics under the label of "Contentious Issues." The final selection of maps was based on the importance and timeliness of the particular subject.

The emphasis in this book is upon the domestic American scene, although several international problems that impinge upon domestic concerns are included under "Contentious Issues."

Some subjects of importance are not included because up-to-date information was not available at the time of publication, e.g., interracial marriages, reports of alleged child abuse, political corruption in state houses and city halls, the quality of public-school education, and incidents of discrimination in the workplace (although maps showing the proportion of management jobs held by women and minorities are included in the chapter on "Contentious Issues"). A map showing people of mixed racial heritage would have been interesting, but unfortunately the U.S. Bureau of the Census asks respondents to decide whether they are white, black, Chinese, American Indian, etc., with no place (at least no official place) to point out that he or she is both black and white with a touch of Sioux, or half-Swedish-Norwegian-American and half-Vietnamese, with a strain of Chinese going back to a great-grandmother.

In designing the maps, the guiding principle has been simplicity. Most are based on the *choropleth* design, in which data are ranked from highest to lowest and then divided into several ranges, with each range being represented by a different color. For example, Figure 1-1 shows the number of people per square mile by county, according to the 1990 Census, in four ranges: fewer than 10, 10 to 999, 1,000 to 9,999, and 10,000 or more.

A few of the maps follow the *isopleth* design, in which contour lines indicate the boundaries of values. For example, the lines in Figure 3-12 indicate the average tornado frequency, with the darkest colored areas being those with 9 or more tornadoes annually per 10,000 square miles, the next darkest being those with 7 to 8.9 per 10,000 square miles, and so on.

In constructing the maps, I have used county data wherever practical, since they bring out regional patterns better than do state or metropolitan area data.

A WORD ABOUT DATA SOURCES

More than a third of the maps are based on tabulations of 1990 U.S. Census data specially prepared for use in this atlas. The term "census" implies that everyone is counted, and indeed this is the aim of the U.S. Bureau of the Census in its decennial counts. However, some people, such as illegal aliens, members of minority groups, the homeless, and the rootless, tend to be undercounted. Estimates from the Bureau of the Census put the overall coverage at about 98 percent, with coverage of blacks estimated at 94 to 96 percent, that of Hispanics and Native Americans at 95 percent, and that of Asian-Americans at 98 percent. Coverage of non-Hispanic white Americans is about 99 percent. The Census also undercounts men more than women, and, in addition, its method of questioning produces a bias in the data for certain ancestry groups. However, none of these flaws grossly distorts the maps. Where flaws in the data are pertinent to the interpretation of a map, they are noted.

Some questions in the decennial census are asked only of 17 percent of the population. For example, the ancestry data used in preparing the maps of Chapter 2 are based on the 17 percent sample data. (The data on race and Hispanic origin are based on the full count.) Data gathered in the 17 percent sample are no less reliable for the purposes of the maps than data gathered in the full sample. Appendix A shows the questionnaire used by the Census in 1990 for both the full count and the 17 percent sample.

The U.S. Census of Population unfortunately does not gather information on religion, and so cannot provide statistics on the location of Irish Protestants or the ethnic and racial profile of fundamentalist church members or of the unchurched. However, the Glenmary Research Center of Atlanta, Georgia, conducts a decennial survey of church organizations, which are asked to supply data on the number of their adherents. The Glenmary census, which is used as the basis for several maps in Chapter 2, is timed to coincide with the U.S. decennial census. Some church groups, particularly those that are large and well established, keep excellent records. Others do not mandate regular reporting on membership and so are less apt to provide complete information. Some denominations report only the number of members with full membership status, excluding from their

1990 Population of the United States
(Height of States Is Proportional to Population)

FIG. A

Connecticut, Delaware, Kansas, Oklahoma, New Hampshire, and Vermont are completely obscured by neighboring states.

The 75 Largest Metropolitan Areas in 1990*

*Includes 20 consolidated metropolitan statistical areas with their 71 component primary areas and an additional 55 metropolitan statistical areas with population of 485,000 or more. The names of some metropolitan areas are omitted.

count members' children and participants who are not confirmed, baptized, or eligible for communion. The Glenmary Research Center attempts to estimate total adherents for these denominations. Of the 246 denominations asked to participate in the Glenmary study, only 133—mostly the larger denominations—actually participated. These 133 denominations, however, account for over 90 percent of all church adherents in the United States.

More than a score of the maps are based on votes by U.S. representatives and senators as tabulated by the *Congressional Record* or by Americans for Democratic Action, a Washington-based liberal advocacy organization. (Similar tabulations are provided by the American Conservative Union and, if substituted, would have caused little change in the patterns as shown on the maps.) The congressional maps do not show the names of representatives and senators, but by referring to Appendix B, you can see how they voted.

The maps in Chapter 6 showing mortality data are based on tabulations from the National Center for Health Statistics, which releases raw data with a lag of two to three years. These raw data are then age-adjusted and mapped by epidemiologists, a process that takes several more years. Although these mortality maps are dated, they are still useful as indicators of the current situation, because geographical mortality patterns, at least for the diseases shown in this atlas, do not change suddenly over time.

Several maps suffer from a lack of complete data. This is probably true of the one showing covert attempts by the U.S. government to overthrow third-world regimes (Figure 7-50), which was pieced together from publicly available information. I suspect that several additional countries will have to be added when and if the federal government fully declassifies its covert activities in the Cold War era. Other maps, such as those showing schoolbook censorship (Figure 7-21) and anti-Semitic crimes (Figure 7-17), may also suffer from underreporting.

Some map viewers may unconsciously fall into the trap of equating real estate with importance. Wyoming, for example, which covers 13 times as much territory as New Jersey, has only one-seventeenth the number of people. The cartogram in Figure A will help the reader visualize the importance of the 50 states in terms of population.

In looking at some of the maps, it is helpful to know the location of metropolitan areas. Figure B shows the location of the 75 largest areas according to the 1990 Census.

For those who want more information, I have given the sources for each map. Those who want a nongeographical insight into the subjects of the maps should look at the Bibliography, which lists those publications that were most useful in designing this atlas. Those interested in the craft of mapmaking will find Judith Tyner's *Introduction to Thematic Cartography* (Prentice Hall, 1992) of value.

1

Demographic Patterns

Population Density

According to the 1990 census, there are 70.3 people per square mile in the United States, the most densely populated state being New Jersey with 1,042, followed by Rhode Island with 960. The least densely populated state is Alaska, with 1.0 people per square mile. The most densely populated counties are New York County (Manhattan), with 52,419 people per square mile; Kings County, New York (Brooklyn), with 32,619; Bronx County, New York, with 28,641; Queens County, New York, with 17,839; and San Francisco County, California, with 15,502.

Number of People Per Square Mile by County, 1990

FIG. 1–1

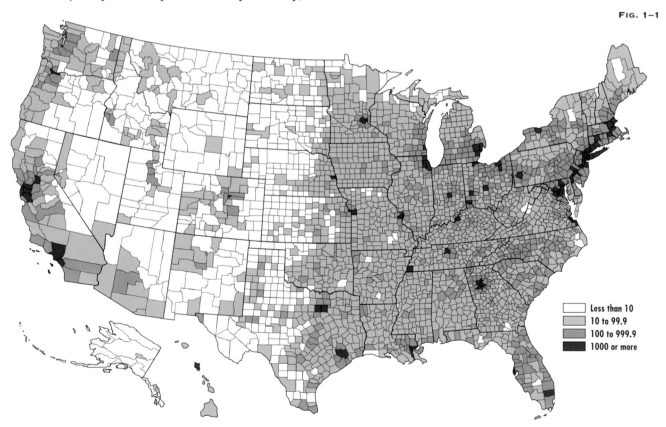

Less than 10
10 to 99.9
100 to 999.9
1000 or more

Percent Change in Population, 1980 to 1990, by County

FIG. 1–2

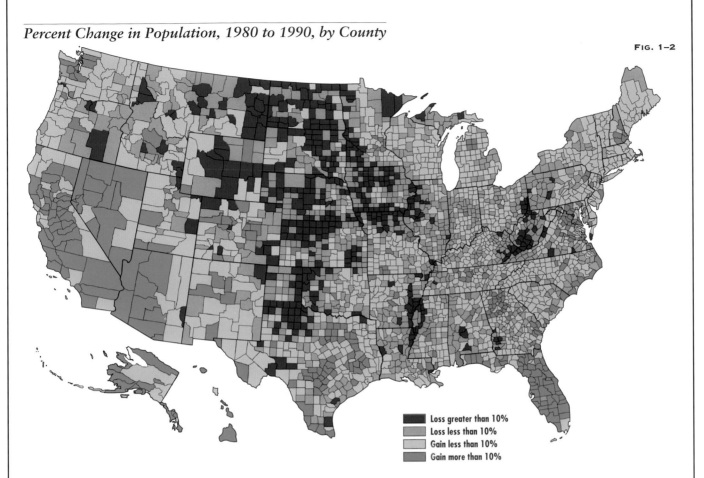

- ■ Loss greater than 10%
- ■ Loss less than 10%
- ■ Gain less than 10%
- ■ Gain more than 10%

The 1980s, like prior decades, was a time of massive population shifts. The big winners were California, which gained 6.1 million people, equivalent to the population of Massachusetts; Florida, which gained 3.2 million, equivalent to the population of Oklahoma; and Texas, which gained 2.8 million, equivalent to the population of Iowa. These three states accounted for more than half the population gain of the entire United States in the 1980s. Four states—Iowa, North Dakota, West Virginia, and Wyoming—lost population from 1980 to 1990.

According to the U.S. Census Bureau, the center of population is that place on "an imaginary, flat, weightless, and rigid map of the United States [that] would balance perfectly if all 248,709,873 residents were of identical weight." Since 1910, the center of population of the United States has shifted toward the Southwest. As of April 1, 1990, the center was in a heavily wooded area near Steelville, Missouri, which is approximately 75 miles southwest of St. Louis.

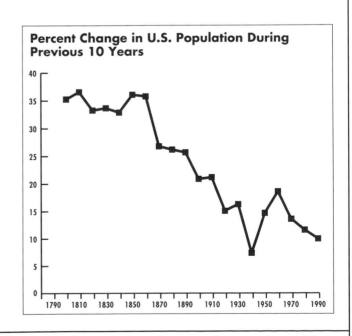

Percent Change in U.S. Population During Previous 10 Years

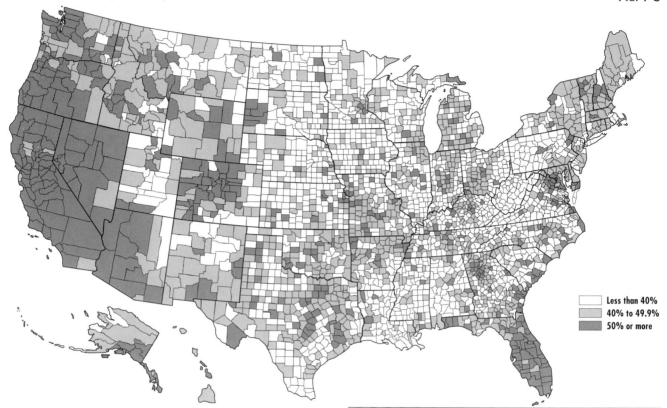

Percent of People 5 Years and Over Who Moved to a Different House in 1985–1990, by County

FIG. 1–3

	Less than 40%
	40% to 49.9%
	50% or more

T he average American occupies 12 or 13 homes in the course of a lifetime, roughly twice as many as the average person in France or Britain, and four times as many as the typical Irish person.

Why are Americans so mobile? One reason is the U.S. divorce rate, which is among the highest in the world. Also, economic opportunity is more dispersed geographically in the United States than in many other countries, where the locus of economic, political, and cultural life may be a single big city. Alexis de Tocqueville observed in 1835 that the absence of rigid class distinctions in America, which gave the average man greater opportunity than he would have had in Europe, also produced in him "anxiety, fear, and regret," and led him "perpetually to change his plans and his abode."

As the map shows, people in the western states and Florida are considerably more mobile than their countrymen elsewhere. This is due in part to the rela-

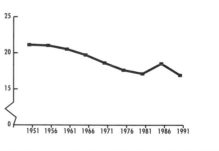

Percent of People Who Moved to a Different House in a Twelve-Month Period

tively high divorce rate in the West and in Florida and in part to the booming economy in much of the Sunbelt in the late 1980s, which lured many people from other areas. An influx of long-distance migrants eventually leads to an increase in short-distance moving: Long-distance migrants tend to move yet again, locally, when they become more familiar with their new place of residence.

Where Young and Old Are Most Numerous

Number of People

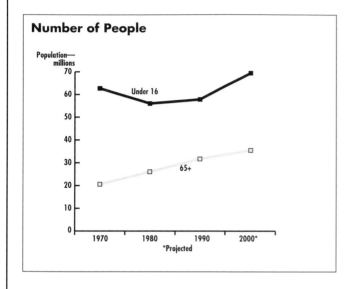

The Plains states have a higher proportion of elderly people because young job seekers tend to leave this area. Florida is a magnet for the retired. Those under 16 tend to be relatively more numerous in Alaska, the Mountain states, areas with a large Mexican-American population, and parts of the Mississippi River delta region. Counties with a high proportion of people under 16 tend to be those with the highest fertility rate. Arlington County, Virginia (suburban Washington), has the lowest proportion of people under 16 (8 percent), while the Wade Hampton Census Area in Alaska has the highest (42 percent). The lowest proportion of those 65 and over is in the Aleutian West Census Area of Alaska (0.9 percent), while the highest proportion is in Llano County, Texas (34 percent).

Counties with Highest Proportion of Young and Old People, 1990

FIG. 1–4

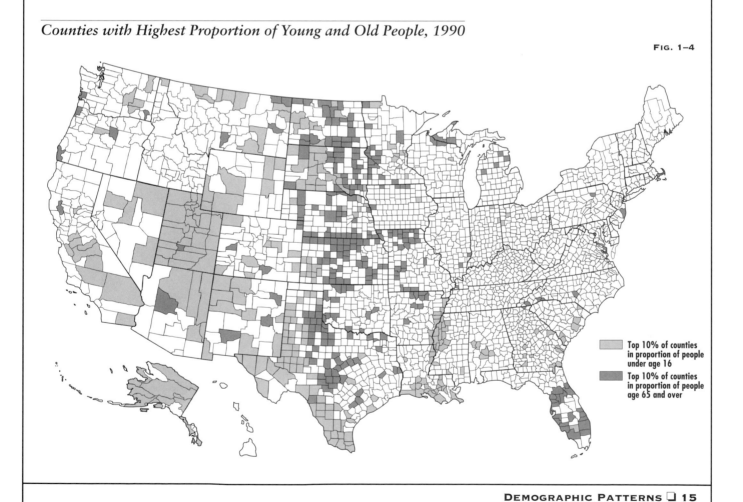

Top 10% of counties in proportion of people under age 16

Top 10% of counties in proportion of people age 65 and over

Two-Parent Families with Children

In 1960 there were about 23.8 million married couples with children under 18, but in 1989 there were only 24.7 million, despite an increase of 62 percent in the number of women of childbearing age. Areas where traditional values are held in high esteem, such as Utah and the Hispanic areas of southern Texas, have a high proportion of two-parent families with children. Some areas, such as the Mississippi River delta region, where a large number of families are headed by women, have a low proportion of two-parent families. Other areas, such as Florida, have a low proportion of two-parent families because the population is elderly (see Figure 1-4).

Chattahoochee County, Georgia, has the highest proportion of two-parent families with children (73 percent of all families), while Charlotte County, Florida, has the lowest (21 percent).

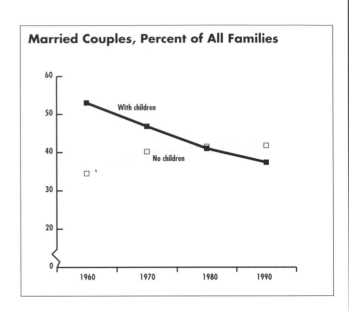

Married Couples, Percent of All Families

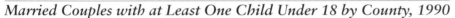

Married Couples with at Least One Child Under 18 by County, 1990

FIG. 1–5

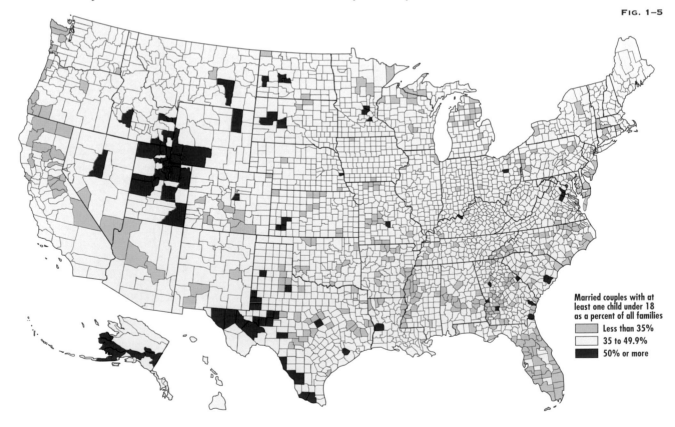

Married couples with at least one child under 18 as a percent of all families

- Less than 35%
- 35 to 49.9%
- 50% or more

Families Headed by Women by County, 1990

FIG. 1–6

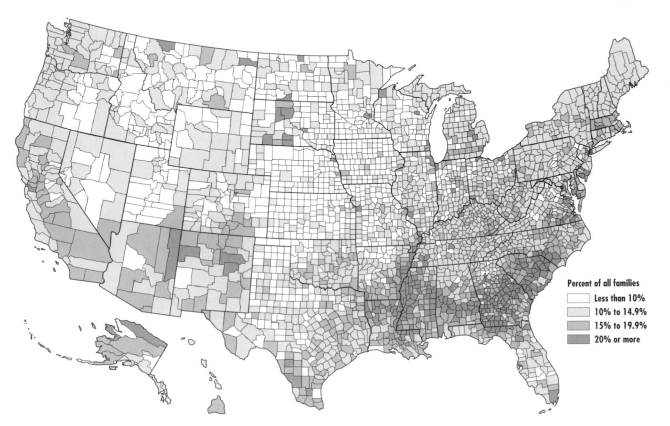

Percent of all families
- Less than 10%
- 10% to 14.9%
- 15% to 19.9%
- 20% or more

In the early 1990s more than one out of six families was headed by a woman. Roughly one-third of these were single, one-third divorced or separated, and one-third widowed. Two-thirds had children under 18. Woman-headed families accounted for four out of 10 poor people in the United States and more than half the poor children. About 45 percent of all black families are headed by women, compared to about 15 percent of white families and 25 percent of Hispanic families. More than half of all female-headed families are white. The concentration of female-headed families in the Southeast reflects the large black population in that area. According to the 1990 U.S. Census, Bronx County, New York, had the highest proportion of families headed by women (41 percent), and Loving County, Texas, the lowest (0 percent).

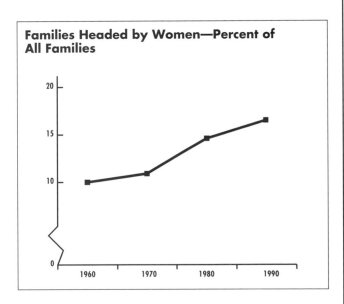

Families Headed by Women—Percent of All Families

Working Mothers

In the early 1990s about six out of 10 mothers of children under six years of age were employed. The concentration of these working mothers in certain areas of the Southeast probably reflects the traditional employment of women in the textile and other manu-

Women 16 and Over with Children Under 6—Percent Employed by County, 1990

FIG. 1–7

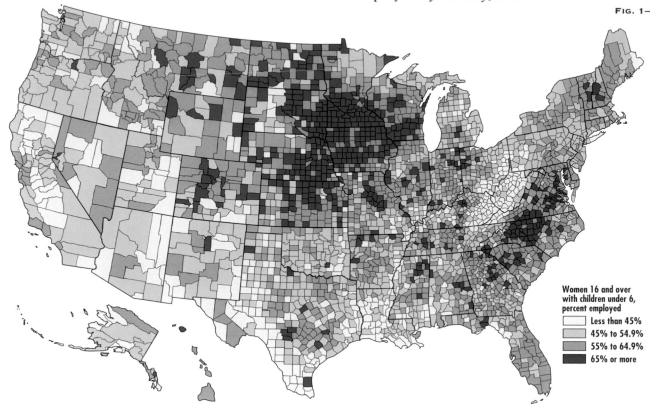

Women 16 and over with children under 6, percent employed

- [ ] Less than 45%
- [ ] 45% to 54.9%
- [ ] 55% to 64.9%
- [ ] 65% or more

facturing industries, which are important in cities like Danville, Virginia, and Lexington, North Carolina. The availability of good-paying factory jobs in this region may explain why so many mothers are attracted to working outside the home.

The high concentration of young working mothers in the West-Central states probably reflects the strong work ethic in rural areas and the large number of farm wives, who, even though they are not paid, are counted as employed. (The typical farm wife spends as much as 40 hours a week on such tasks as bookkeeping, picking up farm supplies, and milking cows.) The employment rate of mothers of young children tends to be low in areas with high rates of poverty and low educational attainment, such as Appalachia, parts of the Mississippi Delta, and the southern border counties of Texas. Most poor women with children have few marketable skills and therefore are more apt to stay out of the job market, particularly if working would result in loss of welfare benefits.

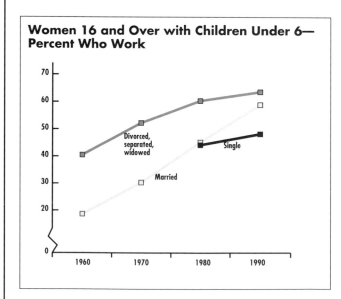

Women 16 and Over with Children Under 6—Percent Who Work

Divorced, separated, widowed

Single

Married

Fertility tends to be high in areas with large minority populations, such as the Mexican border region, certain parts of the Southeast, and in areas where traditional family values predominate, such as the upper Plains states and Utah. The total U.S. population continues to increase because of immigration, and because births still outnumber deaths by a wide margin. The highest number of children born to women 35 to 44 is found in Madison County, Idaho (4.3 average), and the lowest is in Arlington, Virginia, a suburb of Washington (1.0 average).

The number of very young children—under 5 years of age—reached a peak of more than 20 million in the 1960s and in 1989 stood at 18.8 million. The prospect is for a decline to about 16 to 17 million in the first decades of the 21st century.

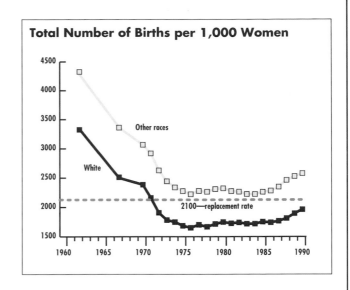

Total Number of Births per 1,000 Women

Average Number of Children Ever Born to Women Age 30 to 44 by County, 1990

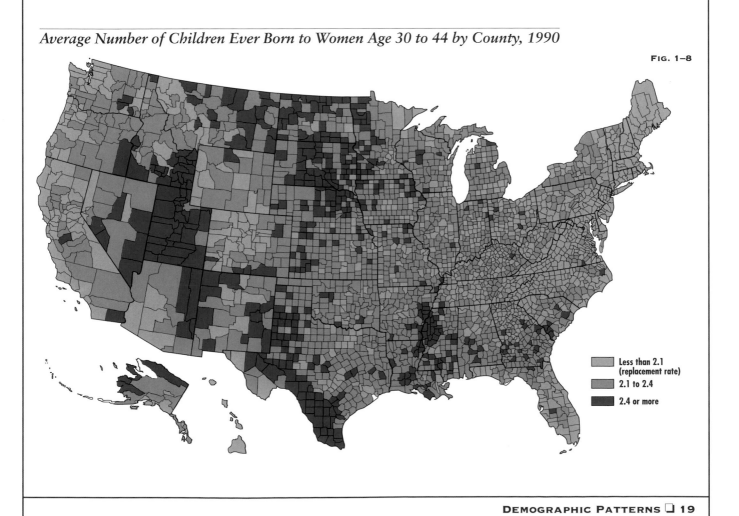

FIG. 1–8

Less than 2.1
(replacement rate)

2.1 to 2.4

2.4 or more

Divorce

America has the highest divorce rate among Western nations, and within America, the rates vary markedly by region for reasons that are not entirely clear. A clue to the regional variation may lie in church membership patterns. The proportion of Americans who are divorced tends to be low in areas where church membership is high, such as the upper Plains states, Utah, the Hispanic areas of Texas, and parts of the Southeast. Conversely, divorced people are more prevalent in areas such as the West Coast and in Ohio, Illinois, Michigan, and Florida, which have low church membership. (Compare Figure 1-9 to Figure 2-49, "Percent of Population Belonging to a Church.")

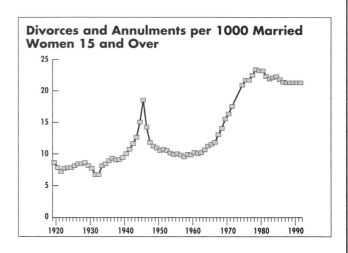

Divorces and Annulments per 1000 Married Women 15 and Over

Percent of People 15 and Over Divorced by County, 1990

FIG. 1–9

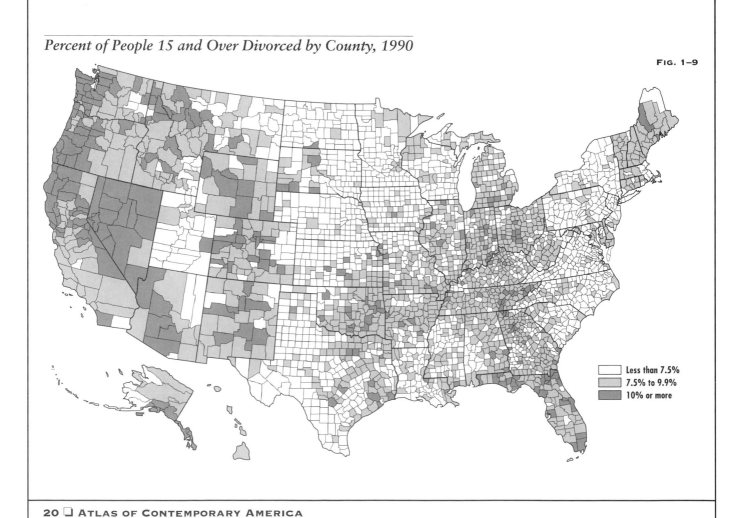

Less than 7.5%
7.5% to 9.9%
10% or more

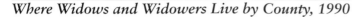

Where Widows and Widowers Live by County, 1990

FIG. 1–10

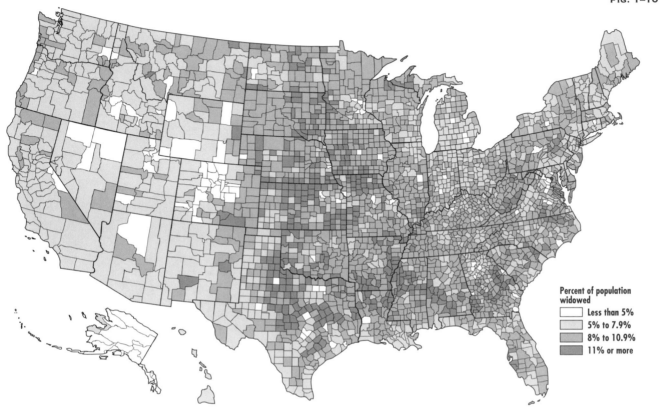

Percent of population
widowed
- Less than 5%
- 5% to 7.9%
- 8% to 10.9%
- 11% or more

In 1990 there were about 14 million widows and widowers in the United States, of which 83 percent were women. Seventy-two percent of all widowed people were 65 or over and 33 percent were 75 or over. The relative importance of the widowed population has declined in recent years, due in part to improved longevity of men, who have suffered progressively fewer deaths from cardiovascular disease. The lowest proportion of widows and widowers is found in the Aleutian West Census Area of Alaska (1.0 percent), and the highest in Worth County, Missouri (16.3 percent).

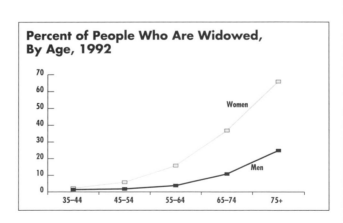

Percent of People Who Are Widowed, By Age, 1992

Shortages of Single Men and Women

Among single people in the 20 to 34 age group there are 119 men for every 100 women. This imbalance mainly reflects the tendency of women in this group to marry men 35 and over, but it also reflects the biological fact that males outnumber females at birth by about 5 percent. In the 35 to 44 age group, there are only 91 single men for every 100 single women, and in older groups the ratio declines still further: 73 among the 45 to 54 group; and 52 among the 55 to 64 group. In the older age groups the shortage of single men is due in part to their higher death rate. (The term "single" as used here includes not only those who have never married, but also those who are widowed, divorced, and separated.)

The wide differences among regions in the ratio of single men to single women in part reflect migration patterns, which tend to differ by sex. Men, for example, have been more apt in recent years to move from the South to the West than women. The shortage of single men in the Southeast reflects in part the extremely high mortality rate of black men. Note that there is some distortion in the maps because the Census undercounts men, and particularly black men, to a greater extent than it undercounts women. Thus, the

Counties with Shortages of Single Men or Single Women Age 20–34, 1990

FIG. 1–11

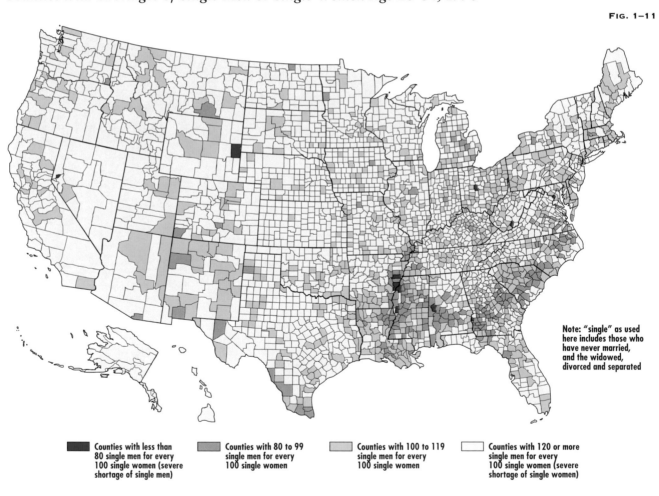

Note: "single" as used here includes those who have never married, and the widowed, divorced and separated

| Counties with less than 80 single men for every 100 single women (severe shortage of single men) | Counties with 80 to 99 single men for every 100 single women | Counties with 100 to 119 single men for every 100 single women | Counties with 120 or more single men for every 100 single women (severe shortage of single women) |

Counties with Shortages of Single Men or Single Women Age 35–44, 1990

FIG. 1–12

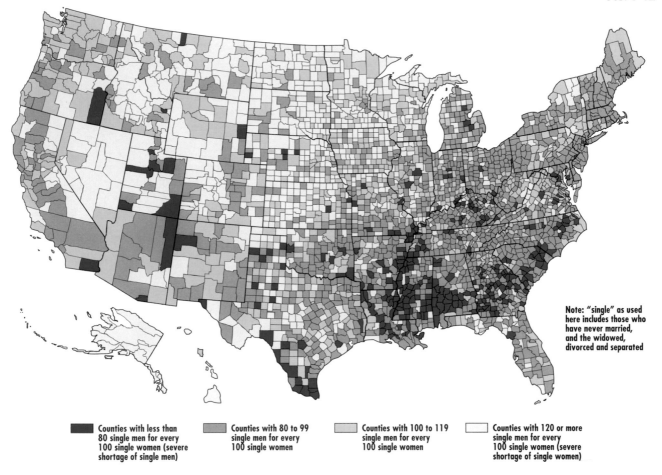

Note: "single" as used here includes those who have never married, and the widowed, divorced and separated

Counties with less than 80 single men for every 100 single women (severe shortage of single men)	Counties with 80 to 99 single men for every 100 single women
Counties with 100 to 119 single men for every 100 single women	Counties with 120 or more single men for every 100 single women (severe shortage of single women)

maps, especially in those areas with large black populations, such as the Mississippi River delta, tend to show a somewhat greater shortage of men than is actually the case. Despite this distortion, the maps provide a rough approximation of the true pattern.

In the 20 to 34 age groups, Alaska has the highest ratio of single men to single women (152 to 100), followed by Hawaii (142 to 100), North Dakota (139 to 100), Nevada (136 to 100), Idaho (135 to 100), California and Wyoming (both 133 to 100), and South Dakota (131 to 100). States with low ratios of single men to single women in the 20 to 34 age group are Mississippi (105 to 100), Louisiana (108 to 100), New York, Massachusetts, Maryland, Delaware, and Alabama (all 111 to 100), and Ohio and Michigan (both 112 to 100). The ratios for the 35 to 44 and older age groups follow much the same pattern.

People 35 and Over Who Have Never Married

People 35 and Over Who Have Never Married by County, 1990

FIG. 1–13

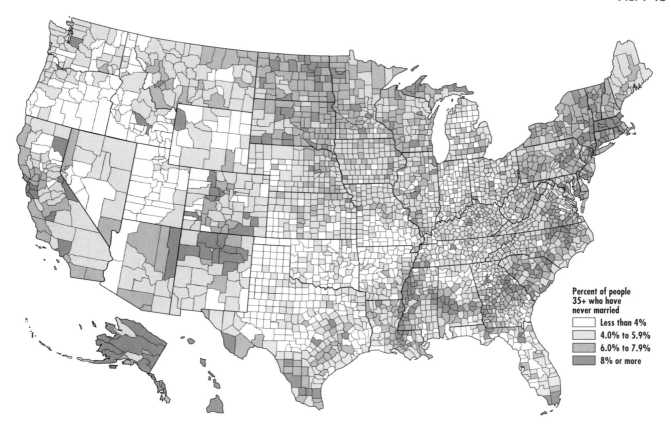

Percent of people 35+ who have never married
- Less than 4%
- 4.0% to 5.9%
- 6.0% to 7.9%
- 8% or more

About 9 million Americans 35 years of age and over have never married, and every year the number grows. In part, the trend reflects the growing number of college-educated women, who have traditionally married later than other American women, and are more likely never to marry at all. The high proportion of never-marrieds in New England and New York State, as well as in Chicago and the larger West Coast cities, reflects in part the concentration of female college graduates in these areas.

The places with the highest proportion of never-married people—20 percent or more—are Manhattan, Boston, the District of Columbia, and San Francisco, where the ranks of the never-married are augmented by large numbers of gays and lesbians and also of blacks.

About 15 percent of blacks over 34 have never married, versus 8 percent of whites. The low marriage

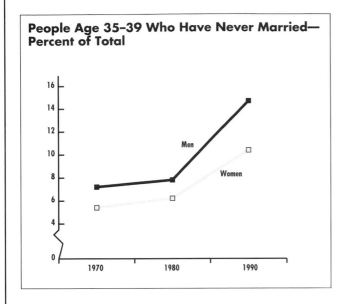

**People Age 35–39 Who Have Never Married—
Percent of Total**

16
14
12
10
8
6
4
0

Men

Women

1970   1980   1990

rate of blacks is related to the high rates of mortality and incarceration of black men and to the widespread inability of poor black men to find jobs that pay enough to support a stable family life. These factors contribute to the high proportion of never-marrieds in the predominantly black areas of the Mississippi River delta and the Southeast.

As for the clusters of never-marrieds in the upper North Central states, marriage prospects for the men of the region have been diminished by the flight of women to metropolitan areas to find service jobs. Marriage rates are similarly low in Alaska, as they have been since the influx of male oil-field workers in the 1960s.

Current estimates are that 10 percent of young men and women will never marry at all, but this is certainly not true of Utah, where Mormons have high marriage rates, nor is it true of the region stretching from northwest Texas through Oklahoma and northern Arkansas into southern Missouri. Like Utah, this is an area of conservative, church-going people who traditionally marry at an early age.

Of the 9 million people 35 or over who have never married, almost a fifth currently live with a member of the opposite sex.

College Graduates

In 1870 a little more than 9,000 Americans graduated from college. The number of graduates remained under 100,000 each year until the late 1920s, and under a million until 1990. As of 1990, about 22 percent of whites, 12 percent of blacks, and 10 percent of Hispanics were college graduates. As recently as 1950 male graduates outnumbered female graduates three to one; but the proportion of females increased, and by 1982, women outnumbered men on college campuses. Since then the proportion of women has increased. College graduates tend to concentrate in areas with better-paying jobs, such as the West and Northeast coasts. Areas with the highest concentration of college graduates are Los Alamos County, New Mexico, home of the Los Alamos National Laboratory (53 percent of those 25 and over), and the suburban Washington, D.C., counties of Arlington, Virginia (52 percent) and Montgomery, Maryland (50 percent).

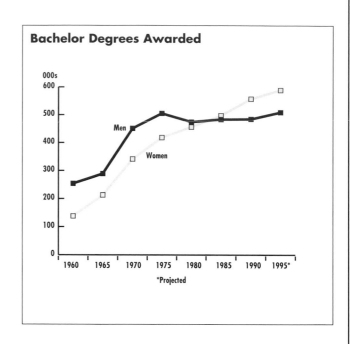

Bachelor Degrees Awarded

Percent of People 25 and Over With Bachelor Degrees by County, 1990

FIG. 1–14

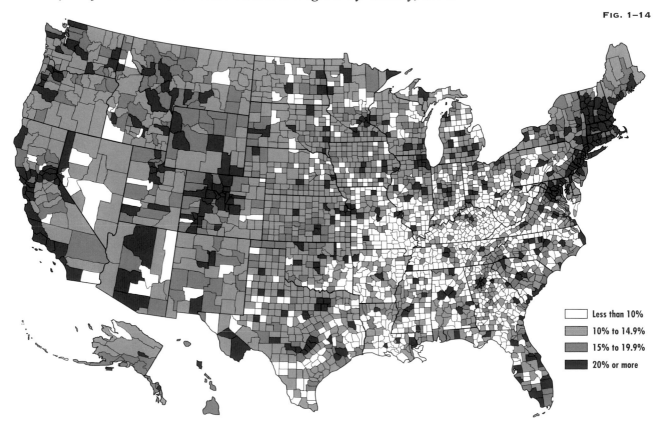

Less than 10%
10% to 14.9%
15% to 19.9%
20% or more

Percent of People 16 to 19 Not Enrolled in School and Not High School Graduates by County, 1990

FIG. 1–15

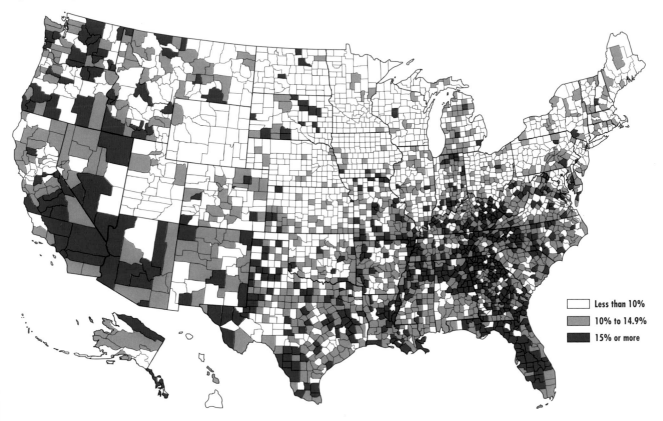

Less than 10%

10% to 14.9%

15% or more

The unemployment rate for high school dropouts in the early 1990s was more than twice that of high school graduates of the same age. Dropout rates for blacks are only slightly above those for whites, and both are much lower than those of Hispanics. The high dropout rates in the Southwest reflect in part the concentration of Hispanics in that region. The high rates in parts of the Southeast and Appalachia probably reflect the higher poverty level in the area. (The dropout rate in low-income families is 10 times that of high-income families.)

The highest proportion of dropouts is in Holmes County, Ohio, where 51 percent of those 16 to 19 are not enrolled in school and not high school graduates. Thirty-six counties, mostly in North Dakota, Montana, and Nebraska, have virtually no dropouts.

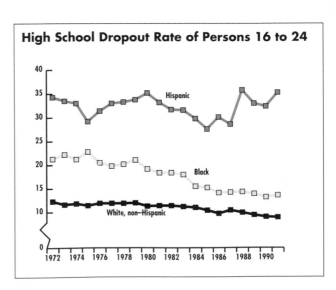

High School Dropout Rate of Persons 16 to 24

Hispanic

Black

White, non–Hispanic

2

Ethnic, Linguistic, and Religious Divisions

The 1990 Census found that 75.6 percent of Americans classified themselves as non-Hispanic white, 12.1 percent as black, 2.9 percent as Asian or Pacific Islanders, and 0.8 percent as Native American. Americans of Hispanic origin, who can be of any race, accounted for 9.0 percent. Fifty-two percent of Hispanics classify themselves as white.

Major Groups in the United States by County, 1990

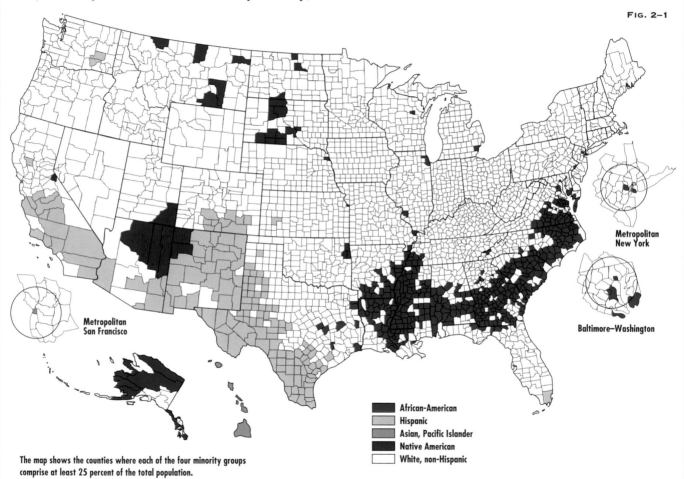

FIG. 2–1

Metropolitan New York

Baltimore–Washington

Metropolitan San Francisco

- ■ African-American
- ▨ Hispanic
- ▦ Asian, Pacific Islander
- ■ Native American
- ☐ White, non-Hispanic

The map shows the counties where each of the four minority groups comprise at least 25 percent of the total population.

*Most of the maps in this chapter are based on ancestry, race, and Hispanic origin data from the 1990 U.S. Census of Population. Respondents answered three sets of questions, one pertaining to ancestry, the second to race, and the third to Hispanic origin. In answering the ancestry question, respondents could list more than one group, for example, English and Irish, or French, German, and Scottish. In preparing the maps, the first ancestry listed has been used. In answering the question on race, respondents could choose only one category, such as white, black, Native American, Japanese, or Chinese. Similarly, in answering the question on Hispanic origin, respondents could choose only one category, such as Mexican or Cuban. Because of the differences in the way the ancestry and race/Hispanic origin questions were asked, these data are not strictly comparable with ancestry data.

Where Americans of English Ancestry Are Concentrated by County, 1990

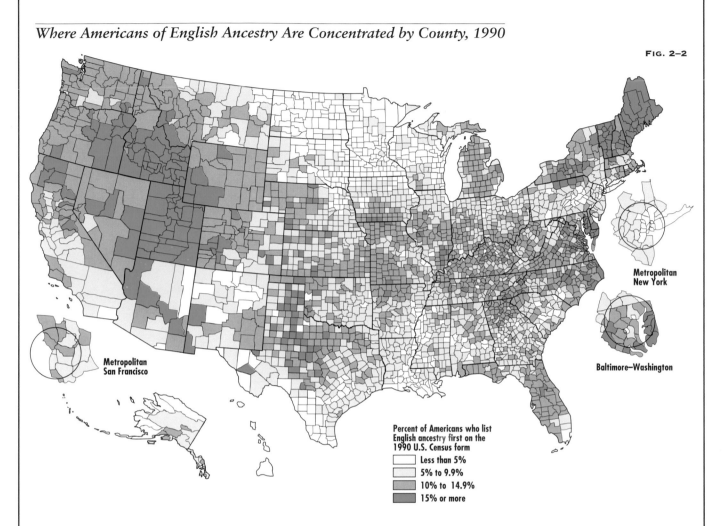

FIG. 2-2

Metropolitan New York

Metropolitan San Francisco

Baltimore–Washington

Percent of Americans who list English ancestry first on the 1990 U.S. Census form

- Less than 5%
- 5% to 9.9%
- 10% to 14.9%
- 15% or more

The early British colonists arrived in North America in four major waves. The first was in 1629-1640, when 20,000 or more English Puritans from East Anglia migrated to the Massachusetts Bay Colony. In the second wave, about 45,000 English cavaliers and their servants, from the south and west of England, colonized Virginia between 1642 and 1675. Next, about 23,000 English and Welsh Quakers from the North Midlands colonized the Delaware Valley in the years 1675-1715. The fourth wave came between 1717 and 1775, when about a quarter-million tenant farmers and impoverished artisans from northern England, Scotland, and Ulster migrated to the back country of Appalachia. Those from Ulster, the Scotch-Irish, are descendants of lowland Scottish Presbyterians who had migrated to

Ulster in Northern Ireland beginning in 1610. They did not, as their name might imply, intermarry with the native, Celtic Irish to any extent.

Subsequent waves of British immigration to America were much greater—more than 5 million came between 1820 and 1990—but it is the earlier immigrants who put their stamp on the country. Each of these four groups established a distinctive culture, traces of which persist to this day. Generally speaking, the Puritan and Quaker cultures encouraged a work ethic, the cavalier culture encouraged a leisure ethic, and the back-country culture encouraged a warrior ethic. In gender relations, the back-country settlers, and to a lesser extent the cavaliers, emphasized male dominance. The Puritans and the Quakers abhorred violence far more than the back-country folk.

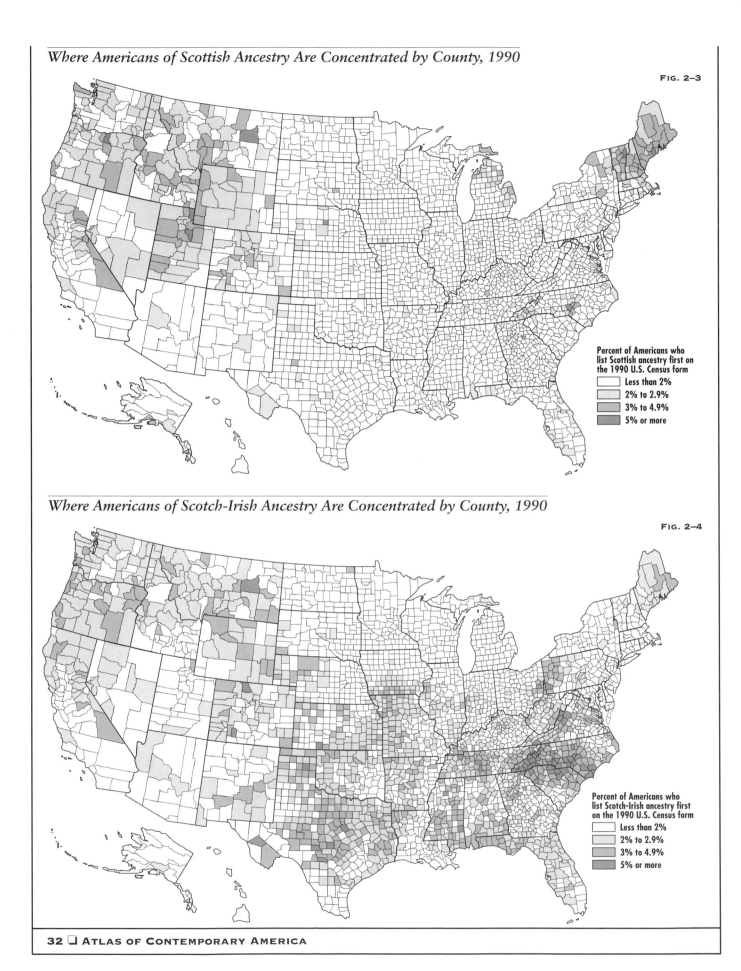

Where Americans of Scottish Ancestry Are Concentrated by County, 1990

FIG. 2–3

Percent of Americans who list Scottish ancestry first on the 1990 U.S. Census form

Less than 2%
2% to 2.9%
3% to 4.9%
5% or more

Where Americans of Scotch-Irish Ancestry Are Concentrated by County, 1990

FIG. 2–4

Percent of Americans who list Scotch-Irish ancestry first on the 1990 U.S. Census form

Less than 2%
2% to 2.9%
3% to 4.9%
5% or more

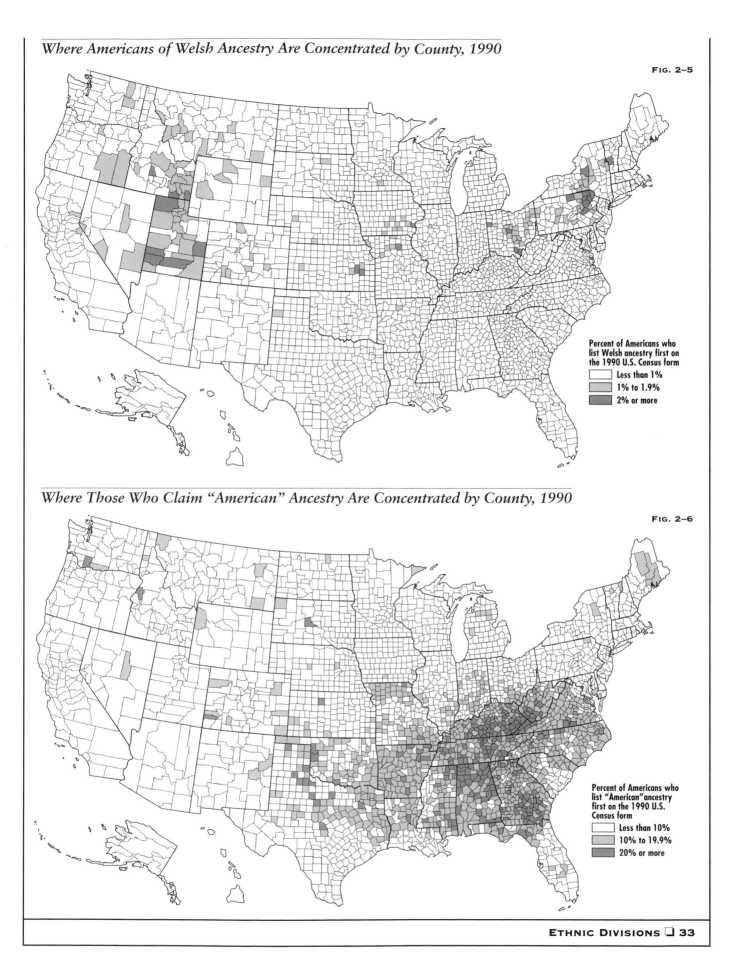

Where Americans of Welsh Ancestry Are Concentrated by County, 1990

FIG. 2–5

Percent of Americans who
list Welsh ancestry first on
the 1990 U.S. Census form

Less than 1%

1% to 1.9%

2% or more

Where Those Who Claim "American" Ancestry Are Concentrated by County, 1990

FIG. 2–6

Percent of Americans who
list "American" ancestry
first on the 1990 U.S.
Census form

Less than 10%

10% to 19.9%

20% or more

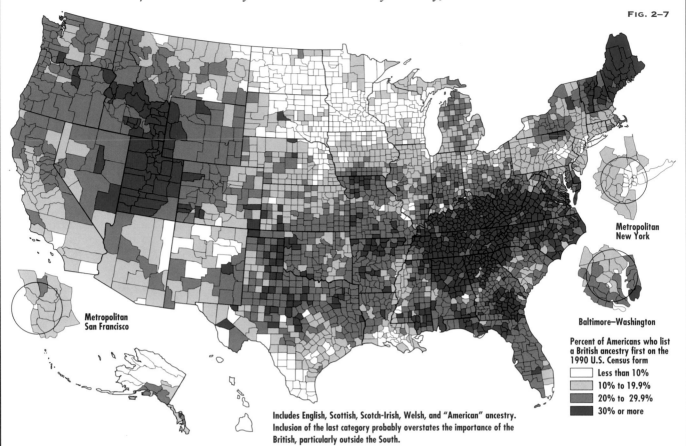

Metropolitan
New York

Metropolitan
San Francisco

Baltimore–Washington

Percent of Americans who list
a British ancestry first on the
1990 U.S. Census form

☐ Less than 10%
▨ 10% to 19.9%
▨ 20% to 29.9%
■ 30% or more

Includes English, Scottish, Scotch-Irish, Welsh, and "American" ancestry.
Inclusion of the last category probably overstates the importance of the
British, particularly outside the South.

The large patch of English ancestry in the West reflects the 1840s migration of the Mormons, who were predominantly of English descent.

Except for Martin Van Buren, Dwight Eisenhower, and John Kennedy, all American presidents have been of predominantly British ancestry. British-Americans imported or established most of the major Protestant denominations—Baptist, Presbyterian, Episcopal, Congregational, Methodist, Pentecostalist, and Mormon. They are the only ancestry group that is spread in force from coast to coast. And despite their relative decline, they are still the most powerful group—to judge by the prevalence of British surnames in Congress and on the Forbes list of the richest Americans.

Despite a large influx of non-English speakers, the British still predominated in 1790, when they accounted for more than 60 percent of the non-Indian population. The English accounted for 46 percent, Scots for 7 percent, Scotch-Irish for 5 percent, and Welsh for 3 percent. The 1990 Census showed only 18.4 percent who listed British ancestry first on the census form. English ancestry was listed by 13.1 percent, Scottish by 2.2 percent, Scotch-Irish by 2.3 per-

cent, and Welsh by 0.8 percent. In 1990, 32.7 million Americans listed English ancestry first on the Census form. The comparable figures for other groups are: Scotch-Irish, 5.6 million; Scottish, 5.4 million; and Welsh, 2.0 million. In addition, 1.1 million claimed British ancestry but did not specify a specific ancestry group. Finally, about 12.4 million listed their ancestry as "American," a category that is primarily of British origin. The map showing Americans of British descent (Figure 2-7) includes those claiming "American" ancestry, and therefore probably overstates the importance of the British.

The two leading ancestry groups in America are the British and the Germans, but because of the way the ancestry question was asked in the 1990 Census, it is not clear which group is larger. Differences between the number of British and Germans in the census should not be given undue weight.*

*In the 1990 Census question on ancestry, "German" was given as an example of the type of information requested, while English was not given as an example. As a consequence, "German" was probably listed first by many who would otherwise have placed it second or third.

Americans who claim Irish ancestry are generally descendants of Catholic immigrants from Southern Ireland or of Protestant immigrants from Northern Ireland. The latter are more or less the same as those who claim Scotch-Irish ancestry. More than half of all people who claim Irish ancestry are Protestant. Figure 2-8 shows those who list Irish ancestry, while Figure 2-9 shows those who list either Irish or Scotch-Irish ancestry.

Irish people immigrated to America in substantial numbers throughout the colonial period. Most were peasants and unskilled laborers, many of them indentured. According to one estimate, there were about 400,000 people of Irish descent in the United States in 1790, of which about half were from the southern counties and half from Ulster. Migration to the United States rose considerably from the late 1820s to the late 1840s, with sometimes as many as 50,000 coming in one year. But with the potato famine of the late 1840s, Irish arrivals in the United States grew dramatically, reaching a peak of 221,000 immigrants in 1851. In the period 1845–1851,

Where Americans of Irish Ancestry Are Concentrated by County, 1990

FIG. 2–8

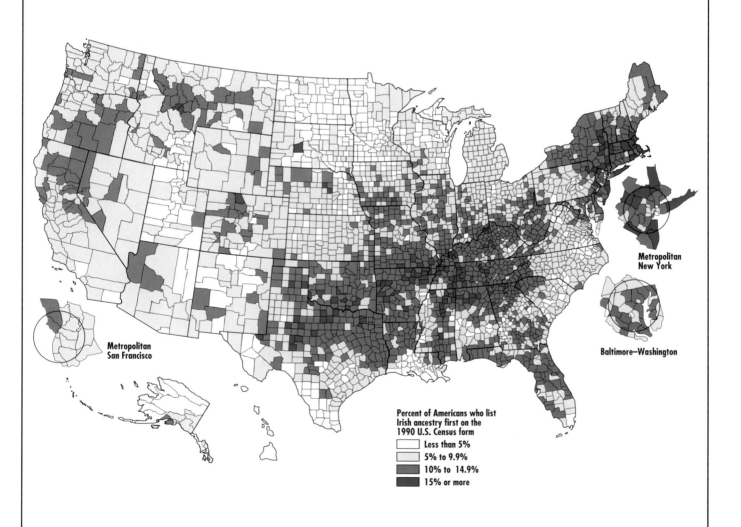

Metropolitan
New York

Metropolitan
San Francisco

Baltimore–Washington

Percent of Americans who list
Irish ancestry first on the
1990 U.S. Census form

Less than 5%
5% to 9.9%
10% to 14.9%
15% or more

Where Those of Either Irish or Scotch-Irish Ancestry Are Concentrated by County, 1990

FIG. 2–9

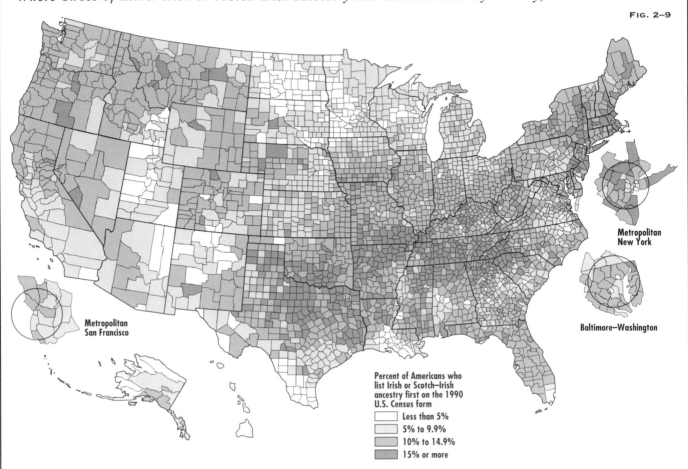

Metropolitan New York

Baltimore–Washington

Metropolitan San Francisco

Percent of Americans who list Irish or Scotch–Irish ancestry first on the 1990 U.S. Census form

☐ Less than 5%
☐ 5% to 9.9%
☐ 10% to 14.9%
☐ 15% or more

Ireland lost 2 million people, half through starvation and half through emigration. Irish immigration to the United States continued at a brisk pace until World War I. In the period 1820–1990, more than 4.7 million Irish entered the United States. The 1990 Census counted more than 38.7 million who listed Irish ancestry first on the census form, making this group the third-largest after the British and the Germans.

A few Germans came to America in the 17th century, but the first big wave began in the 1720s and continued up to the time of the American Revolution, with most settling in Pennsylvania, New Jersey, and New York. In 1790, Germans accounted for 7 percent of the total population of the United States, according to one estimate. A second and much larger wave of German migration started in the 1830s and continued until 1930. In all, almost 6 million came during this century-long period. About a third of German immigrants were Roman Catholic, and most of the balance were Lutheran, Reformed, Evangelical, or Jewish.

Today, Americans of German descent form a majority or a large minority of those living in a broad area stretching from eastern Pennsylvania to Montana—about one-third of the land area of the 48 contiguous states. Early in the 20th century, German culture vied with British culture in this area, so much so that there was even talk of a separate German national state. However, German-Americans as an ethnic community lost their cohesion as they became more affluent and as the second and third generations abandoned the German language. Ethnic German solidarity was given a severe blow in the hysteria of World War I and its aftermath, when

Where Americans of German Ancestry Are Concentrated by County, 1990

FIG. 2–10

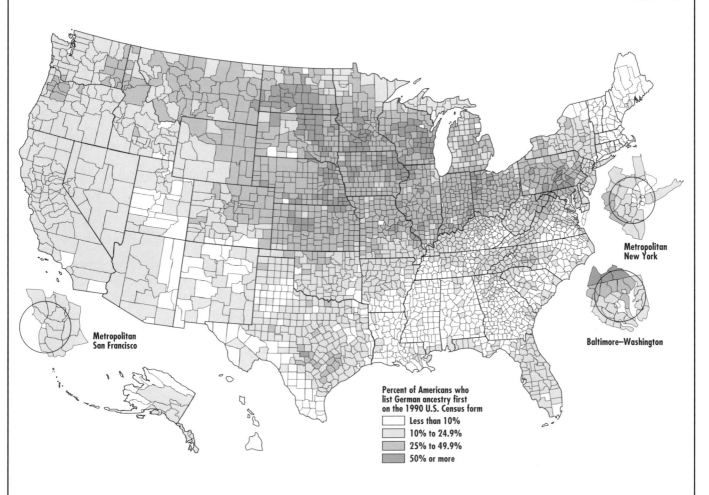

Metropolitan New York

Metropolitan San Francisco

Baltimore–Washington

Percent of Americans who list German ancestry first on the 1990 U.S. Census form

☐ Less than 10%
☐ 10% to 24.9%
☐ 25% to 49.9%
☐ 50% or more

Where Americans of Austrian and Swiss Ancestry Are Concentrated by County, 1990

FIG. 2-11

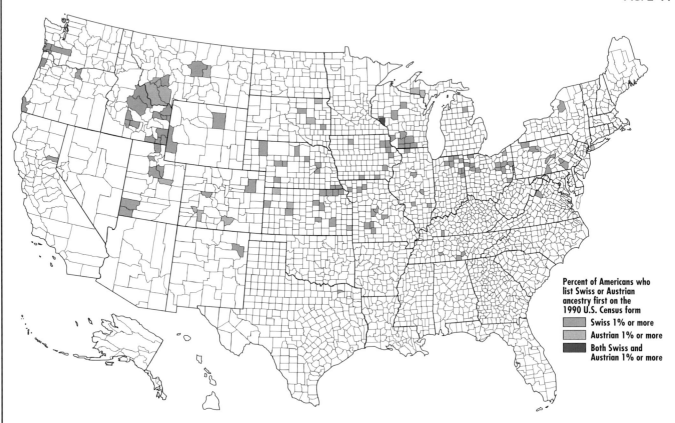

Percent of Americans who list Swiss or Austrian ancestry first on the 1990 U.S. Census form

█ Swiss 1% or more

█ Austrian 1% or more

█ Both Swiss and Austrian 1% or more

German-language newspapers, schools, and social organizations were closed or severely restricted.

Austrians were German-speakers who came from what is now the Austrian republic, which was established after World War I. In 1850 there were few Austrians in the United States, but by 1900 there were several hundred thousand, most of them peasants seeking greater economic opportunity. Most of these early migrants were Catholic and a minority were Lutheran. During the emigration of the 1930s, most Austrians coming to America were Jewish.

A few Swiss came to British North America before 1700, and by the time of the American Revolution 25,000 to 30,000 had arrived. Swiss immigration rose slowly in the 19th century, reaching a peak in the 1880s, and then declined until 1920. By 1990 more than 410,000 Swiss had entered the United States. Some of those who came in the colonial period were religious dissidents seeking a more tolerant atmosphere, such as the Mennonites and Swiss Amish, who settled in Pennsylvania. Many members of the Swiss Reformed Church, the dominant Protestant denomination, also came in the colonial period, attracted by the lure of rich farmland and freedom from taxes. Most Swiss immigrants were German-speaking.

The 1990 Census counted 58 million who listed German ancestry first on the census form, 0.9 million who listed Austrian ancestry first, and 1 million who listed Swiss ancestry first.

Figure 2-12 shows the concentration of Americans who list any French ancestors, including those from France, the French colonies, and Canada. Although those of French-Canadian stock may differ considerably in cultural terms from those with roots in France, they are combined in the map because, in answering the census question, many apparently did not distinguish between Canadian and continental French origin.

The first substantial movement of French people to what is now the United States came in 1685, when Louis XIV revoked the Edict of Nantes (which had protected the religious and civil rights of French Protestants), forcing tens of thousands of Huguenots to emigrate. The Huguenots, who were mostly tradesmen and artisans, settled in urban areas from Massachusetts to South Carolina. They were Calvinist, but the majority converted to the Anglican Church during the colonial period. The French Revolution produced a migration of more than 10,000 refugees to America, including many Catholic priests. Thousands of French Jews came to the United States after the fall of France in 1940. In between these traumatic events that propelled so many in France out of their homeland, there was a more or less steady stream of French migrants to America. Unlike French-speaking immigrants from Canada, those who came directly from France were rarely

Where Americans of French and French-Canadian Ancestry Are Concentrated by County, 1990

FIG. 2-12

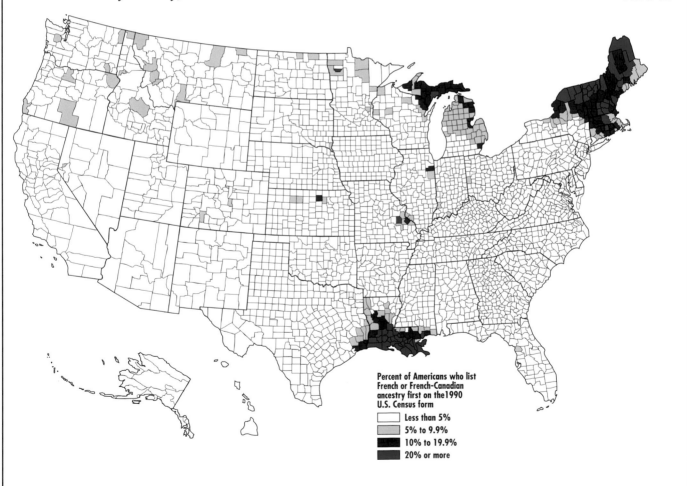

Percent of Americans who list French or French-Canadian ancestry first on the1990 U.S. Census form

- Less than 5%
- 5% to 9.9%
- 10% to 19.9%
- 20% or more

peasants, but mostly middle-class and usually well-educated.

In 1755 the British, for reasons that are not clear, forced 6,000 French-speaking Catholics, or Acadians, out of their homes in the Maritime Provinces of Canada. The Acadians were dispersed to other parts of the British Empire and to France, but many eventually found their way to Louisiana, then a French colony, where their descendants are called Cajuns. Louisiana was ceded to Spain in 1762, but a sympathetic Spanish administration encouraged Acadian settlement. Acadians maintained their devotion to the French language and to the Catholic Church. This, together with their life in isolated farming communities and their reluctance to intermarry with non-Cajuns, delayed their assimilation into the dominant Protestant culture. Indeed, it was not until the early 20th century that Cajun culture began to change,

when industrial jobs lured many away from the farms, and roads linked their isolated settlements to the outside world.

Some Acadians went to northern Maine in the mid-18th century, but the principal migration of French-Canadians to Maine (and other parts of New England) originated in Quebec and occurred mainly in the last half of the 19th century. They came to work in a variety of industries, including the textile mills of New England and the copper mines of Michigan.

In the past four centuries perhaps as many as 800,000 French people, excluding French-Canadians, immigrated to America. The 1790 U.S. Census counted about 50,000 people of French ancestry, while the 1990 Census counted 12.5 million who listed French ancestry first on the census form, including 2.8 million who listed French-Canadian ancestry first.

Where Americans of Dutch Ancestry Are Concentrated by County, 1990

FIG. 2–13

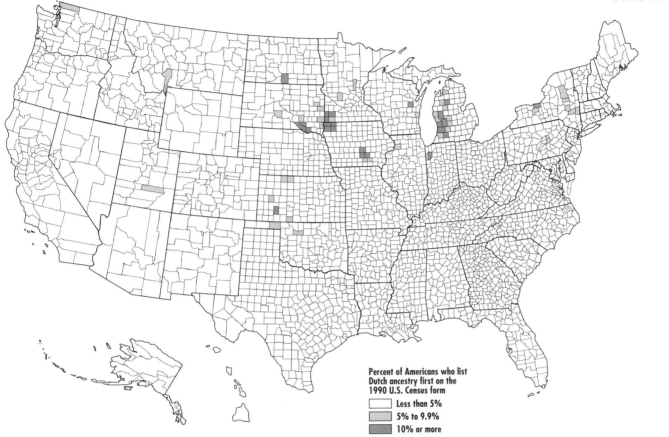

Percent of Americans who list Dutch ancestry first on the 1990 U.S. Census form

☐ Less than 5%
▨ 5% to 9.9%
■ 10% or more

The first Dutch settlement in America was Fort Nassau, near present-day Albany, New York, in 1614. New Amsterdam (now Manhattan) was founded in 1626, and Dutch settlers soon spread out along the Hudson and Delaware rivers. At the time of the English conquest in 1664, the population of the Dutch-held territory amounted to less than 10,000, of which 70 percent were Dutch. The first U.S. Census, in 1790, counted about 100,000 people of Dutch ancestry, 70 percent of them living within 50 miles of New York City. The first mass immigration of Dutch came in 1845-1920, when Dutch peasants and workmen came to the United States and settled largely in the Midwest, where most took up farming. In the period since World War II, more than 100,000 Dutch have come to the United States. Over 80 percent of Dutch immigrants were members of the Dutch Reformed Church, and most of the others were Catholic. A few of those who came from the Netherlands were not actually Dutch, but Frisian, a minority from the northern Netherlands who speak a Germanic language similar to Dutch.

When the southern provinces of the Netherlands rebelled in 1830, the major countries of Europe created the new state of Belgium. The people of northern Belgium speak Flemish, which is virtually the same as Dutch, while the Walloons of southern Belgium speak French. Most of the emigrants from Belgium to the United States were Flemish-speaking Catholics who did not often mix with the Protestant Dutch.

The 1990 Census counted 6.2 million people who listed Dutch ancestry first on the census form and 0.4 million who listed Belgian ancestry first.

Where Americans of Belgian Ancestry Are Concentrated by County, 1990

FIG. 2–14

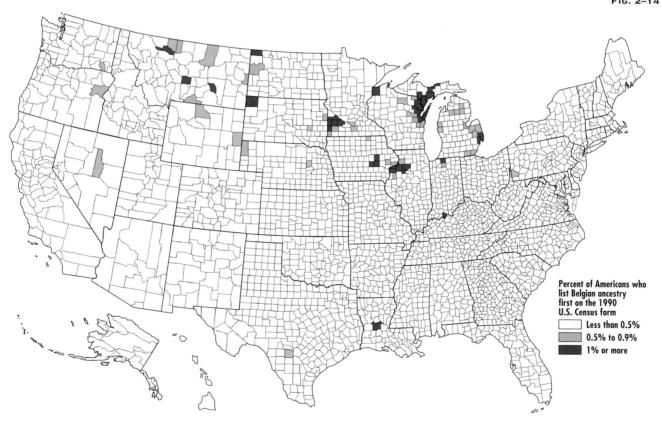

Percent of Americans who list Belgian ancestry first on the 1990 U.S. Census form

☐ Less than 0.5%
▨ 0.5% to 0.9%
■ 1% or more

Swedes founded New Sweden in 1638 at the mouth of the Delaware River, but this venture came to an end in 1655, when the Dutch took over the colony. Few Swedes came to America in the next two centuries, the total number living in the United States in 1790 being well under 20,000. It was not until the late 1840s, when the Swedish economy was depressed, that substantial numbers immigrated to America. In 1865 a truly mass migration started and continued, with little interruption, into the 1920s. The Swedish immigrants were mostly farmers and rural laborers, and therefore it is not surprising that they settled in Illinois, Minnesota, and other states where new land was still available. Many also went to the cities, and indeed for a while in the late 19th century there were more Swedes in Chicago than in any other city except Stockholm. In the 1840s and 1850s, when public worship outside the Church of Sweden was not allowed, Swedish immigrants, adherents of the Jansenist sect, sought religious freedom in Illinois. Most other Swedish immigrants were Lutherans, although there was a liberal sprinkling of Methodists, Mormons, and others.

In the 17th century, a few Norwegians settled in New Amsterdam and on the site of present-day Albany, but there was no major immigration to

Where Americans of Swedish Ancestry Are Concentrated by County, 1990

FIG. 2–15

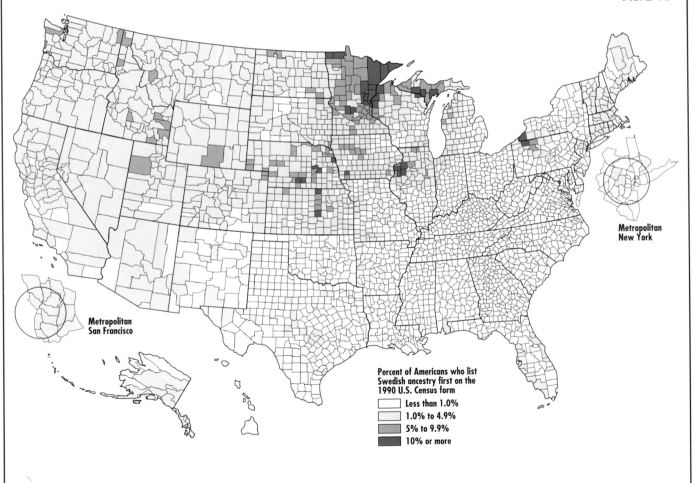

Metropolitan New York

Metropolitan San Francisco

Percent of Americans who list Swedish ancestry first on the 1990 U.S. Census form

- Less than 1.0%
- 1.0% to 4.9%
- 5% to 9.9%
- 10% or more

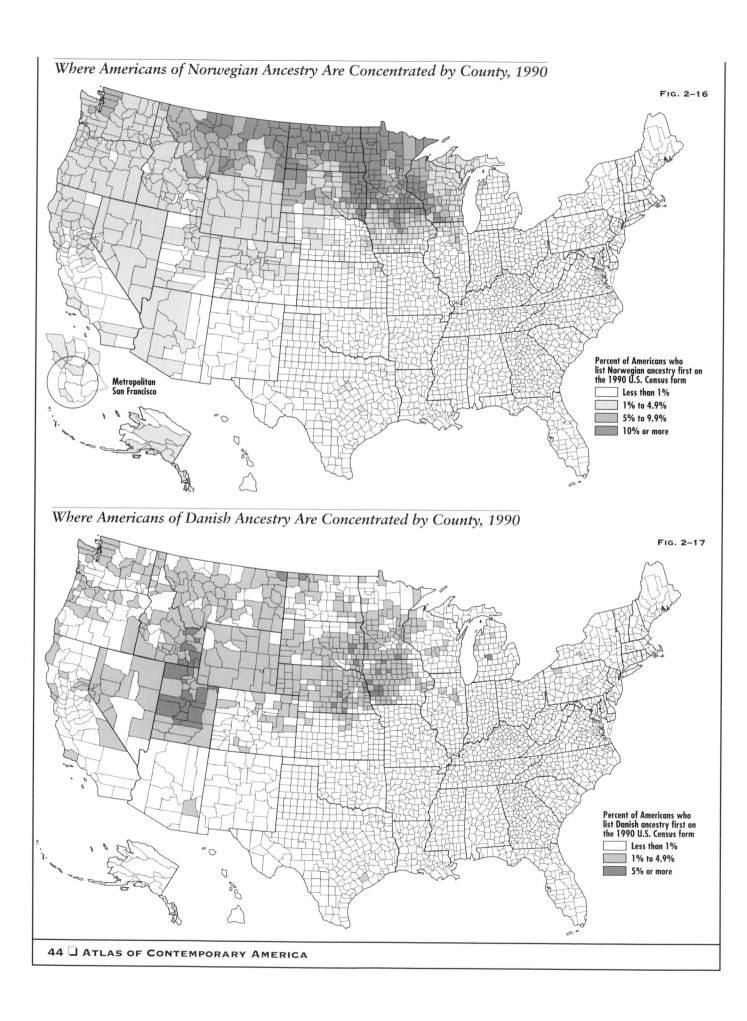

Where Americans of Norwegian Ancestry Are Concentrated by County, 1990

Fig. 2-16

Metropolitan
San Francisco

Percent of Americans who
list Norwegian ancestry first on
the 1990 U.S. Census form

Less than 1%
1% to 4.9%
5% to 9.9%
10% or more

Where Americans of Danish Ancestry Are Concentrated by County, 1990

Fig. 2-17

Percent of Americans who
list Danish ancestry first on
the 1990 U.S. Census form

Less than 1%
1% to 4.9%
5% or more

Where Americans of Scandinavian Ancestry Are Concentrated by County, 1990

FIG. 2–18

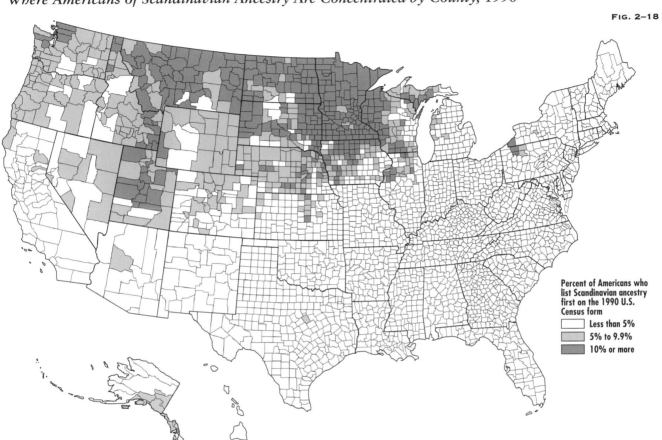

Percent of Americans who list Scandinavian ancestry first on the 1990 U.S. Census form

☐ Less than 5%
▨ 5% to 9.9%
▆ 10% or more

America until the 1840s, when large numbers, mostly peasants driven by a combination of economic necessity and a thirst for more equality, immigrated to the United States. Like the Swedes, they took up farming, particularly in the Midwest, but many also settled in cities. Indeed, Brooklyn, New York, at one time had the largest number of Norwegian-Americans of any city in America. Norwegian immigrants were mostly Lutheran, but many became Methodists, Baptists, and Mormons in America. Danes came to New Amsterdam early in the 17th century, and one of them, Jonas Bronck (d. 1643), gave his name to the Bronx. Their number was minuscule and was to remain so until the 1870s. Many of those who immigrated to America fled German repression in north Schleswig, which had been annexed by Prussia in

1864. The concentration of Danes in Utah resulted from the influx of 17,000 Danish Mormons to America in the late 19th century. (The missionary efforts of the Mormons were more successful in Denmark than in any other European country except England.)

About 11 million Americans listed Scandinavian ancestry first on the Census form, making them about as numerous as those who claim French or Polish ancestry. The 1990 U.S. Census counted 4.7 million who listed Swedish ancestry first on the census form, 3.9 million who listed Norwegian ancestry first, and 1.6 million who listed Danish ancestry first. An additional 0.7 million said they were "Scandinavian," and 40,000 said they were Icelandic. (Icelandic-Americans are not shown on the maps.)

Finnish-Americans

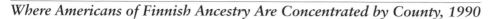

Where Americans of Finnish Ancestry Are Concentrated by County, 1990

FIG. 2-19

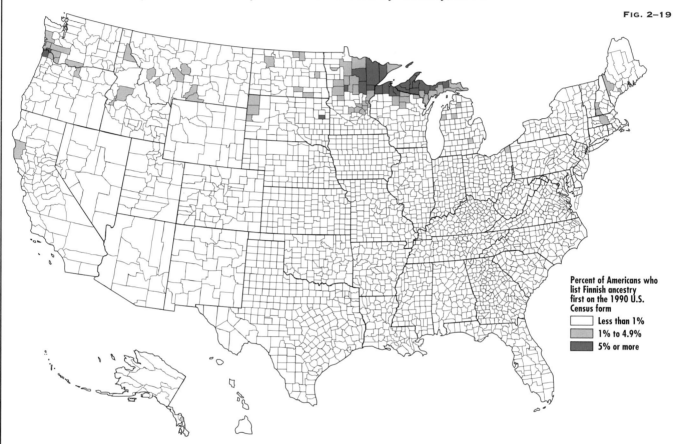

Percent of Americans who list Finnish ancestry first on the 1990 U.S. Census form

☐ Less than 1%

▨ 1% to 4.9%

■ 5% or more

Finns first appeared in America at the founding of New Sweden in Delaware early in the 17th century. (Finland was then a part of Sweden, but in 1809 was ceded to Russia.) During the Civil War, when there was a shortage of labor, Finns were recruited to work in the copper mines of upper Michigan, Minnesota, and Wisconsin, but Finns did not immigrate to the United States in substantial numbers until the mid-1880s, when many left because of economic conditions or to avoid conscription. Most who came to America were Lutheran. About 0.7 million listed Finnish ancestry first on the 1990 census form.

The first major wave of Portuguese immigrants did not arrive in the United States until the 1870s. The majority of these were not from continental Portugal but from the Azores, where they practiced farming. Portuguese laborers went as far west as Hawaii, but most favored lower New England, where typically they went into fishing, truck gardening, dairy farming, and the building trades. A second wave of Portuguese came to the United States in the post-World War II period, particularly after the economic crisis following the 1974 revolution, when democracy was restored to Portugal. About 4,000 Portuguese from Macao migrated to California following unsettled conditions in China after World War II. Most Portuguese immigrants to America were Catholics, although a few were Protestants from Madeira who fled the island in the late 1840s because of religious persecution. Most Portuguese are Caucasian, but a few—mostly from the now independent Cape Verde Islands—are of mixed Portuguese and African descent.

Between 1820, when records were first kept, and 1990, about half a million Portuguese came to the United States. The 1990 Census counted about 1.2 million who listed Portuguese ancestry first on the 1990 Census form.

Where Americans of Portuguese Ancestry Are Concentrated by County, 1990

FIG. 2–20

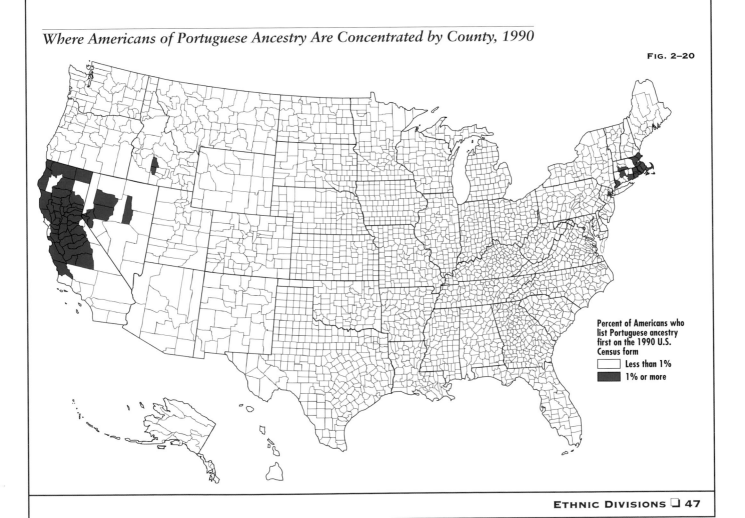

Percent of Americans who list Portuguese ancestry first on the 1990 U.S. Census form

Less than 1%

1% or more

Italian-Americans

Beginning in the 17th century, a few Italians, largely artisans and professionals and mostly from northern Italy, settled on the eastern seaboard from Connecticut to Georgia. A mass migration of peasants and laborers, mostly from southern Italy and Sicily, began in the 1880s as economic conditions worsened. Although these newer immigrants were used to living close to the soil, they usually avoided farming regions in favor of better-paying jobs in building construction and road work, occupations that did not require literacy. The peak of Italian migration came between 1900 and 1914, when more than 3 million entered. From 1820 to 1990, over 5.3 million Italians migrated to the United States. Italians, together with the Irish and immigrants from eastern Europe, formed the core of the blue-collar working class. Unlike the Irish, the Jews, and the Germans, Italian immigrants were more apt to return to their native country, and this slowed their assimilation. The 1990 Census counted 14.7 million people who listed Italian ancestry first on the census form.

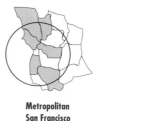

Metropolitan San Francisco

Metropolitan New York

Baltimore–Washington

Where Americans of Italian Ancestry Are Concentrated by County, 1990

FIG. 2–21

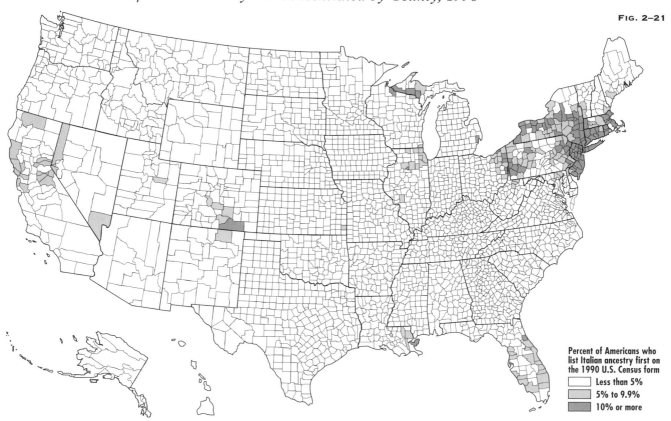

Percent of Americans who list Italian ancestry first on the 1990 U.S. Census form

☐ Less than 5%
☐ 5% to 9.9%
☐ 10% or more

Where Americans of Greek Ancestry Are Concentrated by County, 1990

FIG. 2–22

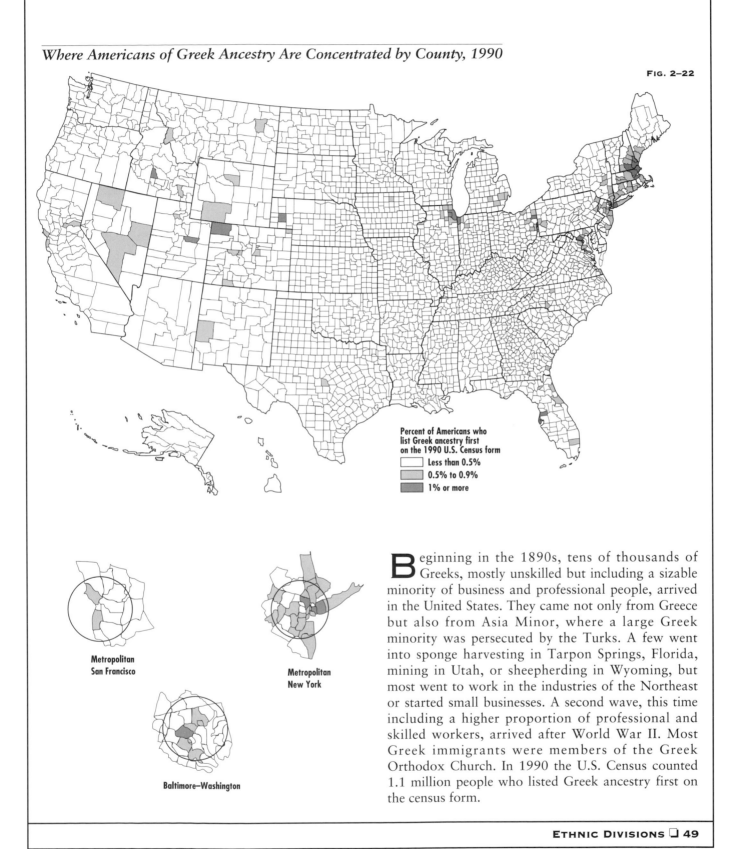

Percent of Americans who
list Greek ancestry first
on the 1990 U.S. Census form

☐ Less than 0.5%
▨ 0.5% to 0.9%
▨ 1% or more

Metropolitan
San Francisco

Metropolitan
New York

Baltimore–Washington

Beginning in the 1890s, tens of thousands of Greeks, mostly unskilled but including a sizable minority of business and professional people, arrived in the United States. They came not only from Greece but also from Asia Minor, where a large Greek minority was persecuted by the Turks. A few went into sponge harvesting in Tarpon Springs, Florida, mining in Utah, or sheepherding in Wyoming, but most went to work in the industries of the Northeast or started small businesses. A second wave, this time including a higher proportion of professional and skilled workers, arrived after World War II. Most Greek immigrants were members of the Greek Orthodox Church. In 1990 the U.S. Census counted 1.1 million people who listed Greek ancestry first on the census form.

Polish-Americans

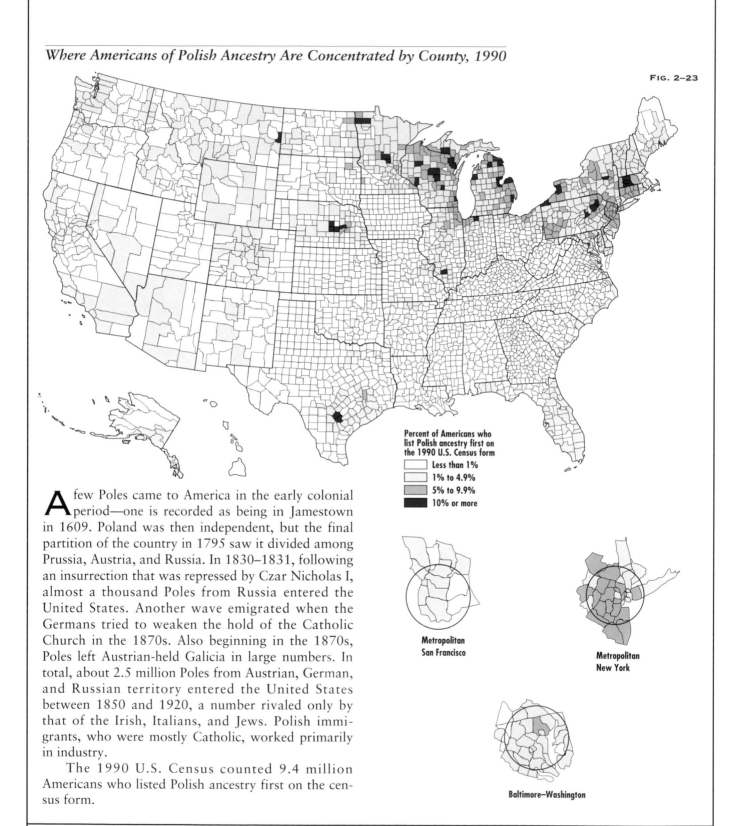

Where Americans of Polish Ancestry Are Concentrated by County, 1990

FIG. 2-23

Percent of Americans who list Polish ancestry first on the 1990 U.S. Census form

- Less than 1%
- 1% to 4.9%
- 5% to 9.9%
- 10% or more

Metropolitan San Francisco

Metropolitan New York

Baltimore–Washington

A few Poles came to America in the early colonial period—one is recorded as being in Jamestown in 1609. Poland was then independent, but the final partition of the country in 1795 saw it divided among Prussia, Austria, and Russia. In 1830–1831, following an insurrection that was repressed by Czar Nicholas I, almost a thousand Poles from Russia entered the United States. Another wave emigrated when the Germans tried to weaken the hold of the Catholic Church in the 1870s. Also beginning in the 1870s, Poles left Austrian-held Galicia in large numbers. In total, about 2.5 million Poles from Austrian, German, and Russian territory entered the United States between 1850 and 1920, a number rivaled only by that of the Irish, Italians, and Jews. Polish immigrants, who were mostly Catholic, worked primarily in industry.

The 1990 U.S. Census counted 9.4 million Americans who listed Polish ancestry first on the census form.

The Czech homeland, Bohemia and Moravia, had long been a part of the Hapsburg Empire when the first few Czechs came to America in the 1630s, but a mass migration did not start until after the Revolution of 1848, when it became easier to leave the country. In the 100 years following 1850, almost 400,000 Czechs, mostly peasants, but including many intellectuals and skilled artisans, came to America. They were the first Slavic people to arrive in the United States in large numbers. Because they came at a time when land was still plentiful they took to farming, unlike the Slovaks, Poles, Ukrainians, and Russians, who generally went into industrial work. However, a substantial number of the early Czech immigrants went to the cities, particularly Chicago. In their homeland, Czechs were almost all Catholics, a result of their forcible conversion back from Protestantism in the 1620s. The fragility of

Where Americans of Czech Ancestry Are Concentrated by County, 1990

FIG. 2–24

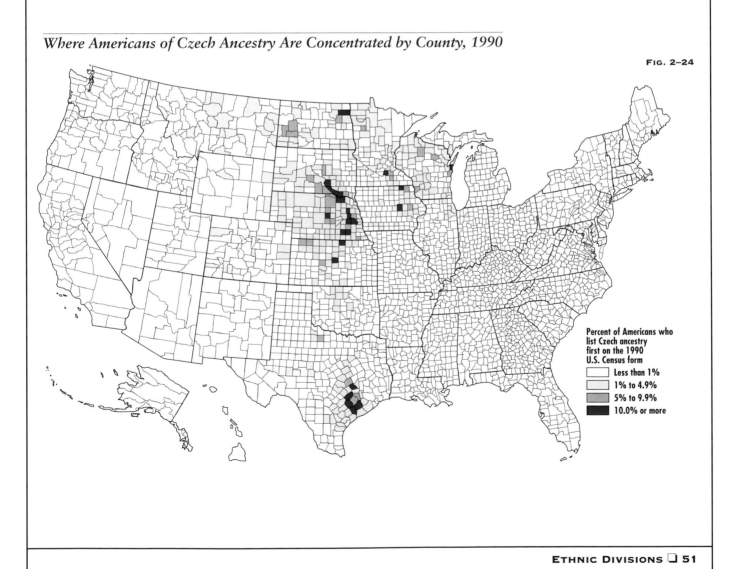

Percent of Americans who list Czech ancestry first on the 1990 U.S. Census form

Less than 1%
1% to 4.9%
5% to 9.9%
10.0% or more

their allegiance to Catholicism was evident in America, where large numbers joined other churches or became Freethinkers. The most recent waves of Czechs to arrive in America came after 1948, when Czechoslovakia fell under Soviet influence, and in 1968, when Warsaw Pact troops invaded the country. These later immigrants were mostly professionals and skilled craftsmen.

Slovakia, like Bohemia and Moravia, had long been a part of the Hapsburg Empire. There was not enough land for the peasants, and therefore, begin-

ning in the 1860s, Slovaks came to the United States to work in the mines, on the railroads, and in other industries. In the 19th century Slovakia was about 80-percent Catholic and 15-percent Lutheran. Slovaks in America split roughly in the same proportion.

The 1990 U.S. Census counted 1.3 million who listed Czech ancestry first on the census form and 1.9 million who listed Slovak ancestry first. In addition, there were 0.3 million who said they were Czechoslovakian.

Where Americans of Slovak Ancestry Are Concentrated by County, 1990

FIG. 2–25

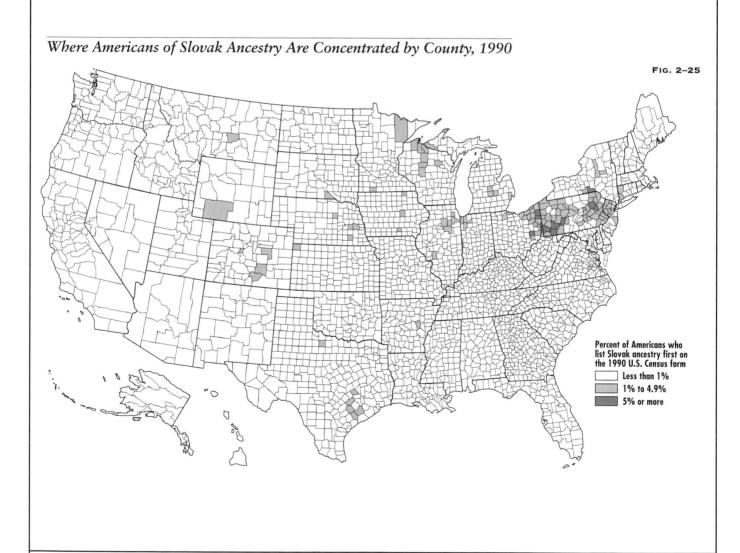

Percent of Americans who list Slovak ancestry first on the 1990 U.S. Census form

Less than 1%
1% to 4.9%
5% or more

Where Americans of Lithuanian Ancestry Are Concentrated by County, 1990

FIG. 2–26

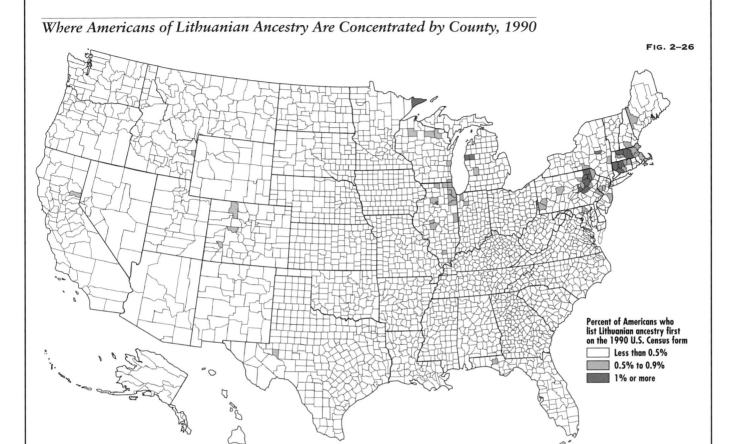

Percent of Americans who
list Lithuanian ancestry first
on the 1990 U.S. Census form

- Less than 0.5%
- 0.5% to 0.9%
- 1% or more

In the 19th century most Lithuanians lived under czarist rule, but some lived in East Prussia. The first wave of Lithuanian immigration to America began in the late 1860s, when thousands of peasants, mostly from Russia, fled to avoid famine and conscription into the czar's army. Later in the century, the worldwide depression of agriculture spurred many more to emigrate. Although most of the emigrants were peasants, few became farmers in America; most started out as unskilled laborers, usually in the Northeast. Later in the 19th century some members of the small but growing Lithuanian professional class came to America, and after World War II a smaller number, including much of the intelligentsia, came to escape Soviet authority. The U.S. Census of 1990 counted 0.8 million who listed Lithuanian ancestry first on the census form.

Russian- and Ukrainian-Americans

Russians first came to Alaska in 1741, when the Danish sailor Vitus Bering, in the service of the Russian monarchy, landed on the Aleutian Islands. Their settlements, devoted mainly to the fur trade, were sparsely populated and far-flung, extending south from the Aleutians to Fort Ross, 100 miles north of San Francisco. In 1867, when the Russian government sold Alaska to the United States, several hundred Russians elected to remain on U.S. territory. Large numbers of Russians first came to America between 1880 and 1914, when peasants and unskilled laborers emigrated because of poor economic conditions. They settled mostly in the East, where they went into a variety of industrial occupations. Between 1920 and 1940 there was a second major wave, this time composed of priests, aristocrats, and others

Where Americans of Russian and Ukrainian Ancestry Are Concentrated by County, 1990

FIG. 2–27

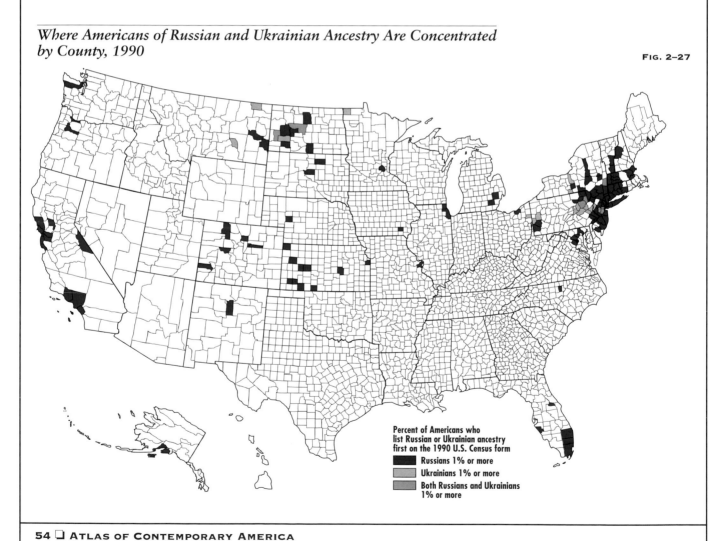

Percent of Americans who
list Russian or Ukrainian ancestry
first on the 1990 U.S. Census form

■ Russians 1% or more

▨ Ukrainians 1% or more

▨ Both Russians and Ukrainians
1% or more

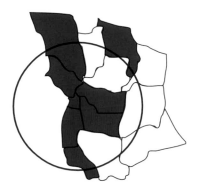

**Metropolitan
San Francisco**

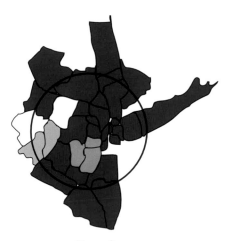

**Metropolitan
New York**

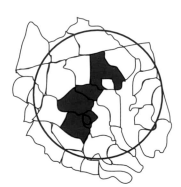

Baltimore—Washington

fleeing the Bolshevik Revolution. A third wave arrived between 1945 and 1955, following World War II. Some groups, such as the Molokan sect, left Russia for specifically religious reasons and settled in California beginning in 1904. The 1990 U.S. Census counted about 3 million Americans who listed Russian ancestry first on the census form. Over two-thirds of these are of Jewish heritage, while most of the balance are descended from Russian Orthodox Church immigrants.

The first large-scale migration of Ukrainians took place between 1880 and 1914, when about a quarter of a million, largely peasants and unskilled laborers, arrived in the United States. They were mostly from the Austrian-dominated provinces of Galicia and Bukovina, and the Transcarpathial region of northeastern Hungary, lands that are now mainly in the far western section of the independent Ukrainian republic. Like the Russians, they came because of poor economic conditions, and, again like the Russians, they went primarily into industry. Additional waves of Ukrainians arrived between 1920 and 1939 and in the decade following World War II. Eighty-five percent of the early Ukrainian immigrants were Catholic. But the American Catholic hierarchy was unsympathetic to their customs, which included priestly marriage, and many went over to the Eastern Orthodox Church. This, together with a high proportion of Orthodox immigrants in more recent years, reduced the proportion of Catholics among Ukrainian-Americans to only 40 percent. Most Ukrainians in the United States in the early 20th century did not have a strong national identity and were often called Russians, Little Russians, Rusyns, or Ruthenians. The 1990 Census counted about 0.7 million who listed Ukrainian ancestry first on the census form.

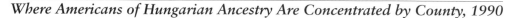

Where Americans of Hungarian Ancestry Are Concentrated by County, 1990

FIG. 2–28

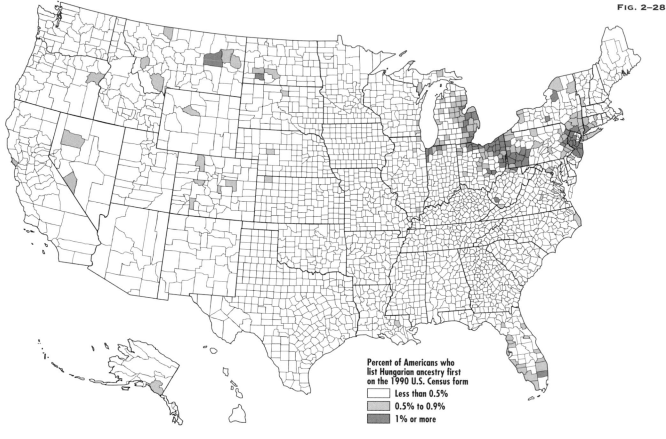

Percent of Americans who
list Hungarian ancestry first
on the 1990 U.S. Census form

	Less than 0.5%
	0.5% to 0.9%
	1% or more

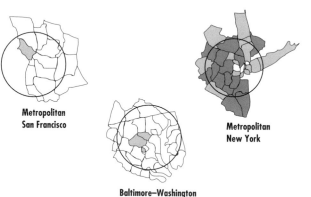

Metropolitan
San Francisco

Baltimore–Washington

Metropolitan
New York

A few Hungarians were in America in colonial times, and some fought on the American side in the Revolutionary War. A substantial number of political dissidents fled the country following the failure of the 1848 uprising against the Hapsburg monarchy, but a far bigger wave—almost 460,000—came to the United States between 1899 and 1914, seeking economic opportunity, which they found in the coal mines, steel mills, and other industries of the East and Midwest. Unlike most immigrants of the period, they were mostly literate. A third wave of about 35,000 arrived following the Soviet suppression of the 1956 Hungarian uprising. In all, roughly 100,000 Hungarians came to the United States from 1945 to 1990. Hungary's population before World War I was about 60 percent Catholic, 25 percent Protestant (mostly members of the Reformed Church of Hungary), and about 5 percent Jewish. Ten percent belonged to various Eastern Orthodox sects. Proportionately more Protestants immigrated to the United States.

The 1990 U.S. Census counted 1.6 million people who listed Hungarian ancestry first on the census form.

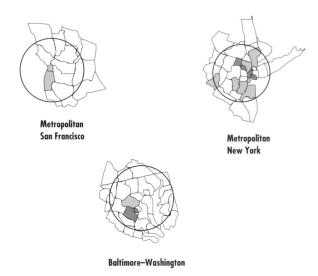

Metropolitan San Francisco

Metropolitan New York

Baltimore–Washington

A rab-Americans can be classified into two general groups, Christians and Muslims. The Christians, who generally don't consider themselves Arabs, began migrating from the Lebanon area in the last quarter of the 19th century. (Lebanon was then a part of the Syrian province of the Ottoman Empire, and became a separate state only after World War I.) The immigrants were mostly from rural areas, but in America they took to trade, beginning as peddlers and later going into conventional retailing, where they prospered. Christians from other Middle Eastern countries also came to the United States.

Muslim Arabs, who came from a variety of Middle Eastern countries, including Egypt, Jordan, Syria, and Iraq, began migrating to the United States in the late 1870s.

The 1990 Census counted 860,000 who listed Arab ancestry first on the census form. Of these, about 45 percent are of Lebanese origin.

Where Americans of Arab Ancestry Are Concentrated by County, 1990

FIG. 2–29

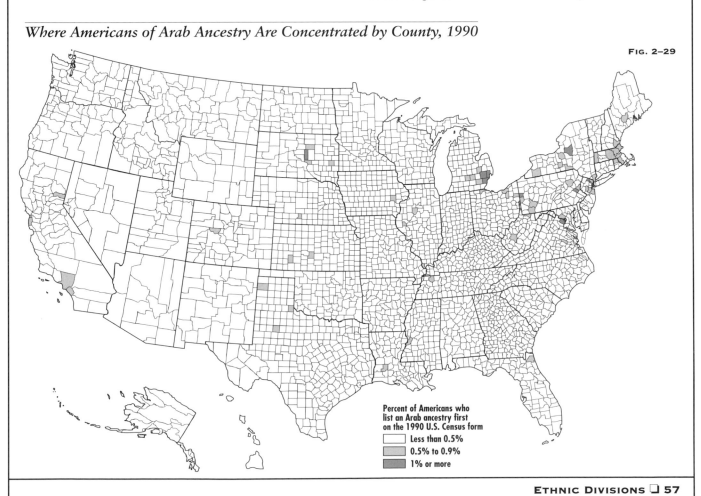

Percent of Americans who list an Arab ancestry first on the 1990 U.S. Census form

☐ Less than 0.5%
▨ 0.5% to 0.9%
▧ 1% or more

African-Americans

There were African slaves in Jamestown as early as 1619, but the majority of the 417,000 Africans brought to the British colonies of North America and to Louisiana arrived between 1741 and 1807. Slave importing was declared illegal by act of Congress in 1807. The slaves came from the west coast of Africa, particularly from what is now southern Nigeria, Ghana, Senegal, Gambia, and Sierra Leone. The U.S. Census of 1790 counted almost 757,000 individuals of African ancestry, and by 1860 there were more than 4.4 million African-Americans, of which 488,000 were free.

At first, African slaves were concentrated in Virginia, Maryland, and North and South Carolina, but in the decades before the Civil War, when these areas were in decline, more than 800,000 were transported to the newer cotton-growing states on the Gulf of Mexico—Alabama, Mississippi, Louisiana, and Texas. An even greater shift of the black population began during World War I, when hundreds of thousands left the South to take jobs in the urban North. New workers were needed to replace the flow of immigrants cut off by the war and later by the restrictive immigration acts of the 1920s.

The African-American population is growing at a faster rate than the Caucasian—13 percent vs. 6 percent from 1980 to 1990—and in 90 counties it is the majority. The 1990 Census counted almost 30 million who classified themselves as African-American. African-Americans accounted for 12.1 percent of the U.S. population in 1990.

Where Americans of African Ancestry Are Concentrated by County, 1990

FIG. 2–30

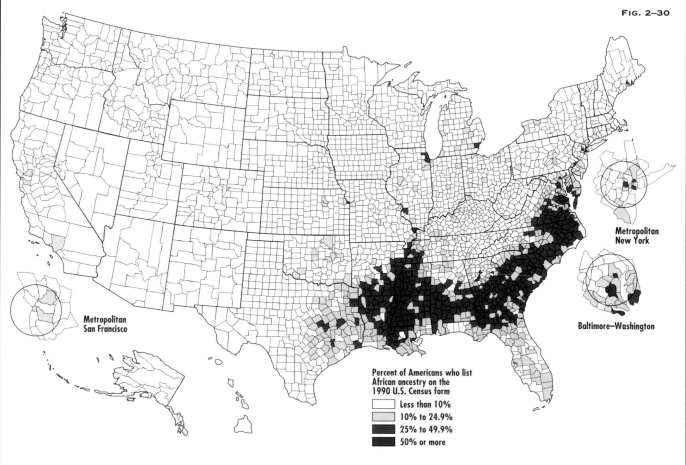

Metropolitan New York

Baltimore–Washington

Metropolitan San Francisco

Percent of Americans who list African ancestry on the 1990 U.S. Census form

- Less than 10%
- 10% to 24.9%
- 25% to 49.9%
- 50% or more

Where Americans of Chinese Ancestry Are Concentrated by County, 1990

FIG. 2–31

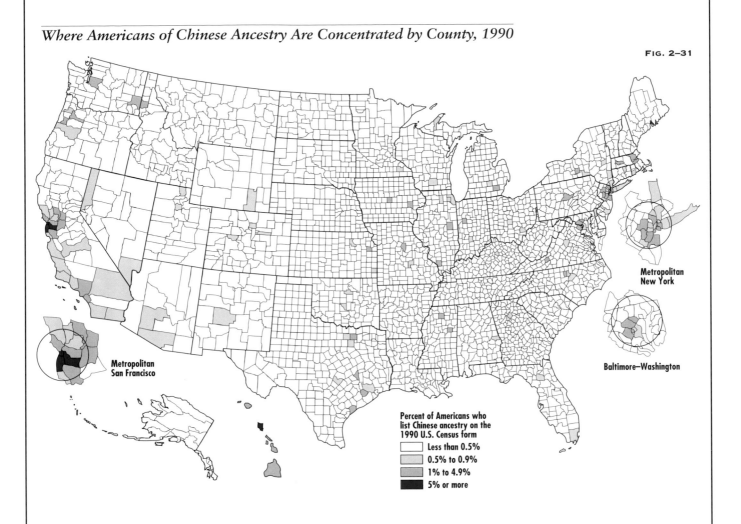

Metropolitan
New York

Metropolitan
San Francisco

Baltimore–Washington

Percent of Americans who
list Chinese ancestry on the
1990 U.S. Census form

Less than 0.5%

0.5% to 0.9%

1% to 4.9%

5% or more

Chinese visited Baltimore in 1785, and apparently a few were in Los Angeles and Monterey in the 1780s. But it wasn't until after the 1848 discovery of gold in California that a substantial number immigrated to the United States. About 320,000 arrived between 1850 and 1882, although many later returned to their homeland. They came mostly from south China, which was wracked by civil war and economic chaos, and they were attracted to Hawaii and California because of the demand for cheap labor. Tens of thousands worked on the railroads, including the transcontinental line completed in 1869. When the lines were finished, they stayed on in railroad towns from Texas to Washington state. Some went into light industry such as the cigar and shoe factories of San Francisco, and others worked in the mines of the West Coast and of Nevada, Wyoming, and Utah.

The Chinese Exclusion Act, passed by Congress in 1882, barred entry of Chinese laborers for the next 10 years. Other federal acts extended the exclusion and put further restrictions on Chinese immigration. It was not until 1943 that Congress repealed the exclusion acts. The immigration laws were further liberalized in 1968, and more than 650,000 Chinese came to America in the 1970s and 1980s. The 1990 U.S. Census counted 1.6 million Chinese, the largest Asian-origin group in the United States.

Filipino-Americans

Where Americans of Filipino Ancestry Are Concentrated by County, 1990

FIG. 2-32

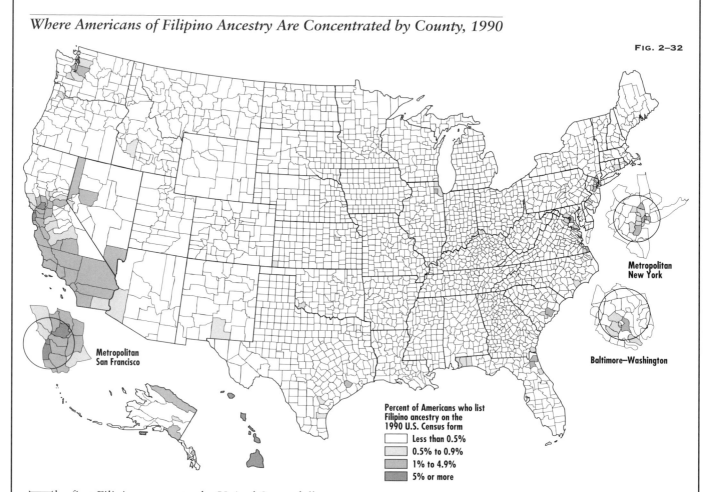

Metropolitan New York

Metropolitan San Francisco

Baltimore–Washington

Percent of Americans who list
Filipino ancestry on the
1990 U.S. Census form

- Less than 0.5%
- 0.5% to 0.9%
- 1% to 4.9%
- 5% or more

The first Filipinos came to the United States follow-ing the Treaty of Paris (1899), which made the Philippines an American possession. The earliest to come were students, who went to mainland colleges and universities. They were followed in the first decade of this century by peasants, who came to work on Hawaii's sugar plantations and later on California farms. By the 1950s, Filipinos and Mexicans held most of the migrant farm jobs in California, and together they were the backbone of the United Farm Workers Organizing Committee, led by Cesar Chavez.

Most Filipinos in the United States are nominally Catholic and know English and Tagalog, the language of central Luzon, which was proclaimed the official language of the Philippines in 1946. The majority of immigrants to the United States, however, do not have Tagalog origins, but come from the Llocano- and Visayan-speaking groups. Ethnic identification, at least among first-generation immigrants, tended to be with their language group and not with a Philippine nationality. At least partly for this reason, Filipinos in America have been less united than other Asian groups here. The 1990 Census counted almost 1.4 million Filipinos in the United States, making them the largest Asian group after the Chinese.

In 1868 the Emperor Meiji ended Japan's policy of isolation, making possible the exodus of Japanese to work on Hawaiian sugar plantations. Japanese immigrants went in lesser numbers to California, where they worked in a variety of jobs, such as railroad construction, farming, and fish canning. By 1890, more than 12,000 Japanese were in Hawaii and more than 2,000 on the mainland. Between 1890 and 1924 more than 300,000 Japanese came to the United States, although many subsequently returned. The number entering the United States slowed to a trickle after the restrictive immigration law of 1924 was passed.

In 1942, after the Japanese attack on Pearl Harbor, more than 110,000 Japanese-Americans in the Pacific states, two-thirds of them American citizens, were moved to internment camps in California, Arizona, Idaho, Utah, and Arkansas, where they remained until 1944, when the Supreme Court ruled this internment illegal. Most of the internees returned to the West Coast, but some remained near the camps or moved on to Midwestern or Eastern cities. The Japanese in Hawaii did not suffer mass internment.

During the 1970s and 1980s, following the enactment of more liberal immigration laws in the 1960s, over 85,000 Japanese came to the United States. According to the 1990 Census, there were 848,000 Japanese-Americans in the United States, making them the third largest Asian group after the Chinese and Filipinos.

Where Americans of Japanese Ancestry Are Concentrated by County, 1990

FIG. 2–33

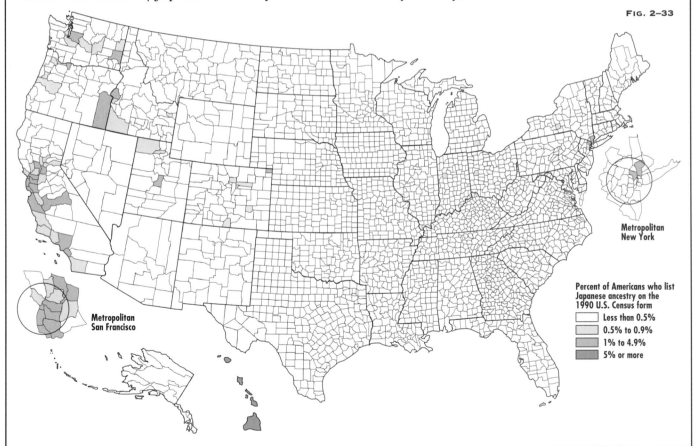

Metropolitan New York

Metropolitan San Francisco

Percent of Americans who list Japanese ancestry on the 1990 U.S. Census form

- Less than 0.5%
- 0.5% to 0.9%
- 1% to 4.9%
- 5% or more

East Indian-Americans

East Indians, sometimes called Asian Indians, have their roots in the subcontinent of India. Most are Caucasian and came from the Ganges region of the northeast, Gujarat in the northwest, or the Dravidian region of southern India. A few came by way of other countries, such as Uganda, which expelled its Indian citizens in 1972. Although their mother tongues may differ—India recognizes 15 national languages—most speak English. Most East Indians are Hindu, but Sikhs make up a large minority of the East Indians in California.

The first East Indian in the United States was recorded in 1820. In the next 140 years fewer than 14,000 arrived, mostly as agricultural workers, railroad laborers, and other unskilled workers, but there was a substantial number of merchants and students, as well as a sprinkling of political dissidents opposed to British rule. East Indian migration to the United States did not swell until liberalization of the immigration laws in the 1960s. In the 1970s and 1980s, more than 417,000 came to the United States, where they had a relatively easy adjustment to American life, not only because legal barriers to racial discrimination were falling but also because a high proportion of the immigrants since the 1960s were professionals. By 1990, according to the U.S. Census, there were 815,000 Americans of East Indian descent.

Where Americans of East Indian Ancestry Are Concentrated by County, 1990

FIG. 2–34

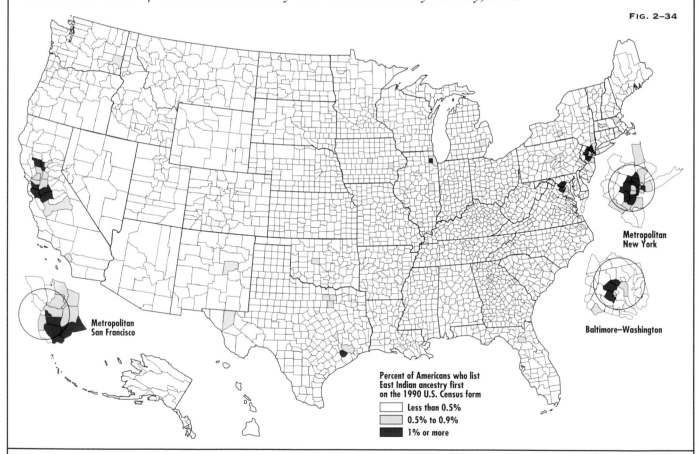

Metropolitan San Francisco

Metropolitan New York

Baltimore–Washington

Percent of Americans who list East Indian ancestry first on the 1990 U.S. Census form

- Less than 0.5%
- 0.5% to 0.9%
- 1% or more

Where Americans of Korean Ancestry Are Concentrated by County, 1990

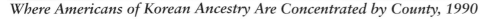

FIG. 2–35

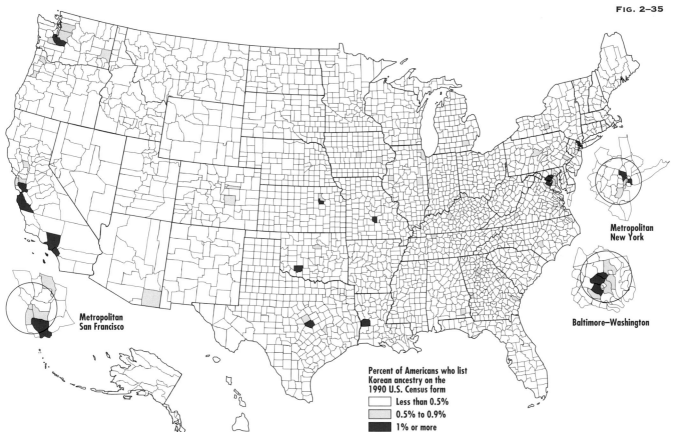

Metropolitan New York

Metropolitan San Francisco

Baltimore–Washington

Percent of Americans who list Korean ancestry on the 1990 U.S. Census form
- Less than 0.5%
- 0.5% to 0.9%
- 1% or more

A few Koreans settled in the United States in the late 19th century, mostly in Hawaii, where, like other Asian immigrants, they worked on the sugar plantations. In 1905, when Korea became a Japanese protectorate, Japan forbade emigration. In 1910, the U.S. Census counted fewer than 5,000 Koreans, and in 1940, about 8,300, mostly in Hawaii. Barely 30,000 Koreans came to the United States from the end of World War II through 1969; but following liberalization of the immigration laws, 587,000 arrived between 1970 and 1990. In 1990, according to the U.S. Census, there were about 800,000 Korean-Americans.

Immigrants from Korea, unlike those from other parts of Asia, are mostly Christians, a circumstance that traces to the zeal of Methodist, Presbyterian, and other missionaries in the late 19th century. Recent Korean immigrants tend to be well educated and middle class. Many are professionals who left their homeland to seek greater economic opportunity or because of opposition to the political regime in Seoul. Many of these were unable to practice their professions and instead founded small businesses, typically retail stores.

Vietnamese- and Cambodian-Americans

Where Americans of Vietnamese and Cambodian Ancestry Are Concentrated by County, 1990

Fig. 2–36

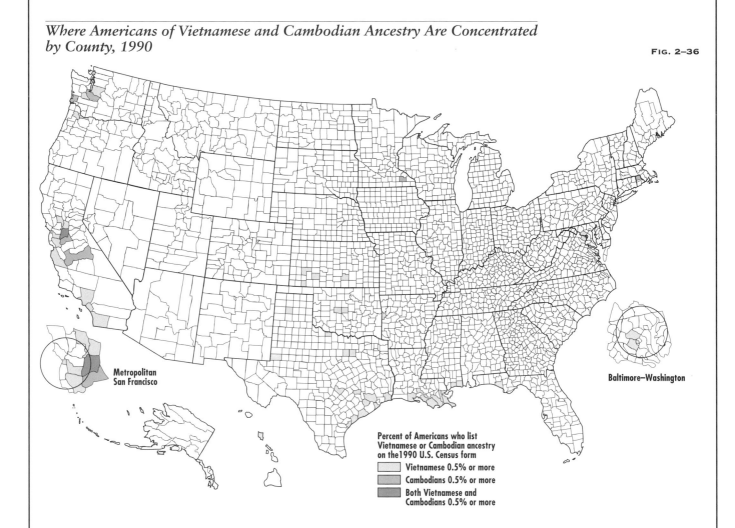

Metropolitan
San Francisco

Baltimore–Washington

**Percent of Americans who list
Vietnamese or Cambodian ancestry
on the 1990 U.S. Census form**

Vietnamese 0.5% or more

Cambodians 0.5% or more

Both Vietnamese and
Cambodians 0.5% or more

Before 1975 few Vietnamese immigrated to the United States, but with the fall of the U.S.-backed government of South Vietnam, 125,000 came in 1975 alone and by 1990, more than 425,000 more Vietnamese had come to the United States. Most of these immigrants had been in the military or employed as professionals, managers, technicians, or office workers. Few were farmers or fishermen. In the United States many went into similar occupations. About 50 percent were Buddhists, 30 percent to 40 percent were Catholic, and the remainder belonged to other religions or were unchurched. The 1990 Census counted 0.6 million Vietnamese in the United States.

Cambodians started coming to America in large numbers in 1980, following the Vietnamese invasion of the country in 1978 and the continuing civil war. Between 1975 and 1990 almost 150,000 entered the United States. They tended to be less literate than the Vietnamese and had fewer occupational skills. Most were Buddhist. The 1990 Census counted 147,000 Cambodian-Americans.

Mexican-Americans, sometimes called Chicanos or Latinos, are overwhelmingly of mixed Spanish and Indian ancestry. A few settled in New Mexico beginning in the late 16th century, and about 80,000 of their descendants became Americans when the United States annexed Texas and much of the northern part of Mexico in the late 1840s. The Mexican-American population in this area, which extends from California to Texas and as far north as southern Wyoming, was perhaps half a million by 1900. This was to grow over the next 30 years when hundreds of thousands of Mexicans came north seeking greater economic opportunity or fleeing unsettled conditions during the Mexican Revolution. Another great wave of Mexican immigration to the United States began in the 1950s and continues to this day. Between 1960 and 1990, more than 2 million Mexican immigrants entered the United States legally, in addition to a large number of illegal immigrants, perhaps as many as 2 to 3 million.

According to the 1990 U.S. Census, Mexican-Americans account for about 20 percent of the combined population of California, Arizona, New Mexico, and Texas, and are in the majority in 30 counties. The 1990 Census counted a total of 13.5 million Mexican-Americans, not including illegal aliens.

Where Americans of Mexican Ancestry Are Concentrated by County, 1990

FIG. 2–37

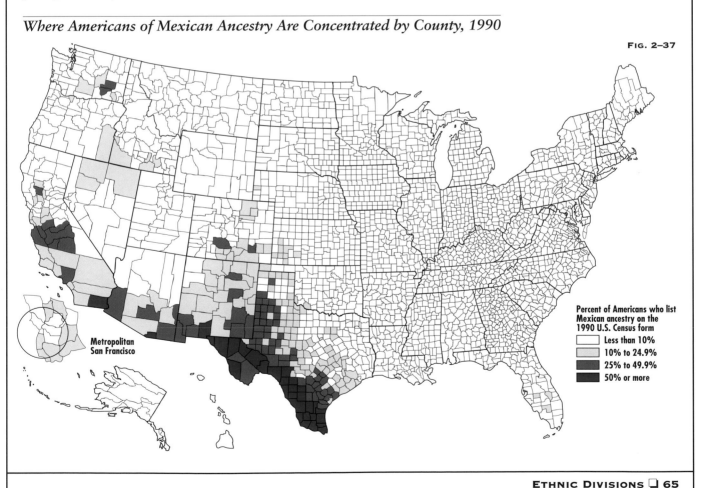

Metropolitan San Francisco

Percent of Americans who list Mexican ancestry on the 1990 U.S. Census form

- Less than 10%
- 10% to 24.9%
- 25% to 49.9%
- 50% or more

Puerto Rican-Americans

Afew Puerto Ricans came to the United States in the late 19th century. The Jones Act of 1917, which declared that all Puerto Ricans were citizens of the United States, encouraged immigration, which was mostly to the large eastern cities, particularly New York, where more than half of Puerto Rican immigrants settled. The biggest wave of immigration began in the late 1940s, when cheap air fares and high unemployment on the island brought millions to the mainland. Most Puerto Ricans who came to the United States went into factory and service work requiring little skill. The 1990 Census counted 2.7 million Puerto Ricans in the United States, compared with 3.5 million in Puerto Rico. Of those in the United States, 46 percent classified themselves as white.

Cuban-Americans

Cubans were in Florida as early as the 1500s, but it was not until the late 1950s, during the last years of the Batista era and the first years of Castro's rule, that large numbers arrived. Between January 1959, when the revolution triumphed, and the end of 1962, more than 155,000 Cubans, mostly upper and upper-middle class, came to the United States. Later waves of Cubans were less affluent and included many blue-collar workers. The 1990 Census counted 1.0 million Americans of Cuban ancestry in 1990. Eighty-four percent of Cubans in the United States classified themselves as white in the Census.

Where Americans of Puerto Rican Ancestry Are Concentrated by County, 1990   **FIG. 2–38**

Where Americans of Cuban Ancestry Are Concentrated by County, 1990   **FIG. 2–39**

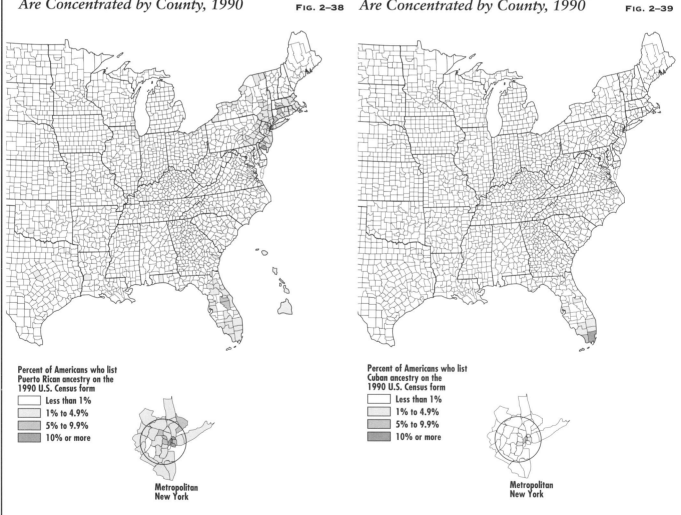

Percent of Americans who list Puerto Rican ancestry on the 1990 U.S. Census form

- Less than 1%
- 1% to 4.9%
- 5% to 9.9%
- 10% or more

Metropolitan New York

Percent of Americans who list Cuban ancestry on the 1990 U.S. Census form

- Less than 1%
- 1% to 4.9%
- 5% to 9.9%
- 10% or more

Metropolitan New York

Where Americans of Other Hispanic Ancestry Are Concentrated by County, 1990

FIG. 2–40

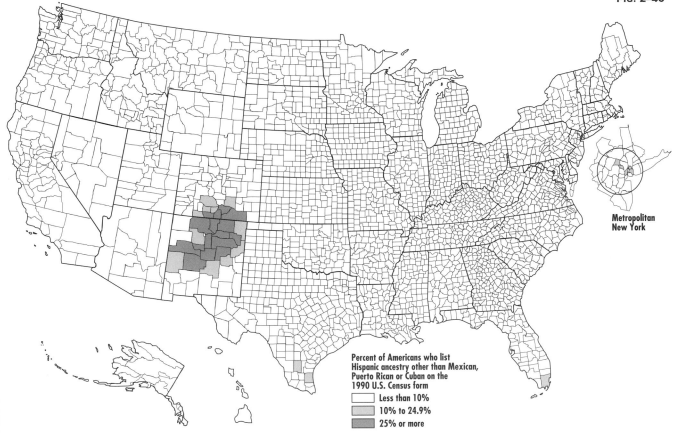

Metropolitan
New York

Percent of Americans who list
Hispanic ancestry other than Mexican,
Puerto Rican or Cuban on the
1990 U.S. Census form

☐ Less than 10%
▢ 10% to 24.9%
■ 25% or more

The "Other Hispanic" group is composed of Spanish-speaking people who listed a non-specific Hispanic origin or a Hispanic origin other than Mexican, Cuban, or Puerto Rican. Most of those in the "Other Hispanic" group are Salvadorans, Nicaraguans, Guatemalans, Colombians, and other Latin Americans who settled in California, Florida, New York, and the Washington, D.C., area. Many, particularly Salvadorans, came as a result of the civil wars in Central America.

Most of the "Other Hispanics" in New Mexico are descendants of people from the Spanish colony of New Spain, which extended from what is now Costa Rica to California, and who came to New Mexico between 1598 and 1821, the year Mexico gained independence. Some in the "Other Hispanic" group emigrated from the Canary Islands and settled in southern Louisiana.

The 1990 U.S. Census counted almost 5.1 million "Other Hispanics," which does not, of course, include illegal aliens.

Where Americans of West Indian Ancestry Are Concentrated by County, 1990

FIG. 2–41

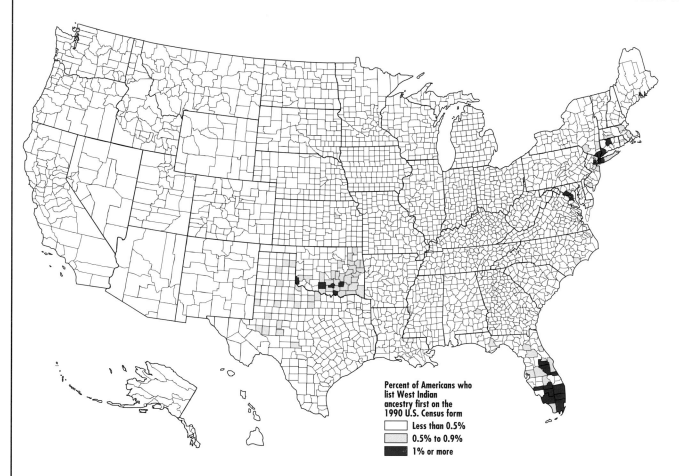

Percent of Americans who
list West Indian
ancestry first on the
1990 U.S. Census form

☐ Less than 0.5%

▨ 0.5% to 0.9%

■ 1% or more

This map shows the distribution of West Indian-Americans, defined here as non-Spanish-speaking people from the Caribbean. There are two main groups, the English-speakers from such places as Jamaica, Trinidad, Tobago, Barbados, and Belize, and the French and Creole-speakers from Haiti. By census definition, all West Indians are black or mulatto.

A few English-speaking West Indians came to the United States in the nineteenth century, but substan-

tial numbers did not arrive until after 1900. The largest migration came between 1970 and 1990. Almost all were literate, and a high proportion were professionals and skilled workers. Those coming from Trinidad, Tobago, and St. Lucia were usually Catholic, while those from the other islands, the majority, were members of the Anglican Church.

Haitians fought on the American side in both the Revolutionary War and the War of 1812. In the

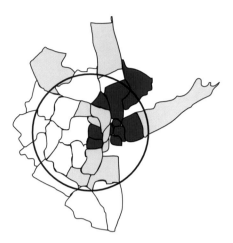

**Metropolitan
New York**

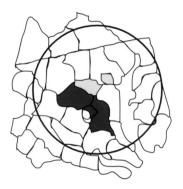

Baltimore–Washington

Haitian Revolution of 1791-1803, when French domination was cast off, many of the black population fled to the United States, settling in Eastern Seaboard cities, particularly Philadelphia. Between 1915 and 1934, when American troops occupied Haiti, some Haitians, mostly the well-educated, immigrated to the United States. The largest emigration began in 1957, when Francois "Papa Doc" Duvalier became president, causing many urban middle-class people to flee for political reasons. Beginning in the 1970s, the "boat people," largely illiterate peasants and unskilled workers, began arriving in the United States. In 1991, after the overthrow of Jean-Bertrand Aristide, the first legally elected president of Haiti in many years, another wave of boat people came to the United States. Middle-class refugees, who are usually mulatto, tend to be Catholic and speak standard French. Lower-class refugees from Haiti, who are usually black, practice Voodoo or Catholicism (sometimes both) and speak Creole French.

The map shows West Indian-Americans living in eastern Oklahoma and western Texas. Most of these are probably Native American Indians who choose to call themselves "West Indians."

The 1990 Census counted 1,157,000 West Indians, of which 805,000 were from English-speaking areas, 290,000 from Haiti, and 62,000 from the Dutch West Indies. More than half of the English-speakers were from Jamaica.

Hawaiian-Americans and Native Americans

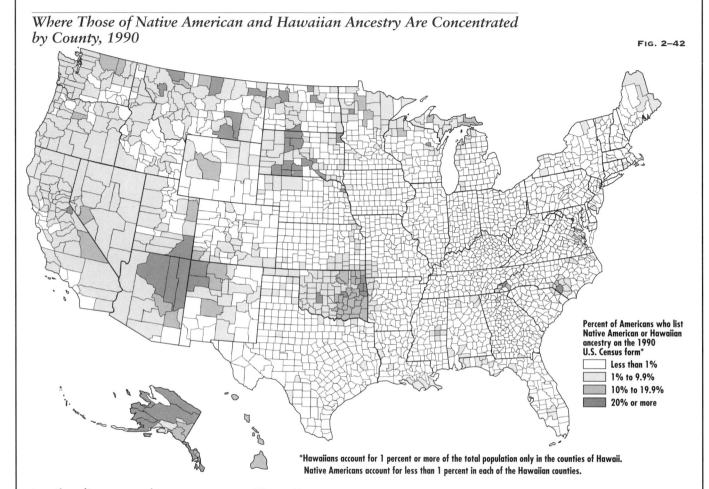

Where Those of Native American and Hawaiian Ancestry Are Concentrated by County, 1990

FIG. 2–42

Percent of Americans who list Native American or Hawaiian ancestry on the 1990 U.S. Census form*

- Less than 1%
- 1% to 9.9%
- 10% to 19.9%
- 20% or more

*Hawaiians account for 1 percent or more of the total population only in the counties of Hawaii.
Native Americans account for less than 1 percent in each of the Hawaiian counties.

The first people to come to Hawaii were Polynesians from the Marquesas and other Pacific islands who arrived about A.D. 400. Four hundred to 500 years later immigrants from Tahiti added a different cultural strain. By 1778, when Captain James Cook landed on the islands, Hawaiians numbered about 300,000. But they lacked immunity to European diseases, and so the population fell to 71,000 by 1853 and to 38,500 by 1910. In 1900, 24 percent of the population on the islands claimed some Hawaiian ancestry. After American annexation in 1898, the islands were dominated politically by a combination of Hawaiians and Caucasians, but after World War II, Asian-Americans became dominant. In 1990, the total number of people claiming Hawaiian ancestry was 211,000, of which 139,000 lived on the islands. Most of these are of mixed ancestry, and few still speak the native Hawaiian language.

The first inhabitants of North America began crossing the broad glacial plain of what is now the Bering Strait 12,000 to 20,000 years ago. Recent research has distinguished three broad groups of Native American languages: Amerind, which covers all of South and Central America, and most of the lower 48 states; Na-Dene, which covers parts of the American Southwest and northern Mexico in addition to eastern Alaska and northwest Canada; and Eskimo-Aleut, found in western Alaska and most of the inhabited Arctic. These three groups suggest that there were three waves of migration into the Western Hemisphere, with the Amerind being the first to enter and the Eskimo-Aleut being the last.

By 1492, according to one estimate, the descendants of the three groups numbered 7 million or more in the area north of the Rio Grande. As white settlers pushed Native Americans out of their hunting grounds onto less desirable land, generally to the West, the Indian population shrank. From 1816 to 1850, there was a massive migration, largely involuntary, of almost 100,000 Native Americans from the eastern states to the area west of the Mississippi. Many of them went to the Indian Territory, or what is now Oklahoma. The western lands were in turn soon coveted by whites, resulting in more conflict, with the U.S. Army pitted against native warriors. Native Americans had some successes, notably the defeat of General Custer in 1876, but this was their last victory. By the spring of 1877, the U.S. Army was in control. By 1885, the buffalo herds, which had been the major food source of the Plains tribes, had all but disappeared. In the Southwest, which was under Spanish domination until the 1840s, Native Americans fared better. The Spanish, unlike the British and the Americans, were interested in making Christian converts and did not ordinarily push natives off the land. By an act of Congress, Native Americans became U.S. citizens in 1924.

The 1990 U.S. Census counted almost 2 million Native Americans, of whom 57,000 were Eskimos and 24,000 were Aleuts. Native Americans are a majority in 22 counties.

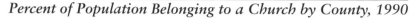

Percent of Population Belonging to a Church by County, 1990

FIG. 2–43

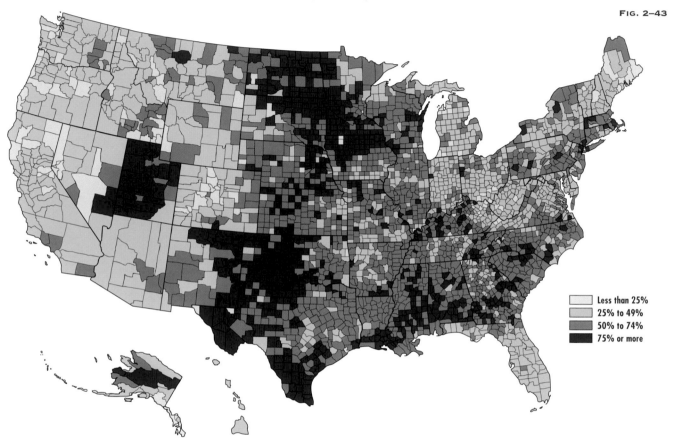

Less than 25%
25% to 49%
50% to 74%
75% or more

Americans are far more religious than Europeans. Seventy percent are church members and 40 percent attend church every week. Weekly attendance in England, France, Italy, and Germany is about 10 percent. (The only Western country in which attendance exceeds that of the United States is Ireland, where the rate is 60 percent.) Almost 90 percent of Americans believe in the existence of God. Seventy-five percent believe in the effectiveness of prayer; 80 percent believe that they will be called before God on Judgment Day to answer for their sins; and 80 percent believe that God performs miracles, even today. Only 14 percent of Americans feel that religion is "not very important" in their lives.

The areas with the highest concentrations of church adherents are in the South, particularly those parts dominated by Baptists and other conservative groups; in the upper North Central states, where Lutherans are strong; and in Utah, which is dominated by Mormons.

Figure 2-44 shows the areas dominated by the six leading Christian religious groups. The largest of these, the Catholics, has 55 million adherents. Roman Catholicism came to what is now Florida in 1565 and to the Southwest in 1598, when the Spaniards converted thousands of American Indians. Although the thinly populated Southwest became predominantly Protestant in the 19th century, as settlers from the East gradually took control, the influx of Mexicans in the 20th century has made Catholicism again the leading religion in this area. In 1634 Maryland was established by Lord Baltimore as a Roman Catholic colony, but one in which freedom of religion was guaranteed for all Christians. However, relatively few Catholics from northern Europe migrated to Maryland or other British colonies. Louisiana was populated by French-speaking Catholic refugees from Canada in the mid-18th century, but it was not until the 1840s that Catholics came to the United States in large numbers, when Irish, Italian, German, and Polish Catholics settled mainly in the industrial Northeast and Midwest.

The Baptists, who are direct theological descendants of the 17th-century English Puritans, are the second largest group, with 28 million adherents in 24 denominations; the largest, the Southern Baptist Convention, accounts for half of all the Baptists in the country. Half or more of all Baptists are fundamentalists—believers in Biblical infallibility.

Major Denominational Families by County, 1990

FIG. 2–44

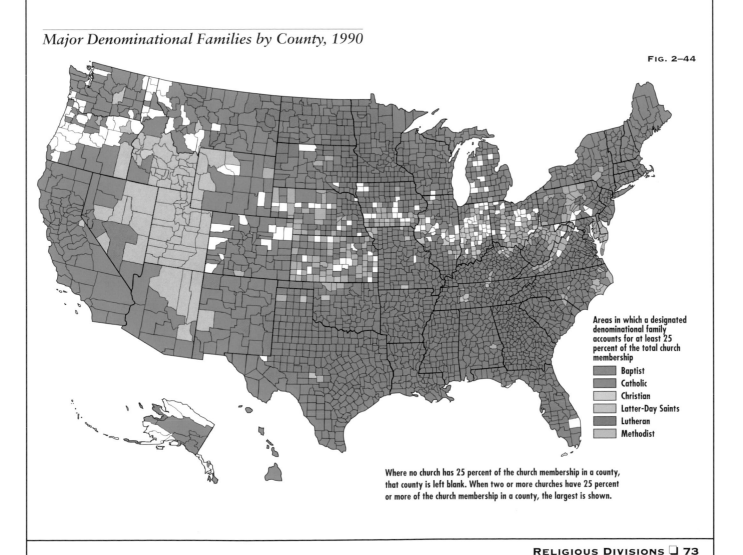

Areas in which a designated denominational family accounts for at least 25 percent of the total church membership

- Baptist
- Catholic
- Christian
- Latter-Day Saints
- Lutheran
- Methodist

Where no church has 25 percent of the church membership in a county, that county is left blank. When two or more churches have 25 percent or more of the church membership in a county, the largest is shown.

The Christian Churches, a group of three denominations tracing to the early 19th century, have an affinity with Baptist doctrine but consider themselves distinct. Their adherents are estimated at 3.8 million.

Methodism, which was founded by John Wesley in the early 18th century as a reform movement within the Church of England, drew its inspiration mainly from Puritanism. Methodists were practicing in America as early as 1769, and by the early 19th century were one of the leading denominations in the new republic. Adherents number over 13 million in 13 denominations, of which the United Methodist Church accounts for 9 million.

Among the non-Puritan Protestant denominations, the Lutherans are the most numerous. American Lutherans, who are mostly descendants of 19th-century German and Scandinavian immigrants, number about 8.4 million in 13 denominations, of which the largest is the Evangelical Lutheran Church in America, with 5.3 million adherents.

The Church of Jesus Christ of Latter-Day Saints was founded by Joseph Smith in upstate New York in 1830, but because of persecution, his followers moved west, settling finally in Utah in 1847. Adherents, who number 4.2 million, are also known as the Mormons.

Other important Christian denominations not shown on the map include the Presbyterian Church (USA), with 3.5 million adherents; the United Church of Christ, with 2 million; the Episcopal Church, with 2.5 million; and the Assemblies of God, with 2.2 million.

Liberal, Moderate, and Conservative Protestant Churches by County, 1990

FIG. 2–45

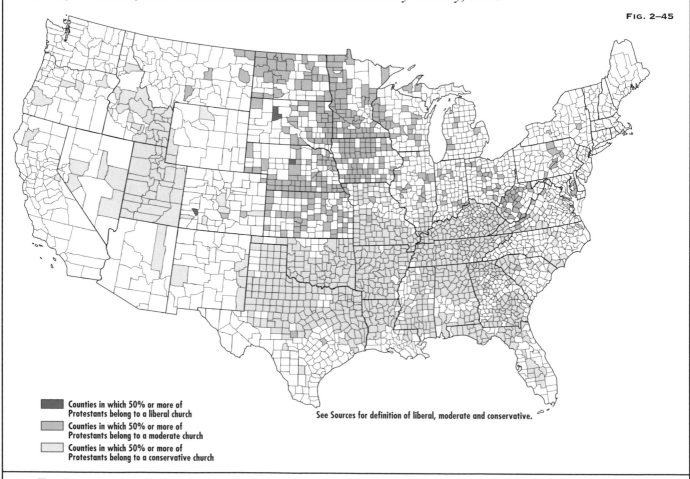

Counties in which 50% or more of Protestants belong to a liberal church

Counties in which 50% or more of Protestants belong to a moderate church

Counties in which 50% or more of Protestants belong to a conservative church

See Sources for definition of liberal, moderate and conservative.

Where Jews Are Concentrated by County, 1990

FIG. 2–46

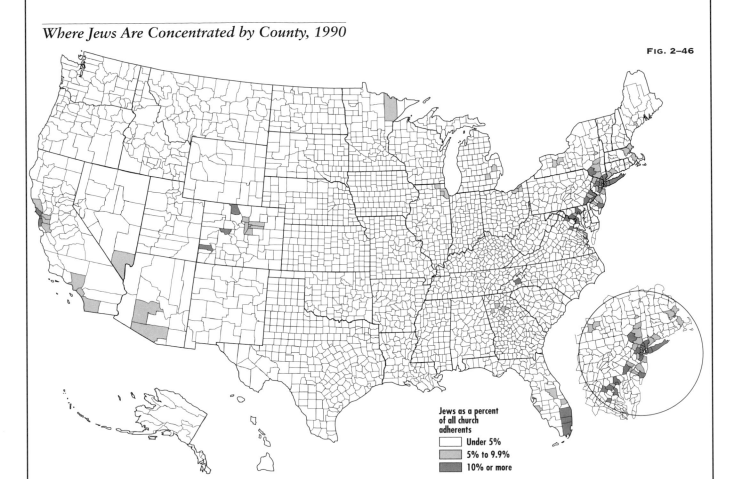

Jews as a percent
of all church
adherents

☐ Under 5%
☐ 5% to 9.9%
☐ 10% or more

Jews migrated to North America throughout the 17th and 18th centuries, but in such small numbers that they totaled only 6,000 by 1830. These early arrivals were mostly Sephardim—Jews from Spain and Portugal. Ashkenazim—Jews from the rest of Europe—began immigrating in substantial numbers around 1830. Until 1880, when the Jewish population of the United States totaled a quarter of a million, most Ashkenazim were German- and/or Yiddish-speaking. From 1880 to the 1920s, Ashkenazim from eastern Europe arrived in huge numbers, and today they and their descendants account for most of the Jews in the United States.

Reform Judaism, which has its roots in early 19th-century Germany, modified or abandoned many traditional beliefs and practices in order to adapt Judaism to the modern world. Conservative Judaism, which also originated in 19th-century Germany,

sought a middle ground between the radical Reform movement and traditional Orthodox practice. Orthodox Judaism encompasses several sects, including the Hasidim, who oppose any change from the old ways in speech, dress, or education. There are about 5.5 million Americans of Jewish heritage, of whom 38 percent are Reform, 35 percent Conservative, 6 percent Orthodox, and 20 percent secular.

Cities Where Minorities Are a Majority

O f the 400 largest cities, 21 now have African-American majorities, 17 have Hispanic majorities, and one—Honolulu—has an Asian majority. In addition, there are 37 cities in which no group has a majority.

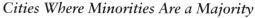

Cities Where Minorities Are a Majority

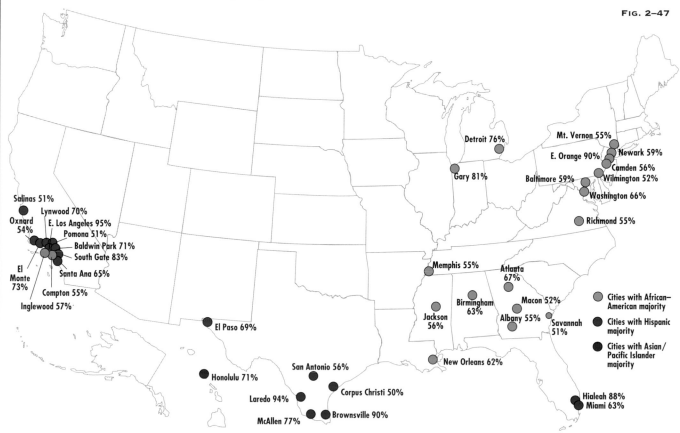

FIG. 2–47

Detroit 76%

Mt. Vernon 55%

E. Orange 90% Newark 59%

Camden 56%

Gary 81% Baltimore 59% Wilmington 52%

Washington 66%

Richmond 55%

Salinas 51%

Lynwood 70%

Oxnard 54% E. Los Angeles 95%

Pomona 51%

Baldwin Park 71%

South Gate 83%

El Monte 73% Santa Ana 65%

Compton 55%

Inglewood 57%

Memphis 55% Atlanta 67%

Macon 52%

Birmingham 63%

Jackson 56% Albany 55% Savannah 51%

El Paso 69%

Honolulu 71%

San Antonio 56%

New Orleans 62%

Corpus Christi 50%

Laredo 94%

McAllen 77% Brownsville 90%

Hialeah 88%
Miami 63%

Cities with African-American majority

Cities with Hispanic majority

Cities with Asian/Pacific Islander majority

1990 U.S. Census data for the top 400 cities and towns in the U.S. were analyzed in preparing the map.

Percent Speaking a Language Other Than English at Home by County, 1990

FIG. 2–48

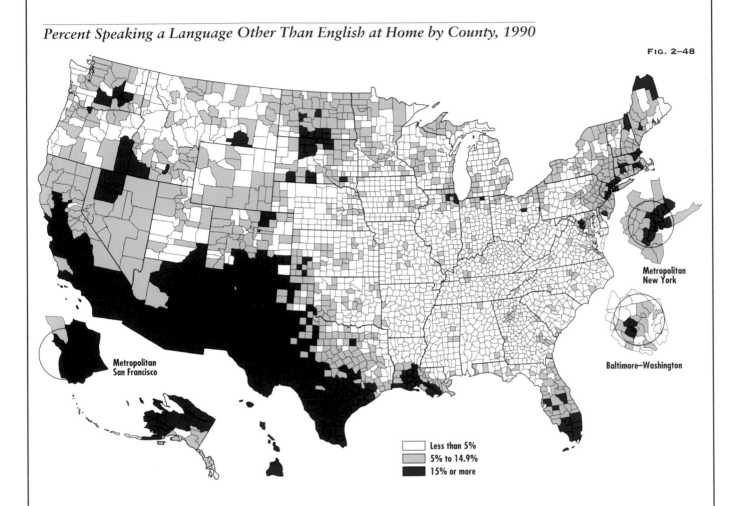

Metropolitan
New York

Metropolitan
San Francisco

Baltimore–Washington

Less than 5%
5% to 14.9%
15% or more

Almost 32 million Americans aged five and over speak a language other than English at home. Of these, 54 percent speak Spanish, 6 percent French, 5 percent German, 4 percent Italian, 4 percent Chinese, 3 percent Tagalog (the official language of the Philippines), 2 percent Polish, and 2 percent a language of the Indian subcontinent.

American Regional Dialects

Major Dialect Regions

FIG. 2-49

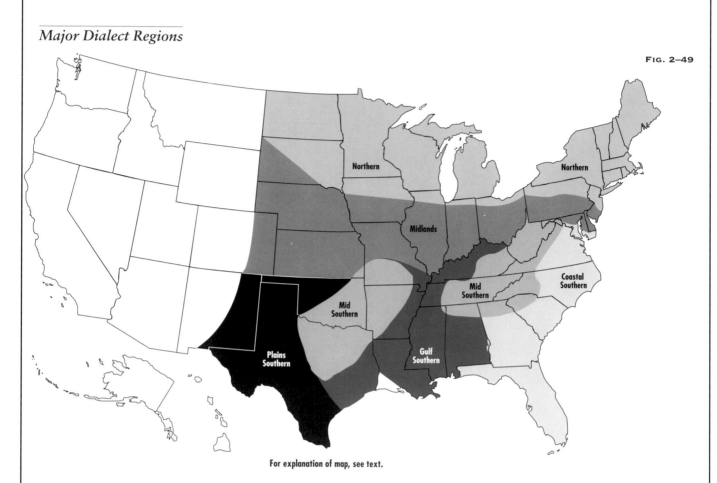

For explanation of map, see text.

Figure 2-49 shows the major dialect regions of the eastern United States as defined by Professor Gordon R. Wood of Southern Illinois University at Carbondale. The Northern dialect originated with the Puritan immigration to Massachusetts beginning in 1620, and the Midland dialect with the Quaker immigration to eastern Pennsylvania beginning in 1670. The New England dialect, with its dropped *r*'s ("pa'k the cah in the ya'd") remains more resistant to homogenization than any other dialect outside the South. New Englanders who migrated west had an important effect upon the speech of New York, the Midwest, the Rocky Mountain area, and the Pacific states, particularly the Northwest. In the Northern region, for example, people tend to say *greasy*, while in the Midlands they are apt to say *greazy*. Within both regions there are many local distinctions, such as the nasal sound of Rochester, New York, natives, and the *oi* sound in words like *girl*, *bird*, and *heard*, found in so-called Brooklynese. This pronunciation is not peculiar to New York City for it can be heard in New Orleans and Charleston, South Carolina, two other areas that, like New York City, were heavily influenced by immigration of lower-class Londoners in the 17th and 18th centuries.

The Coastal Southern dialects radiated from the Tidewater region of Virginia, where the English settled beginning in 1607, and from Charleston, South Carolina, where a mixed group of English, French, Dutch, and others settled beginning in 1670. Gulf Southern dialects radiated from New Orleans, founded by the French in 1717. Midsouthern dialects originated with Scotch-Irish and German immigrants beginning in the 1730s. The South, like the North, is a patchwork of local accents. In Alabama, there are some who say "ass" meaning "eyes." South Carolinians, like Senator Strom Thurmond, would stand "foim" against this way of speaking.

3

The Environment and Quality of Life

Air Pollution

Since enactment of the Clean Air Act of 1970, the Environmental Protection Agency has attempted, with some success, to reduce air pollution. The focus has been on six substances emitted by industrial plants and motor vehicles: (1) carbon monoxide, which in sufficiently high concentrations can kill; (2) lead, which affects blood-forming organs, kidneys, and the nervous system; (3) suspended particulates, which clog the lungs and carry carcinogens and toxic metals; (4) nitrogen dioxide, which lowers resistance to respiratory infection; (5) sulfur dioxide, which is associated with coughs, colds, asthma, and bronchitis;

and (6) ozone, which impairs lung function. (The thinning of the ozone layer in the upper atmosphere is a different problem.) Two of these compounds, nitrogen dioxide and sulfur dioxide, also contribute to acid rain.

The EPA has set maximum acceptable health standards for each of these contaminants and measures their concentration in the air. Areas that failed to attain these standards are shown in Figure 3-1. In the last decade or so, concentrations of toxic air pollutants have been reduced, particularly in the case of lead.

Counties with Areas That Do Not Meet EPA Standards for Six Contaminants, 1990

FIG. 3–1

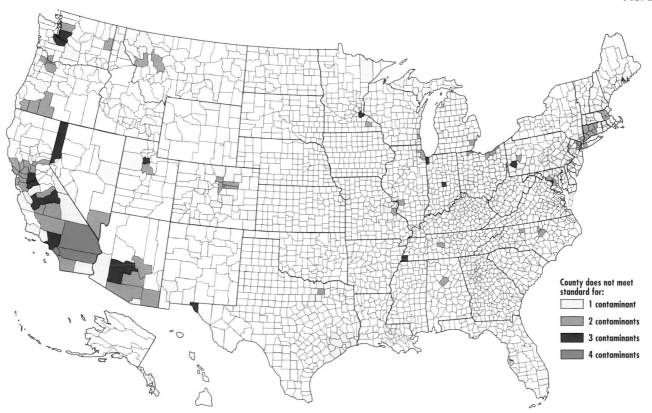

County does not meet standard for:
- 1 contaminant
- 2 contaminants
- 3 contaminants
- 4 contaminants

Map is based on measurements made in 1990 by the Environmental Protection Agency of six substances: ozone, carbon monoxide, particulate matter, sulfur dioxide, lead, and nitrogen dioxide.

According to the greenhouse theory, planetary temperatures are greatly affected by atmospheric gases, notably carbon dioxide, which come mainly from the burning of fossil fuels. Other "greenhouse" gases include nitrous oxide (mainly from fertilizer), methane (from a variety of synthetic and natural sources), and chlorofluorocarbons (from synthetic chemicals used in aerosol cans and in industry). An increase of these gases in the atmosphere traps heat and thereby causes a rise in global temperature. (Venus, which has an excess of CO_2, is very hot, while Mars, which lacks CO_2, is very cold.) During the past century, the amount of carbon dioxide in the atmosphere has been rising because of the increased burning of fossil fuels and is now more than 25 percent greater than a century ago. Global temperatures have risen over the past century, but whether this rise is due to increased CO_2 is not clear.

The possible effects of a warmer earth in the 21st century include decreased rainfall in grain-producing areas of North America, erosion of the West Atlantic ice sheet, with a consequent rise in sea level, and the destruction of species unable to adapt to rapid changes in their habitats.

The greenhouse theory is widely accepted by climatologists, but because many aspects of the climate system are not well understood, there is considerable uncertainty about the future course of global temperature. In order to understand climatic trends, several groups of scientists have constructed computer models that attempt to predict how the global climate may change decades or more in the future. One of the best known is the model devised by James Hansen and his colleagues at NASA's Goddard Space Institute in New York. It features global maps showing predicted changes in temperature for various dates, including the year 2000. Figure 3-2 shows the North American portion of this map. The map is remarkable not for its precision—Dr. Hansen says that there are major uncertainties in the underlying computer model—but for the fact that serious scientists would actually make predictions that only a few years ago would have been considered science fiction. The temperature changes shown on the map are

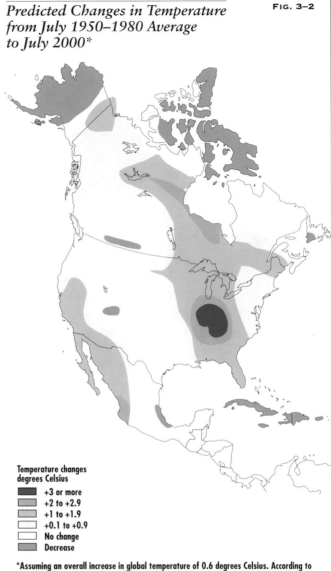

Predicted Changes in Temperature from July 1950–1980 Average to July 2000*

FIG. 3–2

Temperature changes degrees Celsius

- +3 or more
- +2 to +2.9
- +1 to +1.9
- +0.1 to +0.9
- No change
- Decrease

*Assuming an overall increase in global temperature of 0.6 degrees Celsius. According to James E. Hansen, the leader of the group that produced the global map on which the above map is based, "specific temperature patterns for any given month and year should not be viewed as predictions for that specific time, because they depend on unpredictable weather fluctuations."

Changes in Geographical Range of Sugar Maple Trees Assuming Doubled Carbon Dioxide Levels

FIG. 3–3

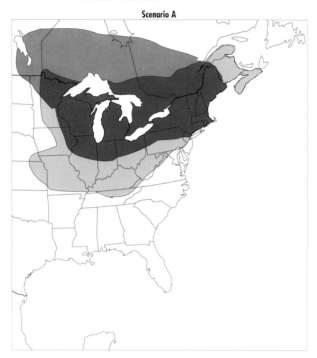

Scenario A

Scenario B

based on the assumption that emissions of greenhouse gases will grow at a decreasing rate. A substantial cut in emissions would result in smaller temperature increases, according to the computer model used by the NASA Goddard group.

It should be noted that, although computer modeling of global climate scenarios is widely accepted as a tool for gaining insight into future trends, some scientists are skeptical of its utility. Sherwood P. Idso of the U.S. Department of Agriculture, for example, believes that the greenhouse effect will be on an order of magnitude less than that predicted by computer models like those used by Dr. Hansen and his colleagues.

The biological effects of global warming cannot be forecast with certainty, given the lack of information on how most plants and animals will respond. Warming could result in the extinction of many species that depend on fragile ecosystems, such as the monarch butterfly and the polar bear, to name only two.

Two scientists from the University of Minnesota, Dr. Margaret B. Davis and Dr. Catherine Zabinskie, have projected the effect of global warming on several species of trees, including sugar maple, using two different climate models, one conservative and the other less so (Figure 3-3). Even under the more conservative model, the geographical distribution of sugar maples would be substantially altered. In the more radical model these trees would virtually disappear from the eastern United States. If the climate change is too fast, sugar maples could not adapt quickly enough to survive. These trees, together with three other susceptible species—beech, hemlock and yellow birch—are the dominant canopy cover in Eastern forests, and so their displacement northward would profoundly affect many animals and smaller plants.

Present geographical range

Potential geographical range with doubled CO_2

The maps show two scenarios. The more conservative—scenario A—predicts higher temperatures throughout eastern North America and slightly increased moisture in the Great Plains. The more radical—scenario B—predicts higher temperatures and decreased soil moisture.

Acid rain is said to cause what the Germans term *Waldsterben*—forest death—but there is no evidence, according to the National Acid Precipitation Assessment Program, that this has happened in the United States on a wide scale. What has happened, says NAPAP, is localized forest damage due to multiple stress factors that include climate and pests, in addition to acid rain. Some high-elevation spruce and fir forests in the eastern U.S., for example, have suffered from the extremely acidic cloud water sometimes found at higher altitudes. NAPAP says that acid rain probably does not kill trees directly but makes them more vulnerable to disease, insects, shortages of water, and extremes of weather and storm damage.

Acid rain has been traced mainly to coal- and oil-burning power plants, which emit nitrous oxides and sulfur dioxide, and motor vehicles, which emit nitrous oxides. These emissions are converted to nitric and sulfuric acids that are then incorporated into cloud droplets. As prevailing weather patterns move the clouds east, they drop acidified moisture into lakes and streams that may be hundreds or even thousands of miles from the source of the chemicals. Certain areas of the East, such as the Adirondacks, have a poor ability to buffer the acid rain, and consequently many lakes and streams become highly acidic and inhospitable to wildlife. This trend has slowed in recent years as air pollution prevention measures have taken effect.

Acid Rain

FIG. 3-4

Sulfate

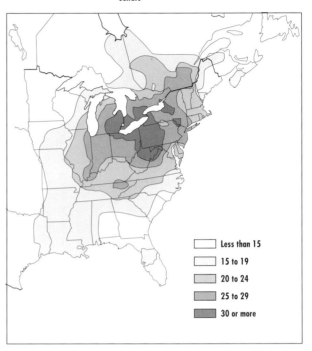

Less than 15
15 to 19
20 to 24
25 to 29
30 or more

Nitrate

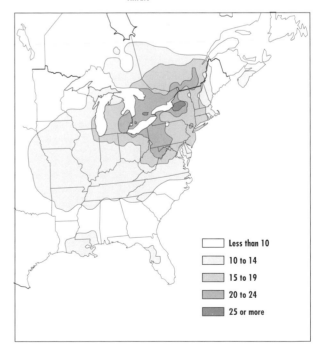

Less than 10
10 to 14
15 to 19
20 to 24
25 or more

The maps show annual wet deposition of sulfate and nitrate in 1985–87 in terms of kilograms per hectare.

Radon

Radon is a colorless, odorless gas produced by the decay of uranium in rocks and soil. Radon gas breaks down into "daughters," products of the radioactive decay process, and it is these that may pose a direct threat to human health. Outdoors, radon is harmless, but it can seep into houses through cracks in concrete floors and walls, floor drains, and sump pumps, and can build up over time. The daughter products adhere to particulate matter in the air. Prolonged exposure to a high concentration of these products causes lung cancer. According to one estimate, radon may contribute to as many as 20,000 lung cancer deaths annually, of which perhaps 5,000 are nonsmokers.

The case for radon as a cancer-causing agent in homes rests not on direct evidence but on epidemiological studies of uranium miners in Colorado, Czechoslovakia, and Ontario, and of iron miners in Sweden. These miners suffered an excess of lung cancer, with the risk being particularly high among those who smoked.

The EPA, together with several state agencies, conducted sample surveys of homes in 46 states to determine levels of radon concentration. The map shows the proportion of homes in these states that had a level high enough to cause concern, that is, 4 picocuries or more per liter of air. The map provides a general indication of the areas most prone to radon seepage, but individual houses within a state may vary considerably in vulnerability to contamination, depending on location, quality of construction, adequacy of ventilation, and the condition of the soil. In the 46 states studied, about 20 percent of homes had radon levels of 4 picocuries or more, and 1.6 percent had levels of 20 or more.

The EPA recommends that everyone living in a detached house (including trailer homes with a permanent foundation), or in basement or first- or second-floor apartments, test for radon using an inexpensive kit. Radon can be reduced to acceptable levels by proper ventilation and the sealing of basement cracks and openings, usually at a cost of $500 to $2,000 per house, according to the EPA.

*Percent of Homes with High Levels of Radon**

FIG. 3–5

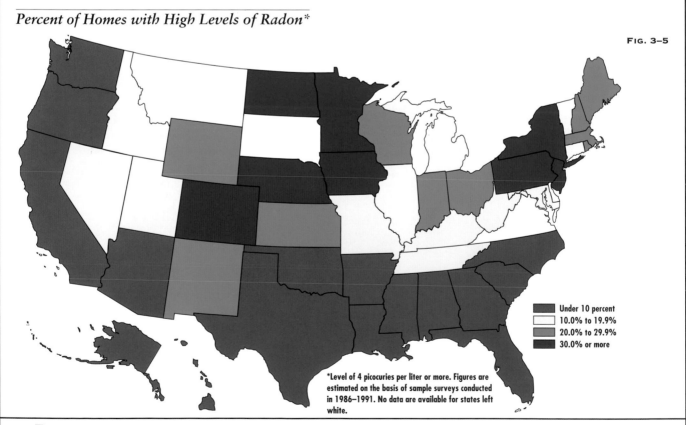

Under 10 percent
10.0% to 19.9%
20.0% to 29.9%
30.0% or more

*Level of 4 picocuries per liter or more. Figures are estimated on the basis of sample surveys conducted in 1986–1991. No data are available for states left white.

Toxic Waste Dumps

FIG. 3–6

The map shows the site of dumps identified by the Environmental Protection Agency for cleanup under the "Superfund" law as of January, 1994.

In the 1890s William T. Love, a visionary industrialist, conceived the idea of an industrial community that would benefit from the electric power of Niagara Falls. As part of his plan, there was to be a canal linking Lake Erie and Lake Ontario. The plan was abandoned in the depression of the 1890s but not before a thousand yards of the canal had been built. For the following 40 years Love Canal was used as a swimming hole, but in 1942 the Hooker Chemical Company (now a part of Occidental Chemical) began using it as a depository for chemical wastes. In the early 1950s, after dumping had stopped, inexpensive tract houses and an elementary school were built on the adjacent land, and 2,600 people, oblivious to the hazard, moved in. It was only in 1978 that the residents awoke to the potential danger of their situation.

Largely because of Love Canal, Congress in 1980 created the Superfund, designed to clean up toxic waste dumps throughout the country. Then began the search to identify the most hazardous sites. Many dumps had been abandoned years earlier and their locations and contents all but forgotten. Ordinary citizens, unable to evaluate the danger from nearby dump sites, became overanxious. In at least one case—this was in a suburb of Memphis—there were highly charged protests regarding an area that local residents felt certain was filled with deadly chemical wastes. But on closer examination, it was found that no such chemical dump existed.

The Environmental Protection Agency has identified over 24,000 hazardous dumps, of which well over a thousand are on its priority list for removal or containment. Few of the sites pose a direct risk to householders in the way that Love Canal did, but they are sources of pollution for streams and groundwater. Many of the chemicals found in the dumps, such as benzidene, benzene, carbon tetrachloride, and polychlorinated biphenols are known or suspected carcinogens.

Erosion of Cropland

Erosion of Cropland, 1987

FIG. 3-7

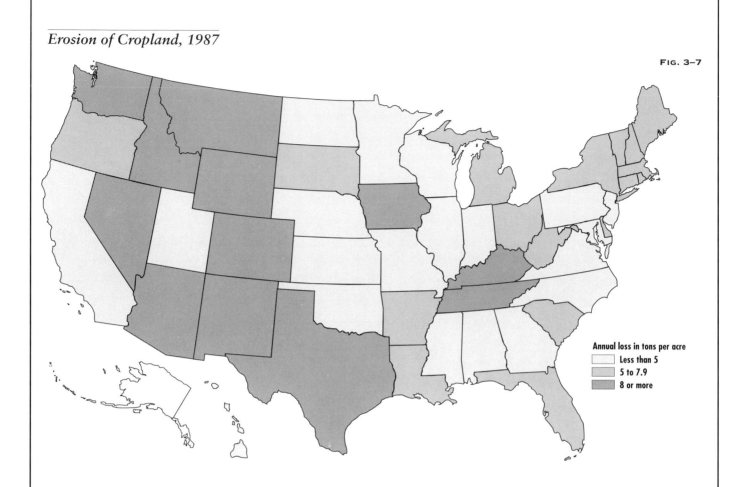

Annual loss in tons per acre
- Less than 5
- 5 to 7.9
- 8 or more

There is considerable concern that American agriculture will eventually decline because of soil erosion. Land with deep topsoil can lose up to five tons an acre annually with no harmful effect. However, on a third of all cropland the loss is greater than five tons. An inch of topsoil that can be blown away in an hour may take nature a hundred years to replace.

The problem of soil erosion traces partly to use of the traditional moldboard plow, which digs into the soil, turning it over, making it more dispersible by wind. The chisel plow, recommended by conservation-ists, exposes only enough soil for planting. In another conservation method—slit planting—deep but narrow seed trenches are cut. Herbicides promote conservation to the extent that they replace mechanical methods of weeding that turn up the soil. Technologies like these, together with contour ploughing and terracing, are probably the solution to America's soil conservation problem. However, poorer farmers are less able to take advantage of these methods. Herbicides could have serious, adverse effects on the environment, although most experts believe that the damage will prove to be relatively minor.

Overgrazing of rangeland by cattle is a prime contributor to the increase in desert land in the western United States. Another important factor is salinization of the soil due to poor drainage on irrigated land. Dr. Harold Dregne of Texas Tech University, working with the United Nations Environment Program, measured the productivity of cropland and rangeland west of the 100th meridian (North Dakota through central Texas). Based on this, Dr. Dregne created a map showing areas of desertification.

Dr. Dregne identified 13 million acres in Texas, New Mexico, and Arizona that have suffered "very severe" desertification. These areas, which have lost more than 50 percent of their productivity, are in his words "irreversibly degraded and cannot be economically rehabilitated or improved." According to Dr. Dregne, an additional 430 million acres have experienced a 25 percent to 50 percent decline in productivity. Part of the problem is caused by the northern European cattle that were imported into the western United States. Unlike the indigenous bison, these herds require wet places and high-protein forage, both scarce in the West. A cow that requires one acre in the East might need as much as 200 acres in the Southwest. The cattle destroy the fragile topsoil, exposing the ground underneath to water and wind erosion.

Estimated Desertification

FIG. 3–8

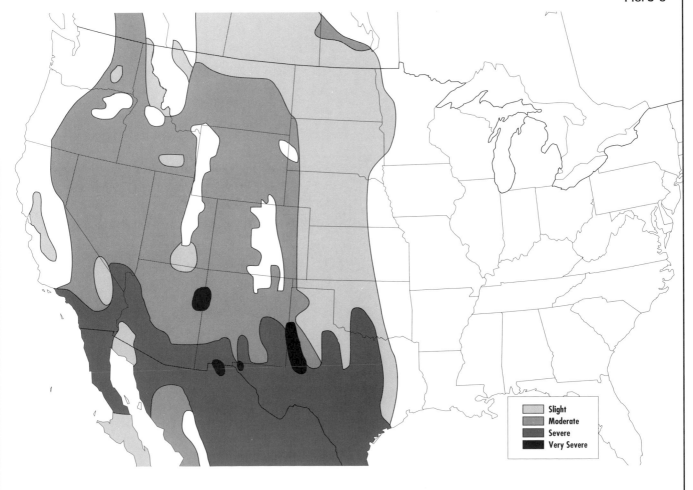

Slight
Moderate
Severe
Very Severe

Chief Type of Fuel Used in Home Heating

The Northeast and the Upper South have long depended on oil for heating and air-conditioning, and so are vulnerable to sudden world oil shortages, as in 1973-1974. Any plan to make the United States energy-sufficient would probably have to emphasize domestic natural gas and wind and solar power.

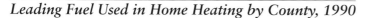

Leading Fuel Used in Home Heating by County, 1990

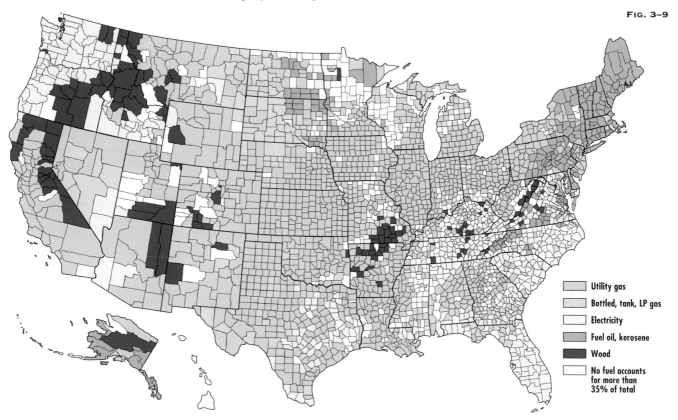

FIG. 3–9

Utility gas
Bottled, tank, LP gas
Electricity
Fuel oil, kerosene
Wood
No fuel accounts for more than 35% of total

The 25 Nuclear Plants with the Lowest Safety Ratings

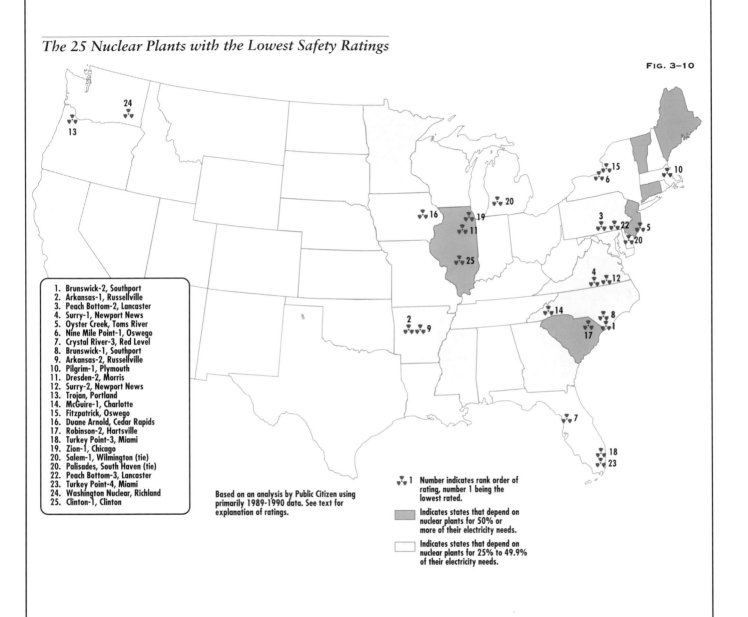

FIG. 3–10

1. Brunswick-2, Southport
2. Arkansas-1, Russellville
3. Peach Bottom-2, Lancaster
4. Surry-1, Newport News
5. Oyster Creek, Toms River
6. Nine Mile Point-1, Oswego
7. Crystal River-3, Red Level
8. Brunswick-1, Southport
9. Arkansas-2, Russellville
10. Pilgrim-1, Plymouth
11. Dresden-2, Morris
12. Surry-2, Newport News
13. Trojan, Portland
14. McGuire-1, Charlotte
15. Fitzpatrick, Oswego
16. Duane Arnold, Cedar Rapids
17. Robinson-2, Hartsville
18. Turkey Point-3, Miami
19. Zion-1, Chicago
20. Salem-1, Wilmington (tie)
20. Palisades, South Haven (tie)
22. Peach Bottom-3, Lancaster
23. Turkey Point-4, Miami
24. Washington Nuclear, Richland
25. Clinton-1, Clinton

Based on an analysis by Public Citizen using primarily 1989-1990 data. See text for explanation of ratings.

1   Number indicates rank order of rating, number 1 being the lowest rated.

Indicates states that depend on nuclear plants for 50% or more of their electricity needs.

Indicates states that depend on nuclear plants for 25% to 49.9% of their electricity needs.

Public Citizen, a Ralph Nader-affiliated consumer organization, has raised the question: Which commercial nuclear reactors in the United States are at the greatest risk of having a major accident? To answer the question, a team from Public Citizen headed by David J. Trickett and Ken Bossong analyzed the records of nuclear plants.

The analysis was based on 14 criteria, such as the number of mishaps reported to the Nuclear Regulatory Commission, the number of emergency reactor shutdowns, the total amount of radioactive effluents released into air and water, and the amount of high-level nuclear waste stored at reactor sites. The 25 least safe reactors as listed in the Public Citizen report are shown on the map.

Wind-Powered Electricity

Proportion of Total U.S. Electricity Needs That Could Be Generated by Wind

FIG. 3–11

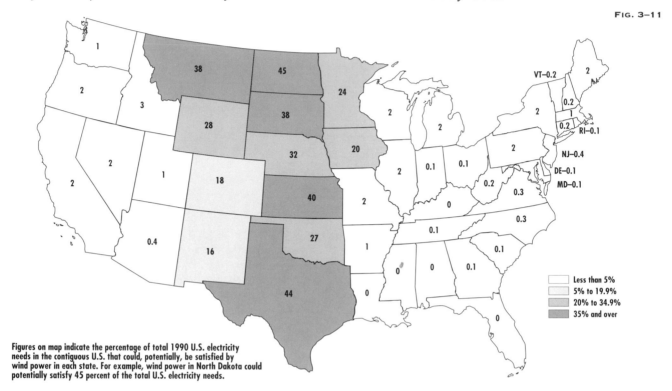

Figures on map indicate the percentage of total 1990 U.S. electricity needs in the contiguous U.S. that could, potentially, be satisfied by wind power in each state. For example, wind power in North Dakota could potentially satisfy 45 percent of the total U.S. electricity needs.

Legend:
- Less than 5%
- 5% to 19.9%
- 20% to 34.9%
- 35% and over

The potential for wind-powered electricity is substantial. Current technology, such as the high-tech windmills used successfully in certain areas of California, can generate electricity on a cost-effective basis from what is called class-5 wind power (speed of 14.3 miles per hour at a height of 33 feet, and 17.9 miles per hour at 164 feet). About 0.6 percent of the land area in the contiguous United States—about 175,000 square miles—has class-5 or greater wind power. Full utilization of this potential would satisfy about 20 percent of U.S. electric consumption or about 7 percent of the total consumption of energy from all sources, including imported oil.

This substantial amount of renewable energy is dwarfed by the potential that could be tapped with improved technology, according to a report issued in 1991 by D.L. Elliott and his colleagues at the Pacific Northwest Laboratory of the Battelle Memorial Institute. Taller and larger-diameter turbines with superior airfoil designs and better controls could tap the potential of class-3 wind power (speed of 12.5 miles per hour at 33 feet, and 15.7 miles per hour at 164 feet). Class-3 power, which is present on about 13 percent of the contiguous U.S. land area, has the potential of *quadrupling the current electrical power generation in the United States*. It is equivalent to 125 percent of total energy consumption in the nation. Storing the energy for use in peak periods in distant locations presents problems, but it is possible that a substantial portion of the potential could be utilized.

Dr. Elliott and his colleagues have calculated the proportion of total U.S. electricity needs that could be satisfied by class-3 wind power generated in each state. Figure 3-11 shows their estimates, which are based on the assumption that 35 percent of the total area with class-3 wind power will be excluded for environmental and land-use reasons. The map shows that North Dakota, South Dakota, and Nebraska combined have the potential of generating electricity equivalent to 115 percent of total U.S. electricity consumption. The potential in these three states is equivalent to 40 percent of the total U.S. energy consumption.

Tornadoes form when there is a highly unstable distribution of humidity and temperature, when winds in the upper atmosphere favor strong updrafts, and when strong cold fronts provide the lift to start convection. These conditions are likely to occur when humid tropical air meets a polar air mass. The two masses of air meet most forcefully during the spring in the central part of the country.

The diameter of a tornado funnel is rarely greater than 600 feet. Typically, tornadoes last for less than an hour and achieve winds upward of 100 miles an hour. In the most violent kind, winds may reach 300 miles an hour. Tornado-producing thunderstorms in most cases have only one funnel, but sometimes there are multiple funnels spread out over hundreds of miles. The most destructive tornado ever recorded in the United States occurred in March 1925 and cut a 300-mile path through southern Missouri, Illinois, and southern Indiana, killing 689 people. On average, 100 Americans die every year in tornadoes.

There is nothing that can be done about this weather phenomenon except to provide better shelters and earlier warnings. The National Weather Service expects, by the mid-1990s, to complete installation of a new Doppler radar detection system that will increase warning time throughout the United States.

Tornadoes

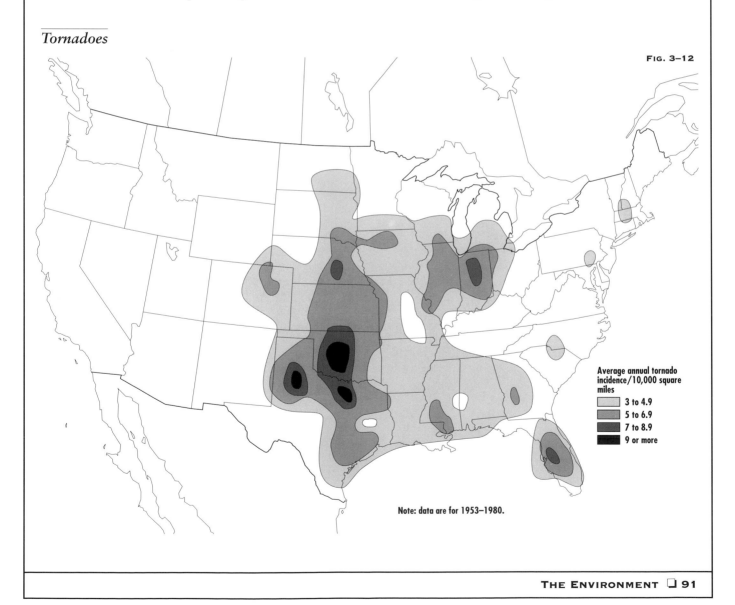

FIG. 3–12

Average annual tornado incidence/10,000 square miles

3 to 4.9
5 to 6.9
7 to 8.9
9 or more

Note: data are for 1953–1980.

Earthquakes

It may come as a surprise to many that large areas of the East are candidates for major earthquakes. Eighteen years after the Pilgrims landed in Plymouth in 1620, New England was shaken by a strong earthquake. The most widely felt earthquake ever recorded in North America occurred in New Madrid, Missouri, in 1811-12. Shocks from this earthquake, which was more severe than the San Francisco quake of 1906, were felt from the Atlantic to the Rocky Mountains and from Canada to the Gulf of Mexico. The 1886 earthquake in Charleston, South Carolina, was felt in Chicago and New York. California, however, gets 55 percent of the earthquakes in the United States that are strong enough to be felt. In a typical year, 100 to 200 quakes in the United States are strong enough to cause destruction. On average, 18 of these register 7.0 or more on the Richter scale, and 1 or 2 register 8.0 or more. The San Francisco quake of 1906 registered 8.2 and the Alaska quake of 1964 registered 8.5.

The earliest accurate record of an earthquake was in A.D. 856 at Corinth, Greece, where 45,000 were killed. The greatest toll was in China's Shensi province in 1556, when 830,000 perished. The Tokyo quake of 1923 took 143,000 lives. In the past 100 years, a million people worldwide have died in earthquakes.

Earthquakes can generate tsunamis (tidal waves), which occur mostly in the Pacific. In 1946 a tsunami killed 170 people in Hilo, Hawaii, and in the Alaskan quake of 1964, most of the 131 dead were victims of a tsunami.

Potential Earthquake Damage

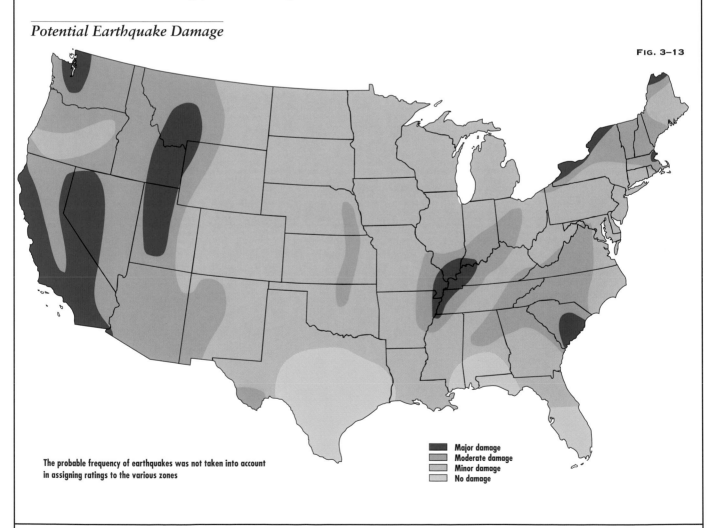

FIG. 3–13

The probable frequency of earthquakes was not taken into account in assigning ratings to the various zones

- ■ Major damage
- ■ Moderate damage
- ■ Minor damage
- ■ No damage

Climatic Stress Zones

FIG. 3–14

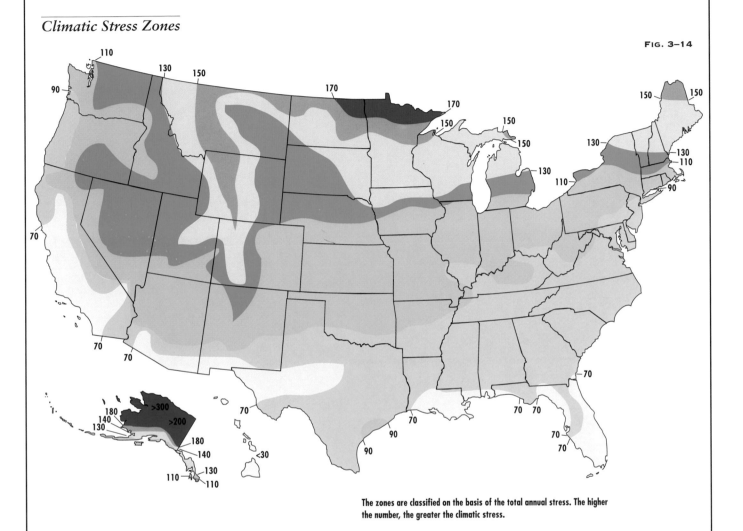

110
130
150
90
170
170
150
150
150
150
130
130
110
130
110
110
70
90
70
70
70
70
180
140
130
>300
>200
180
140
130
110
110
<30
70
70
90
90
70
70
70
70
70
70

The zones are classified on the basis of the total annual stress. The higher the number, the greater the climatic stress.

The climatic stress zone map takes into account human physiological reactions to heat and humidity as revealed in laboratory tests. It shows that the less stressful areas are in the Sunbelt, a finding that may not seem intuitively correct in view of its reputation for oppressive summers. However, according to Professor Werner H. Terjung of the University of California at Los Angeles, who constructed the map, this is a fallacy based on generalizations about annual conditions from a relatively few days of oppressive heat. The low values in the South stem from the mild winters.

Skyscrapers

Tall buildings obstruct views and can turn streets into perpetual twilight zones. They increase the density of population, which may promote gridlock. But at what point does urban architecture begin to affect the quality of life? Any judgment is subjective, but it's likely that negative reactions will be more frequent where the density of skyscrapers is greatest.

Manhattan, the scene of the first great surge in skyscraper construction in the late 1920s and early 1930s, has always had the world's greatest density of tall buildings. Chicago, the home of the first true skyscraper (the 14-story Home Insurance building, built in 1883), has only one-third as many as New York. San Francisco has one-sixth as many; moreover, its tallest building is only 52 stories compared with 110 in both New York and Chicago. Those who are intimidated by skyscrapers would feel comfortable in Washington, D.C., where by law all buildings must be lower than the apex of the Capitol dome.

Skyscrapers

FIG. 3–15

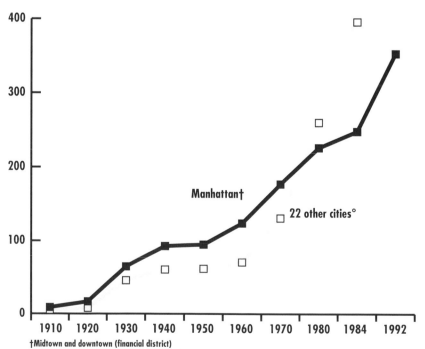

†Midtown and downtown (financial district)
°Atlanta, Baltimore, Boston, Chicago, Cleveland, Dallas, Denver, Detroit, Fort Worth, Houston, Los Angeles, Miami, Minneapolis, Newark, Philadelphia, Pittsburgh, St. Louis, St. Paul, San Diego, San Francisco, Seattle and Tampa

The federal role in environmental protection has been declining since 1980, as an increasing part of the regulatory task has been placed on the states. Renew America, a Washington-based research group, rates state environmental programs on air pollution, soil conservation, waste recycling, hazardous-waste management, groundwater protection, and energy conservation. The results of their latest assessment are shown in Figure 3-16.

Ratings of State Environmental Programs

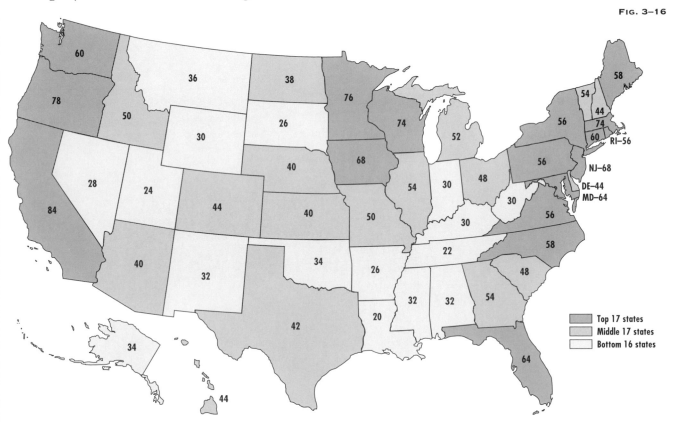

FIG. 3–16

The ratings shown on the map were developed by Renew America, a non-profit educational organization dedicated to environmental improvement. The ratings are based on measures of state government effectiveness in dealing with five areas of concern: forest management, solid waste re-cycling, drinking water quality, food safety, and the effect of population and industrial growth on the environment. A perfect score is 100 percent. The data apply to 1989.

Ratings of U.S. Representatives on Environmental Issues, 1992

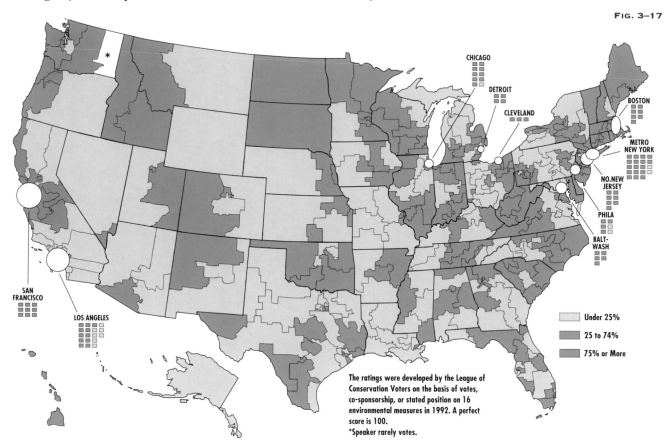

FIG. 3–17

CHICAGO
DETROIT
CLEVELAND
BOSTON
METRO NEW YORK
NO.NEW JERSEY
PHILA
BALT-WASH
SAN FRANCISCO
LOS ANGELES

Under 25%
25 to 74%
75% or More

The ratings were developed by the League of Conservation Voters on the basis of votes, co-sponsorship, or stated position on 16 environmental measures in 1992. A perfect score is 100.
*Speaker rarely votes.

Environmental legislation affects the pocketbooks of many disparate groups like union members and stockholders, renters and householders, and so it is not surprising that members of Congress differ on such matters as water management, global warming, population limitation, air pollution, and energy conservation. The League of Conservation Voters measures such differences in its annual rating of the members of Congress, which is based on their votes and stated opinions.

In general, Democrats in Congress have given far more support to league-backed measures than Republicans. Members of Congress from the North Atlantic region and from the larger cities tend to be stronger supporters of environmental controls than members from other areas.

Ratings of U.S. Senators on Environmental Issues, 1992

FIG. 3–18

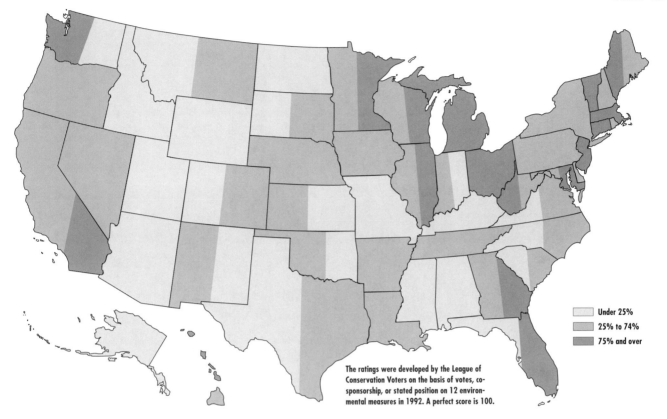

Under 25%

25% to 74%

75% and over

The ratings were developed by the League of
Conservation Voters on the basis of votes, co-
sponsorship, or stated position on 12 environmental measures in 1992. A perfect score is 100.

Leading Cultural Institutions

For many, the quality of life depends on access to cultural institutions such as orchestras, museums, and universities. Figures 3-19 through 3-21 show where the leading institutions of these types are located. If your favorite institution does not appear on these maps, bear in mind that the selection was based not only on quality, but also on size and resources.

Leading Musical Institutions

FIG. 3–19

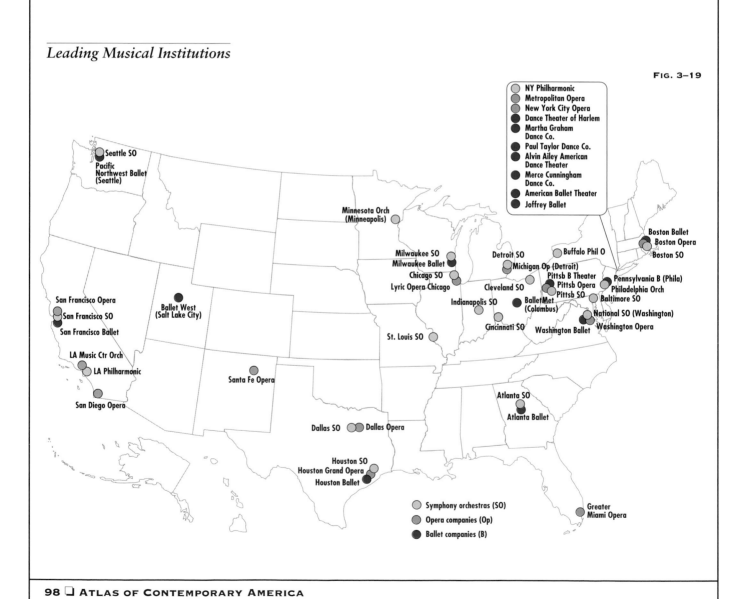

NY Philharmonic
Metropolitan Opera
New York City Opera
Dance Theater of Harlem
Martha Graham Dance Co.
Paul Taylor Dance Co.
Alvin Ailey American Dance Theater
Merce Cunningham Dance Co.
American Ballet Theater
Joffrey Ballet

Seattle SO
Pacific Northwest Ballet (Seattle)

Minnesota Orch (Minneapolis)

Milwaukee SO
Milwaukee Ballet
Chicago SO
Lyric Opera Chicago

Detroit SO
Michigan Op (Detroit)

Buffalo Phil O

Boston Ballet
Boston Opera
Boston SO

Cleveland SO

Pittsb B Theater
Pittsb Opera
Pittsb SO

Pennsylvania B (Phila)
Philadelphia Orch
Baltimore SO

San Francisco Opera
San Francisco SO
San Francisco Ballet

Ballet West (Salt Lake City)

Indianapolis SO

BalletMet (Columbus)

National SO (Washington)
Washington Ballet   Washington Opera

Cincinnati SO

LA Music Ctr Orch
LA Philharmonic

St. Louis SO

Santa Fe Opera

San Diego Opera

Atlanta SO
Atlanta Ballet

Dallas SO   Dallas Opera

Houston SO
Houston Grand Opera
Houston Ballet

Symphony orchestras (SO)
Opera companies (Op)
Ballet companies (B)

Greater Miami Opera

Leading Fine Arts Museums

FIG. 3-20

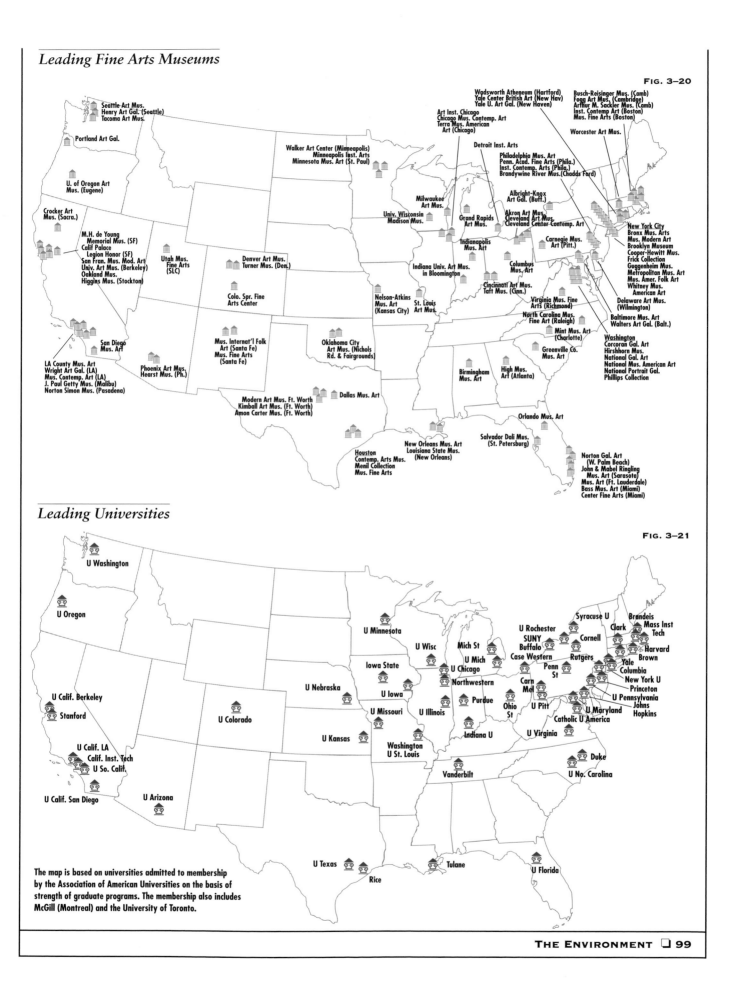

Seattle Art Mus.
Henry Art Gal. (Seattle)
Tacoma Art Mus.

Portland Art Gal.

U. of Oregon Art
Mus. (Eugene)

Crocker Art
Mus. (Sacra.)

M.H. de Young
Memorial Mus. (SF)
Calif. Palace
Legion Honor (SF)
San Fran. Mus. Mod. Art
Univ. Art Mus. (Berkeley)
Oakland Mus.
Higgins Mus. (Stockton)

San Diego
Mus. Art

LA County Mus. Art
Wright Art Gal. (LA)
Mus. Contemp. Art (LA)
J. Paul Getty Mus. (Malibu)
Norton Simon Mus. (Pasadena)

Phoenix Art Mus.
Hearst Mus. (Ph.)

Utah Mus.
Fine Arts
(SLC)

Colo. Spr. Fine
Arts Center

Mus. Internat'l Folk
Art (Santa Fe)
Mus. Fine Arts
(Santa Fe)

Denver Art Mus.
Turner Mus. (Den.)

Walker Art Center (Minneapolis)
Minneapolis Inst. Arts
Minnesota Mus. Art (St. Paul)

Milwaukee
Art Mus.

Univ. Wisconsin
Madison Mus.

Grand Rapids
Art Mus.

Nelson-Atkins
Mus. Art
(Kansas City)

St. Louis
Art Mus.

Oklahoma City
Art Mus. (Nichols
Rd. & Fairgrounds)

Modern Art Mus. Ft. Worth
Kimball Art Mus. (Ft. Worth)
Amon Carter Mus. (Ft. Worth)

Dallas Mus. Art

Houston
Contemp. Arts Mus.
Menil Collection
Mus. Fine Arts

New Orleans Mus. Art
Louisiana State Mus.
(New Orleans)

Birmingham
Mus. Art

High Mus.
Art (Atlanta)

Indiana Univ. Art Mus.
in Bloomington

Indianapolis
Mus. Art

Columbus
Mus. Art

Cincinnati Art Mus.
Taft Mus. (Cinn.)

Detroit Inst. Arts

Art Inst. Chicago
Chicago Mus. Contemp. Art
Terra Mus. American
Art (Chicago)

Akron Art Mus.
Cleveland Art Mus.
Cleveland Center Contemp. Art

Albright-Knox
Art Gal. (Buff.)

Carnegie Mus.
Art (Pitt.)

Wadsworth Atheneum (Hartford)
Yale Center British Art (New Hav)
Yale U. Art Gal. (New Haven)

Philadelphia Mus. Art
Penn. Acad. Fine Arts (Phila.)
Inst. Contemp. Arts (Phila.)
Brandywine River Mus. (Chadds Ford)

Busch-Reisinger Mus. (Camb)
Fogg Art Mus. (Cambridge)
Arthur M. Sackler Mus. (Camb)
Inst. Contemp. Art (Boston)
Mus. Fine Arts (Boston)

Worcester Art Mus.

New York City
Bronx Mus. Arts
Mus. Modern Art
Brooklyn Museum
Cooper-Hewitt Mus.
Frick Collection
Guggenheim Mus.
Metropolitan Mus. Art
Mus. Amer. Folk Art
Whitney Mus.
American Art

Delaware Art Mus.
(Wilmington)

Baltimore Mus. Art
Walters Art Gal. (Balt.)

Washington
Corcoran Gal. Art
Hirshhorn Mus.
National Gal. Art
National Mus. American Art
National Portrait Gal.
Phillips Collection

Virginia Mus. Fine
Arts (Richmond)

North Carolina Mus.
Fine Art (Raleigh)

Mint Mus. Art
(Charlotte)

Greenville Co.
Mus. Art

Orlando Mus. Art

Salvador Dali Mus.
(St. Petersburg)

Norton Gal. Art
(W. Palm Beach)
John & Mabel Ringling
Mus. Art (Sarasota)
Mus. Art (Ft. Lauderdale)
Bass Mus. Art (Miami)
Center Fine Arts (Miami)

Leading Universities

FIG. 3-21

U Washington

U Oregon

U Calif. Berkeley

Stanford

U Calif. LA
Calif. Inst. Tech
U So. Calif.

U Calif. San Diego

U Arizona

U Colorado

U Nebraska

U Kansas

U Texas

Rice

U Minnesota

U Wisc

Iowa State

U Iowa

U Missouri

Washington
U St. Louis

Vanderbilt

Tulane

Mich St

U Mich

U Chicago

Northwestern

U Illinois

Purdue

Indiana U

Ohio
St

U Rochester

SUNY
Buffalo

Case Western

Carn
Mel

U Pitt

Penn
St

U Virginia

U Maryland

Catholic U America

U Florida

Duke

U No. Carolina

Syracuse U

Cornell

Rutgers

Yale
Columbia

New York U

Princeton

U Pennsylvania

Johns
Hopkins

Brandeis
Clark
Mass Inst
Tech
Harvard
Brown

The map is based on universities admitted to membership
by the Association of American Universities on the basis of
strength of graduate programs. The membership also includes
McGill (Montreal) and the University of Toronto.

4

Politics

The Geography of One-party Rule

House Races in Which There Was No Major Party Challenger or in Which a Major Party Candidate Was Outspent by at Least 3 to 1 in the 1990 General Election

FIG. 4–1

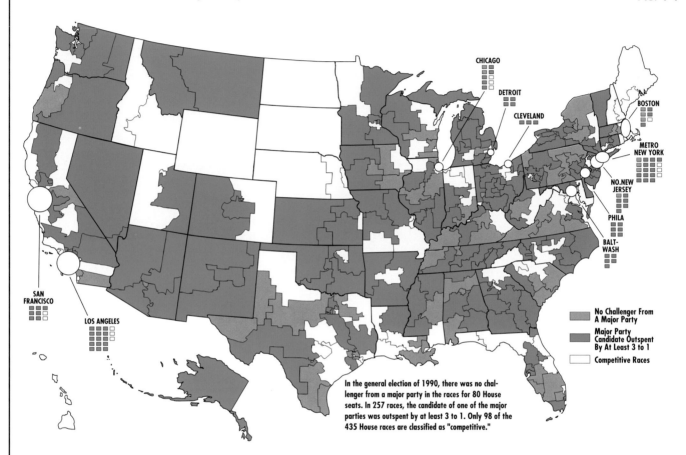

No Challenger From A Major Party

Major Party Candidate Outspent By At Least 3 to 1

Competitive Races

In the general election of 1990, there was no challenger from a major party in the races for 80 House seats. In 257 races, the candidate of one of the major parties was outspent by at least 3 to 1. Only 98 of the 435 House races are classified as "competitive."

Incumbency has always given representatives and senators an enormous advantage over challengers, and in recent years this advantage has been reinforced by the ability of incumbents to attract campaign funds. Unless there is evidence of improper behavior, incumbents can normally count on reelection. In some years, however, voters are stirred to such unusual levels of dissatisfaction that many incumbents lose their seats. This happened in the Johnson-Goldwater race of 1964, when 44 House incumbents (mostly Republicans) were defeated. The voters were stirred up again in 1966 when 40 House members (this time

Senate Races in Which There Was No Major Party Challenger or in Which a Major Party Candidate Was Outspent by at Least 3 to 1 in the 1986, 1988 or 1990 General Elections

FIG. 4–2

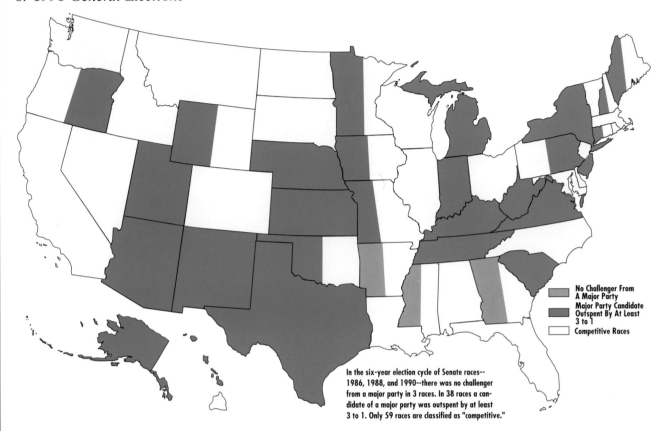

No Challenger From A Major Party

Major Party Candidate Outspent By At Least 3 to 1

Competitive Races

In the six-year election cycle of Senate races-- 1986, 1988, and 1990--there was no challenger from a major party in 3 races. In 38 races a candidate of a major party was outspent by at least 3 to 1. Only 59 races are classified as "competitive."

mostly Democrats) lost their seats. Following the Watergate scandal in 1974, 40 members (mostly Republicans) lost their seats. In 1992, a year of widespread revulsion against Congress, 90 House incumbents—an unusually high number—decided not to run or were defeated in primaries. The Senate presents a similar picture. The worst election for senatorial incumbents in recent years was in 1958, when a third of those up for reelection—11 senators (all Republicans)—lost their seats.

Figure 4-1 shows House races that were not competitive either because there was no challenger from the other major party or because the challenger was unlikely to mount an effective campaign due to insufficient funds. (In constructing the map, challengers who were outspent by 3 to 1 or more were deemed to be insufficiently funded.) Figure 4-2 shows comparable information for a full six-year cycle of Senate races.

Campaign Expenditures in Congressional Races

In the mid-1970s, following the Watergate scandal, there was an extraordinary organizational change in Congress, particularly in the House of Representatives. Younger members revolted, dispossessing many of the old-line barons who had controlled key committees through seniority. Power was taken from the committees and spread among scores of subcommittees. This occurred at a time when members of Congress were becoming increasingly more independent of their parties, largely by finding more opportunities for self-promotion. Through television they could appeal directly to the voters and bypass local power brokers—party bosses, business-

men, union leaders, church spokesmen—who traditionally influenced the candidates. They could afford television ads, poll-takers, media consultants, and the other necessities of modern campaigning because of the increasingly large campaign contributions by political action committees (PACs) and wealthy individuals. The consequence, as detailed in Figure 4-3, has been a substantial increase in campaign spending by both House and Senate candidates.

Average Campaign Expenditures per Candidate in Congressional Races (1990 Dollars)

FIG. 4–3

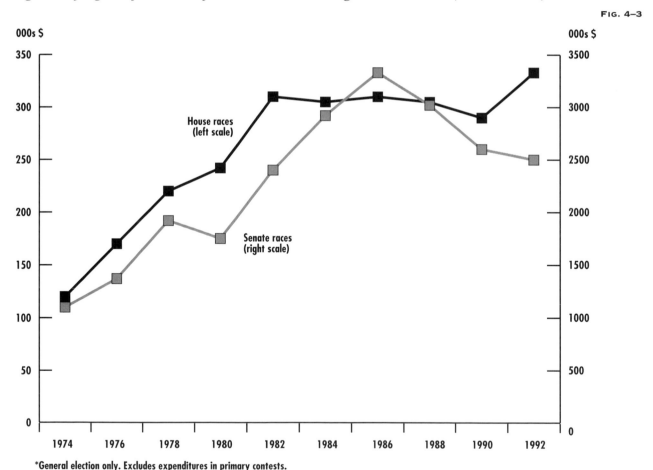

*General election only. Excludes expenditures in primary contests.

Percent of People 18 and Over Who Voted for a Presidential Candidate in the November 1992 General Election

FIG. 4–4

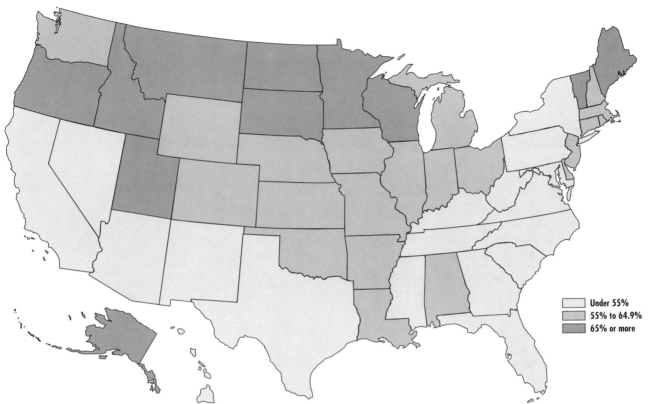

- Under 55%
- 55% to 64.9%
- 65% or more

The map shows the proportion of eligible voters who actually voted in the last Presidential election. In general, Northerners are more apt to vote than Southerners, but even in the North, the average turnout—about 65 to 70 percent in recent presidential election years—is below the level of European countries. Because of the low turnout, Washington politicians are rarely elected by a majority of those eligible to vote. The typical congressman in 1990, for example, was elected by fewer than 20 percent of eligible voters. Ronald Reagan, at the height of his popularity in 1984, was reelected by only 32 percent, and Bill Clinton, in 1992, was elected by less than 24 percent of the eligible voters.

The decline in voter turnout since the 1960s occurred despite the easing of registration restrictions and a dramatic increase in educational levels, factors that ordinarily promote voting. On the other hand, there have been forces at work that depress turnout,

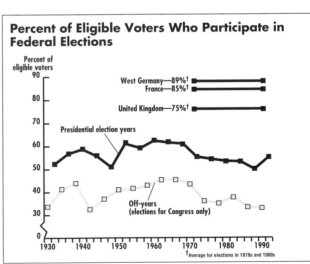

Percent of Eligible Voters Who Participate in Federal Elections

Percent of eligible voters

West Germany—89%†
France—85%†

United Kingdom—75%†

Presidential election years

Off-years
(elections for Congress only)

†Average for elections in 1970s and 1980s

of which the most important may have been the increasingly skeptical attitude of voters toward Washington politicians.

New Congressional Districts in the 1990s

State legislatures, in drawing the new congressional district boundaries based on the 1990 Census, had to take into account the Voting Rights Act as amended in 1982, which in effect mandated that minority candidates be elected in rough proportion to their share of a state's population. This requirement led to the creation of some of the most grotesquely shaped congressional districts in modern memory, including the 12th District of North Carolina, which stretches from the eastern approaches of Durham to the west of Charlotte, more than 100 miles away (Figure 4-5). By snipping here and adding there, while disregarding the principle of geographic cohesion, the mapmakers were able to construct a district with a 53.4 percent black population. Among the other districts created to achieve a black majority is the 30th District in Texas (Figure 4-6). The 4th District in Illinois (Figure 4-7) was stitched together to provide a majority Hispanic population.

12th Congressional District, North Carolina, 1992　　FIG. 4–5

30th Congressional District, Texas, 1992　　FIG. 4–6

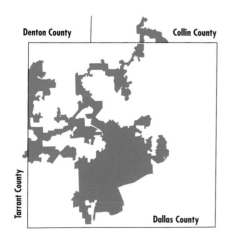

4th Congressional District, Illinois, 1992　　FIG. 4–7

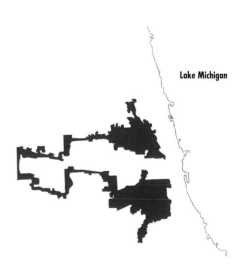

Congressional Districts Where Minorities Are Most Prevalent

FIG. 4–8

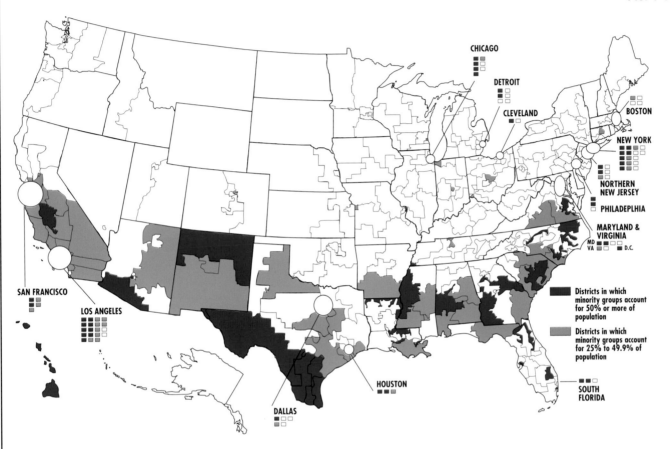

The reapportionment based on the 1990 Census resulted in the creation of 64 congressional districts—15 percent of the total—in which non-whites and Hispanics constituted a majority. Non-whites and Hispanics comprise about one-fourth of the total U.S. population.

The congressional workload, as measured by the number of pages in public bills enacted, has been trending upward for at least two decades. This increase came at the same time that representatives and senators felt compelled to spend more time raising campaign funds from PACs and large individual contributors. Members of Congress naturally would be loath to pass up opportunities for media exposure, and to judge by the sharp growth in the number of journalists accredited by Congress, there has been an increasing number of such opportunities.

Washington Indicators

FIG. 4–9

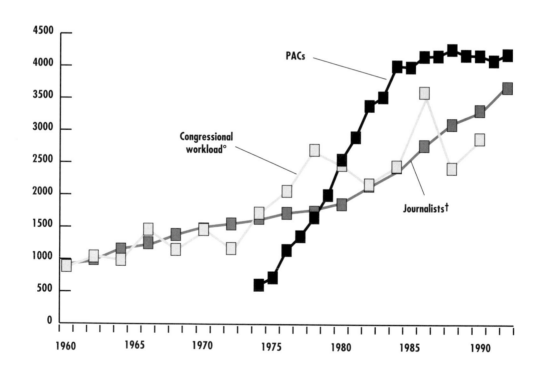

Number of Political Action Committees,
number of congressional journalists, and
congressional workload

†Newspaper, radio and TV journalists accredited by Congress.
°Total number of pages in public bills enacted by Congress per year.

Liberals, Moderates, and Conservatives in Congress

Most Democrats in Congress are "liberal," that is, they believe in the ability of government to solve social and economic problems. They tend to emphasize civil rights, abortion rights, gun control, stricter regulation of business, and preservation of the environment. In theory, they are the party that defends the "little people" against corporations, polluters, and greedy landlords. However, a sizable number of Democrats in Congress take a less than liberal position, and a few are distinctly conservative. In order to gauge the range of their ideology, Democratic representatives and senators were classified as "liberal," "moderate," and "conservative" based on an analysis of voting records made by Americans for Democratic Action, a liberal organization. To qualify as a liberal, a member of Congress had to agree with the ADA's position on at least 70 percent of the bills; and to be classified as a conservative, had to agree on less than 30 percent. Moderates are those who took the ADA's position on 30 to 69 percent of the votes (Figures 4-10, 4-11).

Republicans in Congress tend to be more ideologically homogeneous than their Democratic rivals. Most believe in the power of the free market to produce prosperity, and they have little faith in massive government intervention to solve social and economic problems. In theory, they are the party of the old-fashioned virtues of self-reliance, hard work, and moral integrity—virtues that they believe will promote prosperity. As compared to Democrats, Republicans tend to give less support to abortion rights and gun control, and more support to a strong defense. Most Republicans in Congress are conservative, but conservatives have not always dominated the party. At one time, Eastern moderate Republicans ruled, at least at the presidential level, nominating such middle-of-the-road candidates as Wendell Willkie (1940), Thomas Dewey (1944 and 1948), and Dwight Eisenhower (1952 and 1956).

Democratic Liberals, Moderates, and Conservatives in the House of Representatives

FIG. 4–10

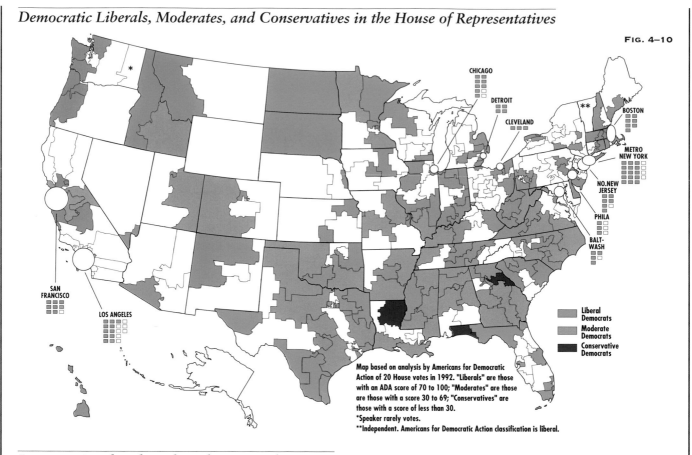

CHICAGO

DETROIT

CLEVELAND

BOSTON

METRO NEW YORK

NO. NEW JERSEY

PHILA

BALT-WASH

SAN FRANCISCO

LOS ANGELES

Liberal Democrats

Moderate Democrats

Conservative Democrats

Map based on analysis by Americans for Democratic Action of 20 House votes in 1992. "Liberals" are those with an ADA score of 70 to 100; "Moderates" are those are those with a score 30 to 69; "Conservatives" are those with a score of less than 30.
*Speaker rarely votes.
**Independent. Americans for Democratic Action classification is liberal.

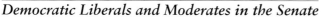

Democratic Liberals and Moderates in the Senate

FIG. 4–11

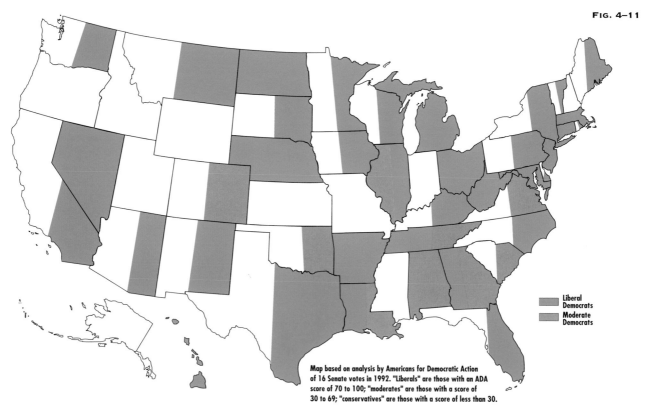

Liberal Democrats

Moderate Democrats

Map based on analysis by Americans for Democratic Action of 16 Senate votes in 1992. "Liberals" are those with an ADA score of 70 to 100; "moderates" are those with a score of 30 to 69; "conservatives" are those with a score of less than 30.

Republican Liberals, Moderates, and Conservatives in the House of Representatives

FIG. 4–12

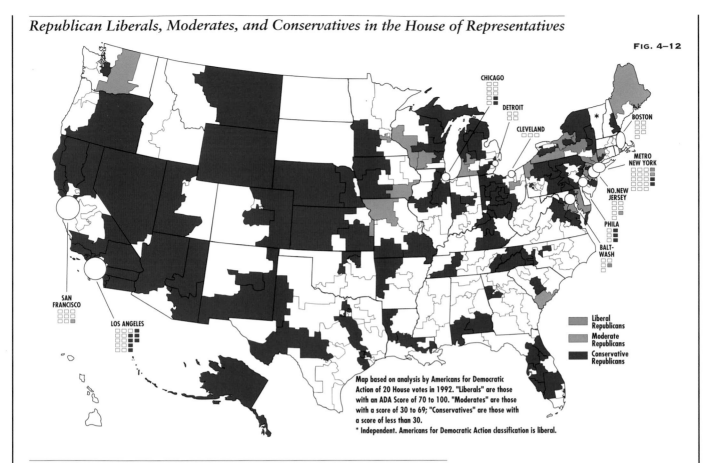

CHICAGO

DETROIT

CLEVELAND

BOSTON

METRO NEW YORK

NO. NEW JERSEY

PHILA

BALT-WASH

SAN FRANCISCO

LOS ANGELES

- Liberal Republicans
- Moderate Republicans
- Conservative Republicans

Map based on analysis by Americans for Democratic Action of 20 House votes in 1992. "Liberals" are those with an ADA Score of 70 to 100. "Moderates" are those with a score of 30 to 69; "Conservatives" are those with a score of less than 30.

* Independent. Americans for Democratic Action classification is liberal.

Republican Liberals, Moderates, and Conservatives in the Senate

FIG. 4–13

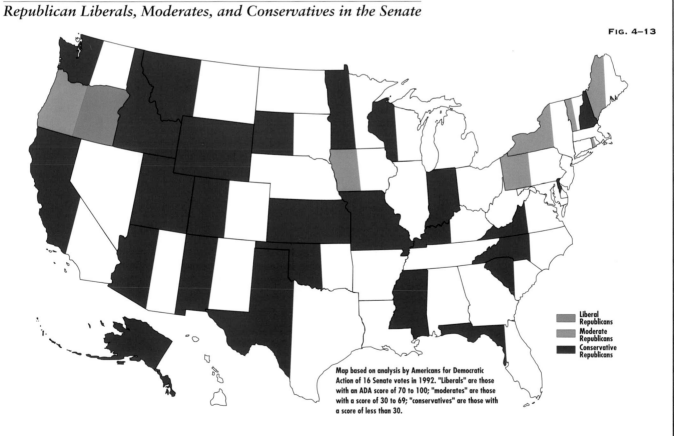

- Liberal Republicans
- Moderate Republicans
- Conservative Republicans

Map based on analysis by Americans for Democratic Action of 16 Senate votes in 1992. "Liberals" are those with an ADA score of 70 to 100; "moderates" are those with a score of 30 to 69; "conservatives" are those with a score of less than 30.

The Two Parties Diverge

Since the late 1970s there has been a significant shift in the position of the parties, at least at the congressional level: The Democrats have become more liberal while the Republicans have become more conservative. Ideology, to some extent, has replaced the power of congressional leaders as the glue holding the parties together.

The shift toward liberalism among the Democrats was partly the result of the unprecedented rise of black voting power. Since the Civil Rights Act of 1964, blacks have been going to the polls in greater numbers, usually supporting liberal Democrats. Some white politicians in areas with a large number of black voters have changed their stance dramatically. Senator John Stennis (D., Miss.) voted against school busing in 1970, but in 1987 he supported home rule for the District of Columbia, a favorite cause of the Congressional Black Caucus.

The Two Parties Diverge

FIG. 4–14

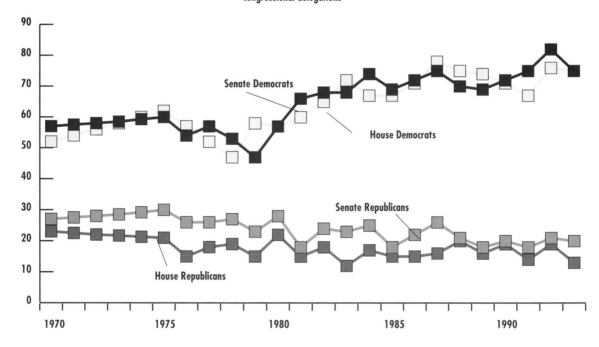

"Liberal Quotient" of Democratic and Republican congressional delegations[†]

†The "Liberal Quotient," which is prepared by Americans for Democratic Action, a liberal political organization, is based on the voting record of all representatives and senators. A high quotient indicates a liberal position and a low quotient, a conservative position.

As recently as the 1970s, big-city mayors were almost exclusively white males, but as Figure 4-15 illustrates, both women and minorities have made considerable progress toward undermining white male hegemony in urban politics.

*Women and Minority Mayors, Cities of 100,00 or More**

FIG. 4–15

*Mayoral status as of January 1994. Mayors in Minneapolis and Washington, D.C. are black and female.

States Where Clinton Was Strongest in the 1992 Presidential Election

FIG. 4–16

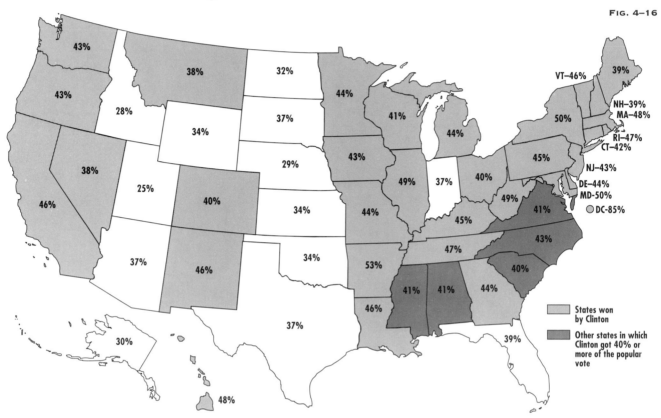

Legend:
- States won by Clinton
- Other states in which Clinton got 40% or more of the popular vote

In the 1992 presidential election, Democrat Bill Clinton got 43 percent of the popular vote and carried 32 states with 370 electoral votes, well above the 270 needed for election. Republican George Bush received 38 percent of the popular vote and 168 electoral votes. Independent candidate Ross Perot got 19 percent of the popular vote and no electoral votes.

In only three states—Arkansas, Maryland, and New York—did Clinton get 50 percent or more of the popular vote. Bush's best performance was in the Deep South states of South Carolina, Alabama, and Mississippi, but only in the last did he get more than half the vote. Perot's best performance was in Maine, where he got 30 percent of the vote.

States Where Bush Was Strongest in the 1992 Presidential Election

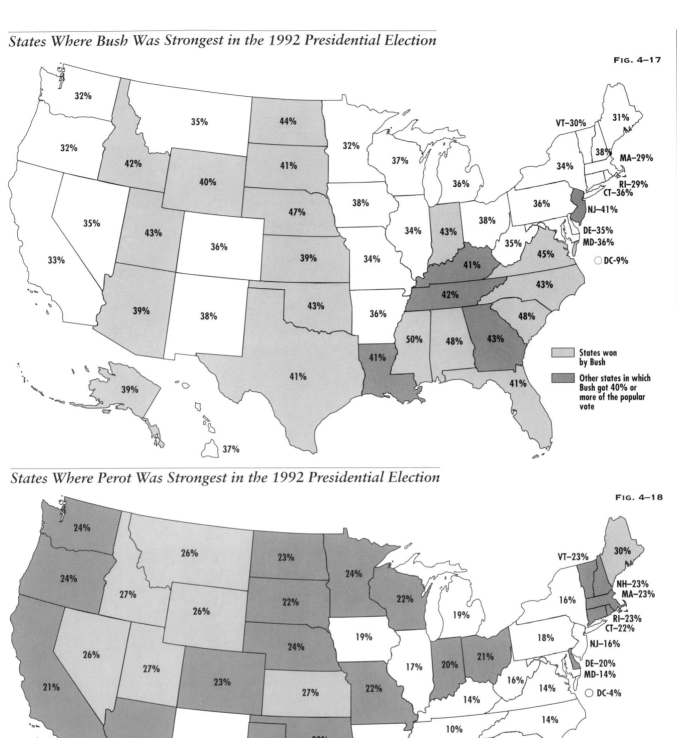

FIG. 4–17

States won by Bush

Other states in which Bush got 40% or more of the popular vote

States Where Perot Was Strongest in the 1992 Presidential Election

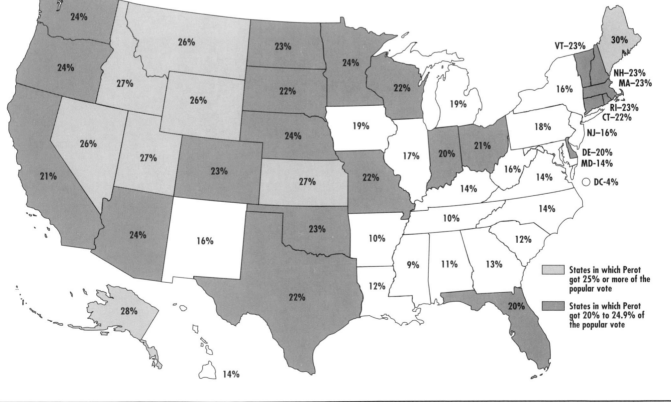

FIG. 4–18

States in which Perot got 25% or more of the popular vote

States in which Perot got 20% to 24.9% of the popular vote

Liberals, Conservatives, Populists and Libertarians in the House of Representatives

FIG. 4–19

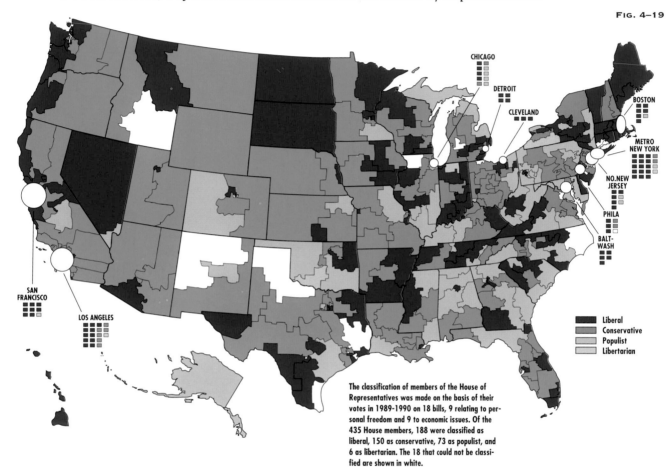

CHICAGO

DETROIT

CLEVELAND

BOSTON

METRO NEW YORK

NO. NEW JERSEY

PHILA

BALT-WASH

SAN FRANCISCO

LOS ANGELES

Liberal
Conservative
Populist
Libertarian

The classification of members of the House of Representatives was made on the basis of their votes in 1989-1990 on 18 bills, 9 relating to personal freedom and 9 to economic issues. Of the 435 House members, 188 were classified as liberal, 150 as conservative, 73 as populist, and 6 as libertarian. The 18 that could not be classified are shown in white.

I f you think that liberals or conservatives are the single largest voter group, you may be wrong. A survey done in 1980 shows that populists outnumber conservatives and are as numerous as liberals. And what are populists? The *American Heritage Dictionary* says that populism is "a political philosophy directed to the needs of the common people and advocating a more equitable distribution of wealth and power." The term often connotes anti-intellectualism and a resentment of the ruling elite—big business, the country club set, "preppies," the "media establishment," and Washington politicians. George Wallace, who waged a populist campaign for president in 1968, castigated "pointy-headed liberals." A useful categorization of populism and other ideologies

Liberals, Conservatives, Populists and Libertarians in the Senate

FIG. 4–20

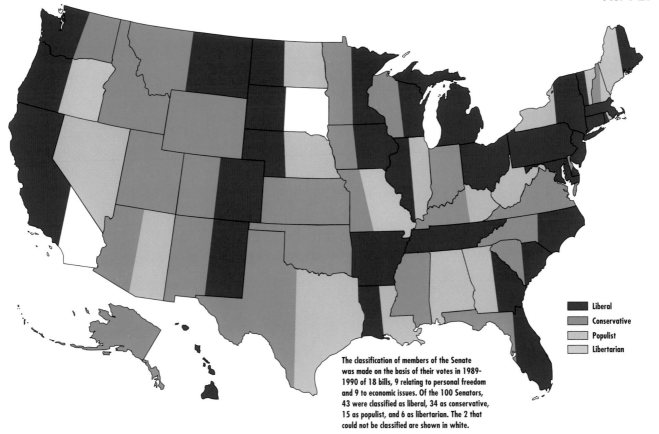

Legend:
- ■ Liberal
- ■ Conservative
- ■ Populist
- ■ Libertarian

The classification of members of the Senate was made on the basis of their votes in 1989-1990 of 18 bills, 9 relating to personal freedom and 9 to economic issues. Of the 100 Senators, 43 were classified as liberal, 34 as conservative, 15 as populist, and 6 as libertarian. The 2 that could not be classified are shown in white.

is given by William S. Maddox and Stuart A. Lilie, of the University of Central Florida. They define *populists* as being for government intervention in economic affairs, but against the expansion of personal freedoms. *Liberals*, they say, are like populists in their attitude toward government intervention, but differ in that they are for the expansion of personal freedoms. *Conservatives* are against both government intervention in economic affairs and the expansion of personal liberties. Maddox and Lilie describe a fourth group, the *libertarians*. Like conservatives, they are against government intervention in economic matters but, unlike conservatives, are for expansion of personal freedoms. According to the Maddox-Lilie scheme, liberals favor both expanded federal funding for health insurance and expanded abortion rights. Conservatives are against both. Populists favor expanded funding of health care but are against abortion. Libertarians oppose the populists on both of these issues. In the Maddox-Lilie scheme, populists are not defined by their attitudes toward the rich or toward intellectuals.

This four-way classification is more precise than the two-way division into liberal and conservative. Under the latter, populists and libertarians lose their distinct identity and are simply classified as "moderates," a label that hides more than it discloses. Some Republicans, usually described as "moderates," are better described as libertarians. Some Southern Democrats tagged as "conservatives" or "moderates" are better described as populists.

Members of Congress can be classified according to the Maddox-Lilie scheme by analyzing their votes. This has been done for members of the House of Representatives and the Senate on the basis of their votes on key domestic bills, both those relating to personal freedom and those relating to economic issues.

5

The Economy

How many Americans live in poverty? Using the federal government standard, which is based on an outdated formula that does not adequately take into account the increase in housing costs of recent years, 12 percent of the population lives in poverty. Others say that when the true cost of housing is taken into account, this figure would be 18 percent. By another measure, which factors in benefits like Medicaid, the estimate is 9 percent. According to the standard federal definition of poverty, 32 million Americans lived in poverty in 1989. The maps (Figures 5-1 and 5-2), which are based on questions in the 1990 U.S. Census, show the concentration of families in poverty in 1989 according to the standard definition. At that time a single person with income of less than $6,311 and a family of four with income less than $12,675 lived in official poverty. Bear in mind that these figures are applied in all areas of the country uniformly, without regard to differences in living cost, which vary considerably by area. For this

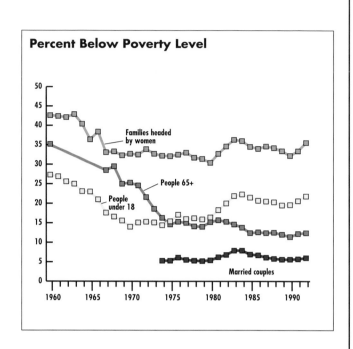

Percent Below Poverty Level

Families headed by women

People 65+

People under 18

Married couples

Percent of Families Below Poverty Level by County, 1989

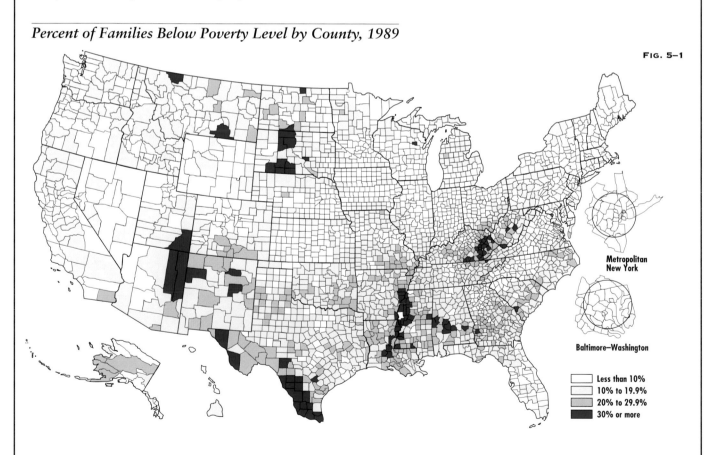

FIG. 5-1

Metropolitan New York

Baltimore–Washington

Less than 10%
10% to 19.9%
20% to 29.9%
30% or more

Percent of Black Families Below Poverty Level by County, 1989

FIG. 5–2

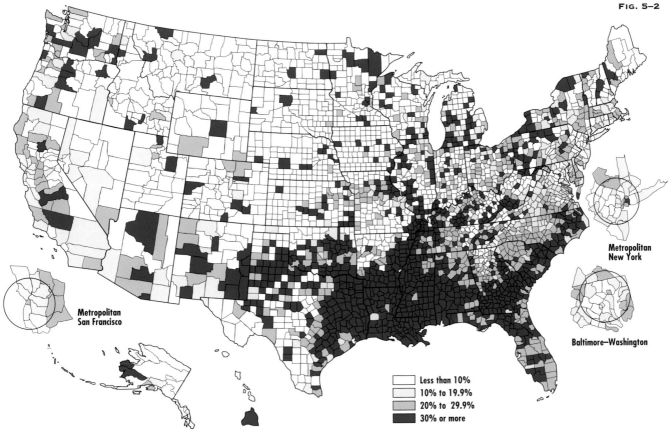

Metropolitan
New York

Metropolitan
San Francisco

Baltimore–Washington

Less than 10%
10% to 19.9%
20% to 29.9%
30% or more

reason, the maps probably overstate the extent of poverty in certain areas, such as the Southeast, where the cost of living is low, and understate the extent in areas where the cost of living is high, such as West Coast and North Atlantic coast cities.

Of those heading poverty-stricken families, about two-thirds are non-Hispanic whites and two-thirds are women. Families headed by women were much more likely to be poverty-stricken than married couple families. About half of all people below the poverty line lack a high school diploma and half lack a steady year-round job.

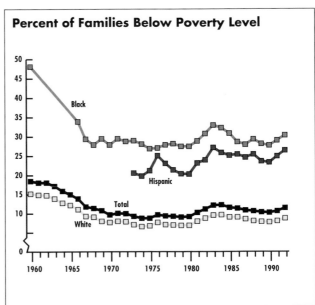

Percent of Families Below Poverty Level

Black

Hispanic

Total

White

1960   1965   1970   1975   1980   1985   1990

Where the Homeless Are

Where the Homeless Are

FIG. 5–3

Seattle
Portland

Minneapolis St. Paul
Milwaukee
Detroit
Rochester Buffalo
Boston

Oakland
Sacramento
Stockton
Fresno
San Jose
Riverside
San Francisco
Las Vegas
Anaheim
Los Angeles
Long Beach
Santa Ana
San Diego
Phoenix Mesa
Tucson

Denver Aurora
Colorado Springs

Omaha

Chicago Toledo Akron Pittsburgh
Indianapolis
Columbus
Cinncinnati

Cleveland
Jersey City New York
Newark
Philadelphia
Baltimore
Washington

Kansas City
St. Louis
Wichita
Louisville Lexington
Richmond Virginia Beach
Norfolk
Raleigh

Tulsa
Oklahoma City
Memphis
Nashville
Charlotte

Albuquerque
El Paso

Ft. Worth Dallas
Arlington
Austin
San Antonio
Corpus Christi
Houston
Baton Rouge
New Orleans

Birmingham
Atlanta
Jacksonville
St. Petersburg Tampa
Miami

Anchorage
Honolulu

Proportion of homeless in population
○ Lowest Third
◐ Middle Third
● Highest third

Cities of over 200,000 population classified according to proportion of population that was homeless in the U.S. Census count of March 1990 (see text).

Periodically throughout American history the homeless have been seen as a problem. First it was the "wandering poor" of Colonial times, then the Skid Row bums of the 1870s and 1880s, and later the hoboes of the Great Depression. The latest wave of homeless people started in the 1980s when the supply of cheap rental housing began to decline. This, together with the emptying of mental hospitals and a "safety net" that works haphazardly for those with no permanent address, contributed to the current homeless population of more than half a million men, women, and children. Some say that the true figure is more than two million. The U.S. Census attempted to count the homeless for the first time in 1990. It found only 228,000, a figure that most authorities believe to be an undercount. However, the Census data do give a clue to the geographical distribution of the homeless.

Who are the homeless? They are the poorest of the poor. For various reasons, they lack the support of family and friends to help provide shelter. Roughly 45 percent are white, 40 percent are black, and 10 percent are Hispanic. Half have a high school diploma. Perhaps as much as a quarter have served time in state or federal prisons. An estimated 15 percent are children, and 20 percent are women. About 15 percent of the homeless are members of families, usually headed by a woman. About a third are mentally ill, a third to one-half are alcoholic, and about 10 percent are drug abusers. The homeless are sicker than other people. As many as 40 percent have serious physical problems.

The people in the middle, the schoolteachers, computer programmers, construction workers, unionized factory workers, small retailers, civil servants—roughly the group with family income from $20,000 to $40,000—are being squeezed. Average pay reached a peak in 1978 but has declined since then in terms of purchasing power. Middle-income people have been able to maintain or improve their purchasing power only by sending a second wage earner into the marketplace.

The map shows average income by metropolitan area adjusted for differences in the cost of living between areas. Some areas, such as the industrial Midwest, are much more hospitable to people with average incomes than other areas, like the East and West coasts.

Purchasing Power of the Average Salary by Metropolitan Area, 1990

FIG. 5–4

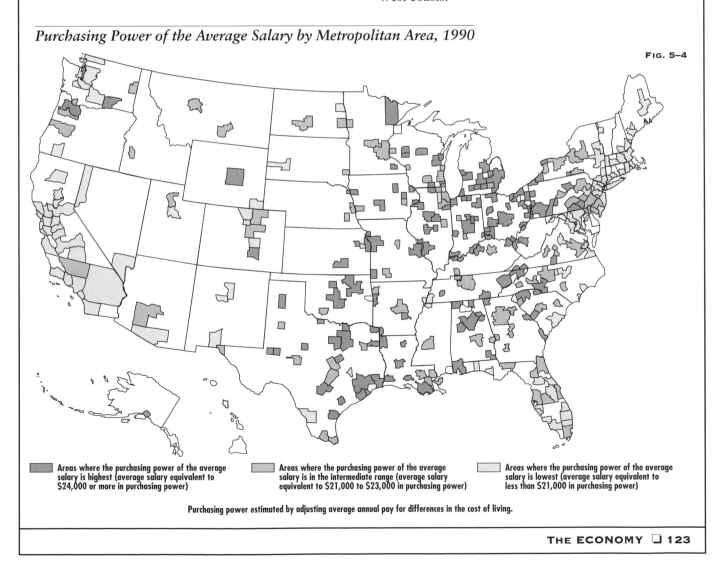

Areas where the purchasing power of the average salary is highest (average salary equivalent to $24,000 or more in purchasing power)

Areas where the purchasing power of the average salary is in the intermediate range (average salary equivalent to $21,000 to $23,000 in purchasing power)

Areas where the purchasing power of the average salary is lowest (average salary equivalent to less than $21,000 in purchasing power)

Purchasing power estimated by adjusting average annual pay for differences in the cost of living.

Where the Affluent Live

The 1990 U.S. Census provides county data on the number of families with an income of $150,000 or more. These families tend to be found more often on the East and West coasts, which throughout the 1980s, were the areas of greatest opportunity for making six- and seven-figure incomes. The increasing prosperity of upper-income America is illustrated in the chart, which shows an extraordinary increase in the number of families with incomes of a million or more.

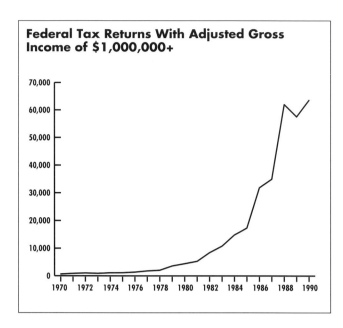

Federal Tax Returns With Adjusted Gross Income of $1,000,000+

Families with Incomes of $150,000 or More as a Percent of All Families, by County, 1989

FIG. 5–5

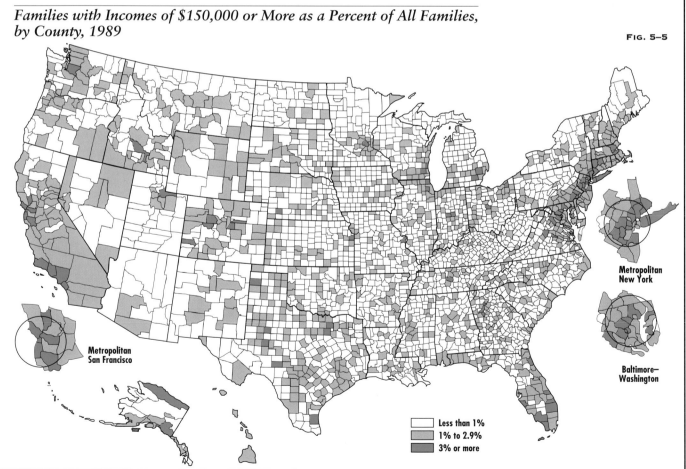

Metropolitan New York

Metropolitan San Francisco

Baltimore–Washington

- Less than 1%
- 1% to 2.9%
- 3% or more

Fairness of State and Local Tax Structure, 1991*

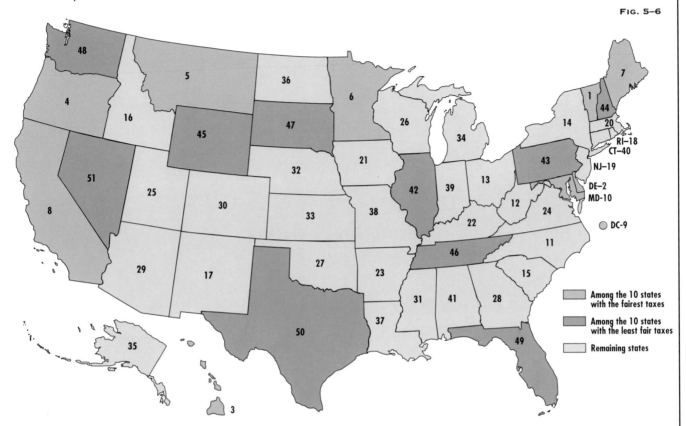

FIG. 5–6

Legend:
- Among the 10 states with the fairest taxes
- Among the 10 states with the least fair taxes
- Remaining states

Fairness of taxes in terms of progressivity, according to Citizens for Tax Justice. Numbers are ranks of states (and the District of Columbia) according to the fairness of their tax structure, 1 being the most fair and 51 being the least fair.

The notion that taxes should be progressive—that is, that the share of income paid in taxes should rise as income rises—has long been a guiding principle for lawmakers. In the early 1990s, the reality is that the total burden of federal, state, and local taxes is *not* progressive.

The federal personal income tax *is* progressive, although less so than in the 1970s. However, much of its progressivity is cancelled by unprogressive levies, such as the social security tax, and by state and local taxes. The state and local tax burden varies considerably, according to a report prepared by Citizens for Tax Justice (CTJ), of Washington, D.C. CTJ ranked the 50 states and the District of Columbia according to the fairness of their taxes in terms of progressivity. In virtually every state the poor (those in the lowest 20 percent of the income scale) pay a greater percentage of their income in state and local taxes than do the rich (those in the top 1 percent). The proportion paid by the poor varies considerably: In some states it is more than 17 percent, in others less than 8 percent. By contrast, there are many states in which the rich pay less than 4 percent. States without income taxes tend to have the most regressive tax structures.

Low and middle income people have suffered from declining real wages in recent years, and so a tax structure that puts a heavy burden on these classes is likely to suffer shortfalls in recessionary periods. A more progressive tax structure would help lessen shortfalls by tapping the rich, whose assets and incomes tend to be more stable.

Minimum Family Income Needed to Buy an Existing Median Priced Single–Family Home in Major Metropolitan Areas, 1992*

FIG. 5–7

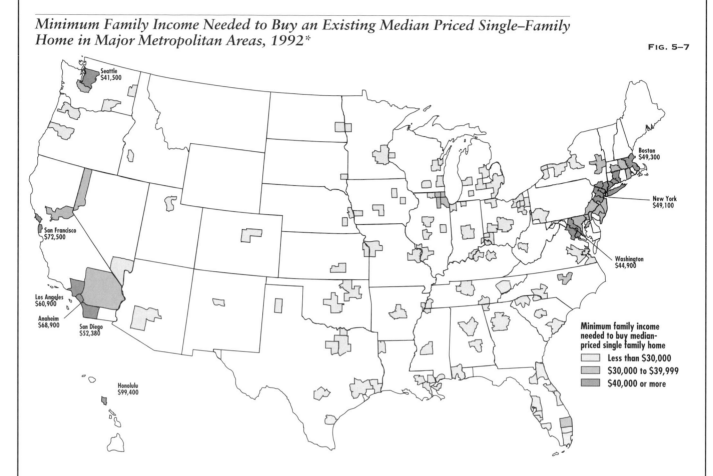

Seattle
$41,500

Boston
$49,300

New York
$49,100

San Francisco
$72,500

Washington
$44,900

Los Angeles
$60,900

Anaheim
$68,900

San Diego
$52,380

Honolulu
$99,400

Minimum family income needed to buy median-priced single family home

☐ Less than $30,000
▨ $30,000 to $39,999
▓ $40,000 or more

*Assuming a 20% down payment and an interest rate of 8.11% in all areas. Local interest rates may vary from the national average. The minimum income required is shown for several of the very high-priced areas.

In most areas of the United States, families qualify for a home mortgage if income is equal to about one-third the purchase price of the house. For example, a family must have income of $40,000 to buy a home costing $120,000. The map shows the minimum income needed to buy the median-priced home in major metropolitan areas.

Metro areas on the North Atlantic coast, California, and Hawaii have the least affordable housing for middle-class families. A likely contributor to the high cost of housing in these areas is the big growth in recent years of personal income of professionals and business people. With their large and rising incomes, they were able to outbid people of lesser means, thus pushing up housing prices beyond the reach of middle-income people.

In this era of cellular telephones, modems, and dedicated fax lines, there are astonishing lacunae in basic telephone service in both rural and urban areas of the United States. According to the 1990 U.S. Census, almost 5 million of the country's 89 million housing units lack basic telephone service. Overall, 5 percent of white households lack a phone, in comparison to 15 percent of black and Hispanic and 20 percent of Native American households.

In most of these cases, a telephone is simply an unaffordable luxury; two-thirds of families below the poverty line do not have a home phone. A majority of phoneless homes are in urban areas, especially the poorer, inner-city sections. Bronx County, New York, among the 100 most populous counties, has the highest proportion of families without phone service (12.5 percent) and of families below the poverty level (26 percent). Nearby Nassau County, comprised of largely middle-class suburbs, has a phone-subscriber rate of 99 percent.

About 200,000 remotely situated houses, many of them in the Rocky Mountain states, are without a phone because service is unavailable; stringing up wires is either physically or financially impossible for many regional phone companies. But, as in urban areas, a far more significant cause of rural area phone gaps is poverty. Poor families that can afford basic services—or receive government subsidies that allow them to—often cannot get a phone owing to bad credit ratings. Rural service is most scarce in Appalachia, which is home to many poor whites, and in areas with large minority populations such as: counties in the Southeast where African-Americans predominate, areas of the Southwest where Mexican-Americans are most concentrated, and Native American enclaves in Alaska, the Southwest, and the West Central states. In rural Apache County, Arizona, which has a large Navajo population, 60 percent of housing units have no phone.

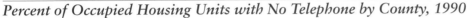

Percent of Occupied Housing Units with No Telephone by County, 1990

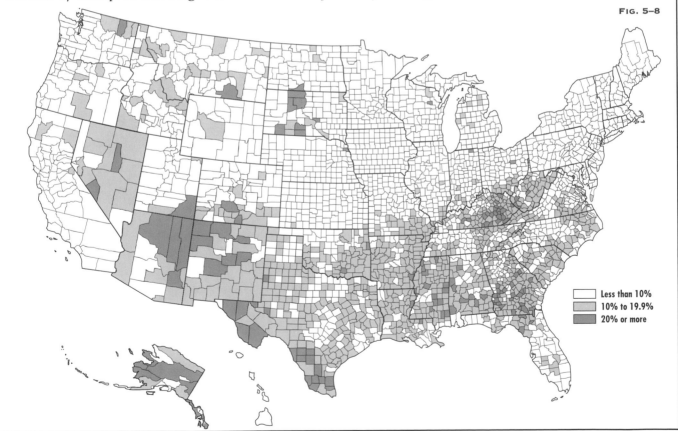

FIG. 5–8

Less than 10%
10% to 19.9%
20% or more

Figure 5-9 shows five indicators of the U.S. competitive position in the world. These were chosen because they measure America's effort in advanced technology, which presumably is the key to future economic growth.

Indicators of U.S. Competitive Position

FIG. 5–9

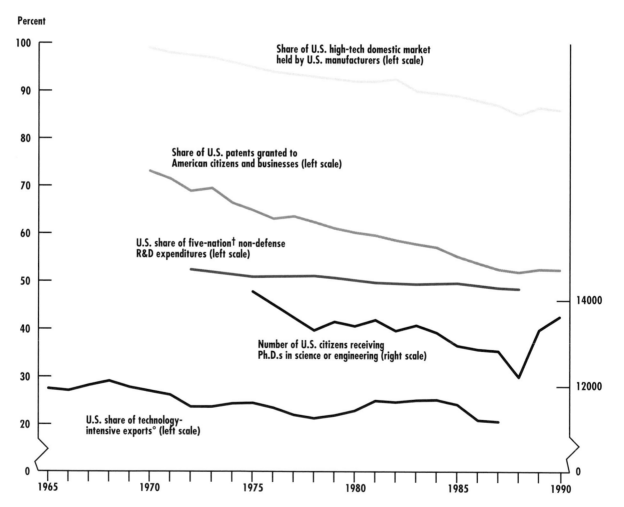

Percent

Share of U.S. high-tech domestic market held by U.S. manufacturers (left scale)

Share of U.S. patents granted to American citizens and businesses (left scale)

U.S. share of five-nation† non-defense R&D expenditures (left scale)

Number of U.S. citizens receiving Ph.D.s in science or engineering (right scale)

U.S. share of technology-intensive exports° (left scale)

†France, Federal Republic of Germany, Britain, Japan and U.S.
°Based on 24 countries.

Labor unions achieved their greatest penetration of the work force in 1953, when one in three of those in non-agricultural work were union members. In the early 1990s, less than one out of five are union members. The decline has been due in part to a shift from manufacturing, where unions have traditionally been strong, to the service sector, which is far harder to organize. The relatively high unemployment rates of the 1980s made employees more concerned about job security, and so less apt to offend management by agitating for union certification.

Unions in Europe, Canada, and Australia have managed to stay far stronger than their American counterparts. The weakness of American unions is due in part to laws such as the Taft-Hartley Act of 1947 and the Landrum-Griffin Act of 1959, which severely restrict the right of unions to use the techniques that were so successful in the 1930s, such as the secondary boycott and mass picketing. The Taft-Hartley Act allows states to enforce right-to-work laws, which make it illegal to require union membership as a condition of employment. (Eighteen states now have such laws.) Laws in most states deprive teachers and other government employees of their most important weapon—the legal right to strike. The weakness of unions was demonstrated in 1981, when President Reagan crushed PATCO, the Professional Air Traffic Controllers Organization, with virtually no opposition from organized labor.

Percent of Manufacturing Workers Who Are Unionized, 1989

FIG. 5–10

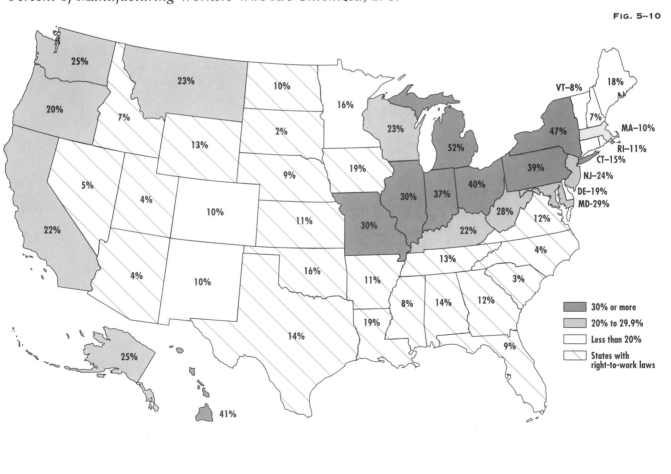

30% or more

20% to 29.9%

Less than 20%

States with right-to-work laws

Department of Commerce Predictions of Changes in Employment During the 1990s, by Metropolitan Area

FIG. 5–11

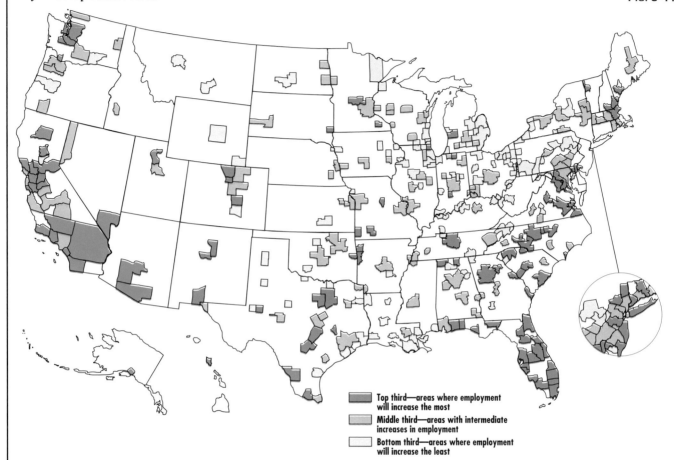

Top third—areas where employment will increase the most

Middle third—areas with intermediate increases in employment

Bottom third—areas where employment will increase the least

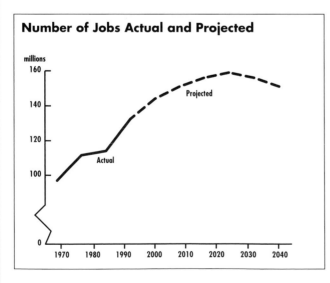

Number of Jobs Actual and Projected

millions

160

140

120

100

0

Projected

Actual

1970 1980 1990 2000 2010 2020 2030 2040

During the 1990s, employment is expected to rise substantially in the states bordering the Atlantic and Pacific, according to the U.S. Department of Commerce, although the Las Vegas, Nevada metropolitan area is forecast to have the greatest growth—30 percent. The Cheyenne, Wyoming, area is predicted to have the least growth—3 percent during the decade. Among the dozen largest metropolitan areas, the biggest gains in jobs over the next decade are forecast for San Francisco and Los Angeles (both 17 percent) and Denver and Washington (both 16 percent). The smallest gains are forecast for New York City (8 percent), Detroit (9 percent), and Philadelphia and Atlanta (both 10 percent). In the intermediate range are Chicago (11 percent), Houston (12 percent), Dallas (13 percent), and Miami (14 percent).

Percent of Employed People 16 and Over Who Work in Manufacturing by County, 1990

FIG. 5-12

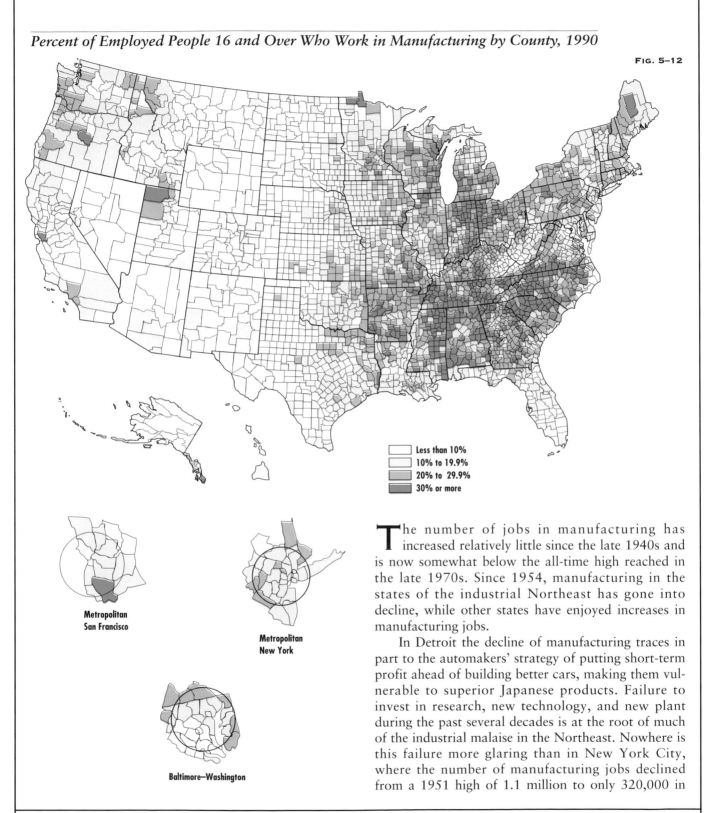

Less than 10%
10% to 19.9%
20% to 29.9%
30% or more

Metropolitan San Francisco

Metropolitan New York

Baltimore–Washington

The number of jobs in manufacturing has increased relatively little since the late 1940s and is now somewhat below the all-time high reached in the late 1970s. Since 1954, manufacturing in the states of the industrial Northeast has gone into decline, while other states have enjoyed increases in manufacturing jobs.

In Detroit the decline of manufacturing traces in part to the automakers' strategy of putting short-term profit ahead of building better cars, making them vulnerable to superior Japanese products. Failure to invest in research, new technology, and new plant during the past several decades is at the root of much of the industrial malaise in the Northeast. Nowhere is this failure more glaring than in New York City, where the number of manufacturing jobs declined from a 1951 high of 1.1 million to only 320,000 in

1990. Jason Epstein, writing in the *New York Review of Books* in 1992, suggested that the decline may have been caused in large part by the attitude of the city's elite, who were more interested in building skyscrapers than in creating industrial jobs. Indeed, their policies discouraged manufacturing, according to Epstein. The elite yearned for a nice clean environment based on industries like banking, stockbroking, and advertising and free of unaesthetic factories and swarms of grimy factory workers who seemed to do nothing but depress property values. Following the loss of manufacturing jobs, the tax base narrowed, tax rates increased, and the middle class fled.

New York is an extreme case, but most sizable cities in the Northeast, including Chicago, Detroit, Cleveland, Boston, Indianapolis, Philadelphia, Buffalo, and Pittsburgh, also lost manufacturing jobs in the post-World War II era.

Manufacturing Employment, 1946–1992

Report Card on City and State Management

Report Card on Management of the States

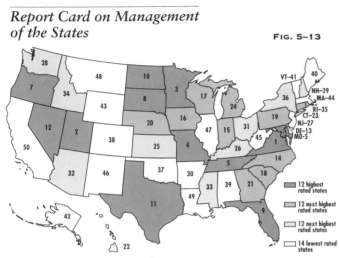

FIG. 5–13

The ratings were made by *Financial World,* and are based on data collected in 1992. The numbers on the map indicate the rank of the states in the ratings.

Legend:
- 12 highest rated states
- 12 next highest rated states
- 12 next highest rated states
- 14 lowest rated states

inancial World magazine makes an annual evaluation of the management of cities and states based on an analysis of accounting practices, budgeting, infrastructure controls, and program evaluation. The ratings are based on questionnaires sent to municipal and state budget offices and public works departments, and interviews with controllers, bond analysts, newspaper reporters, legislators, and others. Among the questions that *Financial World* attempts to answer: Are financial statements prepared in accordance with generally accepted accounting principles? Does the government provide the public with easy-to-read financial statements? How accurate are budget forecasts? Does the government conduct regular assessments of its infrastructure? Do government departments have clearly defined objectives? Is there a system to measure whether government departments meet these objectives?

Report Card on Management of the 30 Largest Cities

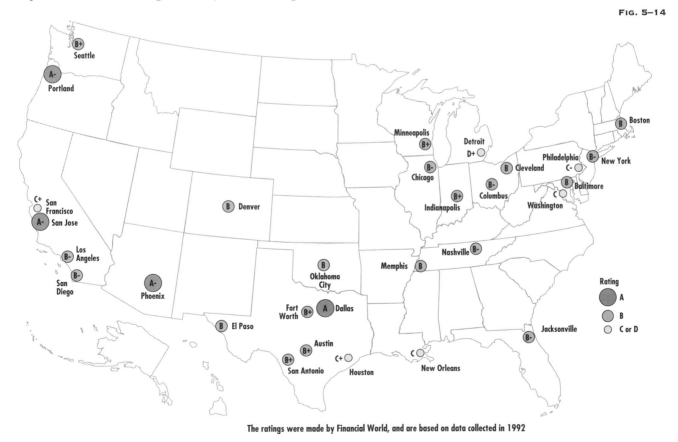

FIG. 5–14

Rating:
- A
- B
- C or D

The ratings were made by Financial World, and are based on data collected in 1992.

American Cultural Penetration

Long before the Cold War ended, America was the dominant superpower of popular culture, with a strong underground following even in the Soviet Union. France, usually zealous in defending Gallic culture, is home to a Disney World complex. Among the few holdouts against American cultural imperialism are fundamentalist Iran, Myanmar (formerly Burma), which tries to bar all foreign influence, and Castro's Cuba. (But even in Cuba baseball continues to be played.)

American Cultural Penetration—Countries Where Pepsi-Cola and McDonald's Hamburgers Are Sold

FIG. 5–15

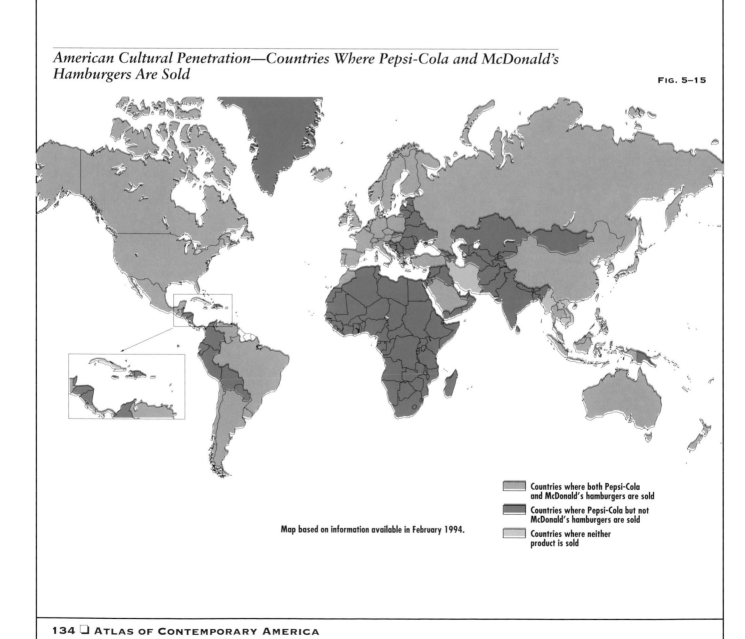

Countries where both Pepsi-Cola and McDonald's hamburgers are sold

Countries where Pepsi-Cola but not McDonald's hamburgers are sold

Countries where neither product is sold

Map based on information available in February 1994.

6

Health

Death Rates

Life expectancy of Americans at birth was about 39 years in 1850, 47 years in 1900, and 76 years in 1990. This remarkable progress came about largely through measures aimed at preventing and treating infectious diseases, such as cholera, typhoid, typhus, smallpox, and tuberculosis. Water was purified, milk was pasteurized, sanitary sewers were installed, people were vaccinated, and antibiotics were introduced.

Because of these and other measures, there has not been a major epidemic of a highly infectious disease in the United States since 1918-1919, when half a million Americans died from influenza. Instead, Americans have been plagued mostly by chronic ailments that typically afflict the middle-aged and elderly, such as heart disease, which accounts for 37 percent of all deaths, and cancer, which accounts for 21 percent.

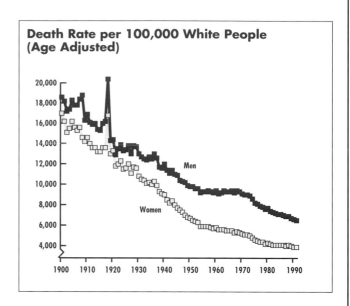

Death Rate per 100,000 White People (Age Adjusted)

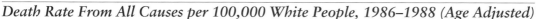

Death Rate From All Causes per 100,000 White People, 1986–1988 (Age Adjusted)

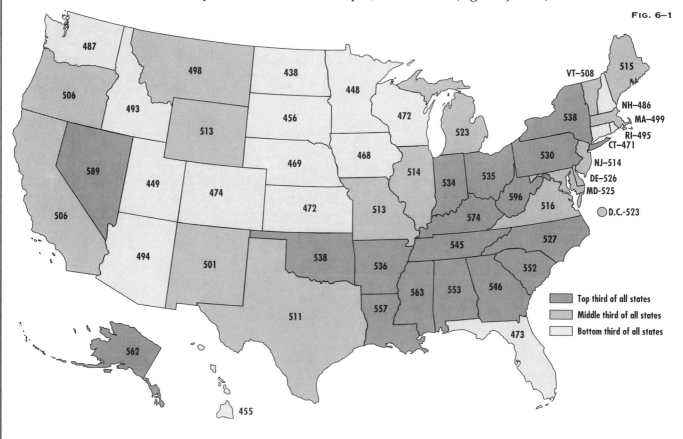

FIG. 6–1

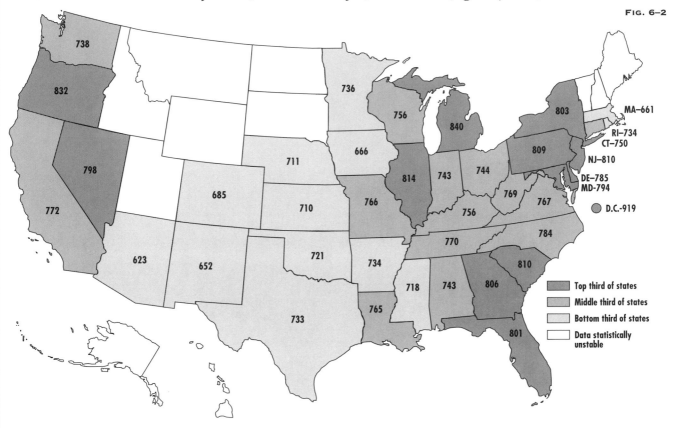

FIG. 6–2

738
832
756
840
803
MA–661
RI–734
CT–750
NJ–810
809
DE–785
MD–794
D.C.–919
798
772
711
666
814
743
744
766
769
767
685
710
784
756
623
652
721
734
770
810
733
718
743
806
765
801

Top third of states
Middle third of states
Bottom third of states
Data statistically unstable

Susceptibility to these chronic diseases is highest in the eastern half of the country, and this helps explain why the death rate among whites from all causes is so high in this area (Figure 6-1). The all-cause death rate among blacks tends to follow the same pattern, but at a higher level (Figure 6-2). In every state, the rate for blacks is higher than for whites, a disparity that can be traced largely to poorer quality medical care, cigarette-smoking (more blacks smoke), and the risks of inner-city living.

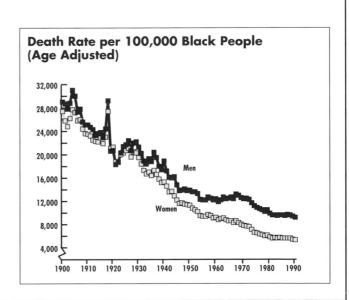

Death Rate per 100,000 Black People (Age Adjusted)

Coronary Heart Disease Death Rate—White Males 35–74, 1968–1978 (Age Adjusted)

FIG. 6–3

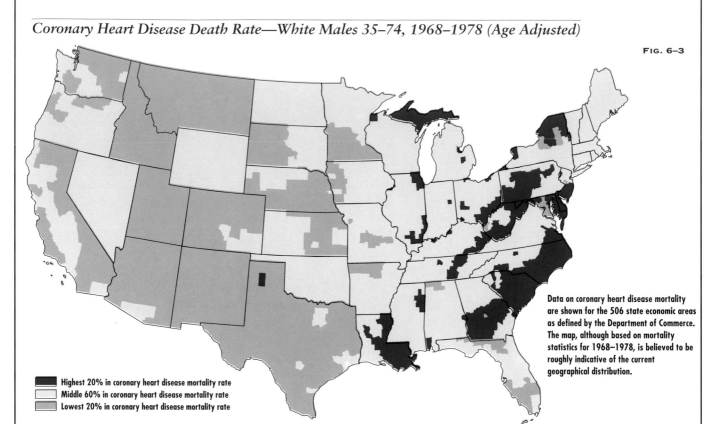

Highest 20% in coronary heart disease mortality rate
Middle 60% in coronary heart disease mortality rate
Lowest 20% in coronary heart disease mortality rate

Data on coronary heart disease mortality are shown for the 506 state economic areas as defined by the Department of Commerce. The map, although based on mortality statistics for 1968–1978, is believed to be roughly indicative of the current geographical distribution.

Coronary Heart Disease Mortality Rate per 100,000 White Men

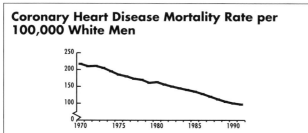

Coronary heart disease (CHD), the dominant form of heart ailment, is the leading killer of men in the United States and in many other industrialized countries. CHD arises when the coronary arteries, which supply oxygen-rich blood to the heart, become blocked, usually through the process of atherosclerosis (degenerative narrowing of the arteries) or thrombosis (blood clotting). This may result in a heart attack—the sudden destruction of part of the heart muscle and wild, uncontrolled heartbeats. Below age 65, men are three times more likely to get the disease than women, but among the elderly, the disparity between men and women decreases with age.

There are several factors that greatly increase risk of CHD: cigarette smoking, high blood pressure, a high level of cholesterol (low-density lipoproteins) in the blood, and diabetes. Sedentary living may also contribute to the disease. The decline of CHD mortality in recent years may have been due to less cigarette smoking, programs to reduce blood pressure, and possibly changes in diet that could have reduced average blood cholesterol levels.

Coronary heart disease exhibits some puzzling regional patterns. Mortality from the disease among white males is heaviest in Appalachia, along the South Atlantic coast, and in a few large cities. Appalachia may lag in the sophisticated coronary care that has saved so many lives in recent years, but it is not clear what accounts for the high CHD rates in cities like Chicago, Buffalo, and Amarillo, Texas. Also, it is not clear why places like Houston and San Diego have exceptionally low rates. (The map shows the CHD mortality rates for white men. The rates for women and nonwhites follow similar patterns.)

Stroke is the third leading cause of death in the United States, surpassed only by coronary heart disease and lung cancer. A stroke may occur when an artery bringing blood to the brain is blocked by a clot or when a vessel in the brain or on the brain surface ruptures. The principal risk factors for stroke are high blood pressure, smoking, high red blood cell count, a previous history of heart disease, and transient ischemic attacks, so-called "little strokes" that occur when a blood clot temporarily clogs an artery. Deaths from the disease have been declining for many years, perhaps in part due to better control of blood pressure.

Stroke affects primarily those over 55. Men have a slightly higher rate than women, but blacks have much higher rates than whites. For reasons that are not clear, blacks are far more likely to have high blood pressure, the preeminent risk factor for stroke.

Stroke mortality rates for white men are shown in Figure 6-4. The geographic patterns for white females and for nonwhites are similar to those of white males. The Southeast is the poorest region of the country, and it is poor people who are most likely to suffer hypertension and stroke.

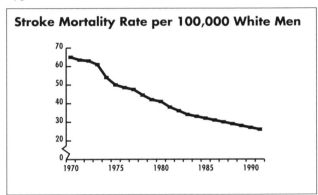

Stroke Mortality Rate per 100,000 White Men

Stroke Death Rate—White Males 35–74, 1976–1982 (Age Adjusted)

FIG. 6–4

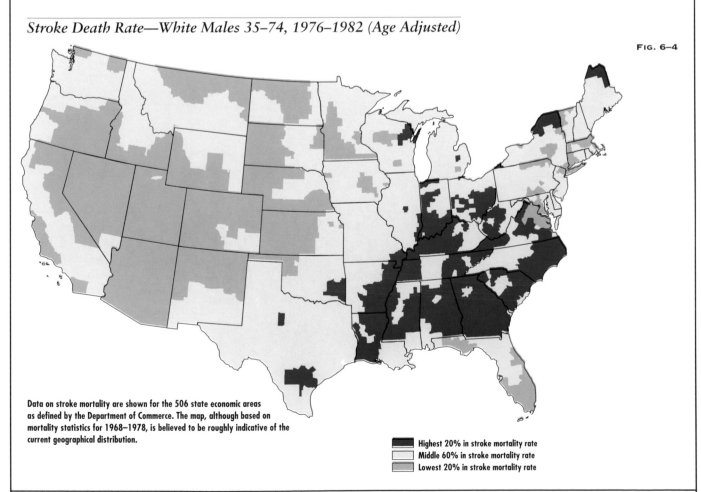

Data on stroke mortality are shown for the 506 state economic areas as defined by the Department of Commerce. The map, although based on mortality statistics for 1968–1978, is believed to be roughly indicative of the current geographical distribution.

■ Highest 20% in stroke mortality rate
□ Middle 60% in stroke mortality rate
▨ Lowest 20% in stroke mortality rate

Since 1950 the death rate from cancer has risen markedly among American men, mostly because of rising rates of lung cancer among cigarette smokers. The recent upturn in cancer death rates among women is also due to smoking-induced lung cancer. The rates for both men and women and both whites and nonwhites would be much higher were it not for improved detection and treatment of many types of cancer in recent decades.

Total cancer mortality rates for white men (Figure 6-5) are particularly high in the Northeast, the cities of the industrial Midwest, coastal areas of the South, and in Louisiana and other parts of the Mississippi Delta. The rates are particularly low in the Mountain states. The rates for white women (Figure 6-6) follow a similar pattern, except that they are low in the South and high in California. These patterns reflect the distribution of specific types of cancer, particularly cancer of the lung, colon, and breast, which together account for about half of all cancer deaths.

Lung cancer, which traces primarily to cigarette smoking, is the most widespread type of cancer. Deaths from this disease among white men (Figure 6-7) are particularly high in the band of states stretching from Virginia through Louisiana and Arkansas, an area where smoking among males tends to be very high despite the anti-smoking bias of the Baptists, who are especially strong in this region. Southern Louisiana is an area of high cancer mortality among men owing in part to the tobacco habits of the Cajuns, who smoke large quantities of hand-rolled cigarettes and other high-tar products.

In the Mississippi Delta region of Louisiana, Mississippi, and Arkansas, one of the poorest areas of the country, the high rate of lung cancer among men may be exacerbated by poor nutrition and lack of medical care. (Diets in the South are low in vitamin A, a nutrient that may be protective against lung cancer among smokers.) The high rate of lung cancer among men in the Atlantic coast areas of Virginia, Georgia, and Florida followed exposure to chemicals

Mortality Rate per 100,000 White Males—All Types of Cancer, 1970–1980 (Age Adjusted)

FIG. 6–5

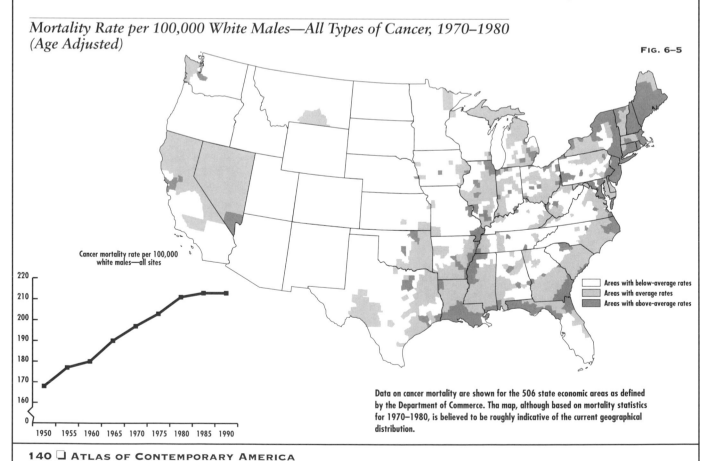

Cancer mortality rate per 100,000 white males—all sites

220
210
200
190
180
170
160
0

1950 1955 1960 1965 1970 1975 1980 1985 1990

Areas with below-average rates
Areas with average rates
Areas with above-average rates

Data on cancer mortality are shown for the 506 state economic areas as defined by the Department of Commerce. Tha map, although based on mortality statistics for 1970–1980, is believed to be roughly indicative of the current geographical distribution.

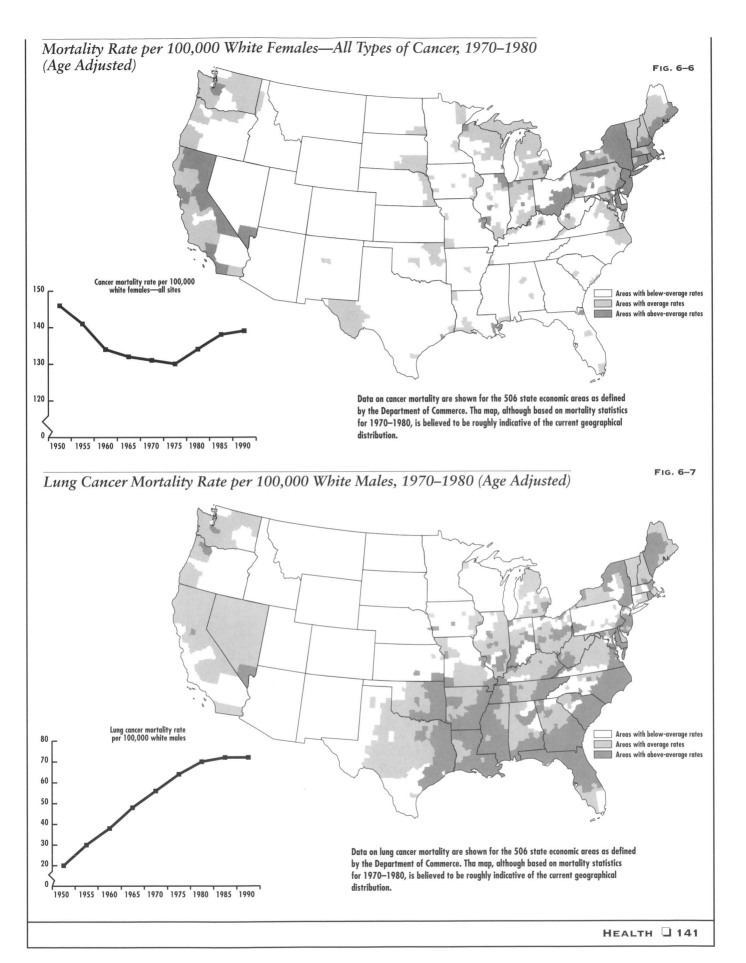

Mortality Rate per 100,000 White Females—All Types of Cancer, 1970–1980 (Age Adjusted)

FIG. 6–6

Cancer mortality rate per 100,000 white females—all sites

150
140
130
120
0

1950 1955 1960 1965 1970 1975 1980 1985 1990

Areas with below-average rates
Areas with average rates
Areas with above-average rates

Data on cancer mortality are shown for the 506 state economic areas as defined by the Department of Commerce. Tha map, although based on mortality statistics for 1970–1980, is believed to be roughly indicative of the current geographical distribution.

FIG. 6–7

Lung Cancer Mortality Rate per 100,000 White Males, 1970–1980 (Age Adjusted)

Lung cancer mortality rate per 100,000 white males

80
70
60
50
40
30
20
0

1950 1955 1960 1965 1970 1975 1980 1985 1990

Areas with below-average rates
Areas with average rates
Areas with above-average rates

Data on lung cancer mortality are shown for the 506 state economic areas as defined by the Department of Commerce. Tha map, although based on mortality statistics for 1970–1980, is believed to be roughly indicative of the current geographical distribution.

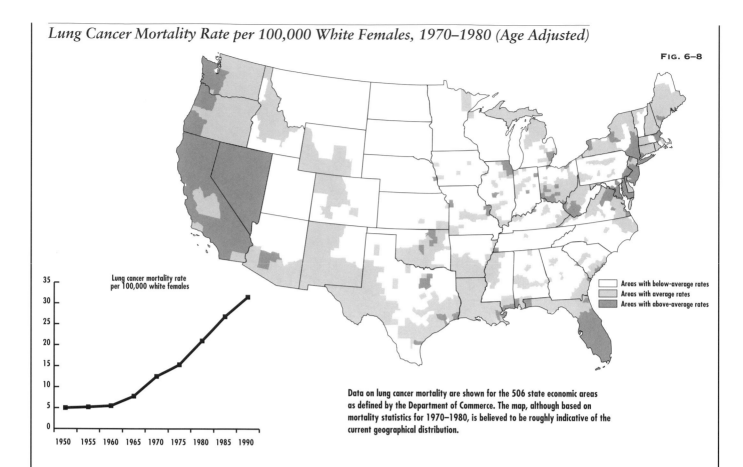

Lung Cancer Mortality Rate per 100,000 White Females, 1970–1980 (Age Adjusted)

FIG. 6–8

Lung cancer mortality rate
per 100,000 white females

- Areas with below-average rates
- Areas with average rates
- Areas with above-average rates

Data on lung cancer mortality are shown for the 506 state economic areas as defined by the Department of Commerce. The map, although based on mortality statistics for 1970–1980, is believed to be roughly indicative of the current geographical distribution.

in shipbuilding yards, mostly during World War II. There is also evidence that people in these coastal areas who work in paper, chemical, and petroleum industries are at greater than average risk for lung cancer. The high rates of lung cancer in some cities in the North, such as Cincinnati and Indianapolis, may also be due to industrial chemical exposure.

It is not surprising that the Mountain and Plains states, where cigarettes are relatively unpopular, have the lowest lung cancer rates in the United States. Utah, home of the nonsmoking, abstemious Mormons, has the lowest lung cancer rate of any state. Lutherans and Methodists, prominent in the Midwest, also tend to discourage smoking. The Mountain and Plains states also benefit from less job exposure to toxic chemicals and radiation than other areas.

The geographical pattern of lung cancer mortality rates among white women (Figure 6-8) differs from that of men. The highest concentration is in the New York-Washington corridor, Florida, and the West Coast. The striking increase in lung cancer deaths among white women over the past 20 years is almost certainly the end result of the sharp increase in smoking among women in the 1940s, 1950s and 1960s.

Air pollution does not seem to contribute to lung cancer. Many cities with low lung cancer rates, such as Minneapolis and Denver, are heavily polluted, while other cities with high lung cancer rates, such as Jacksonville and Norfolk, have relatively little air pollution. However, people living close to certain industrial plants (for example, those disseminating zinc, arsenic, or cadmium) may be at risk.

Colon cancer mortality among men (Figure 6-9) is strongly concentrated in the northeast quadrant of the nation. This concentration may reflect exposure to radiation and cancer-causing chemicals on the job, for this is the most industrialized area of the country and includes most of the nation's chemical industry, particularly important in northern New Jersey. Several industrial substances—for example, asbestos—are associated with colon cancer. Colon cancer mortality among women (not shown) is also concentrated in the northeast quadrant. However, occupational exposure does not help explain the geographical concentration of colon cancer among women, who are far less apt to work in factories.

According to one leading theory, colon cancer is promoted by excessive fat in the diet, but this does not explain the high rate in the Northeast, where consumption of fat is below the national average. According to another theory, colon cancer arises from a diet deficient in fiber, particularly fiber from whole grain cereals. The low level of dietary fiber consumption in the Northeast is consistent with this explanation. Neither the dietary fiber nor the dietary fat theory of colon cancer promotion is fully accepted by medical researchers.

Breast cancer mortality among women (Figure 6-10), like colon cancer, is highest in the northeast quadrant, but rates are also high in San Francisco and Los Angeles. Breast cancer is associated with urban living, higher socioeconomic status, and delayed pregnancy, characteristics that apply to women in the Northeast. According to some researchers, breast cancer may be caused by excessive fat in the diet, but the relatively low fat consumption in the Northeast is not consistent with this theory.

Deaths from other types of cancer (not shown) follow a variety of geographical patterns. Cancers of the stomach, bladder, rectum, and ovary tend to be concentrated in the northeast quadrant. Leukemia and cancers of the pancreas and prostate tend to be less concentrated geographically. Cancers of the mouth, esophagus, and larynx, which are promoted by the combination of cigarette-smoking and alcohol consumption, are particularly low in the Midwest and Mountain states, areas of low cigarette and alcohol use. High rates of oral cancer among men in the coastal areas of Virginia and Georgia are probably due to high consumption of cigarettes and alcohol. Skin cancer, which is caused mainly by exposure to the sun, is found in a broad band of southern states stretching from Virginia through Texas.

Cancer mortality differs markedly by race. As compared to white males, African-American males are 25 percent more likely to die of cancer, Native Americans are 50 percent less likely, Japanese are 33 percent less likely, and Chinese are 20 percent less likely. As compared to white women, black women are about 15 percent more likely to die of cancer, Native American and Japanese women are about 40 percent less likely, and Chinese women are 30 percent less likely. The map (Figure 6-11) shows the total cancer rate among nonwhite males. The geographic pattern is somewhat similar to that of white males except that the nonwhites have a greater susceptibility in eastern Ohio, eastern Pennsylvania, and southern Florida. In part, this reflects greater mortality from lung cancer in these areas.

Colon Cancer Mortality Rate per 100,000 White Males, 1970–1980 (Age Adjusted)

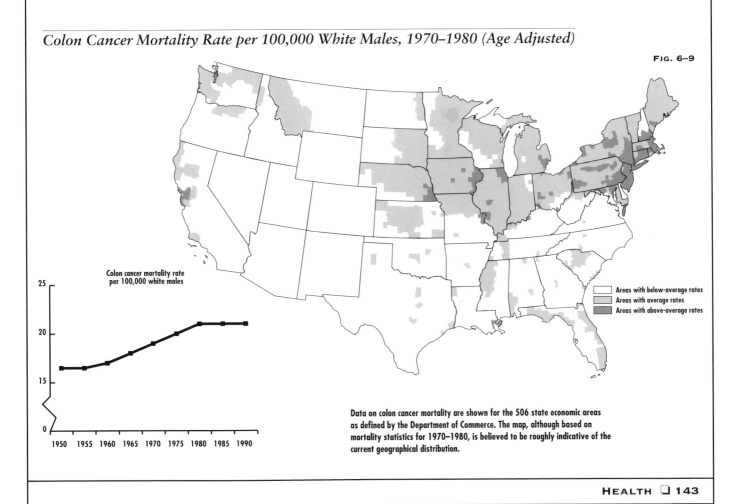

FIG. 6–9

Colon cancer mortality rate per 100,000 white males

Areas with below-average rates
Areas with average rates
Areas with above-average rates

Data on colon cancer mortality are shown for the 506 state economic areas as defined by the Department of Commerce. The map, although based on mortality statistics for 1970–1980, is believed to be roughly indicative of the current geographical distribution.

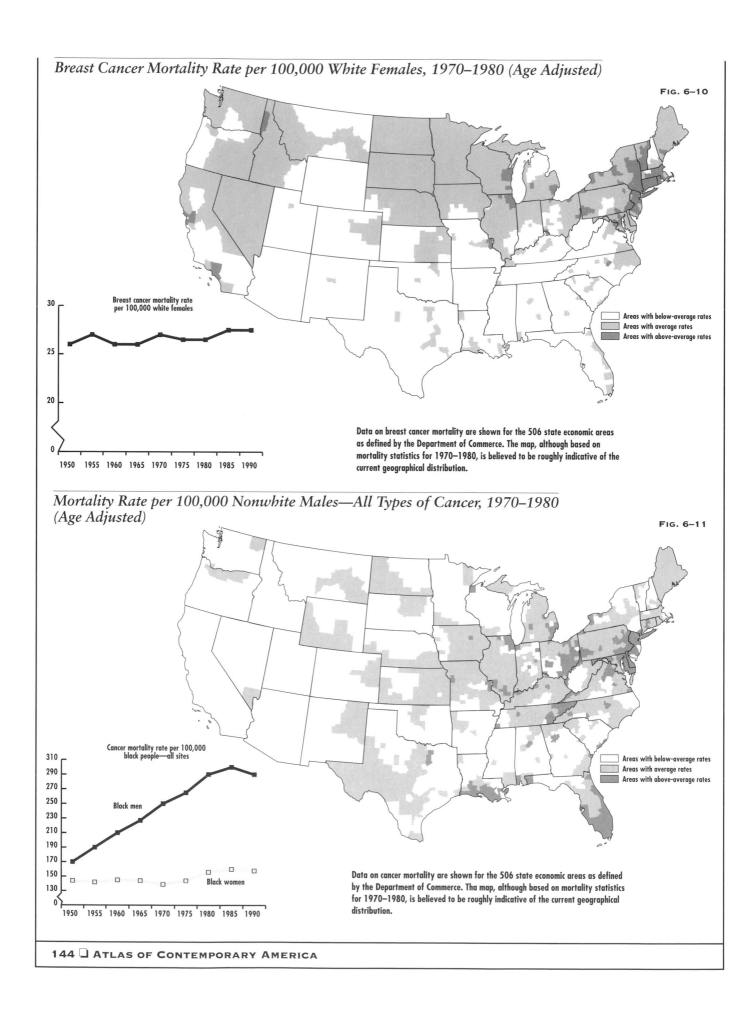

Breast Cancer Mortality Rate per 100,000 White Females, 1970–1980 (Age Adjusted)

FIG. 6–10

Breast cancer mortality rate per 100,000 white females

Areas with below-average rates
Areas with average rates
Areas with above-average rates

Data on breast cancer mortality are shown for the 506 state economic areas as defined by the Department of Commerce. The map, although based on mortality statistics for 1970–1980, is believed to be roughly indicative of the current geographical distribution.

Mortality Rate per 100,000 Nonwhite Males—All Types of Cancer, 1970–1980 (Age Adjusted)

FIG. 6–11

Cancer mortality rate per 100,000 black people—all sites

Black men

Black women

Areas with below-average rates
Areas with average rates
Areas with above-average rates

Data on cancer mortality are shown for the 506 state economic areas as defined by the Department of Commerce. Tha map, although based on mortality statistics for 1970–1980, is believed to be roughly indicative of the current geographical distribution.

The human immunodeficiency virus (HIV) usually enters the body through sexual intercourse or exchange of needles by intravenous drug users. Typically, about three weeks after exposure, the virus causes transient mononucleosis-like symptoms. This is followed by a latency period averaging 8 to 10 years, but which may be as short as a few months or more than 15 years. By the end of the latent period the virus has suppressed the immune system to such an extent that the victim is afflicted by opportunistic ailments like Kaposi's sarcoma, a rare type of cancer; pneumocystis pneumonia; infections of the mouth, intestines, and brain; and dementia. It is these consequences of HIV infection that are called AIDS—acquired immunodeficiency syndrome.

AIDS cases tend to be concentrated in metropolitan areas with large gay communities or large numbers of IV drug users, such as New York, Miami, and San Francisco. San Francisco has by far the highest rate, while New York has the largest number of cases.

One of the most remarkable features of AIDS in the United States is that, until about 1987, most of the cases were non-Hispanic whites. However, beginning in 1991 blacks and Hispanics comprised the majority of cases, and since then their proportion has grown.

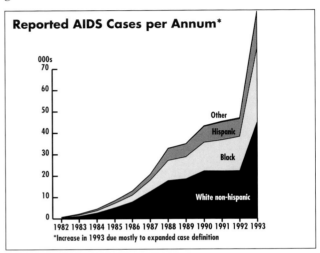

Reported AIDS Cases per Annum*

Increase in 1993 due mostly to expanded case definition

AIDS Cases per 100,000 Population, 1992

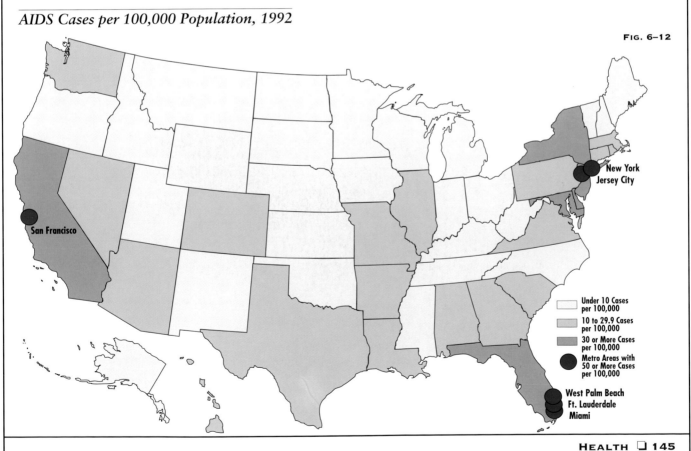

FIG. 6–12

Under 10 Cases per 100,000

10 to 29.9 Cases per 100,000

30 or More Cases per 100,000

Metro Areas with 50 or More Cases per 100,000

San Francisco

New York
Jersey City

West Palm Beach
Ft. Lauderdale
Miami

Syphilis is caused by a spiral-shaped organism, *Treponema pallidum*, which is usually transmitted by sexual contact. The disease, if unchecked, progresses through three phases. In the primary phase, the initial lesion appears, usually 10 to 90 days after sexual contact. In the secondary phase, which may occur weeks after the first phase, victims develop a rash and typically complain of headache, sore throat, fever, and general malaise. (The map shows the combined primary and secondary cases.) In the tertiary phase, which may take up to 25 years after infection to develop, victims may be afflicted by congestive heart disease, paralysis, blindness, and sometimes insanity. Tertiary syphilis may develop within months of infection if the victim is also infected with the human immunodeficiency virus (HIV), the organism that causes AIDS. Penicillin cures primary syphilis in 95 percent of cases.

The highest mortality rate recorded for tertiary syphilis in the United States was in 1917, when more than 20,000 died. In 1989, only 105 deaths from this disease were reported. In recent years the annual number of reported primary and secondary cases has been about 50,000. Among white men, the incidence of syphilis has declined sharply, apparently because homosexuals and bisexuals—groups far more likely to contract the disease than heterosexuals—have been practicing safer sex in response to the AIDS epidemic. The rates for white women, which have always been low, remained largely unchanged during the 1980s, but for blacks of both sexes the rates increased markedly in the late 1980s, possibly because addiction to cocaine and other illegal drugs promotes the sale of sex for drugs.

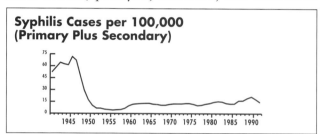

Syphilis Cases per 100,000 (Primary Plus Secondary)

Syphilis Cases per 100,000 Population, 1991 (Primary Plus Secondary)

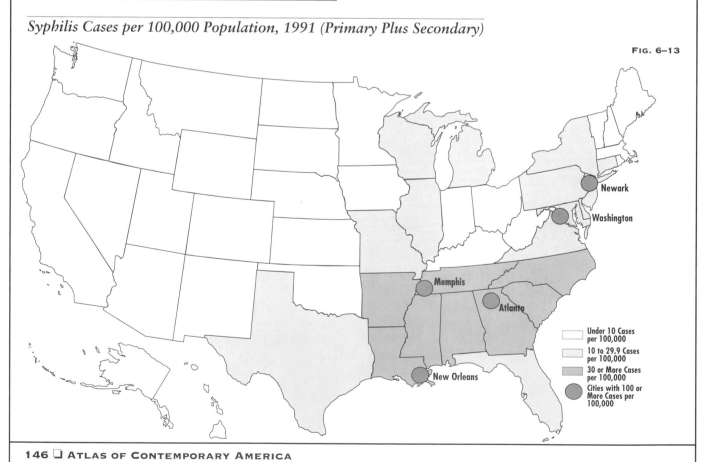

FIG. 6–13

Under 10 Cases per 100,000

10 to 29.9 Cases per 100,000

30 or More Cases per 100,000

Cities with 100 or More Cases per 100,000

Gonorrhea Cases per 100,000 Population, 1991

FIG. 6–14

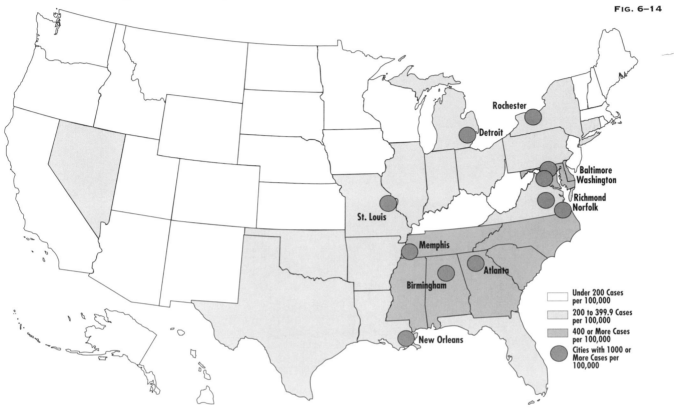

- Under 200 Cases per 100,000
- 200 to 399.9 Cases per 100,000
- 400 or More Cases per 100,000
- Cities with 1000 or More Cases per 100,000

G onorrhea, which is caused by the bacteria *Neisseria gonorrhoeae*, is the most widespread of all the reportable sexually transmitted diseases, with about 700,000 new cases annually in recent years. In men, the first lesion appears within days of infection. If untreated, the infection spreads upward in the urethra to the prostate gland, seminal vesicles, bladder, and related organs. Most infected women who are not treated do not have immediate symptoms, but about half develop pelvic inflammatory disease in about 8 to 10 weeks, with possible infertility a result. Both men and women may develop arthritis as a result of infection.

Epidemics of gonorrhea occurred after World War I and during World War II, when the disease was first treated with penicillin. In recent years the incidence has declined, perhaps in part because gay men have been taking protective measures. However, a disquieting development since 1980 has been the

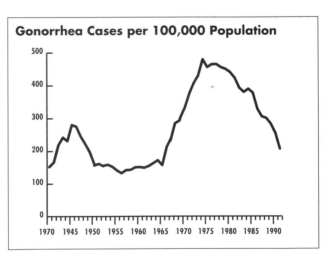

Gonorrhea Cases per 100,000 Population

growth of "super gonorrhea," new strains of the bacteria that are more resistant to antibiotic treatment. Rates for blacks are considerably higher than those for whites.

Suicide

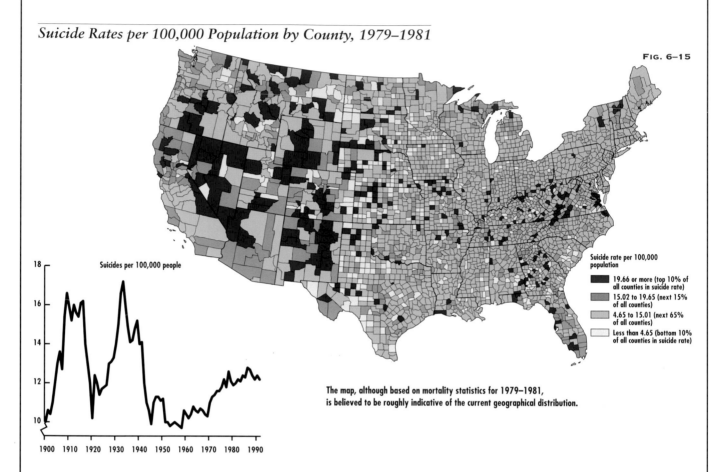

Suicide Rates per 100,000 Population by County, 1979–1981

FIG. 6–15

Suicides per 100,000 people

Suicide rate per 100,000 population

■ 19.66 or more (top 10% of all counties in suicide rate)

■ 15.02 to 19.65 (next 15% of all counties)

■ 4.65 to 15.01 (next 65% of all counties)

□ Less than 4.65 (bottom 10% of all counties in suicide rate)

The map, although based on mortality statistics for 1979–1981, is believed to be roughly indicative of the current geographical distribution.

The French sociologist Emile Durkheim theorized in 1897 that suicide is influenced by the extent to which people are integrated into their society. Suicide rates are higher not only among the unemployed but also among those who do not participate in social and religious organizations and those who are single, widowed, or divorced. The higher rates in the Mountain states are consistent with this theory, for this area has a higher divorce rate than other regions and contains a larger proportion of new residents than any other region. People who emigrate disrupt their social relationships and may be more prone to suicide than those who are less mobile.

Suicide rates have varied dramatically since 1900, with peaks around 1910 and in the early 1930s. The reasons for the first peak are not clear but may reflect high rates among immigrants, who were coming to America in record numbers at the time. The second peak may be related to the high unemployment of the Great Depression. Gun ownership has increased greatly in the past 40 years and may be responsible for the slow rise in the suicide rate since the low of the 1950s. The overall rate tends to be lower in states with strict gun-control laws and higher in states where the laws are less strict.

Men are more likely than women to commit suicide, and whites more likely than nonwhites. Among white men, the rate rises progressively with age; but with white women, it rises into middle age and then declines. Among blacks of both sexes, it rises until early adulthood and then declines with age. In recent years, the chief means of suicide were, in descending order, guns, hanging, poisoning, and carbon monoxide. Relatively few people kill themselves by overdosing on antidepressant medication. One method frequently used in the past—turning on the kitchen gas—is used much less often now.

Of the top-20 industrialized countries, the United States has the highest infant mortality rate, with more than 38,000 infants dying every year. Many of these deaths are preventable with proper prenatal and infant care. Most of the infants at risk are born to young mothers, mostly single, often undereducated, and usually poor. A disproportionately large number are black (26 percent).

The principal factor in infant mortality is low birth weight—less than 5 1/2 pounds. Such infants are 40 times more likely than those of normal weight to die within a month of birth and, if they survive, are far more likely to suffer from mental retardation, cerebral palsy, epilepsy, chronic lung problems, blindness, deafness, and slow speech development. Low birthweight can be largely prevented by prenatal care beginning early in pregnancy, by good nutrition, and

by avoidance of smoking, alcohol, and drugs. More than a quarter of women of childbearing age lack health insurance, and the system of public health care is inadequate to meet their needs. Medicaid, the health program for the needy, does not provide adequate care for many poor women in the critical early weeks of pregnancy. Many doctors and nurses don't want to work in the overcrowded clinics that serve the inner cities, where infant mortality is highest. Certified nurse midwives and nurse practitioners, who could provide adequate care, are restricted by law in some states from practicing independently.

If America's infant mortality rate were brought down to Japan's level, at least 16,000 additional infants would survive and thousands of additional infants would be born without brain damage or other defects.

Infant Mortality Rate per 1000 Live Births, Children Under One Year, 1989

FIG. 6–16

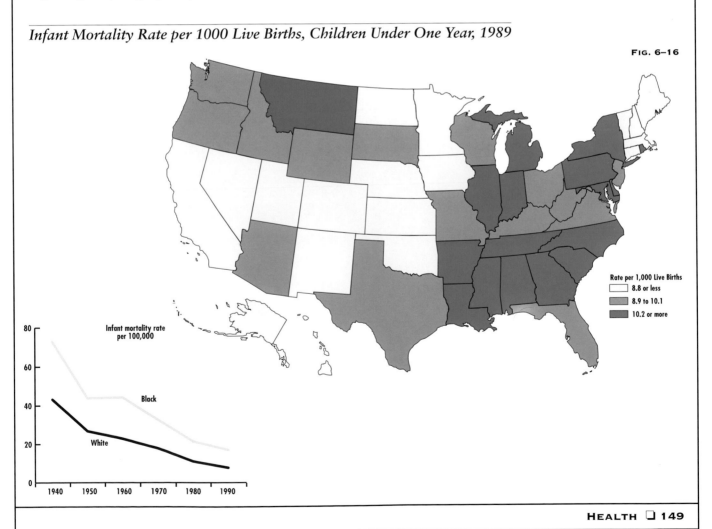

Social Pressures Against Drinking

The Middle-Atlantic states are more tolerant of drinking than other regions, while the South has long been the most intolerant, in part because of church influence. The least tolerant state is Mississippi, and the most tolerant is Nevada. Deaths from cirrhosis of the liver tend to be lower in areas that disapprove of drinking.

Men are four times more likely to be heavy drinkers than women, and whites tend to be heavier drinkers than blacks. There is a gradation by religion, with Catholics tending to be the heaviest drinkers, followed by liberal Protestants, conservative Protestants, and finally Jews, who are the lightest drinkers of all. However, among Catholics, there are big differences, with the Irish tending to be very heavy drinkers and the Italians being more moderate. Of all major groups, the Irish have the highest rate of alcohol-related problems in America, while Italians have one of the lowest. In traditional Italian culture, drinking is associated with food and family festivities, whereas in traditional Irish culture, it is associated with bachelor gatherings, which are uninhibited by family restraints. Observant Jews learn to use alcohol early in life for religious rituals and not for inebriation, which is strongly discouraged.

National drinking patterns can change markedly over time. The early Jews were apparently heavy drinkers, but became moderate drinkers in the fifth and fourth centuries B.C. In 18th-century England, according to one historian, four out of five people who drank were alcoholics, but now England has one of the lowest alcoholism rates in Europe. A similar change may be taking place in America, where hard liquor consumption has declined in recent years. One sign of change is the extraordinary shift among American writers. Of the seven native-born Americans given the Nobel Prize for literature, five were alcoholics—William Faulkner, Ernest Hemingway, John Steinbeck, Eugene O'Neill, and Sinclair Lewis. Dozens of other well-known American writers were also alcoholic, including Jack London, F. Scott Fitzgerald, Hart Crane, Dashiell Hammett, Dorothy Parker, Ring Lardner, John Cheever, Robert Lowell, and Truman Capote.* Among younger American writers, alcoholism seems to be less fashionable.

*Among those who were not alcoholics were T.S. Eliot, Ezra Pound, Edith Wharton, Willa Cather, Robert Frost, and Gertrude Stein.

Social Pressures Against Drinking

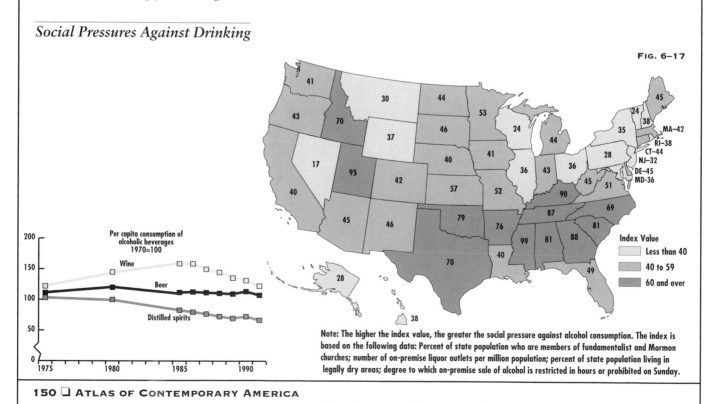

FIG. 6–17

Index Value
- Less than 40
- 40 to 59
- 60 and over

Note: The higher the index value, the greater the social pressure against alcohol consumption. The index is based on the following data: Percent of state population who are members of fundamentalist and Mormon churches; number of on-premise liquor outlets per million population; percent of state population living in legally dry areas; degree to which on-premise sale of alcohol is restricted in hours or prohibited on Sunday.

Percent of People Twenty and Over Who Smoke Cigarettes, 1989

FIG. 6–18

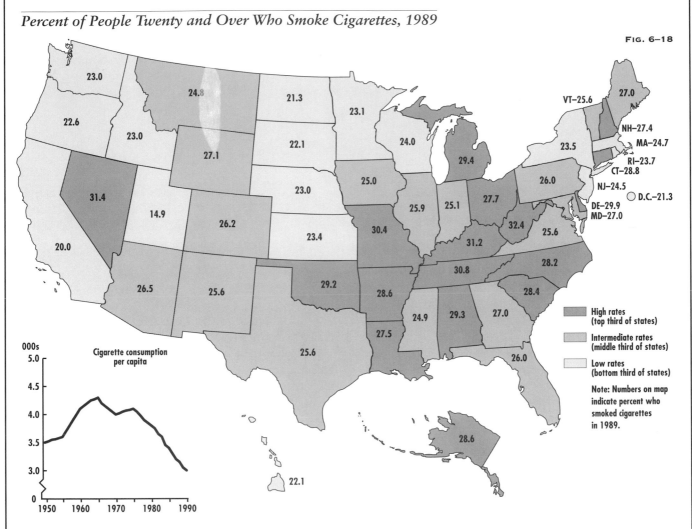

23.0

24.8

21.3

23.1

VT–25.6

27.0

22.6

23.0

27.1

22.1

24.0

NH–27.4

23.5

MA–24.7

29.4

RI–23.7

CT–28.8

31.4

14.9

26.2

23.0

25.0

25.9

25.1

27.7

26.0

NJ–24.5

○ D.C.–21.3

DE–29.9

MD–27.0

20.0

23.4

30.4

31.2

32.4

25.6

26.5

25.6

29.2

28.6

30.8

28.2

28.4

24.9

29.3

27.0

27.5

25.6

26.0

28.6

22.1

High rates
(top third of states)

Intermediate rates
(middle third of states)

Low rates
(bottom third of states)

Note: Numbers on map
indicate percent who
smoked cigarettes
in 1989.

000s

5.0

4.5

4.0

3.5

3.0

0

Cigarette consumption
per capita

1950   1960   1970   1980   1990

Cigarette-smoking is a worldwide epidemic; 200 million children now under 20 years of age will eventually die from it. In the United States, cigarette smoking kills about 400,000 every year, including about 120,000 from lung cancer, 100,000 from coronary heart disease, and 27,000 from stroke. Cigarette smoking also contributes to cancer of the larynx, mouth, esophagus, bladder, pancreas, and kidney, and to stroke, peripheral vascular disease, growth retardation in the womb, low-birthweight babies, increased infant mortality, peptic ulcer, and probably also miscarriage. Rates of smoking have come down considerably over the past 25 years due in large part to anti-smoking campaigns by the U.S. Surgeon General and others. In the past 30 years, roughly a

million smoking-related deaths were avoided or postponed because Americans decided to quit smoking or were persuaded not to try cigarettes.

Most people who smoke cigarettes begin in their teens, typically in their 17th year. Any effort to further reduce cigarette consumption by a large amount would therefore have to focus on preventing adolescents from taking up the habit.

Smokers tend to be less well educated and poorer than nonsmokers, and this is reflected in the geography of cigarette use, which is higher in the South than in other regions. Utah has the smallest proportion of cigarette smokers and West Virginia the largest. The map shows the geographical pattern of cigarette-smoking for men. The pattern for women is similar.

Areas with a Scarcity or Surplus of Physicians

FIG. 6–19

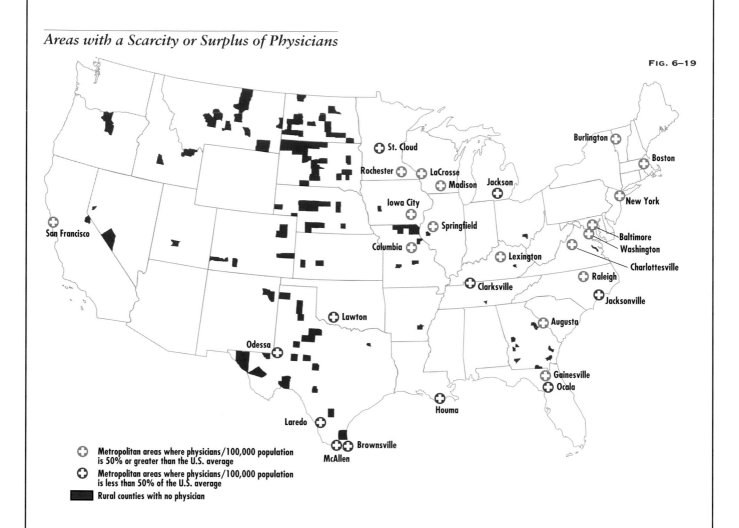

St. Cloud

Burlington
Boston

Rochester LaCrosse
Madison Jackson

New York

Iowa City

Springfield Baltimore
Washington

San Francisco Columbia Charlottesville

Lexington Raleigh

Clarksville Jacksonville

Augusta

Lawton

Gainesville
Odessa Ocala

Houma

Laredo

Brownsville
McAllen

⊕ Metropolitan areas where physicians/100,000 population
   is 50% or greater than the U.S. average
⊕ Metropolitan areas where physicians/100,000 population
   is less than 50% of the U.S. average
■ Rural counties with no physician

Private physicians are hard to find in the inner-city and in rural areas, places where needy patients are most likely to live. People who live in these areas often do not have their own physician but must use clinics and hospital emergency rooms. Many rural patients must travel long distances for care. Over a hundred rural counties have no physician at all. Several metropolitan areas suffer from a shortage of physicians, with several having less than half the number of physicians per 100,000 population than the national average.

arly in the century dental researchers found that people living in areas of Colorado with high natural levels of fluoride in drinking water had remarkably few dental cavities. Tests in cities like Grand Rapids, Michigan, and Newburgh, New York, showed that adding fluoride to the water supply was effective in preventing cavities. In the 1950s, municipalities began to fluoridate their water supply at an average concentration of about 1 part per million. The decision to fluoridate was left to state and local jurisdictions. It was assumed by the public health authorities that fluoridation would be adopted universally, just as water purification was earlier in the century. They were mistaken, because fluoridation opponents were effective in blocking the adoption of this measure in many localities. The anti-fluoridation

Percent of Population with Fluoridated Water Supply, 1985*

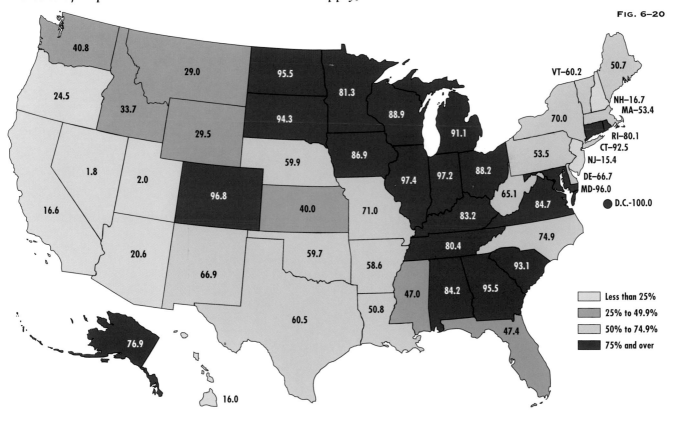

FIG. 6–20

VT–60.2
50.7
NH–16.7
MA–53.4
RI–80.1
CT–92.5
NJ–15.4
DE–66.7
MD–96.0
D.C.–100.0

	Less than 25%
	25% to 49.9%
	50% to 74.9%
	75% and over

40.8
29.0
95.5
81.3
88.9
24.5
33.7
94.3
91.1
70.0
29.5
86.9
53.5
1.8
2.0
59.9
97.4
97.2
88.2
96.8
40.0
71.0
83.2
65.1
84.7
16.6
20.6
59.7
58.6
80.4
74.9
66.9
50.8
47.0
84.2
95.5
93.1
60.5
47.4
76.9
16.0

*Includes both artificially and naturally fluoridated areas.

movement attracted a few scientists and libertarians, and a wide array of crackpots, such as those who saw fluoridation as a communist conspiracy. At one time or another the "antis" have claimed that fluoridation caused skeletal fluorosis, birth defects, kidney disease, allergies, heart disease, various types of cancer, and a variety of other ills. No scientific proof has been offered to back up the charges that fluoridation causes disease. As of the early 1990s, opponents were successful in keeping the water supply unfluoridated for 40 percent of the American population. Among the cities that do not have fluoridated water are Los Angeles, Portland, Oregon, and Salt Lake City.

The prevalence of dental caries among children has declined greatly in recent years, with 50 percent of children caries-free in 1986-87 as compared to 37 percent in 1979-80. In the later period, those who lived in fluoridated areas had 18 percent fewer cavities than those in non-fluoridated areas. However, children in nonfluoridated areas showed a substantial improvement, apparently because they were exposed to fluoride from toothpaste, mouthwash, and other topical applications, as well as from foods processed in areas with fluoridated water.

One of the side-effects of fluoride exposure is fluorosis, or mottling of teeth. This has occurred in both fluoridated and nonfluoridated areas. Such mottling is ordinarily not noticeable and is not a health problem, although potentially an esthetic problem.

7

Contentious Issues

Abortion

No one knows how many illegal abortions were done in the 1960s; estimates range from 200,000 to as high as 1,200,000 a year. Between 1967 and 1972, under pressure from feminists and the medical profession, 19 states loosened restrictions on abortion. Of these, New York was the most liberal, allowing the procedure during the first 24 weeks of gestation. The Supreme Court's *Roe* v. *Wade* decision of 1973 gave women the unrestricted right to abortion in the first trimester of pregnancy. In the second trimester, the Court said, the state could not deny the right to an abortion, but could insist upon certain safeguards; but for the third trimester, the Court recognized the states' right to "proscribe abortion except when necessary to preserve the life or health of the mother." Since 1989 the Court has gradually restricted abortion rights.

In recent years the number of legal abortions in the United States has held steady at slightly under 1.6 million a year. At this rate there is one legal abortion for every two-and-a-half live births. In total, there were more than 20 million legal abortions in the 20 years following the *Roe* v. *Wade* decision.

In recent years about a quarter of abortions were obtained by teenagers and over half by women in their twenties. About eight out of 10 women seeking abortions were unmarried and about a third were nonwhite. About half had already given birth to children. Slightly over half the abortions were performed in the first eight weeks of gestation, and over 90 percent in the first 12 weeks. Six states—California, Florida, Illinois, New Jersey, New York, and Texas accounted for half of all legal abortions in recent years.

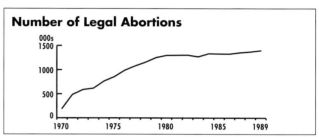

Number of Legal Abortions

Abortion Rate

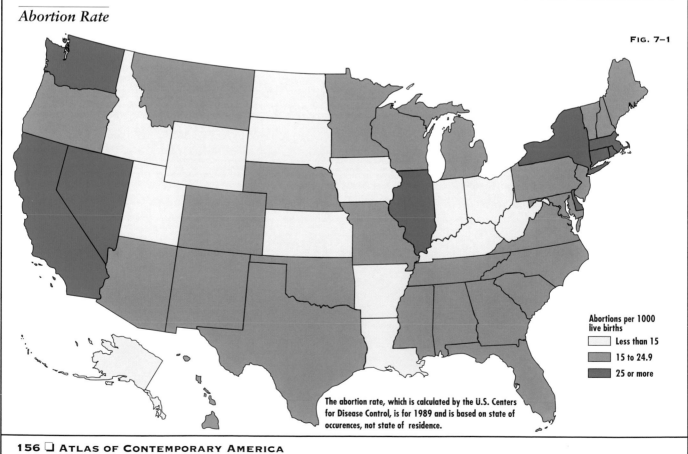

FIG. 7–1

Abortions per 1000 live births
- Less than 15
- 15 to 24.9
- 25 or more

The abortion rate, which is calculated by the U.S. Centers for Disease Control, is for 1989 and is based on state of occurences, not state of residence.

The Political Climate For Abortion Among Governors and State Legislators

FIG. 7–2

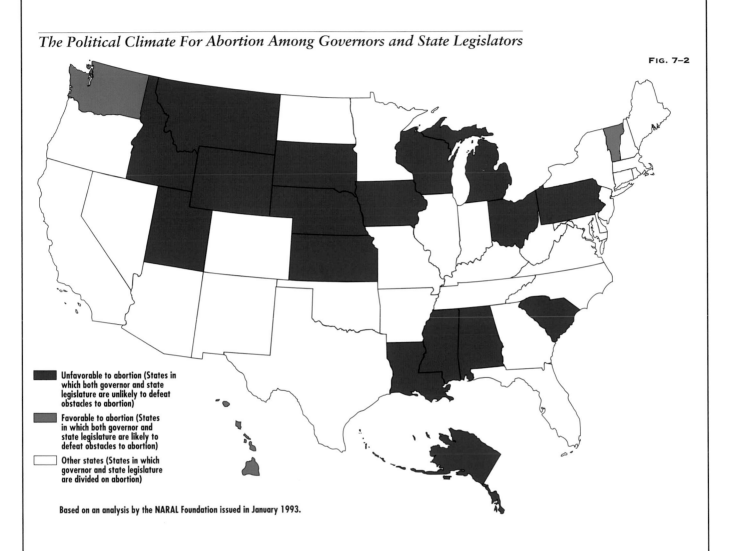

■ Unfavorable to abortion (States in which both governor and state legislature are unlikely to defeat obstacles to abortion)

■ Favorable to abortion (States in which both governor and state legislature are likely to defeat obstacles to abortion)

☐ Other states (States in which governor and state legislature are divided on abortion)

Based on an analysis by the NARAL Foundation issued in January 1993.

The National Abortion Rights Action League (NARAL) has tabulated the position of governors and state legislators on a woman's right to choose. The map shows the political climate for abortion as based on the NARAL tabulation.

Teenage Pregnancy—Births per 1000 Girls 15 to 19, 1990

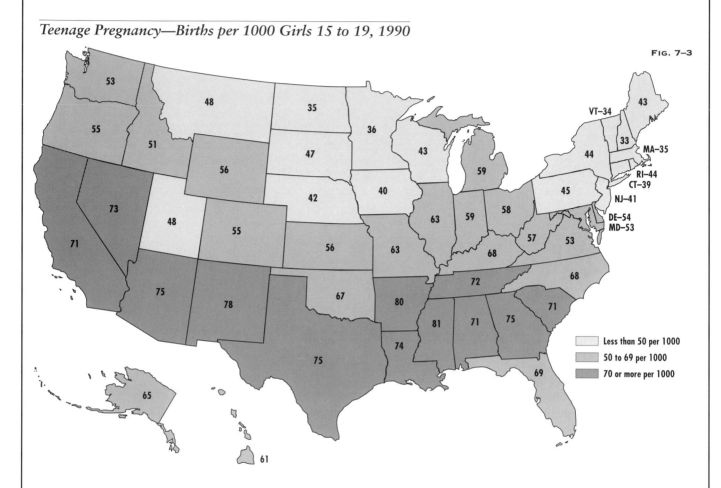

FIG. 7–3

Less than 50 per 1000
50 to 69 per 1000
70 or more per 1000

Of the estimated one million teenagers who become pregnant annually, about one in 10 miscarries, four in 10 have abortions, and five out of 10 give birth. Of the half million or so who give birth, almost two-thirds are unwed. Unmarried teenage mothers tend to be poor and undereducated and have little hope of finding a good-paying job. The large number of unwed teenage mothers helps explain why more than a sixth of all white families and more than half of black families are headed by women.

Pregnant teenagers are less likely to receive early prenatal care than older women. Their babies tend to be smaller than average and suffer a high rate of neonatal mortality. Low-birth-weight babies—about 45,000 of them are born to teenagers every year—are far more likely to die in the first year than those of normal weight. If they survive, they are likely to suffer from congenital abnormalities, neurological prob-

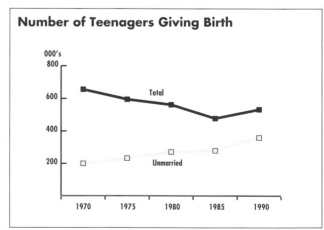

Number of Teenagers Giving Birth

lems, and lung problems. As children, they are likely to have lower IQ test scores and be more prone to emotional problems, drug abuse, and earlier sexual activity than those born in the normal weight range.

Equal Rights Provisions in State Constitutions

In 1972 the National Organization for Women (NOW) took the lead in pressing for an Equal Rights Amendment (ERA) to the Constitution. The proposed amendment, which stated that "Equality of rights under the law shall not be denied or abridged by the United States or by any state on account of sex," was passed by Congress, and by early 1973, 30 states had ratified it. It seemed only a matter of time before three-quarters of the states would approve it, but passage by the necessary 38 states was blocked by a well-organized group of Protestant fundamentalists who believed that the amendment threatened traditional views of a woman's role. The ERA proponents lost the propaganda war in part because they couldn't explain why the amendment was needed in view of the Supreme Court's evolving liberal view on gender issues and because new provisions in state constitutions made sex discrimination illegal.

Sixteen states now have such constitutional provisions, and in nine states the wording of the provisions closely parallels that of the U.S. Equal Rights Amendment. Women are, of course, protected by federal statutes such as the Civil Rights Act of 1964, but the 16 state ERAs, as they are called, have substantially expanded the protections of women against discrimination in employment, education, sports, marital property rights, alimony, and child support. For example, under the Connecticut ERA, limits on the number of hours women can work were repealed in 1972, thus increasing employment opportunities for women. In Hawaii, pregnancy was eliminated as a disqualification for unemployment benefits in 1973. In Illinois, women won the right to equal employment-related death benefits in 1975. In Pennsylvania, the attorney general in 1973 found that the minimum height requirement for state police officers violated the state ERA. In Massachusetts, a scholarship that was previously awarded only to male law students was opened to women in 1977. According to the NOW Legal Defense and Education Fund, the greatest progress has been made in six states—Colorado, Maryland, Massachusetts, New Mexico, Pennsylvania, and Washington.

States with Equal Rights Provisions in Their Constitutions

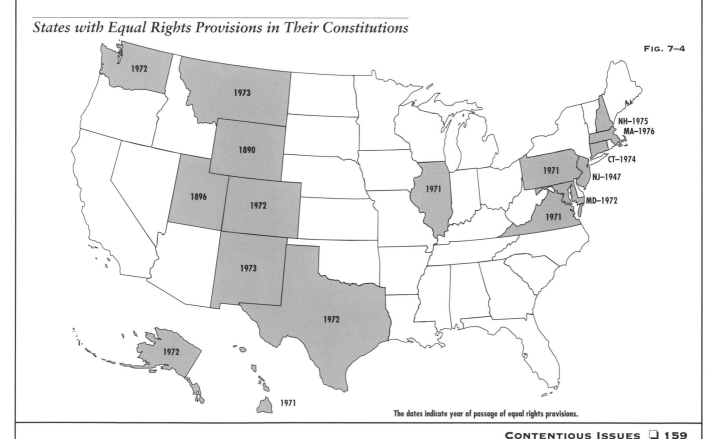

FIG. 7–4

The dates indicate year of passage of equal rights provisions.

Progress Toward Job Equality

The Equal Employment Opportunity Commission collects data on employment status by race and gender from large- and medium-sized firms. These data are used here to measure the success of women and minorities in obtaining the better-paying positions in private industry, those classified as "officials and managers." Success is measured in terms of the proportion of women or minorities in such positions in relation to their share of the total work force. Note that the success rates as computed here do not measure discrimination but simply progress toward equality in holding the better jobs. The chart (Figure 7-5) shows the success rates by gender and racial/ethnic group. The maps (Figures 7-6 and 7-7) show the success rate for two groups, white women and minorities in total.

Progress Toward Job Equality in Private Industry by Women and Minorities, Large and Medium-Sized Firms, 1990

Fig. 7–5

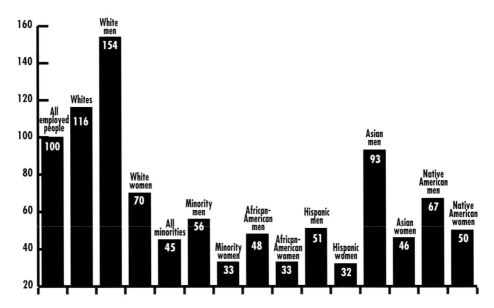

Numbers on chart indicate proportion of women or minorities who are officials and managers in relation to their share in the total workforce. A score of 100 indicates that a group held these jobs at a rate equal to its share of the total workforce. Scores under 100 indicate lesser degrees of achievement. (See text.)

Progress Toward Job Equality in Private Industry by White Women, Large and Medium-Sized Firms, 1990

FIG. 7-6

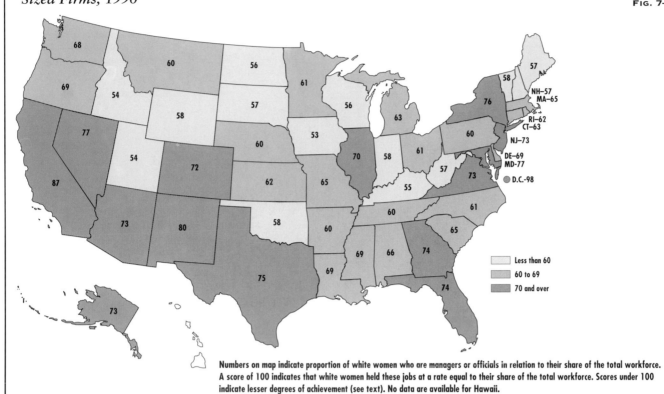

Numbers on map indicate proportion of white women who are managers or officials in relation to their share of the total workforce. A score of 100 indicates that white women held these jobs at a rate equal to their share of the total workforce. Scores under 100 indicate lesser degrees of achievement (see text). No data are available for Hawaii.

Progress Toward Job Equality in Private Industry by Minorities, Large and Medium-Sized Firms, 1990

FIG. 7-7

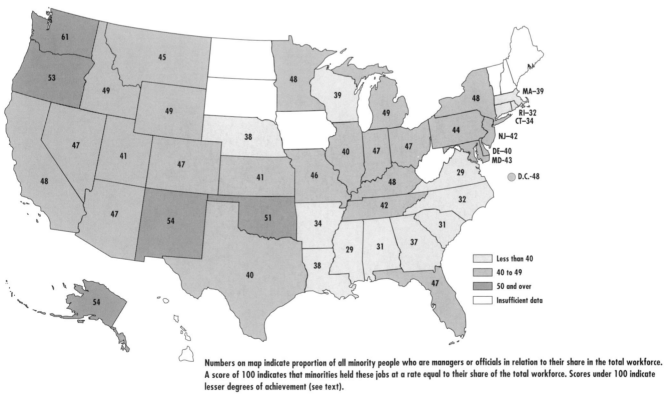

Numbers on map indicate proportion of all minority people who are managers or officials in relation to their share in the total workforce. A score of 100 indicates that minorities held these jobs at a rate equal to their share of the total workforce. Scores under 100 indicate lesser degrees of achievement (see text).

Housing Segregation

Figures 7-8 to 7-11 show housing segregation in metropolitan areas. The measure of segregation was calculated by Roderick J. Harrison and Daniel H. Weinberg of the U.S. Census Bureau, using 1990

African-Americans—Segregation in Housing

FIG. 7–8

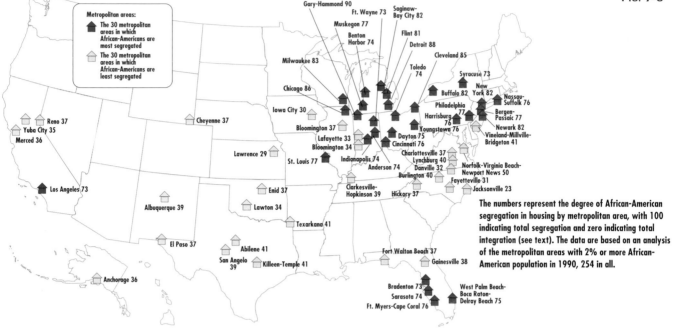

The numbers represent the degree of African-American segregation in housing by metropolitan area, with 100 indicating total segregation and zero indicating total integration (see text). The data are based on an analysis of the metropolitan areas with 2% or more African-American population in 1990, 254 in all.

Hispanic-Americans—Segregation in Housing

FIG. 7–9

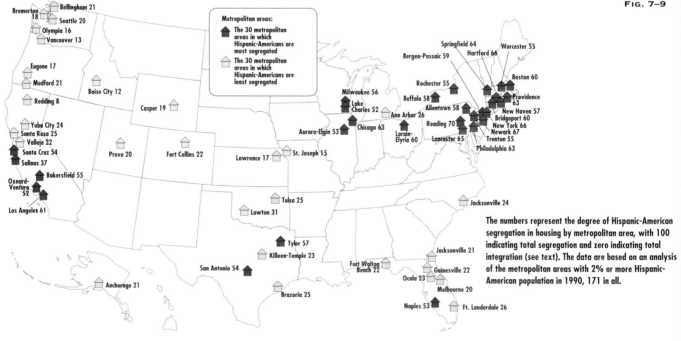

The numbers represent the degree of Hispanic-American segregation in housing by metropolitan area, with 100 indicating total segregation and zero indicating total integration (see text). The data are based on an analysis of the metropolitan areas with 2% or more Hispanic-American population in 1990, 171 in all.

Asians and Pacific Islanders—Segregation in Housing

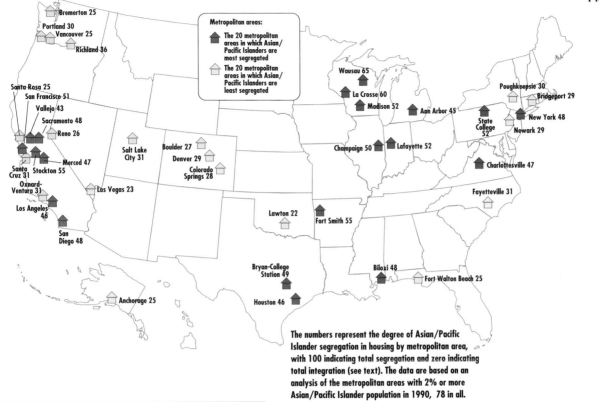

FIG. 7–10

Metropolitan areas:

The 20 metropolitan areas in which Asian/Pacific Islanders are most segregated

The 20 metropolitan areas in which Asian/Pacific Islanders are least segregated

Bremerton 25
Portland 30
Vancouver 25
Richland 36
Santa Rosa 25
San Francisco 51
Vallejo 43
Sacramento 48
Reno 26
Santa Cruz 31
Stockton 55
Merced 47
Oxnard-Ventura 31
Los Angeles 46
San Diego 48
Salt Lake City 31
Boulder 27
Denver 29
Colorado Springs 28
Las Vegas 23
Anchorage 25
Wausau 65
La Crosse 60
Madison 52
Ann Arbor 45
Champaign 50
Lafayette 52
Poughkeepsie 30
Bridgeport 29
State College 52
New York 48
Newark 29
Charlottesville 47
Fayetteville 31
Lawton 22
Fort Smith 55
Bryan-College Station 49
Houston 46
Biloxi 48
Fort Walton Beach 25

The numbers represent the degree of Asian/Pacific Islander segregation in housing by metropolitan area, with 100 indicating total segregation and zero indicating total integration (see text). The data are based on an analysis of the metropolitan areas with 2% or more Asian/Pacific Islander population in 1990, 78 in all.

Native Americans—Segregation in Housing

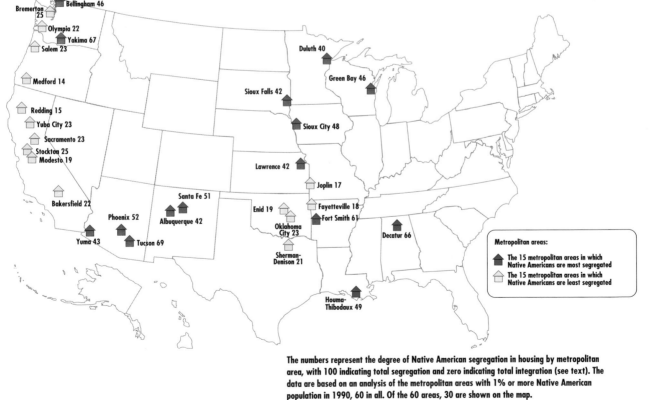

FIG. 7–11

Metropolitan areas:

The 15 metropolitan areas in which Native Americans are most segregated

The 15 metropolitan areas in which Native Americans are least segregated

Bremerton 25
Bellingham 46
Olympia 22
Yakima 67
Salem 23
Medford 14
Redding 15
Yuba City 23
Sacramento 23
Stockton 25
Modesto 19
Bakersfield 22
Phoenix 52
Yuma 43
Tucson 69
Santa Fe 51
Albuquerque 42
Duluth 40
Green Bay 46
Sioux Falls 42
Sioux City 48
Lawrence 42
Joplin 17
Enid 19
Fayetteville 18
Fort Smith 61
Oklahoma City 23
Sherman-Denison 21
Decatur 66
Houma-Thibodaux 49

The numbers represent the degree of Native American segregation in housing by metropolitan area, with 100 indicating total segregation and zero indicating total integration (see text). The data are based on an analysis of the metropolitan areas with 1% or more Native American population in 1990, 60 in all. Of the 60 areas, 30 are shown on the map.

Census tract data. This measure defines segregation as the proportion of each minority group in a given metropolitan area who would have to move to another Census tract to achieve an even racial distribution throughout that metropolitan area.* The scores can range from 100 percent, indicating complete segregation, down to zero percent, indicating complete integration. In actuality, the highest score was 90 percent, which applies to African-Americans in the Gary-Hammond, Indiana, metropolitan area; the lowest score was 8 percent, which applies to Hispanic-Americans in the Redding, California, metropolitan area. Note that the scores measure segregation, not discrimination. Members of minority groups may choose to live among people of similar ancestry and culture.

Of the four groups for which statistics were computed, African-Americans are the most segregated, with an average score of 69 percent in all metropolitan areas. Hispanics are next, with an average score of 51 percent, followed by Asians and Pacific Islanders with a score of 42 percent, and Native Americans with a score of 35 percent.

*Housing segregation of minorities can be measured in many different ways, and indeed Harrison and Weinberg have calculated 19 different measures of segregation, of which the one shown on the maps is the most widely used. In general, the measure used here tends to parallel the other 18 measures.

Drug Arrest Rate in Cities of 100,000 Population and Over

Fig. 7–12

Arrest rate per
100,000 population
○ Less than 600
◐ 600 to 1,099
● 1,100 and over

Data are for 1989. Information for 16 cities, 8 of them in Florida, are estimated on basis of historical record.
All cities of 100,000 or more population in 1989 are shown except for Nashville-Davidson.

Arrests for sale of illegal drugs tend to be highest in cities on the East and West coasts. Two-thirds of all people arrested in urban areas test positive for illegal drugs, including cocaine. Heavy use of illegal drugs (and also alcohol) is associated with criminal activity, but it is not clear that drugs cause crime.

Crime Rates

Violent crime, which includes murder, rape, robbery, and aggravated assault, tends to be higher
in the South, in northeast coastal cities, and in
California than in most parts of the Midwest.
Property crime, which includes burglary, larceny-
theft, and motor vehicle theft, follows a similar pattern. The reasons for the geographical differences are
not clear, but it is likely that poverty, unemployment,
and drug use explain part of the differences. Other
factors, such as the availability of guns, may also play
a role.

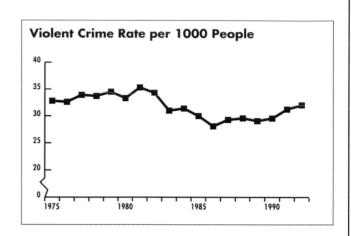

Violent Crime Rate per 1000 People

Violent Crime Rate by Metropolitan Area, 1990

FIG. 7–13

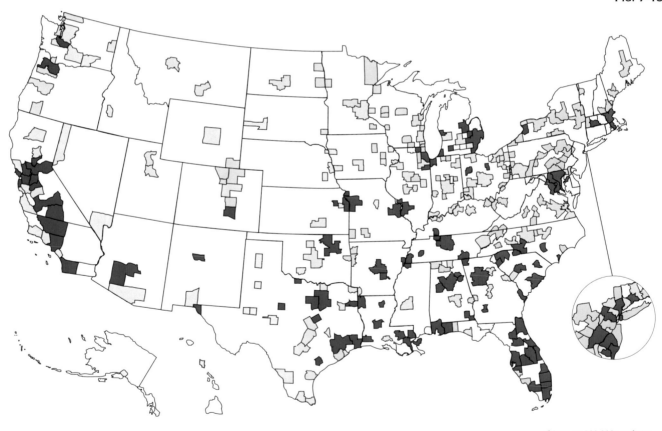

The map shows the combined rate for four types of crime tabulated by the Federal Bureau of Investigation:
murder, forcible rape, robbery, and aggravated assault. The data are for 1990. The chart shows data from
the National Crime Survey conducted by the Bureau of Justice Statistics, U.S. Department of Justice.

Crimes per 100,000 population
- Less than 400
- 400 to 699
- 700+

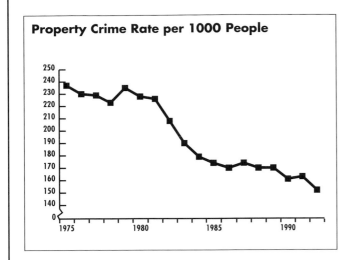

Property Crime Rate per 1000 People

Young people are far more apt to be crime victims than the elderly. People in the 16-to-19-year age group are, for example, 19 times more likely to be victims of violent crime than people 65 and over. Blacks are about 25 percent more likely to be the victims of violent crime than whites. Three-quarters of crimes committed by whites are against other whites. Three-quarters of crimes committed by blacks are against other blacks. The poor are more likely to be victims than the middle class or the rich.

Note that the maps are based on crimes reported by the FBI, while the trend figures accompanying the maps are based on random-sample surveys of the U.S. population conducted by the Bureau of Justice Statistics, a unit of the U.S. Department of Justice. The latter data are more useful as long-term trend indicators because, unlike the FBI data, they are collected on a uniform basis over many years.

Property Crime Rate by Metropolitan Area, 1990

FIG. 7–14

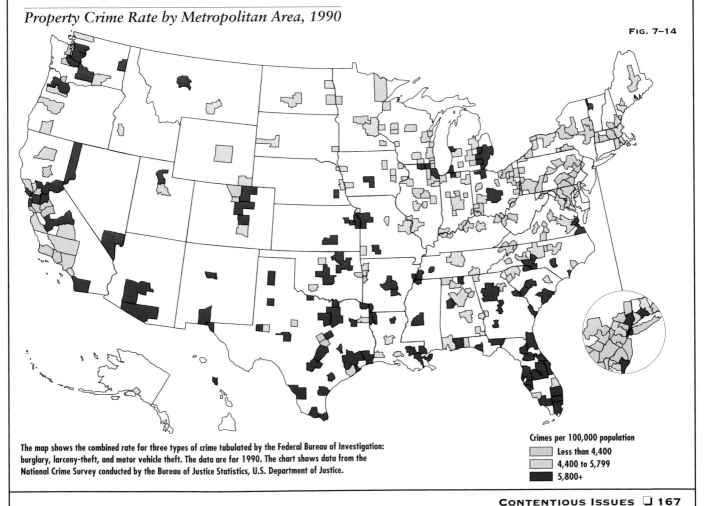

The map shows the combined rate for three types of crime tabulated by the Federal Bureau of Investigation: burglary, larceny-theft, and motor vehicle theft. The data are for 1990. The chart shows data from the National Crime Survey conducted by the Bureau of Justice Statistics, U.S. Department of Justice.

Crimes per 100,000 population
- Less than 4,400
- 4,400 to 5,799
- 5,800+

Handgun Murder Rate, 1990

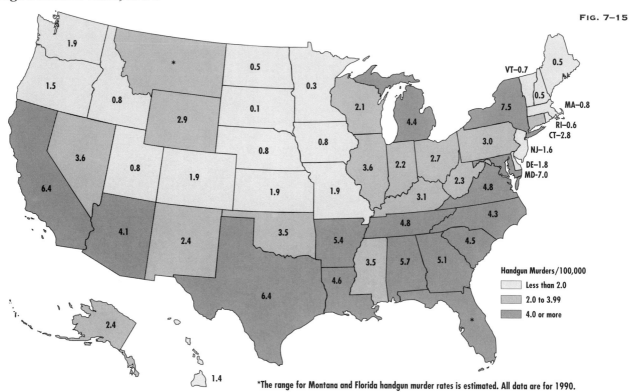

Fig. 7-15

VT–0.7 0.5
0.5
MA–0.8
RI–0.6
CT–2.8
NJ–1.6
DE–1.8
MD–7.0

1.9
1.5
0.8
*
0.5
0.3
0.1
2.9
2.1
7.5
4.4
3.6
0.8
1.9
0.8
0.8
3.6 2.2 2.7 3.0
6.4
1.9 1.9 3.1 2.3 4.8
4.1
2.4
3.5 4.8 4.3
5.4 4.5
3.5 5.7 5.1
4.6
6.4
2.4
1.4

Handgun Murders/100,000
☐ Less than 2.0
☐ 2.0 to 3.99
☐ 4.0 or more

*The range for Montana and Florida handgun murder rates is estimated. All data are for 1990.

Of the more than 20,000 murders in the United States every year, half are committed with handguns and another 15 percent or so with rifles, shotguns, or other types of firearms. The highest rates of murder with a handgun are found in the southern half of the country, but New York and Michigan also had high rates (Figure 7-15).

In at least half the murders committed with guns, the victim is a relative, friend, or acquaintance of the killer, and most of these killings are the result of arguments. Twenty to twenty-five percent of gun murders are committed in the course of a felony, such as robbery or narcotics dealing.

States and municipalities have passed laws restricting guns, but these have not had a major effect in reducing the number of murders because of the difficulty of controlling the flow of guns from other jurisdictions. According to Franklin E. Zimring, head of the Earl Warren Legal Institute of the University of California at Berkeley, the measure most likely to be effective is a federal law restricting the ownership of

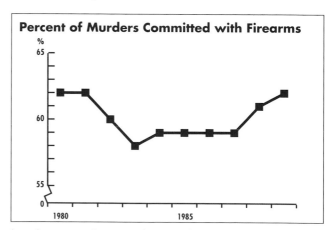

Percent of Murders Committed with Firearms

%
65

60

55
0
1980   1985

handguns to those with special needs. In his opinion, prohibition of sales to felons and the requirement of waiting periods before purchase of guns prevent few murders. Licensing of guns and restrictions on ownership of exotic weapons, such as semi-automatics, according to Zimring, are stronger measures but not as effective as wide-scale restrictions on ownership of handguns.

In the landmark *Furman* v. *Georgia* decision (1972), the Supreme Court said that all death penalty laws then in force were discriminatory and capricious, and it ruled them unconstitutional because they violated the Eighth Amendment prohibition against cruel and unusual punishment and did not meet the requirements of "equal protection" and "due process" prescribed by the Fourteenth Amendment. However, the Court noted that the death penalty per se was not constitutionally "cruel and unusual." Thirty-six states then revised their laws in an effort to make them consistent with the Court's ruling. In 1976, in the *Gregg* v. *Georgia* decision, the Court approved Georgia's revised law that seemed to remove the elements of discrimination and capriciousness. In 1977 executions resumed, the first being in Utah.

Of those executed in the United States since 1977, virtually all were men and all were convicted of

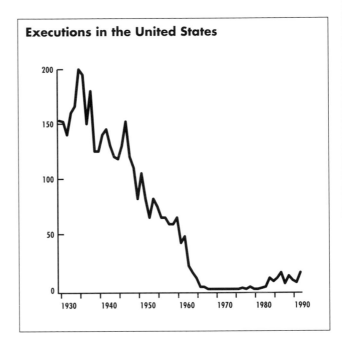

Executions in the United States

States That Allow Capital Punishment

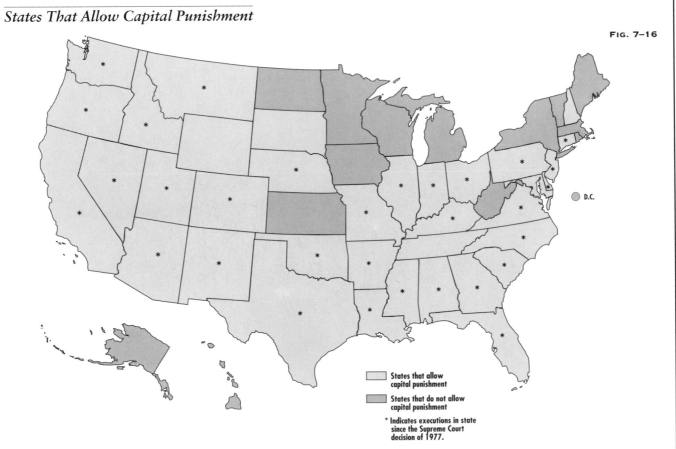

FIG. 7–16

D.C.

□ States that allow capital punishment

■ States that do not allow capital punishment

* Indicates executions in state since the Supreme Court decision of 1977.

murder. About 55 percent were white, 39 percent were black, 5 percent were Hispanic, and 1 percent Native American. In 56 percent of cases, both the defendant and the victim were white, in 24 percent the defendant was black and the victim white, and in 13 percent of cases, both the defendant and the victim were black. In less than 1 percent of the cases, the defendant was white and the victim black.

Several statistical studies have suggested that despite the new laws, blacks are far more likely than whites to receive the death sentence for comparable crimes. Those convicted of murdering whites were far more likely to be given the death sentence than those convicted of murdering blacks. The Supreme Court, in *McCleskey* v. *Kemp* (1987), ruled that such evidence does not "prove that race enters into any capital sentencing decisions . . ."

Opinion polls show that Americans overwhelmingly support the death penalty; but, paradoxically, juries have been reluctant to impose it. Court reviews have resulted in the reversal of about 100 death penalties annually. The result of jury reluctance to impose the penalty and court review has been to keep the number of executions since 1977 well below that of earlier years, despite several thousand convicted felons on death row.

The courts provide extensive review in order to guard against factual and legal errors. Despite this, is it possible that innocent people are executed? Hugo Adam Bedau of Tufts University and Michael L. Radelet of the University of Florida examined all capital cases in the United States from 1900 to 1985 for which information was available. They identified 23 cases in which innocent people were executed and an additional 21 cases in which prisoners were declared innocent in the 72 hours preceding their scheduled execution.

Anti-Semitic Crimes, 1988–1991

FIG. 7–17

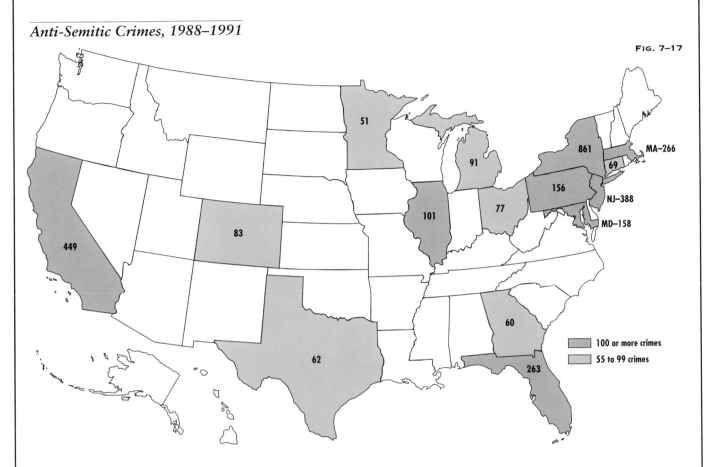

The figures on the map are the number of anti-Semitic crimes during the period 1988–1991.

100 or more crimes	
55 to 99 crimes	

The Anti-Defamation League of B'nai B'rith makes an annual report of anti-Semitic episodes of vandalism, harassment, threats, and assaults, and these are used as the basis for the map. About 2 percent of the incidents reported by the Anti-Defamation League involve serious crime, such as synagogue burnings and plots to bomb meetings of Jewish groups. Other incidents include telephone harassment, sending of hate mail, painting of swastikas on buildings, and distributing hate literature.

Hate Groups

FIG. 7–18

Legend:
- ○ KKK groups
- ▪ Neo-Nazi groups
- ▲ Identity "churches" and other groups
- ● Extreme right publications

The Anti-Defamation League of B'nai B'rith also catalogs organized hate groups such as the various factions of the Ku Klux Klan, pseudo-religious paramilitary organizations, neo-Nazi groups such as the National Socialist Liberation Front, and neo-Nazi Skinhead groups. (Of course, not all young people who adopt skinhead hairstyles are racist or anti-Semitic.) These groups, which share a common hatred of Jews and non-whites, probably have a total active membership well under 10,000, but many others are sympathetic to their cause, as is suggested by the career of David Duke, a former member of the Klan, who won the Republican nomination for governor of Louisiana in 1991.

Until 1961, all 50 states had statutes that criminalized homosexuality and other acts classified as sodomy. Today, 25 states retain such statutes, although they are rarely enforced. Nevertheless, these laws were given renewed life by a 1986 Supreme Court decision. Michael Hardwick, an Atlanta man, was arrested for having consensual oral sex with another male in his home. Although the district attorney refused to prosecute, Hardwick sued the state of Georgia, claiming that his rights of privacy, freedom of association, and freedom of expression had been violated. In a 5 to 4 decision, the Supreme Court ruled against him and upheld the Georgia anti-sodomy statute. Associate Justice Byron White, in the majority opinion, said that the statute does not violate "the fundamental rights of homosexuals" and denied that the Constitution confers "a right of privacy that extends to homosexual sodomy." Associate Justice Harry A. Blackmun, in a dissenting opinion,

State Anti-Sodomy Laws

FIG. 7–19

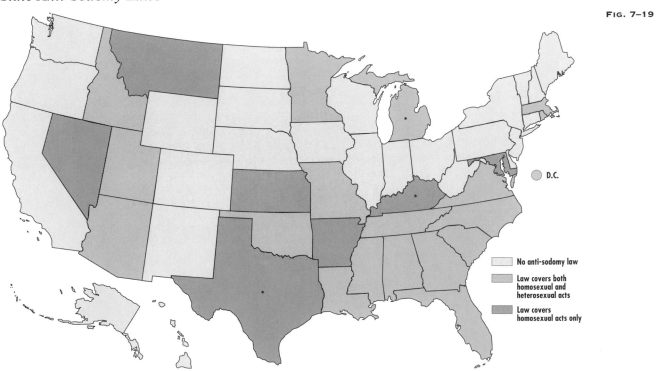

D.C.

No anti-sodomy law

Law covers both homosexual and heterosexual acts

Law covers homosexual acts only

*As of May 1992, lower courts had struck down sodomy laws in Texas, Kentucky, and Michigan on grounds that they were unconstitutional. These decisions are being appealed to higher courts.

said that "the right of an individual to conduct intimate relationships in the intimacy of his or her own home seems to me to be the heart of the Constitution's protection of privacy." The majority made it clear that it was not ruling on whether the Constitution protected *heterosexual* acts of sodomy. It is unlikely that the Supreme Court ruling will lead to prison sentences for homosexuals, but homosexual rights groups fear that it helps promote homophobia.

Gays are subject to considerable harassment, including threats and beatings. Among those implicated are far-right hate groups, such as the Aryan Nation and some skinhead gangs. Gays are subject to discrimination in housing, jobs, credit ratings, and insurance coverage. However, several states, counties, and municipalities now have laws or regulations protecting various aspects of gay activity. Most of the state laws deal only with public employment, but municipal laws tend to be broader and to protect rights of gays in private employment, public accommodations, education, housing, credit, and union practices.

Laws Barring Discrimination on the Basis of Sexual Orientation

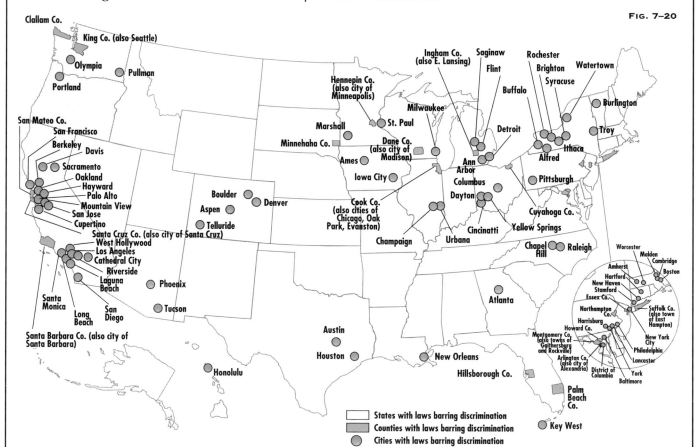

FIG. 7–20

Shown are state, county and local laws that have at least one provision barring discrimination on the basis of sexual orientation in public employment, private employment, public accommodations, education, housing, credit, or union practices. Where there is both a county and a city law, the county is shown on the map and the city is noted parenthetically. The map shows laws in effect as of June 1993. In November 1992, Colorado voters approved a proposition annulling local gay rights laws. This is being appealed in the courts.

Attempts to Censor Schoolbooks

FIG. 7–21

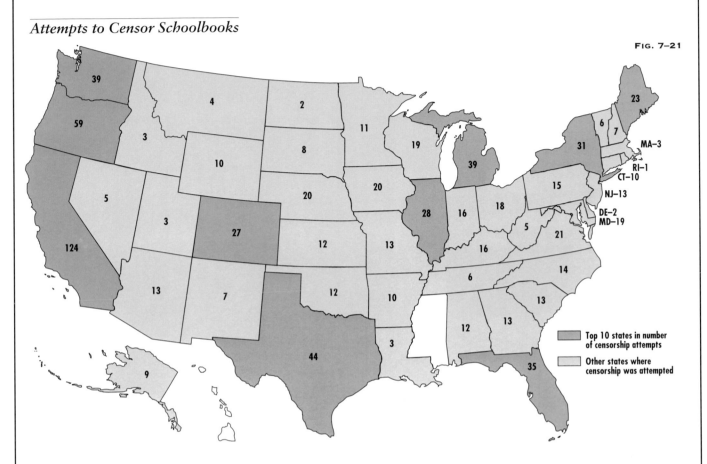

39
59
3
4
2
11
19
23
6 7
31
MA–3
RI–1
CT–10
NJ–13
DE–2
MD–19
10
8
39
15
5
20
20
18
28
16
5
21
124
3
27
12
13
16
14
13
7
12
10
6
13
13
9
44
3
12
35

Top 10 states in number
of censorship attempts

Other states where
censorship was attempted

The map is based on tabulations prepared by People for the American
Way for the five academic years ending 1990–1991 (see text). The
number of attempts during the five-year period are shown on the map.

Censorship of schoolbooks is an American tradition that goes back at least to the beginning of the public school system early in the 19th century. At first, the motivation for censoring books was to protect children from sexual content, and later, from communist ideas. The most recent wave of censorship is somewhat different, springing as it does from the frustration of ultra-fundamentalist Christians threatened by the women's rights and gay rights movements. Ultra-fundamentalists see these movements as undermining their way of life, which emphasizes the sanctity of the family, the traditional role of women as nurturers and keepers of the hearth, and the role of men as providers. They believe that biblical revelation should be the basis of public school teaching. They claim that public schools are not value-neutral but are motivated by secular humanism, that is, the idea that humans are the arbiters of their own fate. In their view, the schools erode traditional culture, including religion, by usurping parents' right to control and mold the moral behavior of their children. Further, they claim that the schools invade the privacy of children through modern pedagogical techniques such as values clarification and behavior modification, while at the same time failing to teach basic skills like writing and math.

Among the books the ultra-fundamentalists have tried to bar in the schools are John Steinbeck's *Of Mice and Men*, J. D. Salinger's *Catcher in the Rye*, *The Diary of Anne Frank*, Bernard Malamud's *The Natural*, Mark Twain's *The Adventures of Huckleberry Finn*, Charlotte Brontë's *Jane Eyre*, Richard Wright's *Native Son*, Gabriel García Márquez's *One Hundred Years of Solitude*, and the children's books of Maurice Sendak. They have consistently been against sex education, the teaching of the Darwinian theory of evolution, and what they perceive as Satanism. As an alternative to scientific theories of evolution, they want the schools to teach creationism, the theory that God created the world in six days.

People for the American Way, a Washington, D.C., public interest group, monitors attempts to remove or restrict school reading materials including textbooks, school library books, school newspapers, or to otherwise prevent information from being given to students. The organization's data are used as the basis for the map (Figure 7-21). According to John Buchanan, chairman of the organization, schools that have an orderly book review process are more apt to avoid censorship, and apparently more schools are adopting this practice in response to the threat of book banning.

In 1900, only 6 percent of Americans graduated from high school, as compared with 29 percent in 1930, 63 percent in 1960, and over 75 percent in the early 1990s. The enormous growth of the public education system was made possible by drawing on the labor of women, who could be paid lower wages than men, a circumstance that partly explains the relatively low prestige of teachers in America. Teachers in the United States are paid about one-fourth as much as physicians.

In constructing the map, teacher salaries were compared to the average salaries of all workers covered by state and federal unemployment insurance. This measure provides a rough index of teacher purchasing power area by area.

What Teachers Are Paid

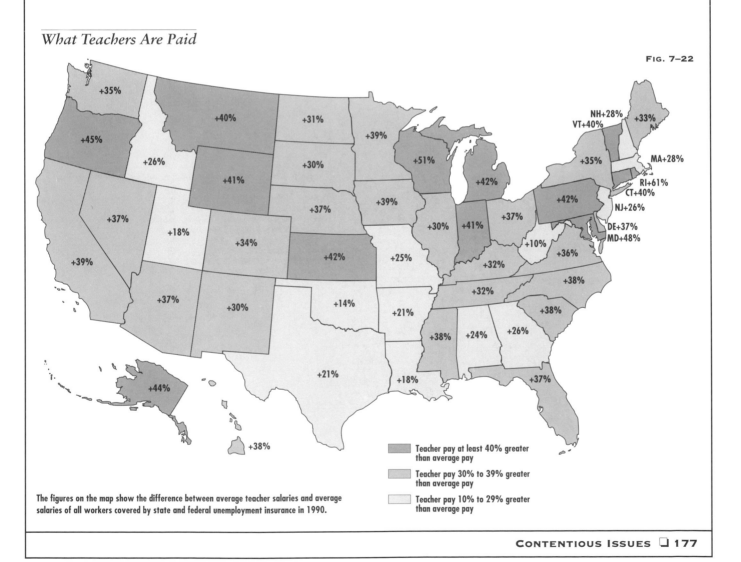

FIG. 7–22

The figures on the map show the difference between average teacher salaries and average salaries of all workers covered by state and federal unemployment insurance in 1990.

Teacher pay at least 40% greater than average pay

Teacher pay 30% to 39% greater than average pay

Teacher pay 10% to 29% greater than average pay

Privacy

Privacy rights came to the fore in the late 1960s in part because the federal government intruded into the lives of citizens protesting for civil rights and against the Vietnam War. There was, for example, the FBI's program of dirty tricks against the Black Panthers, feminists, and public figures like Martin Luther King, Jr. Because of fears raised by such activities, and also by the threat that access to computerized data posed to privacy, Congress passed several laws designed to strengthen individual privacy rights, including: the U.S. Privacy Act of 1974, the Fair Credit Reporting Act of 1970, and the Family Educational Rights and Privacy Act of 1974.

The states have attempted to provide additional protection through a variety of laws. Figures 7-23 through 7-30 show states that have passed pro-privacy laws in eight areas:

Drug testing of employees. The few states that have privacy laws generally specify that drug testing be done only when there is reasonable suspicion.

Library records. The laws generally state that library records can be released only by court order.

Automated telephone solicitation. Prerecorded and computerized phone solicitation is banned or restricted.

Arrest records. Over half of those arrested are either acquitted or have charges dismissed, but the arrest record may remain and be transmitted to potential employers, credit bureaus, state licensing bureaus, and lending institutions.

States With Statutes Making Library Records Confidential

FIG. 7-24

States That Limit Intrusion By Automatic Telephone Solicitation

FIG. 7-25

Note: State laws regulating automatic solicitation vary widely. Some states, including Arkansas, Maryland, Michigan, and Arizona have an outright ban on automated dialing devices. Other states, such as Wisconsin, Alaska, California, Florida, Minnesota and Oregon, require consent of the person called. In Washington, a telephone customer may collect $500 in damages if unsolicited calls are made with an automated device. Connecticut, Nebraska, Texas and Virginia require that automated devices disconnect after the phone is held up. Illinois, Nebraska, and North Carolina require a live operator. Georgia requires a permit to operate automatic dialing devices and prohibits their use after 9 P.M. In Massachusetts and Florida, phone customers can notify the telephone company to stop automated sales calls.

States Where Arrest Record Is Destroyed If There Is No Conviction

FIG. 7-26

Note: Includes states where the arrest record is sealed and cannot be opened except under court order. Maryland and Virginia allow sealing of records three years after arrest or earlier if arrestee waives right to civil claims arising from the incident.

States With Statutes That Limit Random Drug Testing

FIG. 7-23

States With Statutes Protecting Privacy of
Conversations with Clergyman

FIG. 7–27

States Where Employees Have Statutory
Right to See Their Personnel File

FIG. 7–28

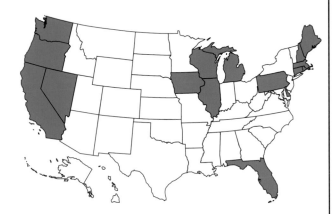

According to the Civil Rights Act of 1964, no one can be denied a job on the basis of an arrest. Some states have attempted to reinforce this act, usually with statutes that expunge or seal arrest records of persons not convicted. A few states, such as New Jersey, allow destruction of conviction records after a certain period of time.

Privacy of conversation with clergy. Confidentiality is universal in the case of patient-physician and client-lawyer conversations. Many states have extended this right to clergy and psychologists.

Personnel files. The federal Occupational Safety and Health Act of 1970 gives employees the right to see their own occupational medical records. Laws in some states allow employees to inspect their personnel files. Some states, such as Connecticut, mandate that the company must correct inaccuracies.

Confidentiality of income tax returns. The Federal Tax Reform Act of 1976 protects the confidentiality of federal tax returns, with certain exceptions, such as on written request by state tax authorities, requests by a committee of Congress, requests by the Departments of Justice or Treasury, or court order by federal investigators in non-tax cases. About a third of the states have passed laws that protect the confidentiality of any tax records, including state records.

Confidentiality of AIDS testing. Laws in 11 states specifically protect the confidentiality of AIDS test results, and an additional five states have general non-disclosure laws that apparently provide the same protection.

Laws in many states also protect the privacy of bank records, social security numbers, school records, and other confidential information.

States with Statutes Protecting Confidentiality
of Income Tax Records

FIG. 7–29

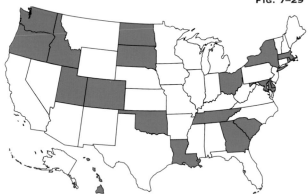

Note: Includes states where tax records can be opened only under court order.

States with Statutes Guaranteeing Confidentiality
of AIDS Test Results

FIG. 7–30

The solid-colored states have statutes that specifically require that AIDS test results be kept confidential. The states with crosshatching do not have such statutes but do guarantee confidentiality of medical records in general or venereal disease test results. The statutes in these states may provide confidentiality for AIDS test results.

U.S. English, an organization founded by the late Senator S.I. Hayakawa of California, advocates the establishment of English as the official language of the United States, a goal that it believes is crucial to "the unity and future well-being of the United States." It would achieve this through an amendment to the Constitution making English the official American language. Critics of the proposed amendment say that, with only two million non-English speakers in the country, the threat to national unity is largely imaginary and that the amendment could do great damage by disenfranchising non-English speakers and would be a direct assault on the cultural integrity of Hispanic-Americans and other minority groups. The critics also believe that a constitutional amendment would impose restrictions on educators that could, paradoxically, inhibit their efforts to teach English as a second language.

Although U.S. English's drive to pass a constitutional amendment appears to be stalled, the organization has been successful in getting more than a dozen states to enact English-as-the-official-language legislation. (Several states, including Nebraska, which passed a language statute in the anti-German climate following World War I, had official English laws on the books prior to the U.S. English campaign.) California's statute, one of the most stringent, permits citizens to sue if they feel that the status of English has been degraded in any way. The most restrictive of all was Arizona's law, which prohibited the use of other languages by the state or its political subdivisions. A federal court in 1990 found this law violated the free speech guarantee of the First Amendment.

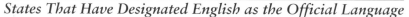

States That Have Designated English as the Official Language

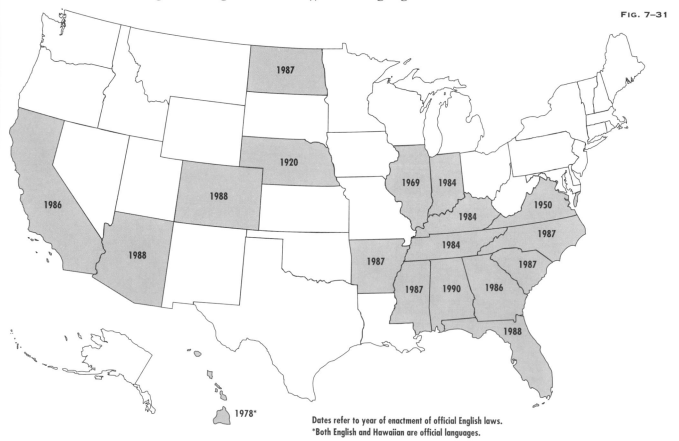

FIG. 7–31

Dates refer to year of enactment of official English laws.
*Both English and Hawaiian are official languages.

Number of Lawyers in Private Practice per 1,000 Population, 1988

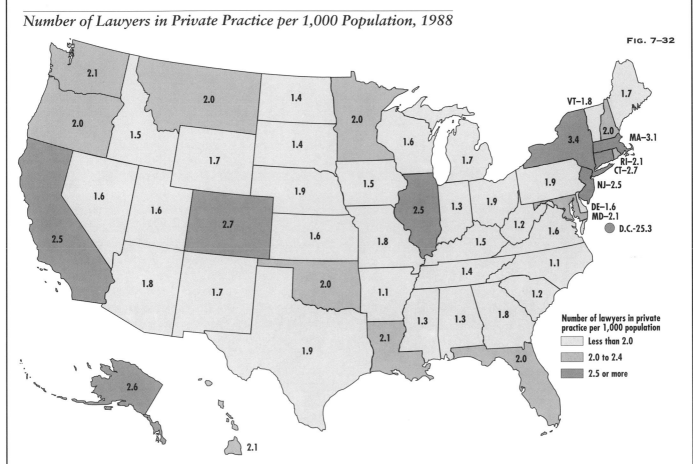

FIG. 7-32

Number of lawyers in private practice per 1,000 population

Less than 2.0

2.0 to 2.4

2.5 or more

Former Vice President Dan Quayle, speaking at the American Bar Association's annual meeting in 1991, claimed that there are too many lawyers in the United States and that American business is at a competitive disadvantage in world markets because of enormous legal costs. In support of this, Quayle said that businesses and individuals pay $80 billion annually for direct costs relating to litigation and an additional $220 billion for indirect costs. He said that there were 18 million civil suits filed annually in the United States and noted that the United States had 70 percent of the world's lawyers.

According to Michael Franck, writing in the January 1991 issue of the *Michigan Bar Journal*, the cost of all tort litigation in the United States was $29 billion to $36 billion in 1985. The 18 million civil cases Quayle referred to, Franck says, include small claims cases, family law cases, and other cases that have little bearing on business liability. Fewer than 10 percent involve product liability, the type that might put a firm at a competitive disadvantage. The United States, according to Franck, has nowhere near 70 percent of the world's lawyers. This figure comes from comparing the number of lawyers in foreign countries who are licensed to appear in court or in all levels of the court system—usually a small fraction of the number of law school graduates—with the total number of American lawyers, all of whom are licensed to litigate after passing the bar exam. When the total number of lawyers is used for comparison, Franck says, the United States has about the same proportion of lawyers relative to population as other countries.

The map is based on counts of U.S. lawyers in private practice made by the American Bar Foundation.

Congressional Votes on Contentious Issues

Every year, Congress considers thousands of bills and motions. A small fraction of these are reported in the newspapers or on television. A still smaller number are discussed in editorial pages or on talk shows. A handful—perhaps 3 to 5 every year—arouse intense popular interest. These are deeply emotional issues, such as perceived sexual harassment (the confirmation hearings of Clarence Thomas to the Supreme Court), fear of foreign competition (the debate over the North American Free Trade Agreement), fear of crime (the debate over tougher penalties for violent crime), mistrust and envy of government officials (the outcry over congressional pay raises), fear of being embroiled in a foreign war (the debate over the Persian Gulf War), freedom of speech or patriotism (the constitutional amendment to ban flag burning), fear of government intrusion into private life (the debate over gun control legislation), hunger for job security (the family leave bill), the desire for fair play (the campaign reform bill), the urge for retribution (the debate over the death penalty), religious belief (the debate over school prayer), and the urge to preserve the "sanctity of life" vs. a "woman's right to choose." The maps on the following pages show recent votes by the House of Representatives and the Senate on several of these contentious issues.

How the House of Representatives Voted on Flag Desecration

FIG. 7–33

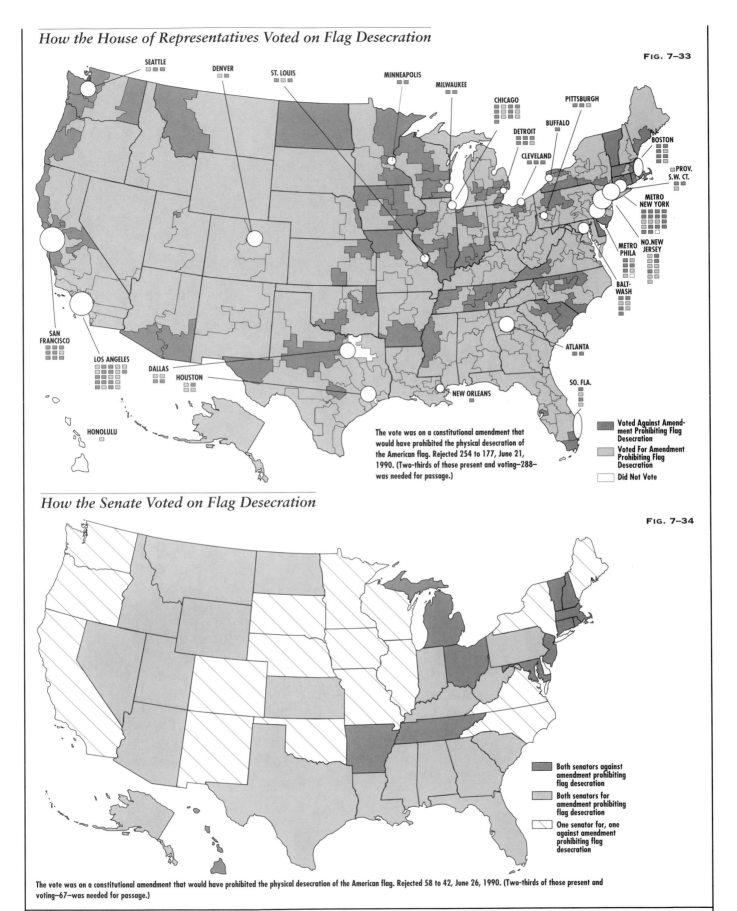

SEATTLE

DENVER

ST. LOUIS

MINNEAPOLIS

MILWAUKEE

CHICAGO

PITTSBURGH

DETROIT

BUFFALO

BOSTON

CLEVELAND

PROV.
S.W. CT.

METRO
NEW YORK

METRO
PHILA

NO. NEW
JERSEY

BALT-
WASH

SAN
FRANCISCO

LOS ANGELES

DALLAS

HOUSTON

ATLANTA

SO. FLA.

NEW ORLEANS

HONOLULU

The vote was on a constitutional amendment that would have prohibited the physical desecration of the American flag. Rejected 254 to 177, June 21, 1990. (Two-thirds of those present and voting—288—was needed for passage.)

Voted Against Amendment Prohibiting Flag Desecration

Voted For Amendment Prohibiting Flag Desecration

Did Not Vote

How the Senate Voted on Flag Desecration

FIG. 7–34

Both senators against amendment prohibiting flag desecration

Both senators for amendment prohibiting flag desecration

One senator for, one against amendment prohibiting flag desecration

The vote was on a constitutional amendment that would have prohibited the physical desecration of the American flag. Rejected 58 to 42, June 26, 1990. (Two-thirds of those present and voting—67—was needed for passage.)

How the House of Representatives Voted on the Persian Gulf War

FIG. 7–35

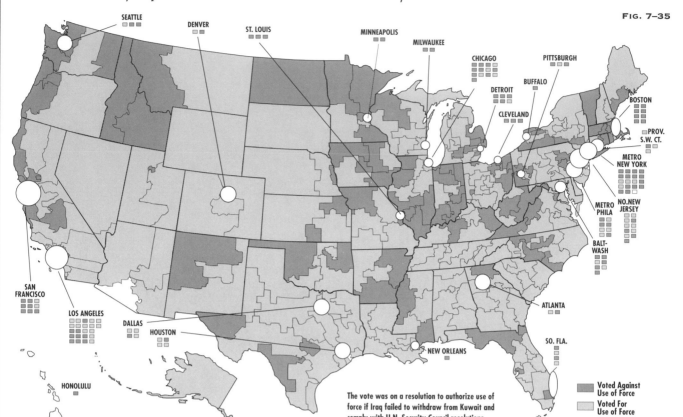

SEATTLE

DENVER

ST. LOUIS

MINNEAPOLIS

MILWAUKEE

CHICAGO

PITTSBURGH

DETROIT

BUFFALO

BOSTON

CLEVELAND

PROV.
S.W. CT.

METRO
NEW YORK

METRO
PHILA

NO.NEW
JERSEY

BALT-
WASH

SAN
FRANCISCO

LOS ANGELES

DALLAS

HOUSTON

ATLANTA

NEW ORLEANS

SO. FLA.

HONOLULU

The vote was on a resolution to authorize use of
force if Iraq failed to withdraw from Kuwait and
comply with U.N. Security Council resolutions.
Passed 250 to 183, January 12, 1991.

Voted Against
Use of Force

Voted For
Use of Force

Did Not Vote

How the Senate Voted on the Persian Gulf War

FIG. 7–36

Both senators
voted against
use of force

Both senators
voted for
use of force

One senator for,
one against use
of force

The vote was on a resolution to authorize use of force if Iraq failed to withdraw from Kuwait
and comply with U.N. Security Council resolutions. Passed 52 to 47, January 12, 1991.

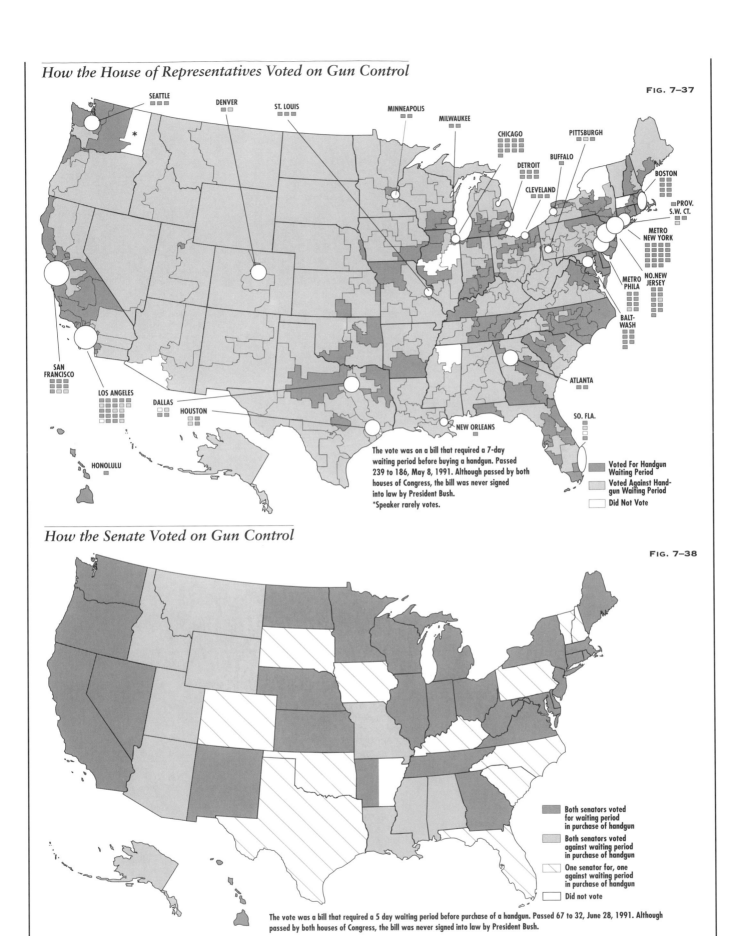

How the House of Representatives Voted on Gun Control

FIG. 7–37

SEATTLE

DENVER

ST. LOUIS

MINNEAPOLIS

MILWAUKEE

CHICAGO

PITTSBURGH

DETROIT

BUFFALO

BOSTON

CLEVELAND

PROV.
S.W. CT.

METRO
NEW YORK

METRO
PHILA

NO.NEW
JERSEY

BALT-
WASH

ATLANTA

SO. FLA.

SAN
FRANCISCO

LOS ANGELES

DALLAS

HOUSTON

NEW ORLEANS

HONOLULU

The vote was on a bill that required a 7-day waiting period before buying a handgun. Passed 239 to 186, May 8, 1991. Although passed by both houses of Congress, the bill was never signed into law by President Bush.
*Speaker rarely votes.

Voted For Handgun Waiting Period

Voted Against Hand-gun Waiting Period

Did Not Vote

How the Senate Voted on Gun Control

FIG. 7–38

Both senators voted for waiting period in purchase of handgun

Both senators voted against waiting period in purchase of handgun

One senator for, one against waiting period in purchase of handgun

Did not vote

The vote was a bill that required a 5 day waiting period before purchase of a handgun. Passed 67 to 32, June 28, 1991. Although passed by both houses of Congress, the bill was never signed into law by President Bush.

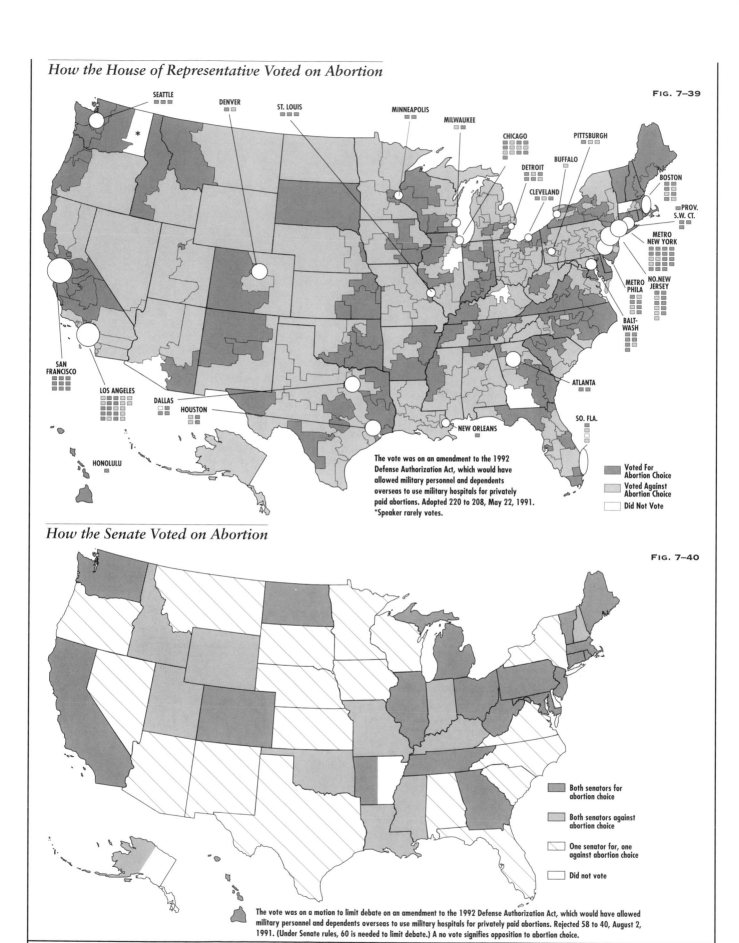

How the House of Representative Voted on Abortion

FIG. 7–39

SEATTLE

DENVER

ST. LOUIS

MINNEAPOLIS

MILWAUKEE

CHICAGO

PITTSBURGH

DETROIT

BUFFALO

BOSTON

CLEVELAND

PROV.
S.W. CT.

METRO
NEW YORK

SAN
FRANCISCO

METRO
PHILA

NO.NEW
JERSEY

LOS ANGELES

DALLAS

BALT-
WASH

HOUSTON

ATLANTA

NEW ORLEANS

SO. FLA.

HONOLULU

The vote was on an amendment to the 1992
Defense Authorization Act, which would have
allowed military personnel and dependents
overseas to use military hospitals for privately
paid abortions. Adopted 220 to 208, May 22, 1991.
*Speaker rarely votes.

Voted For
Abortion Choice

Voted Against
Abortion Choice

Did Not Vote

How the Senate Voted on Abortion

FIG. 7–40

Both senators for
abortion choice

Both senators against
abortion choice

One senator for, one
against abortion choice

Did not vote

The vote was on a motion to limit debate on an amendment to the 1992 Defense Authorization Act, which would have allowed
military personnel and dependents overseas to use military hospitals for privately paid abortions. Rejected 58 to 40, August 2,
1991. (Under Senate rules, 60 is needed to limit debate.) A no vote signifies opposition to abortion choice.

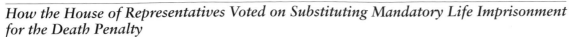

How the House of Representatives Voted on Substituting Mandatory Life Imprisonment for the Death Penalty

FIG. 7–41

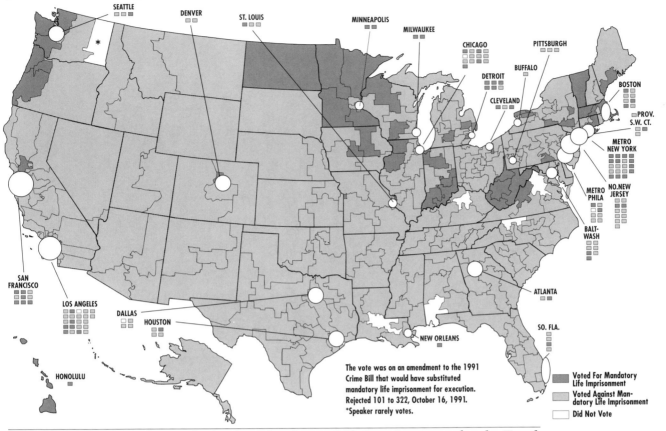

SEATTLE

DENVER

ST. LOUIS

MINNEAPOLIS

MILWAUKEE

CHICAGO

PITTSBURGH

DETROIT

BUFFALO

BOSTON

CLEVELAND

PROV.
S.W. CT.

METRO
NEW YORK

METRO
PHILA

NO. NEW
JERSEY

BALT-
WASH

ATLANTA

SO. FLA.

SAN
FRANCISCO

LOS ANGELES

DALLAS

HOUSTON

NEW ORLEANS

HONOLULU

The vote was on an amendment to the 1991
Crime Bill that would have substituted
mandatory life imprisonment for execution.
Rejected 101 to 322, October 16, 1991.
*Speaker rarely votes.

Voted For Mandatory
Life Imprisonment

Voted Against Man-
datory Life Imprisonment

Did Not Vote

How the Senate Voted on Substituting Mandatory Life Imprisonment for the Death Penalty

FIG. 7–42

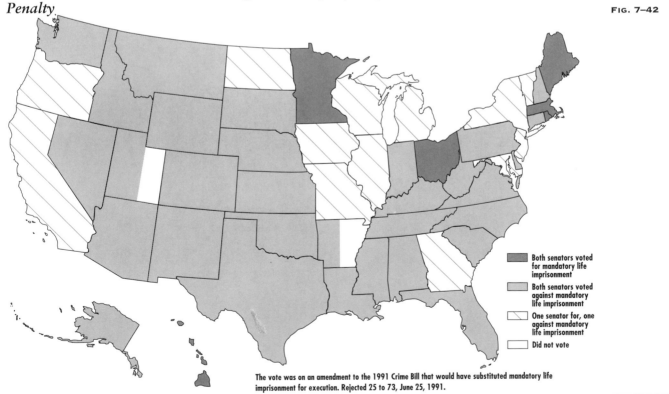

Both senators voted
for mandatory life
imprisonment

Both senators voted
against mandatory
life imprisonment

One senator for, one
against mandatory
life imprisonment

Did not vote

The vote was on an amendment to the 1991 Crime Bill that would have substituted mandatory life
imprisonment for execution. Rejected 25 to 73, June 25, 1991.

How the House of Representatives Voted on Campaign Finance Reform

FIG. 7–43

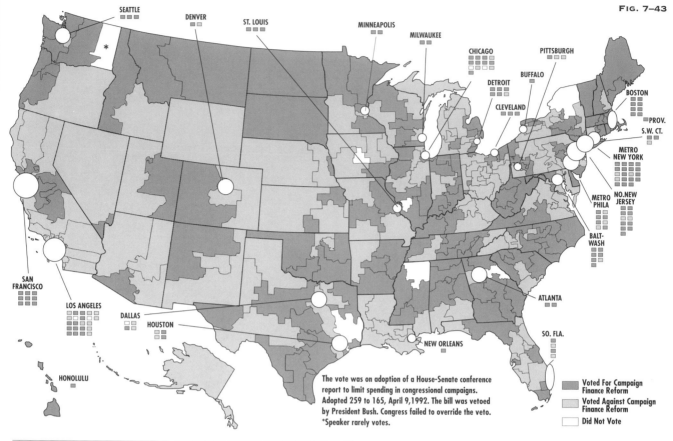

SEATTLE

DENVER

ST. LOUIS

MINNEAPOLIS

MILWAUKEE

CHICAGO

PITTSBURGH

DETROIT

BUFFALO

CLEVELAND

BOSTON

PROV.

S.W. CT.

METRO
NEW YORK

METRO
PHILA

NO. NEW
JERSEY

BALT-
WASH

ATLANTA

SO. FLA.

SAN
FRANCISCO

LOS ANGELES

DALLAS

HOUSTON

NEW ORLEANS

HONOLULU

*

The vote was on adoption of a House-Senate conference
report to limit spending in congressional campaigns.
Adopted 259 to 165, April 9, 1992. The bill was vetoed
by President Bush. Congress failed to override the veto.
*Speaker rarely votes.

■ Voted For Campaign
Finance Reform
■ Voted Against Campaign
Finance Reform
□ Did Not Vote

How the Senate Voted on Campaign Finance Reform

FIG. 7–44

■ Both senators voted
for campaign finance
reform

■ Both senators voted
against campaign
finance reform

▨ One senator voting
for, one against
campaign finance
reform

□ Did not vote

The vote was on whether to override President Bush's veto of a bill to limit spending in congressional campaigns. Rejected 57 to 42,
May 13, 1992. (Two-thirds of those present and voting, or 66 votes, were required to override the veto.)

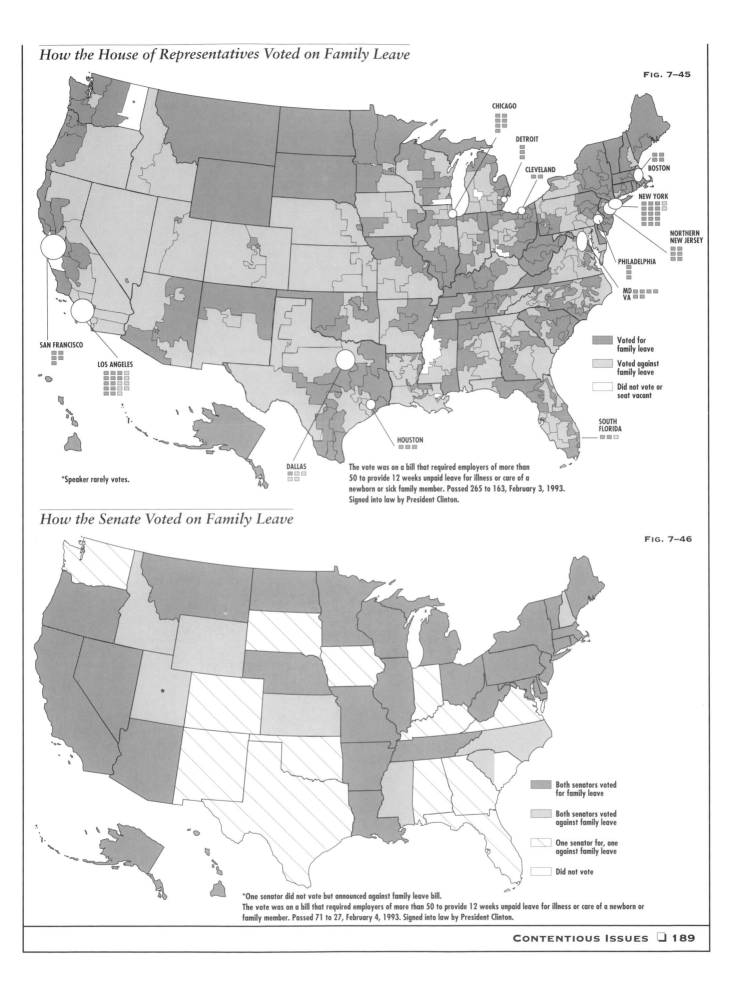

How the House of Representatives Voted on Family Leave

FIG. 7–45

CHICAGO

DETROIT

CLEVELAND

BOSTON

NEW YORK

NORTHERN NEW JERSEY

PHILADELPHIA

MD
VA

Voted for family leave

Voted against family leave

Did not vote or seat vacant

SAN FRANCISCO

LOS ANGELES

SOUTH FLORIDA

HOUSTON

DALLAS

*Speaker rarely votes.

The vote was on a bill that required employers of more than 50 to provide 12 weeks unpaid leave for illness or care of a newborn or sick family member. Passed 265 to 163, February 3, 1993. Signed into law by President Clinton.

How the Senate Voted on Family Leave

FIG. 7–46

Both senators voted for family leave

Both senators voted against family leave

One senator for, one against family leave

Did not vote

*One senator did not vote but announced against family leave bill.
The vote was on a bill that required employers of more than 50 to provide 12 weeks unpaid leave for illness or care of a newborn or family member. Passed 71 to 27, February 4, 1993. Signed into law by President Clinton.

Although the United States has declined economically relative to other powers in the last 30 years, it remains the leader in terms of gross domestic product, foreign trade volume, and manufactures. Militarily, the United States has grown relative to other NATO powers and Russia since 1980 and remains preeminent in naval ships and naval bases, which allow it to project power to all areas of the globe bordering the seas, although at a lower force level than previously, due to budget cuts.

How will this unprecedented power be used in the post-Cold War era? An official answer comes from a classified Pentagon document leaked to the *New York Times* in 1992. This document, known as the "Defense Planning Guidance for the 1994-99 Fiscal Years," declared that it is U.S. policy to deal with threats to its national interest primarily through cooperative efforts rather than unilateral actions.* To this end, it would strengthen the system of military alliances built during the Cold War and build new alliances with other democratic countries, including those of the former Soviet Union. It would emphasize the importance of working through the United Nations and other international organizations. A chief goal of American policy, according to the document, is to deter hostile powers from dominating strategically important regions, such as the Persian Gulf, Western Europe, and East Asia. America would not be the policeman of the world, but would continue to maintain a strong military presence abroad, including a sizable military force in Europe and a commitment to the security of Israel.

*An earlier and more chauvinistic version of the Pentagon document gave considerable weight to preserving the U.S. capability for unilateral military intervention. It stated that it was U.S. policy to prevent the emergence of rivals to American global supremacy and, specifically, to prevent Japan, Germany, and indeed Western Europe from becoming strong, independent military powers. In the earlier version, the United States would discourage India's efforts to become the dominant power in South Asia and the Indian Ocean. This version was soundly criticized by many, including those who said that the cost of the military machine required to support the policy was more than the country could afford.

U.S. Strategic Position

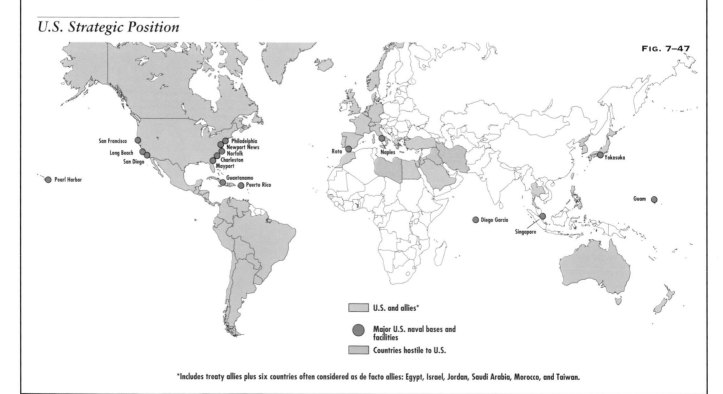

FIG. 7–47

San Francisco
Long Beach
San Diego
Pearl Harbor
Philadelphia
Newport News
Norfolk
Charleston
Mayport
Guantanamo
Puerto Rico
Rota
Naples
Yokosuka
Guam
Diego Garcia
Singapore

U.S. and allies*

● Major U.S. naval bases and facilities

Countries hostile to U.S.

*Includes treaty allies plus six countries often considered as de facto allies: Egypt, Israel, Jordan, Saudi Arabia, Morocco, and Taiwan.

Arms Imports by Developing Countries, 1985–1989

FIG. 7–48

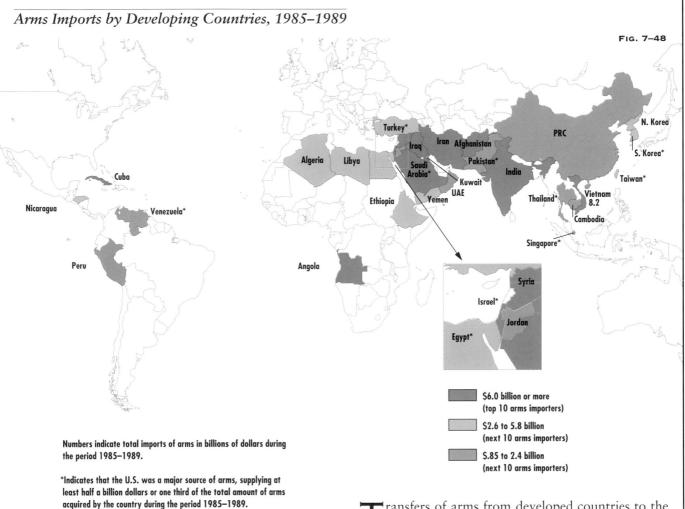

Numbers indicate total imports of arms in billions of dollars during the period 1985–1989.

*Indicates that the U.S. was a major source of arms, supplying at least half a billion dollars or one third of the total amount of arms acquired by the country during the period 1985–1989.

$6.0 billion or more (top 10 arms importers)

$2.6 to 5.8 billion (next 10 arms importers)

$.85 to 2.4 billion (next 10 arms importers)

Transfers of arms from developed countries to the less developed played a key role in the Afghanistan and Cambodian civil wars and in the Iran-Iraq War. In recent years, developed countries have funneled $40 billion annually in arms to developing countries. The chief buyers have been Saudi Arabia, Iraq, and India. Many developing countries, particularly those in the Middle East, devote a large proportion of their expenditure to medium-range ballistic missiles, which by their nature are highly threatening weapons.

In recent years, the leading suppliers of arms to developing countries were, in descending order, Russia, the United States, France, China, the United Kingdom, and West Germany. The largest American shipments to any country went to Israel; indeed, the United States is the only arms supplier to that country.

Nuclear Proliferation

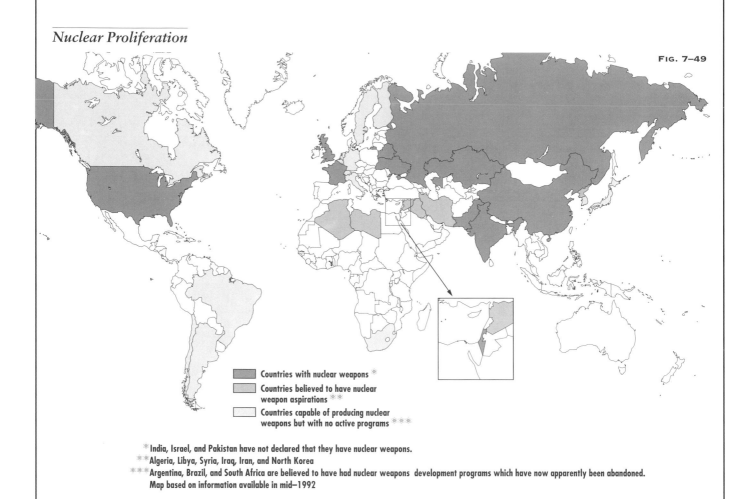

Nuclear Proliferation

FIG. 7–49

Countries with nuclear weapons *

Countries believed to have nuclear weapon aspirations **

Countries capable of producing nuclear weapons but with no active programs ***

* India, Israel, and Pakistan have not declared that they have nuclear weapons.
** Algeria, Libya, Syria, Iraq, Iran, and North Korea
*** Argentina, Brazil, and South Africa are believed to have had nuclear weapons development programs which have now apparently been abandoned.
Map based on information available in mid–1992

Since 1964, when the People's Republic of China announced that it had nuclear weapons, no additional country has announced its membership in the nuclear club. However, at least three others—India, Pakistan, and Israel—are strongly suspected of having such weapons, or the capability to assemble them in short order. In 1974 India detonated a nuclear device and is now thought capable of assembling up to 60 bombs. Pakistan started its program in the early 1970s and now has the capability of producing up to 10 bombs. Israel started its nuclear research program in the late 1950s and now has at least 100 bombs and possibly more than 300.

At least six other states have nuclear ambitions—Algeria, Libya, Syria, Iraq, Iran, and North Korea—either by developing their own programs or through buying material from industrialized nations. France was the major supplier to Israel, and German firms have supplied nuclear technology to India, Iran, Iraq, Libya, and Pakistan, among others. There are a thousand or more scientists in former Soviet countries who are capable of designing nuclear weapons, and these countries have an estimated 700 to 1,000 tons of weapons-grade fissionable material that could be sold or stolen. South Africa had a stockpile of weapons-grade uranium, but has now discontinued its nuclear weapons program. Brazil and Argentina, which were once in the preliminary stages of a nuclear weapons race, have now abandoned it. Almost all of the developing countries that now have nuclear weapons or hope to have them, also have ballistic missiles, some of them capable of delivering a nuclear warhead more than 2,000 miles away.

Major Foreign Interventions by the United States Since 1945

Since 1945, the United States has fought three major wars, against North Korea, North Vietnam, and Iraq, and seven lesser military actions in Lebanon (1958 and 1983), the Persian Gulf (1987), Grenada, Panama, Libya, and the Dominican Republic. In addition, the United States conducted a proxy war in El Salvador in the 1980s and the Somali peacekeeping mission of 1993–1994.

Of these 12 episodes, seven were successful: the Korean War (1950-53); the Lebanon intervention of 1958; the Dominican intervention of 1965; the Grenada invasion of 1983; the Libyan air strike of 1986; the Panama invasion of 1989; and the Gulf War of 1991. Two were military failures: the Vietnam War and the Lebanese action of 1983. It is not clear what the Persian Gulf intervention of 1987 or the Somali action of 1993–1994 accomplished. The El Salvador proxy war was ended by negotiation in 1992.

In addition to these overt interventions, the United States also mounted at least 13 major covert efforts in third world countries to overturn or destabilize unfriendly governments.* Some of these operations, such as those in Afghanistan and Nicaragua, began as covert actions but eventually became overt.

*There are several other cases in which the U.S. government allegedly tried to overturn legal governments—for example, those of Syria and Brazil—but information on such cases is sketchy. Alleged attempts like these are not shown on the map.

Major Foreign Interventions by the United States Since 1945

FIG. 7–50

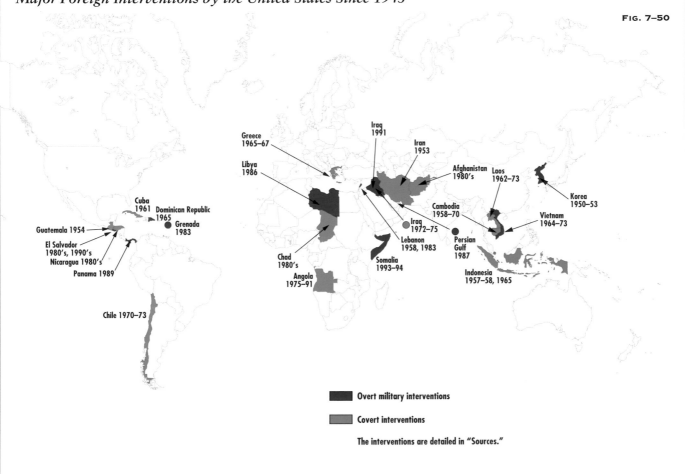

Overt military interventions

Covert interventions

The interventions are detailed in "Sources."

Of the 13 covert efforts, those in six countries—Iran, Guatemala, Chile, Greece, Afghanistan, and Angola—were successful in their immediate objectives. In four cases—Indonesia, Cuba, Libya, and Nicaragua—the efforts were unsuccessful. In three other cases—Cambodia, Laos, and Iraq—the results were uncertain.

Several initially successful covert operations turned out to be counterproductive in the long run. U.S. intervention in Iran in 1953 contributed to Iranian mistrust of the United States, which has long prevented rapprochement between the two countries. The failed Bay of Pigs invasion of 1961 has poisoned U.S.-Cuban relations for more than three decades. In Guatemala, the reformist government of Arbenz, overthrown by the CIA in 1953, was soon succeeded by a series of military rulers who killed more than 100,000 of their own people. In Greece, CIA actions in the 1960s helped prepare the way for the notorious Colonels' Junta. In Chile, American actions in the early 1970s contributed to the overthrow of Allende, who was succeeded by the repressive Pinochet. In Angola during the 1980s, the CIA joined South Africa in supporting the insurgent UNITA faction against a Marxist government that, paradoxically, encouraged American business interests.

Covert actions designed to destabilize foreign governments violate several agreements to which the United States is a signatory, including the United Nations Charter and the Charter of the Organization of American States.

The Future

Over the next decade, it's unlikely that the patterns shown on the maps will change radically. Minorities and old people will grow in importance and there are likely to be more women in public office. Single motherhood will still be widespread, poverty will still be a problem, and the same disease patterns will still be apparent despite probable improvements in the health care system. Unless there is a major war or a profound change in the economy, it's likely that many contentious issues of today, such as abortion, housing segregation, capital punishment, and rights to privacy, will still be boiling. If this atlas were to be updated in 2004 the most radical change would likely be in its physical appearance: It wouldn't be a book anymore, but a disc or a tape, or something that you play on your computer.

Appendix A

1990 United States Census Questionnaire

The Census questionnaire below was sent to all households in March 1990. Everyone was required to answer the first seven population and housing questions. A select sample of 17 percent of all households was sent a longer form that included additional questions as shown on the following pages.

PERSON 1 / PERSON 7

	PERSON 1	PERSON 7
	Last name	Last name
	First name Middle initial	First name Middle initial

Please fill one column for each person listed in Question 1a on page 1.

2. How is this person related to PERSON 1?

Fill ONE circle for each person.

If Other relative of person in column 1, fill circle and print exact relationship, such as mother-in-law, grandparent, son-in-law, niece, cousin, and so on.

START in this column with the household member (or one of the members) in whose name the home is owned, being bought, or rented.

If there is no such person, start in this column with any adult household member.

If a RELATIVE of Person 1:
- ○ Husband/wife
- ○ Natural born or adopted son/daughter
- ○ Stepson/ stepdaughter
- ○ Brother/sister
- ○ Father/mother
- ○ Grandchild
- ○ Other relative

If NOT RELATED to Person 1:
- ○ Roomer, boarder, or foster child
- ○ Housemate, roommate
- ○ Unmarried partner
- ○ Other nonrelative

3. Sex

Fill ONE circle for each person.

○ Male   ○ Female

4. Race

Fill ONE circle for the race that the person considers himself/herself to be.

If Indian (Amer.), print the name of the enrolled or principal tribe.

If Other Asian or Pacific Islander (API), print one group, for example: Hmong, Fijian, Laotian, Thai, Tongan, Pakistani, Cambodian, and so on.

If Other race, print race.

- ○ White
- ○ Black or Negro
- ○ Indian (Amer.) (Print the name of the enrolled or principal tribe.)

Eskimo
Aleut   Asian or Pacific Islander (API)
- ○ Chinese   ○ Japanese
- ○ Filipino   ○ Asian Indian
- ○ Hawaiian   ○ Samoan
- ○ Korean   ○ Guamanian
- ○ Vietnamese   ○ Other API

○ Other race (Print race)

5. Age and year of birth

a. Print each person's age at last birthday. Fill in the matching circle below each box.

b. Print each person's year of birth and fill the matching circle below each box.

a. Age   b. Year of birth

6. Marital status

Fill ONE circle for each person.

- ○ Now married   ○ Separated
- ○ Widowed   ○ Never married
- ○ Divorced

7. Is this person of Spanish/Hispanic origin?

Fill ONE circle for each person.

If Yes, other Spanish/Hispanic, print one group.

- ○ No (not Spanish/Hispanic)
- ○ Yes, Mexican, Mexican-Am., Chicano
- ○ Yes, Puerto Rican
- ○ Yes, Cuban
- ○ Yes, other Spanish/Hispanic (Print one group, for example: Argentinian, Columbian, Dominican, Nicaraguan, Salvadoran, Spaniard, and so on.)

FOR CENSUS USE

○ ○

Housing Questions

H1a. Did you leave anyone out of your list of persons for Question 1a on page 1 because you were not sure if the person should be listed — for example, someone temporarily away on a business trip or vacation, a newborn baby still in the hospital, or a person who stays here once in a while and has no other home?

- ○ Yes, please print the name(s) and reason(s).
- ○ No

b. Did you include anyone in your list of persons for Question 1a on page 1 even though you were not sure that the person should be listed — for example, a visitor who is staying here temporarily or a person who usually lives somewhere else?

- ○ Yes, please print the name(s) and reason(s).
- ○ No

H2. Which best describes this building? Include all apartments, flats, etc., even if vacant.

- ○ A mobile home or trailer
- ○ A one-family house detached from any other house
- ○ A one-family house attached to one or more houses
- ○ A building with 2 apartments
- ○ A building with 3 or 4 apartments
- ○ A building with 5 to 9 apartments
- ○ A building with 10 to 19 apartments
- ○ A building with 20 to 49 apartments
- ○ A building with 50 or more apartments
- ○ Other

H3. How many rooms do you have in this house or apartment? Do NOT count bathrooms, porches, balconies, foyers, halls, or half-rooms.

- ○ 1 room   ○ 4 rooms   ○ 7 rooms
- ○ 2 rooms   ○ 5 rooms   ○ 8 rooms
- ○ 3 rooms   ○ 6 rooms   ○ 9 or more rooms

H4. Is this house or apartment —

- ○ Owned by you or someone in this household with a mortgage or loan?
- ○ Owned by you or someone in this household free and clear (without a mortgage)?
- ○ Rented for cash rent?
- ○ Occupied without payment of cash rent?

H5a. If this is a ONE-FAMILY HOUSE — Is this house on ten or more acres?

○ Yes   ○ No

b. Is there a business (such as a store or barber shop) or a medical office on this property?

○ Yes   ○ No

H6. Answer only if you or someone in this household OWNS OR IS BUYING this house or apartment — What is the value of this property; that is, how much do you think this house and lot or condominium unit would sell for if it were for sale?

- ○ Less than $10,000
- ○ $10,000 to $14,999
- ○ $15,000 to $19,999
- ○ $20,000 to $24,999
- ○ $25,000 to $29,999
- ○ $30,000 to $34,999
- ○ $35,000 to $39,999
- ○ $40,000 to $44,999
- ○ $45,000 to $49,999
- ○ $50,000 to $54,999
- ○ $55,000 to $59,999
- ○ $60,000 to $64,999
- ○ $65,000 to $69,999
- ○ $70,000 to $74,999
- ○ $75,000 to $79,999
- ○ $80,000 to $89,999
- ○ $90,000 to $99,999
- ○ $100,000 to $124,999
- ○ $125,000 to $149,999
- ○ $150,000 to $174,999
- ○ $175,000 to $199,999
- ○ $200,000 to $249,999
- ○ $250,000 to $299,999
- ○ $300,000 to $399,999
- ○ $400,000 to $499,999
- ○ $500,000 or more

H7a. Answer only if you PAY RENT for this house or apartment— What is the monthly rent?

- ○ Less than $80
- ○ $80 to $99
- ○ $100 to $124
- ○ $125 to $149
- ○ $150 to $174
- ○ $175 to $199
- ○ $200 to $224
- ○ $225 to $249
- ○ $250 to $274
- ○ $275 to $299
- ○ $300 to $324
- ○ $325 to $349
- ○ $350 to $374
- ○ $375 to $399
- ○ $400 to $424
- ○ $425 to $449
- ○ $450 to $474
- ○ $475 to $499
- ○ $500 to $524
- ○ $525 to $549
- ○ $550 to $599
- ○ $600 to $649
- ○ $650 to $699
- ○ $700 to $749
- ○ $750 to $999
- ○ $1,000 or more

b. Does the monthly rent include any meals?

○ Yes   ○ No

PLEASE ALSO ANSWER THESE

H8. When did the person listed in column 1 on page 2 move into this house or apartment?

- ○ 1989 or 1990
- ○ 1985 to 1988
- ○ 1980 to 1984
- ○ 1970 to 1979
- ○ 1960 to 1969
- ○ 1959 or earlier

■

H9. How many bedrooms do you have; that is, how many bedrooms would you list if this house or apartment were on the market for sale or rent?

- ○ No bedroom
- ○ 1 bedroom
- ○ 2 bedrooms
- ○ 3 bedrooms
- ○ 4 bedrooms
- ○ 5 or more bedrooms

■

H10. Do you have COMPLETE plumbing facilities in this house or apartment; that is, 1) hot and cold piped water, 2) a flush toilet, and 3) a bathtub or shower?

- ○ Yes, have all three facilities
- ○ No

H11. Do you have COMPLETE kitchen facilities; that is, 1) a sink with piped water, 2) a range or cookstove, and 3) a refrigerator?

- ○ Yes
- ○ No

■

H12. Do you have a telephone in this house or apartment?

- ○ Yes
- ○ No

H13. How many automobiles, vans, and trucks of one-ton capacity or less are kept at home for use by members of your household?

- ○ None
- ○ 1
- ○ 2
- ○ 3
- ○ 4
- ○ 5
- ○ 6
- ○ 7 or more

■

H14. Which FUEL is used MOST for heating this house or apartment?

- ○ Gas: from underground pipes serving the neighborhood
- ○ Gas: bottled, tank, or LP
- ○ Electricity
- ○ Fuel oil, kerosene, etc.
- ○ Coal or coke
- ○ Wood
- ○ Solar energy
- ○ Other fuel
- ○ No fuel used

■

H15. Do you get water from —

- ○ A public system such as a city water department, or private company?
- ○ An individual drilled well?
- ○ An individual dug well?
- ○ Some other source such as a spring, creek, river, cistern, etc.?

H16. Is this building connected to a public sewer?

- ○ Yes, connected to public sewer
- ○ No, connected to septic tank or cesspool
- ○ No, use other means

H17. About when was this building first built?

- ○ 1989 or 1990
- ○ 1985 to 1988
- ○ 1980 to 1984
- ○ 1970 to 1979
- ○ 1960 to 1969
- ○ 1950 to 1959
- ○ 1940 to 1949
- ○ 1939 or earlier
- ○ Don't know

■

H18. Is this house or apartment part of a condominium?

- ○ Yes
- ○ No

If you live in an apartment building, skip to H20.

H19a. Is this house on less than 1 acre?

- ○ Yes — *Skip to H20*
- ○ No

b. In 1989, what were the actual sales of all agricultural products from this property?

- ○ None
- ○ $1 to $999
- ○ $1,000 to $2,499
- ○ $2,500 to $4,999
- ○ $5,000 to $9,999
- ○ $10,000 or more

■

H20. What are the yearly costs of utilities and fuels for this house or apartment? If you have lived here less than 1 year, estimate the yearly cost.

a. Electricity

$ __ __ __ __ .00
Yearly cost — Dollars

OR

- ○ Included in rent or in condominium fee
- ○ No charge or electricity not used

b. Gas

$ __ __ __ __ .00
Yearly cost — Dollars

OR

- ○ Included in rent or in condominium fee
- ○ No charge or gas not used

c. Water

$ __ __ __ __ .00
Yearly cost — Dollars

OR

- ○ Included in rent or in condominium fee
- ○ No charge

d. Oil, coal, kerosene, wood, etc.

■

$ __ __ __ __ .00
Yearly cost — Dollars

OR

- ○ Included in rent or in condominium fee
- ○ No charge or these fuels not used

QUESTIONS FOR YOUR HOUSEHOLD

INSTRUCTION:

Answer questions H21 to H26. If this is a one-family house, a condominium, or a mobile home that someone in this household OWNS OR IS BUYING; otherwise, go to page 6.

H21. What were the real estate taxes on THIS property last year?

$ __ __ __ __ .00
Yearly amount — Dollars

OR

- ○ None

H22. What was the annual payment for fire, hazard, and flood insurance on THIS property?

$ __ __ __ __ .00
Yearly amount — Dollars

OR

- ○ None

■

H23a. Do you have a mortgage, deed of trust, contract to purchase, or similar debt on THIS property?

○ Yes, mortgage, deed of trust, or similar debt
○ Yes, contract to purchase } Go to H23b
○ No — Skip to H24a

b. How much is your regular monthly mortgage payment on THIS property? Include payment only on first mortgage or contract to purchase.

```
|$          .00|
Monthly amount — Dollars
```

OR

○ No regular payment required — Skip to H24a

c. Does your regular monthly mortgage payment include payments for real estate taxes on THIS property?

○ Yes, taxes included in payment
○ No, taxes paid separately or taxes not required

d. Does your regular monthly mortgage payment include payments for fire, hazard, or flood insurance on THIS property?

○ Yes, insurance included in payment
○ No, insurance paid separately or no insurance

H24a. Do you have a second or junior mortgage or a home equity loan on THIS property?

○ Yes
○ No — Skip to H25

b. How much is your regular monthly payment on all second or junior mortgages and all home equity loans?

```
|$          .00|
Monthly amount — Dollars
```

OR

○ No regular payment required

c. Answer ONLY if this is a CONDOMINIUM —
What is the monthly condominium fee?

```
|$          .00|
Monthly amount — Dollars
```

H25. Answer ONLY if this is a MOBILE HOME —
What was the total cost for personal property taxes, site rent, registration fees and license fees on this mobil home and its site last year? Exclude real estate taxes.

```
|$          .00|
Yearly amount — Dollars
```

Please turn to page 6. ↗

PERSON 1

```
| Last name | First name | Middle initial |
```

8. In what U.S. State or foreign country was this person born? ⌐
(Name of State or foreign country; or Puerto Rico, Guam, etc.)

9. Is this person a CITIZEN of the United States?

○ Yes, born in the United States — Skip to 11
○ Yes, born in Puerto Rico, Guam, the U.S. Virgin Islands, or Northern Marianas
○ Yes, born abroad of American parent or parents
○ Yes, U.S. citizen by naturalization
○ No, not a citizen of the United States

10. When did this person come to the United States to stay?

○ 1987 to 1990   ○ 1970 to 1974
○ 1985 or 1986   ○ 1965 to 1969
○ 1982 to 1984   ○ 1960 to 1964
○ 1980 or 1981   ○ 1950 to 1959
○ 1975 to 1979   ○ Before 1950

11. At any time since February 1, 1990, has this person attended regular school or college? Include only nursery school, kindergarten, elementary school, and schooling which leads to a high school diploma or a college degree.

○ No, has not attended since February 1
○ Yes, public school, public college
○ Yes, private school, private college

12. How much school has this person COMPLETED? Fill ONE circle for the highest level COMPLETED or degree received. If currently enrolled, mark the level of previous grade attended or highest degree received.

○ No school completed
○ Nursery school
○ Kindergarten
○ 1st, 2nd, 3rd, or 4th grade
○ 5th, 6th, 7th, or 8th grade
○ 9th grade
○ 10th grade
○ 11th grade
○ 12th grade, NO DIPLOMA
○ HIGH SCHOOL GRADUATE — high school DIPLOMA or the equivalent (For example: GED)
○ Some college but no degree
○ Associate degree in college — Occupational program
○ Associate degree in college — Academic program
○ Bachelor's degree (For example: BA, AB, BS)
○ Master's degree (For example: MA, MS, MEng, MEd, MSW, MBA)
○ Professional school degree (For example: MD, DDS, DVM, LLB, JD)
○ Doctorate degree (For example: PhD, EdD)

13. What is this person's ancestry or ethnic origin? ⌐
(See instruction guide for further information.)

(For example: German, Italian, Afro-Amer., Croatian, Cape Verdean, Dominican, Ecuadorean, Haitian, Cajun, French Canadian, Jamaican, Korean, Lebanese, Mexican, Nigerian, Irish, Polish, Slovak, Taiwanese, Thai, Ukrainian, etc.)

14a. Did this person live in this house or apartment 5 years ago (on April 1, 1985)?

○ Born after April 1, 1985 — Go to questions for the next person
○ Yes — Skip to 15a
○ No

b. Where did this person live 5 years ago (on April 1, 1985)?

(1) Name of U.S. State or foreign country ⌐
(If outside U.S., print answer above and skip to 15a.)

(2) Name of county in the U.S. ⌐

(3) Name of city or town in the U.S. ⌐

(4) Did this person live inside the city or town limits?

○ Yes
○ No, lived outside the city/town limits

15a. Does this person speak a language other than English at home?

○ Yes   ○ No — Skip to 16

b. What is this language? ⌐

(For example: Chinese, Italian, Spanish, Vietnamese)

c. How well does this person speak English?

○ Very well   ○ Not well
○ Well   ○ Not at all

16. When was this person born?

○ Born before April 1, 1975 — Go to 17a
○ Born April 1, 1975 or later — Go to questions for the next person

17a. Has this person ever been on active-duty military service in the Armed Forces of the United States or ever been in the United States military Reserves or the National Guard? If service was in Reserves or National Guard only, see instruction guide.

○ Yes, now on active duty
○ Yes, on active duty in past, but not now
○ Yes, service in Reserves or National Guard only — Skip to 18
○ No — Skip to 18

b. Was active-duty military service during — Fill a circle for each period in which this person served.

○ September 1980 or later
○ May 1975 to August 1980
○ Vietnam era (August 1964—April 1975)
○ February 1955—July 1964
○ Korean conflict (June 1950—January 1955)
○ World War II (September 1940—July 1947)
○ World War I (April 1917—November 1918)
○ Any other time

c. In total, how many years of active-duty military service has this person had?

```
|      | Years
```

PLEASE ANSWER THESE QUESTIONS   FOR PERSON 1 ON PAGE 2

18. Does this person have a physical, mental or other health condition that has lasted for 6 or more months and which —

a. Limits the kind or amount of work this person can do at a job?

○ Yes   ○ No

b. Prevents this person from working at a job?

○ Yes   ○ No

19. Because of a health condition that has lasted for 6 or more months, does this person have any difficulty —

a. Going outside the home alone, for example, to shop or visit a doctor's office?

○ Yes   ○ No

b. Taking care of his or her own personal needs, such as bathing, dressing, or getting around inside the home?

○ Yes   ○ No

If this person is a female —

20. How many babies has she ever had, not counting stillbirths? Do not count her stepchildren or children she has adopted.

None 1 2 3 4 5 6 7 8 9 10 11 12 or more
○ ○ ○ ○ ○ ○ ○ ○ ○ ○ ○ ○ ○

21a. Did this person work at any time LAST WEEK?

○ Yes — Fill this circle if this person worked full time or part time. (Count part-time work such as delivering papers, or helping without pay in a family business or farm. Also count active duty in the Armed Forces.)

○ No — Fill this circle if this person did not work, or did only own housework, school work, or volunteer work. — *Skip to 25*

b. How many hours did this person work LAST WEEK (at all jobs)? Subtract any time off; add overtime or extra hours worked.

|___|___| Hours

22. At what location did this person work LAST WEEK?

If this person worked at more than one location, print where he or she worked most last week.

a. Address (Number and street)

|_____|

(If the exact location is not known, give a description of the location such as the building name or the nearest street or intersection.)

b. Name of city, town or post office

|_____|

c. Is the work location inside the limits of that city or town?

○ Yes   ○ No, outside the city/town limits

d. County

|_____|

e. State

|_____|

f. ZIP Code

|_____|

23a. How did this person usually get to work LAST WEEK? If this person usually used more than one method of transportation during the trip, fill the circle of the one used for most of the distance.

○ Car, truck, or van   ○ Motorcycle
○ Bus or trolley bus   ○ Bicycle
○ Streetcar or trolley car ○ Walked
○ Subway or elevated   ○ Worked at home — *Skip to 28*
○ Railroad   ○ Other method
○ Ferryboat
○ Taxicab

If "car, truck, or van" is marked in 23a, go to 23b. Otherwise, skip to 24a.

b. How many people, including this person, usually rode to work in the car, truck, or van LAST WEEK?

○ Drove alone   ○ 5 people
○ 2 people   ○ 6 people
○ 3 people   ○ 7 to 9 people
○ 4 people   ○ 10 or more people

24a. What time did this person usually leave home to go to work LAST WEEK?

|___|___| ○ a.m. ○ p.m.

b. How many minutes did it usually take this person to get from home to work LAST WEEK?

|___|___| Minutes — *Skip to 28*

25. Was this person TEMPORARILY absent or on layoff from a job or business LAST WEEK?

○ Yes, on layoff
○ Yes, on vacation, temporary illness, labor dispute, etc.
○ No

26a. Has this person been looking for work during the last 4 weeks?

○ Yes
○ No — *Skip to 27*

b. Could this person have taken a job LAST WEEK if one had been offered?

○ No, already has a job
○ No, temporarily ill
○ No, other reasons (in school, etc.)
○ Yes, could have taken a job

27. When did this person last work, even for a few days?

○ 1990   Go
○ 1989   to
○ 1988   28
○ 1985 to 1987

○ 1980 to 1984   Skip
○ 1979 or earlier to 32
○ Never worked

28–30. CURRENT OR MOST RECENT JOB ACTIVITY. Describe clearly this person's chief job activity or business last week. If this person had more than one job, describe the one at which this person worked the most hours. If this person had no job or business last week, give information for his/her last job or business since 1985.

---

28. Industry or Employer

a. For whom did this person work?

If now on active duty in the Armed Forces, fill this circle ○ and print the branch of the Armed Forces.

|_____|
(Name of company, business, or other employer)

b. What kind of business or industry was this? Describe the activity at location where employed.

|_____|

(For example: hospital, newspaper publishing, mail order house, auto engine manufacturing, retail bakery)

c. Is this mainly — Fill ONE circle

○ Manufacturing   ○ Other (agriculture,
○ Wholesale trade   construction, service,
○ Retail trade   government, etc.)

29. Occupation

a. What kind of work was this person doing?

|_____|

(For example: registered nurse, personnel manager, supervisor of order department, gasoline engine assembler, cake icer)

b. What were this person's most important activities or duties?

|_____|

(For example: patient care, directing hiring policies, supervising order clerks, assembling engines, icing cakes)

30. Was this person — Fill ONE circle

○ Employee of a PRIVATE FOR PROFIT company or business or of an individual, for wages, salary, or commissions
○ Employee of a PRIVATE NOT-FOR-PROFIT, tax-exempt, or charitable organization
○ Local GOVERNMENT employee (city, county, etc.)
○ State GOVERNMENT employee
○ Federal GOVERNMENT employee
○ SELF-EMPLOYED in own NOT INCORPORATED business, professional practice, or farm
○ SELF-EMPLOYED in own INCORPORATED business, professional practice, or farm
○ Working WITHOUT PAY in family business or farm

31a. Last year (1989), did this person work, even for a few days, at a paid job or in a business or farm?

○ Yes
○ No — *Skip to 32*

b. How many weeks did this person work in 1989? Count paid vacation, paid sick leave, and military service.

|___|___| Weeks

c. During the weeks WORKED in 1989, how many hours did this person usually work each week?

|___|___| Hours

---

32. INCOME IN 1989 —

Fill the "Yes" circle below for each income source received during 1989. Otherwise fill the "No" circle. If "Yes," enter the total amount received during 1989. For income received jointly, see instruction guide. If exact amount is not known, please give best estimate. If net income was a loss, write "Loss" above the dollar amount.

a. Wages, salary, commissions, bonuses or tips from all jobs — Report amount before deductions for taxes, bonds, dues, or other items.

○ Yes → $|_____| .00
○ No   Annual amount — Dollars

b. Self-employment income from own non-farm business, including proprietorship and partnership — Report NET income after business expenses.

○ Yes → $|_____| .00
○ No   Annual amount — Dollars

c. Farm self-employment income — Report NET income after operating expenses. Include earnings as a tenant farmer or sharecropper.

○ Yes → $|_____| .00
○ No   Annual amount — Dollars

d. Interest, dividends, net rental income or royalty income, or income from estates and trusts — Report even small amounts credited to an account.

○ Yes → $|_____| .00
○ No   Annual amount — Dollars

e. Social Security or Railroad Retirement

○ Yes → $|_____| .00
○ No   Annual amount — Dollars

f. Supplemental Security Income (SSI), Aid to Families with Dependent Children (AFDC), or other public assistance or public welfare payments.

○ Yes → $|_____| .00
○ No   Annual amount — Dollars

g. Retirement, survivor, or disability pensions — Do NOT include Social Security.

○ Yes → $|_____| .00
○ No   Annual amount — Dollars

h. Any other sources of income received regularly such as Veterans' (VA) payments, unemployment compensation, child support, or alimony — Do NOT include lump-sum payments such as money from an inheritance or the sale of a home.

○ Yes → $|_____| .00
○ No   Annual amount — Dollars

33. What was this person's total income in 1989? Add entries in questions 32a through 32h; subtract any losses. If total amount was a loss, write "Loss" above amount.

○ None   OR $|_____| .00
                Annual amount — Dollars

Please turn to the next page and answer questions for Person 2 on page 2. If this is the last person listed in question 1 on page 1, go to the back of the form.

Appendix B

Congressional Votes and Ratings Used as the Basis for Various Maps in Chapters 3, 4, and 7

HOUSE OF REPRESENTATIVES

1. League of Conservation Voters ratings, 1992 (Figure 3-15). Highest score is 100.
2. Americans for Democratic Action ratings, 1992 (Figures 4-10, 4-12). Highest score is 100.
3. Persian Gulf War, 1991. A "yes" indicates a vote for war (Figure 7-35).
4. Gun control, 1991. A "yes" indicates a vote for handgun waiting period (Figure 7-37).
5. Abortion, 1991. A "yes" indicates a vote in favor of allowing military personnel to use military hospitals for abortions (Figure 7-39).
6. Death penalty, 1991. A "yes" indicates a vote in favor of substituting life imprisonment for the death penalty (Figure 7-41).
7. Campaign finance reform, 1992. A "yes" indicates a vote in favor of the reform bill (Figure 7-43).
8. Flag desecration, 1990. A "yes" indicates a vote for a constitutional amendment to prohibit flag desecration (Figure 7-33).
9. Family leave, 1993. A "yes" indicates a vote in favor of the family leave bill (Figure 7-45).

SENATE

10. League of Conservation Voters ratings, 1992 (Figure 3-16). Highest score is 100.
11. Americans for Democratic Action ratings, 1992 (Figures 4-11, 4-13). Highest score is 100.
12. Persian Gulf War, 1991. A "yes" indicates a vote for war (Figure 7-36).
13. Gun control, 1991. A "yes" indicates a vote for handgun waiting period (Figure 7-38).
14. Abortion, 1991. A "yes" indicates a vote in favor of allowing military personnel to use military hospitals for abortions (Figure 7-40).
15. Death penalty, 1991. A "yes" indicates a vote in favor of substituting life imprisonment for the death penalty (Figure 7-42).
16. Campaign finance reform, 1992. A "yes" indicates a vote in favor of the reform bill (Figure 7-44).
17. Flag desecration, 1990. A "yes" indicates a vote for a constitutional amendment to prohibit flag desecration (Figure 7-34).
18. Family leave, 1993. A "yes" indicates a vote in favor of the family leave bill (Figure 7-46).

Y = Yes, including those paired for and announced for.
N = No, including paired for and announced for.
X = no vote or seat vacant.
D = Democrat
R = Republican
I = Independent
* Speaker rarely votes

Notes
1. Blackwell replaced Gray in the 1991 session.
2. Johnson replaced Bartlett in the 1991 session.
3. Allen replaced Slaughter in the 1991 session.
4. Wofford replaced Heinz in the 1991 session.

			1.	2.	3.	4.	5.	6.	7.
Alabama									
1	CALLAHAN	R	0	5	Y	N	N	Y	N
2	DICKINSON	R	0	10	Y	N	N	N	N
3	BROWDER	D	44	45	Y	N	N	N	Y
4	BEVILL	D	19	55	Y	N	N	N	Y
5	CRAMER	D	44	55	Y	N	Y	N	Y
6	ERDREICH	D	31	45	Y	N	Y	N	Y
7	HARRIS	D	25	40	Y	N	N	N	Y
Alaska									
	YOUNG	R	0	25	Y	N	N	N	N
Arizona									
1	RHODES	R	0	10	Y	N	N	N	N
2	PASTOR	D	56	85	X	X	X	N	Y
3	STUMP	R	0	0	Y	N	N	N	N
4	KYL	R	0	5	Y	N	N	N	N
5	KOLBE	R	0	25	Y	N	Y	N	N
Arkansas									
1	ALEXANDER	D	38	65	N	N	Y	N	Y
2	THORNTON	D	25	85	Y	N	N	N	Y
3	HAMMERSCHMIDT	R	0	5	Y	N	N	N	N
4	ANTHONY	D	19	45	N	Y	Y	N	Y
California									
1	RIGGS	R	31	25	N	Y	Y	N	N
2	HERGER	R	6	5	Y	N	N	N	N
3	MATSUI	D	69	80	N	Y	Y	N	Y
4	FAZIO	D	56	90	N	Y	Y	Y	Y
5	PELOSI	D	100	90	N	Y	Y	Y	Y
6	BOXER	D	69	60	N	Y	Y	N	Y
7	MILLER	D	75	85	N	Y	Y	Y	Y
8	DELLUMS	D	94	95	N	Y	Y	Y	Y
9	STARK	D	100	95	N	Y	Y	Y	Y
10	EDWARDS	D	100	100	N	Y	Y	Y	Y
11	LANTOS	D	94	95	Y	Y	Y	N	Y
12	CAMPBELL	R	44	30	Y	Y	Y	N	N
13	MINETA	D	81	100	N	Y	Y	Y	Y
14	DOOLITTLE	R	0	5	Y	N	N	N	N
15	CONDIT	D	25	55	Y	N	Y	N	Y
16	PANETTA	D	88	90	N	Y	Y	N	Y
17	DOOLEY	D	50	75	N	Y	Y	N	Y
18	LEHMAN	D	38	60	Y	Y	Y	N	Y
19	LAGOMARSINO	R	6	10	Y	Y	N	N	N
20	THOMAS	R	6	15	Y	Y	Y	N	N
21	GALLEGLY	R	6	15	Y	Y	N	N	N
22	MOORHEAD	R	13	5	Y	N	N	N	N
23	BEILENSON	D	100	85	N	Y	Y	N	Y
24	WAXMAN	D	100	95	N	Y	Y	Y	Y
25	ROYBAL	D	81	95	N	X	Y	Y	Y
26	BERMAN	D	100	85	Y	Y	Y	Y	Y
27	LEVINE	D	44	50	Y	Y	Y	N	X
28	DIXON	D	94	80	N	Y	Y	Y	Y
29	WATERS	D	75	95	N	Y	Y	Y	Y
30	MARTINEZ	D	69	95	N	Y	N	N	Y
31	DYMALLY	D	56	45	N	Y	Y	X	Y

			1.	2.	3.	4.	5.	6.	7.
California (cont.)									
32	ANDERSON	D	31	90	Y	Y	Y	N	Y
33	DREIER	R	6	0	Y	N	N	N	N
34	TORRES	D	94	85	N	Y	Y	N	Y
35	LEWIS	R	0	10	Y	N	N	N	N
36	BROWN	D	81	95	N	Y	Y	Y	Y
37	McCANDLESS	R	6	10	Y	N	N	N	N
38	DORNAN	R	0	5	Y	Y	N	N	N
39	DANNEMEYER	R	6	10	Y	N	N	N	X
40	COX	R	0	5	Y	N	N	N	N
41	LOWERY	R	13	5	Y	Y	N	N	N
42	ROHRABACHER	R	6	20	Y	N	N	N	N
43	PACKARD	R	0	0	Y	Y	N	N	N
44	CUNNINGHAM	R	0	5	Y	N	N	N	N
45	HUNTER	R	0	15	Y	N	N	N	N
Colorado									
1	SCHROEDER	D	94	95	N	Y	Y	N	Y
2	SKAGGS	D	69	90	N	Y	Y	Y	Y
3	CAMPBELL	D	44	55	Y	N	Y	N	Y
4	ALLARD	R	0	5	Y	N	N	N	N
5	HEFLEY	R	0	20	Y	N	N	N	N
6	SCHAEFER	R	0	5	Y	N	N	N	N
Connecticut									
1	KENNELLY	D	88	100	N	Y	Y	N	Y
2	GEJDENSON	D	63	90	N	Y	Y	Y	Y
3	DeLAURO	D	94	90	N	Y	Y	N	Y
4	SHAYS	R	100	65	Y	Y	Y	Y	Y
5	FRANKS	R	31	20	Y	N	Y	N	N
6	JOHNSON	R	38	40	Y	Y	Y	N	N
Delaware									
	CARPER	D	56	75	Y	Y	Y	N	Y
Florida									
1	HUTTO	D	6	15	Y	Y	N	N	N
2	PETERSON	D	38	75	N	N	Y	N	Y
3	BENNETT	D	75	65	N	Y	Y	N	N
4	JAMES	R	19	15	Y	Y	N	N	N
5	McCOLLUM	R	19	15	Y	N	N	N	N
6	STEARNS	R	25	5	Y	Y	N	N	N
7	GIBBONS	D	50	65	N	Y	Y	N	Y
8	YOUNG	R	25	15	Y	Y	N	N	N
9	BILIRAKIS	R	19	20	Y	Y	N	N	N
10	IRELAND	R	6	5	Y	N	N	N	N
11	BACCHUS	D	88	70	Y	Y	Y	N	Y
12	LEWIS	R	19	10	Y	N	N	N	N
13	GOSS	R	31	5	Y	Y	N	N	N
14	JOHNSTON	D	94	90	N	Y	Y	N	Y
15	SHAW	R	19	15	Y	N	N	N	N
16	SMITH	D	88	95	N	Y	Y	N	Y
17	LEHMAN	D	81	85	N	X	X	Y	Y
18	ROS-LEHTINEN	R	56	25	Y	Y	N	N	N
19	FASCELL	D	81	85	Y	Y	Y	N	Y

				1.	2.	3.	4.	5.	6.	7.
Georgia										
1	THOMAS	D		19	40	Y	N	Y	N	Y
2	HATCHER	D		19	60	Y	Y	X	N	Y
3	RAY	D		25	30	Y	N	N	N	Y
4	JONES	D		56	65	Y	Y	Y	N	Y
5	LEWIS	D		88	95	N	Y	Y	Y	Y
6	GINGRICH	R		6	10	Y	N	N	N	N
7	DARDEN	D		38	70	Y	Y	Y	N	Y
8	ROWLAND	D		19	50	Y	Y	Y	N	Y
9	JENKINS	D		38	75	N	N	N	N	Y
10	BARNARD	D		13	0	Y	N	N	N	X
Hawaii										
1	ABERCROMBIE	D		88	95	N	Y	Y	Y	Y
2	MINK	D		100	100	N	Y	Y	Y	Y
Idaho										
1	LaROCCO	D		50	80	N	N	Y	N	Y
2	STALLINGS	D		38	55	N	N	N	N	Y
Illinois										
1	HAYES	D		75	95	N	Y	Y	Y	Y
2	SAVAGE	D		69	90	N	Y	Y	X	Y
3	RUSSO	D		50	70	N	Y	N	N	X
4	SANGMEISTER	D		63	70	N	Y	N	N	Y
5	LIPINSKI	D		38	50	N	Y	N	N	Y
6	HYDE	R		13	15	Y	Y	N	N	N
7	COLLINS	D		56	85	N	Y	Y	Y	Y
8	ROSTENKOWSKI	D		25	95	Y	Y	N	N	Y
9	YATES	D		88	95	N	Y	Y	Y	X
10	PORTER	R		56	30	Y	Y	Y	N	N
11	ANNUNZIO	D		56	85	N	Y	N	N	Y
12	CRANE	R		0	0	Y	N	N	N	N
13	FAWELL	R		44	25	Y	Y	Y	N	N
14	HASTERT	R		13	5	Y	N	N	N	N
15	EWING	R		0	25	Y	X	X	N	N
16	COX	D		75	95	N	Y	Y	Y	Y
17	EVANS	D		100	95	N	Y	Y	Y	Y
18	MICHEL	R		6	10	Y	X	N	N	N
19	BRUCE	D		31	85	N	N	N	N	Y
20	DURBIN	D		69	90	N	Y	Y	N	Y
21	COSTELLO	D		56	60	N	N	N	N	X
22	POSHARD	D		56	65	N	N	N	N	Y
Indiana										
1	VISCLOSKY	D		38	85	N	Y	Y	Y	Y
2	SHARP	D		38	85	N	Y	Y	Y	Y
3	ROEMER	D		44	55	N	Y	N	N	Y
4	LONG	D		44	80	N	N	Y	N	Y
5	JONTZ	D		100	90	N	N	Y	Y	Y
6	BURTON	R		13	10	Y	N	N	N	N
7	MYERS	R		6	0	Y	N	N	N	N
8	McCLOSKEY	D		56	95	N	Y	Y	Y	Y
9	HAMILTON	D		44	80	N	Y	Y	Y	Y
10	JACOBS	D		75	85	N	Y	Y	Y	Y
Iowa										
1	LEACH	R		31	60	Y	Y	Y	N	Y

				1.	2.	3.	4.	5.	6.	7.
Iowa (cont.)										
2	NUSSLE	R		6	25	Y	N	N	N	N
3	NAGLE	D		44	85	N	N	Y	Y	N
4	SMITH	D		25	75	N	N	Y	Y	X
5	LIGHTFOOT	R		0	15	Y	N	N	N	N
6	GRANDY	R		0	15	Y	N	N	N	N
Kansas										
1	ROBERTS	R		0	10	Y	N	N	N	N
2	SLATTERY	D		63	75	Y	N	Y	N	Y
3	MEYERS	R		50	30	Y	Y	Y	N	N
4	GLICKMAN	D		50	75	Y	Y	Y	N	Y
5	NICHOLS	R		0	20	Y	N	Y	N	N
Kentucky										
1	HUBBARD	D		13	45	Y	Y	Y	N	Y
2	NATCHER	D		31	85	N	N	N	N	Y
3	MAZZOLI	D		56	70	N	Y	N	N	Y
4	BUNNING	R		0	10	Y	N	N	N	N
5	ROGERS	R		6	25	Y	N	N	N	N
6	HOPKINS	R		0	15	Y	N	X	X	N
7	PERKINS	D		38	70	N	N	N	N	N
Louisiana										
1	LIVINGSTON	R		0	10	Y	N	N	N	N
2	JEFFERSON	D		63	85	N	Y	Y	Y	Y
3	TAUZIN	D		13	40	Y	N	N	N	N
4	McCRERY	R		13	5	Y	N	N	N	N
5	HUCKABY	D		13	25	Y	N	N	N	N
6	BAKER	R		0	0	Y	N	N	N	N
7	HAYES	D		6	30	Y	N	N	N	N
8	HOLLOWAY	R		0	15	Y	N	N	X	N
Maine										
1	ANDREWS	D		100	100	N	Y	Y	Y	Y
2	SNOWE	R		63	50	Y	N	Y	N	Y
Maryland										
1	GILCHRIST	R		88	30	Y	Y	Y	N	N
2	BENTLEY	R		6	25	Y	Y	N	N	N
3	CARDIN	D		81	95	N	Y	Y	N	Y
4	McMILLEN	D		81	80	Y	Y	Y	N	Y
5	HOYER	D		44	90	N	Y	Y	Y	Y
6	BYRON	D		19	30	Y	N	N	N	Y
7	MFUME	D		75	95	N	Y	Y	Y	Y
8	MORELLA	R		81	70	N	Y	Y	N	Y
Massachusetts										
1	CONTE	R		X	X	N	X	X	X	X
1	OLVER	D		100	100	X	X	X	Y	Y
2	NEAL	D		88	90	N	Y	N	Y	Y
3	EARLY	D		56	85	N	Y	N	N	Y
4	FRANK	D		100	100	N	Y	Y	Y	Y
5	ATKINS	D		88	95	N	Y	Y	N	Y
6	MAVROULES	D		75	85	N	Y	N	N	Y
7	MARKEY	D		88	100	N	Y	Y	Y	Y
8	KENNEDY	D		100	95	N	Y	Y	N	Y
9	MOAKLEY	D		50	85	N	Y	N	N	Y

			1.	2.	3.	4.	5.	6.	7.
Massachusetts(cont.)									
10	STUDDS	D	88	100	N	Y	Y	Y	Y
11	DONNELLY	D	50	75	N	Y	N	N	Y
Michigan									
1	CONYERS	D	81	90	N	Y	Y	Y	Y
2	PURSELL	R	19	5	Y	Y	N	N	N
3	WOLPE	D	94	85	N	Y	Y	Y	Y
4	UPTON	R	25	30	Y	Y	N	N	N
5	HENRY	R	44	35	Y	Y	N	N	N
6	CARR	D	25	70	N	N	Y	X	N
7	KILDEE	D	75	90	N	Y	N	Y	Y
8	TRAYLER	D	38	40	N	N	N	N	Y
9	VANDERJAGT	R	0	5	Y	N	N	N	N
10	CAMP	R	13	5	Y	N	N	N	N
11	DAVIS	R	6	20	Y	N	N	N	N
12	BONIOR	D	69	80	N	Y	N	Y	Y
13	COLLINS	D	63	95	N	Y	Y	Y	Y
14	HERTEL	D	75	85	N	Y	N	Y	Y
15	FORD	D	50	95	N	Y	Y	Y	Y
16	DINGELL	D	38	90	Y	N	Y	N	Y
17	LEVIN	D	75	95	N	Y	Y	Y	Y
18	BROOMFIELD	R	6	10	Y	Y	N	N	N
Minnesota									
1	PENNY	D	69	45	N	N	N	Y	Y
2	WEBER	R	19	10	Y	N	N	Y	N
3	RAMSTAD	R	50	30	Y	N	Y	N	N
4	VENTO	D	94	100	N	Y	Y	Y	Y
5	SABO	D	81	100	N	Y	Y	Y	Y
6	SIKORSKI	D	94	95	N	Y	Y	N	Y
7	PETERSON	D	63	65	N	N	N	Y	Y
8	OBERSTAR	D	88	90	N	N	N	Y	Y
Mississippi									
1	WHITTEN	D	13	50	Y	X	N	N	X
2	ESPY	D	31	75	N	N	Y	N	Y
3	MONTGOMERY	D	6	30	Y	N	N	N	Y
4	PARKER	D	13	30	Y	N	N	N	Y
5	TAYLOR	D	31	30	N	N	N	N	N
Missouri									
1	CLAY	D	75	95	N	Y	Y	Y	Y
2	HORN	D	88	95	N	Y	Y	N	Y
3	GEPHARDT	D	44	85	N	Y	Y	N	Y
4	SKELTON	D	6	45	Y	N	N	N	Y
5	WHEAT	D	88	95	N	Y	Y	Y	Y
6	COLEMAN	R	13	35	Y	Y	N	N	N
7	HANCOCK	R	0	10	Y	N	N	N	N
8	EMERSON	R	6	20	Y	N	N	N	N
9	VOLKMER	D	19	50	Y	N	N	N	Y
Montana									
1	WILLIAMS	D	38	85	N	N	Y	N	Y
2	MARLENEE	R	6	10	Y	N	N	N	Y
Nebraska									
1	BEREUTER	R	25	20	Y	N	N	N	N

			1.	2.	3.	4.	5.	6.	7.
Nebraska (cont.)									
2	HOAGLAND	D	63	85	Y	Y	Y	N	Y
3	BARRETT	R	0	10	Y	N	N	N	N
Nevada									
1	BILBRAY	D	56	70	Y	N	N	N	Y
2	VUCANOVICH	R	19	5	Y	N	N	N	N
New Hampshire									
1	ZELIFF	R	6	20	Y	N	Y	N	N
2	SWETT	D	94	85	Y	Y	Y	N	Y
New Jersey									
1	ANDREWS	D	69	70	N	Y	Y	N	Y
2	HUGHES	D	88	80	Y	Y	Y	N	Y
3	PALLONE	D	88	90	Y	Y	Y	N	Y
4	SMITH	R	44	40	Y	Y	N	Y	Y
5	ROUKEMA	R	38	50	Y	Y	Y	N	N
6	DWYER	D	69	80	N	Y	N	N	Y
7	RINALDO	R	56	45	Y	Y	N	N	Y
8	ROE	D	50	70	N	Y	N	N	Y
9	TORRICELLI	D	63	85	Y	Y	Y	N	Y
10	PAYNE	D	81	95	N	Y	Y	Y	Y
11	GALLO	R	19	25	Y	Y	Y	N	N
12	ZIMMER	R	50	40	Y	N	Y	N	Y
13	SAXTON	R	38	15	Y	Y	N	N	N
14	GUARINI	D	69	75	N	Y	Y	N	Y
New Mexico									
1	SCHIFF	R	13	25	Y	N	Y	N	N
2	SKEEN	R	6	20	Y	N	N	N	N
3	RICHARDSON	D	63	75	N	N	Y	N	Y
New York									
1	HOCHBRUECKNER	D	75	95	N	Y	Y	Y	Y
2	DOWNEY	D	88	85	N	Y	Y	Y	Y
3	MRAZEK	D	88	85	N	Y	Y	Y	Y
4	LENT	R	6	5	Y	Y	N	N	N
5	McGRATH	R	13	25	Y	Y	N	N	N
6	FLAKE	D	75	90	N	Y	Y	Y	Y
7	ACKERMAN	D	75	70	Y	Y	Y	Y	Y
8	SCHEUER	D	94	90	N	Y	Y	Y	Y
9	MANTON	D	38	85	N	Y	N	N	Y
10	SCHUMER	D	88	95	N	Y	Y	N	Y
11	TOWNS	D	69	80	N	Y	Y	Y	Y
12	OWENS	D	94	85	N	Y	Y	Y	Y
13	SOLARZ	D	88	100	Y	Y	Y	N	Y
14	MOLINARI	R	44	35	Y	Y	Y	N	N
15	GREEN	R	75	70	Y	Y	Y	N	Y
16	RANGEL	D	69	95	N	Y	Y	Y	Y
17	WEISS	D	94	100	N	Y	Y	Y	Y
18	SERRANO	D	88	95	N	Y	Y	Y	Y
19	ENGEL	D	94	95	Y	Y	Y	Y	Y
20	LOWEY	D	88	100	N	Y	Y	Y	Y
21	FISH	R	81	40	Y	Y	N	N	Y
22	GILMAN	R	81	75	Y	Y	Y	N	Y
23	McNULTY	D	25	90	Y	Y	N	Y	Y
24	SOLOMON	R	19	15	Y	N	N	N	N

			1.	2.	3.	4.	5.	6.	7.
New York (cont.)									
25 BOEHLERT	R		88	75	Y	Y	Y	N	Y
26 MARTIN	R		6	15	Y	X	N	N	X
27 WALSH	R		50	25	Y	Y	N	N	N
28 McHUGH	D		69	90	N	Y	Y	Y	Y
29 HORTON	R		44	40	Y	N	Y	N	N
30 SLAUGHTER	D		100	95	N	Y	Y	Y	Y
31 PAXON	R		6	10	Y	N	N	N	N
32 LaFALCE	D		44	85	N	Y	N	Y	Y
33 NOWAK	D		56	85	N	Y	N	N	Y
34 HOUGHTON	R		13	30	Y	N	Y	N	N
North Carolina									
1 JONES	D		31	69	Y	Y	Y	N	Y
2 VALENTINE	D		38	45	Y	Y	Y	N	Y
3 LANCASTER	D		25	45	Y	Y	Y	N	Y
4 PRICE	D		56	85	N	Y	Y	N	Y
5 NEAL	D		81	65	N	Y	Y	X	Y
6 COBLE	R		6	10	Y	N	N	N	N
7 ROSE	D		50	95	N	Y	N	N	Y
8 HEFNER	D		13	40	N	Y	Y	N	Y
9 McMILLAN	R		19	15	Y	Y	N	N	N
10 BALLENGER	R		6	10	Y	N	N	N	N
11 TAYLOR	R		6	15	Y	N	N	N	N
North Dakota									
DORGAN	D		56	70	N	N	N	Y	Y
Ohio									
1 LUKEN	D		56	55	Y	Y	N	N	Y
2 GRADISON	R		19	20	Y	Y	N	N	N
3 HALL	D		44	60	N	Y	N	N	Y
4 OXLEY	R		0	5	Y	Y	N	N	N
5 GILLMOR	R		19	20	Y	N	N	N	N
6 McEWEN	R		0	10	Y	N	N	N	N
7 HOBSON	R		13	15	Y	N	N	N	N
8 BOEHNER	R		0	5	Y	N	N	N	N
9 KAPTUR	D		56	75	N	Y	N	N	Y
10 MILLER	R		0	5	Y	N	N	N	N
11 ECKART	D		63	95	N	Y	Y	N	Y
12 KASICH	R		25	15	Y	N	N	N	N
13 PEASE	D		75	100	N	Y	Y	N	Y
14 SAWYER	D		63	95	N	Y	Y	Y	Y
15 WYLIE	R		6	10	Y	Y	N	N	N
16 REGULA	R		25	35	Y	Y	N	N	N
17 TRAFICANT	D		50	85	N	Y	Y	N	N
18 APPLEGATE	D		44	70	N	N	N	N	N
19 FEIGHAN	D		69	80	N	Y	Y	Y	Y
20 OAKAR	D		25	65	N	Y	N	N	Y
21 STOKES	D		81	95	N	Y	Y	Y	Y
Oklahoma									
1 INHOFE	R		0	10	Y	N	N	N	N
2 SYNAR	D		81	95	N	Y	Y	N	Y
3 BREWSTER	D		25	60	Y	N	Y	N	Y
4 McCURDY	D		38	70	Y	Y	Y	N	Y
5 EDWARDS	R		0	10	Y	N	N	N	N
6 ENGLISH	D		38	55	N	N	N	N	Y

			1.	2.	3.	4.	5.	6.	7.
Oregon									
1	AuCOIN	D	69	95	N	Y	Y	Y	Y
2	SMITH	R	0	5	Y	N	N	N	N
3	WYDEN	D	81	95	N	Y	Y	N	Y
4	DeFAZIO	D	75	90	N	N	Y	Y	Y
5	KOPETSKI	D	63	85	N	N	Y	Y	Y
Pennsylvania									
1	FOGLIETTA	D	56	80	N	Y	Y	Y	Y
2	GRAY	D	X	X	N	Y	Y	X	X
2	BLACKWELL[1]	D	69	90	X	X	X	X	Y
3	BORSKI	D	56	80	Y	Y	N	N	Y
4	KOLTER	D	38	60	N	N	N	N	Y
5	SCHULZE	R	13	10	Y	N	N	N	N
6	YATRON	D	44	70	N	N	N	N	Y
7	WELDON	R	38	25	Y	Y	N	N	N
8	KOSTMAYER	D	88	95	N	Y	Y	Y	Y
9	SHUSTER	R	0	5	Y	N	N	N	N
10	McDADE	R	13	15	Y	Y	N	N	N
11	KANJORSKI	D	50	80	N	N	N	N	Y
12	MURTHA	D	25	65	Y	N	N	N	Y
13	COUGHLIN	R	6	25	Y	Y	Y	N	N
14	COYNE	D	63	95	N	Y	Y	N	Y
15	RITTER	R	13	20	Y	N	N	N	N
16	WALKER	R	6	10	Y	N	N	N	N
17	GEKAS	R	19	15	Y	N	N	N	N
18	SANTORUM	R	19	20	Y	N	N	N	N
19	GOODLING	R	19	10	Y	Y	N	Y	N
20	GAYDOS	D	31	60	N	Y	N	N	N
21	RIDGE	R	19	30	Y	N	Y	N	Y
22	MURPHY	D	50	65	N	N	N	N	N
23	CLINGER	R	13	10	Y	N	N	N	N
Rhode Island									
1	MACHTLEY	R	88	55	Y	Y	Y	N	Y
2	REED	D	94	90	N	Y	Y	N	Y
South Carolina									
1	RAVENEL	R	69	40	Y	N	N	N	N
2	SPENCE	R	6	15	Y	N	N	N	N
3	DERRICK	D	44	80	Y	Y	Y	N	Y
4	PATTERSON	D	38	50	Y	N	Y	N	Y
5	SPRATT	D	56	75	Y	Y	Y	N	Y
6	TALLON	D	25	75	Y	N	N	N	Y
South Dakota									
	JOHNSON	D	69	70	N	N	Y	N	Y
Tennessee									
1	QUILLEN	R	6	5	Y	N	N	N	N
2	DUNCAN	R	6	25	Y	N	N	N	Y
3	LLOYD	D	25	45	Y	Y	N	N	Y
4	COOPER	D	63	70	Y	Y	Y	N	Y
5	CLEMENT	D	38	65	Y	Y	Y	N	Y
6	GORDON	D	56	70	Y	Y	Y	N	Y
7	SUNDQUIST	R	6	5	Y	N	N	N	N
8	TANNER	D	25	65	Y	N	Y	N	Y
9	FORD	D	63	85	N	Y	Y	Y	Y

				1.	**2.**	**3.**	**4.**	**5.**	**6.**	**7.**
Texas										
1	CHAPMAN	D		13	75	Y	Y	Y	N	Y
2	WILSON	D		31	65	Y	N	Y	N	X
3	BARTLETT	D		X	X	Y	X	X	X	X
3	JOHNSON[2]	R		0	10	X	X	N	N	N
4	HALL	D		0	40	Y	N	N	N	N
5	BRYANT	D		75	80	N	Y	Y	N	Y
6	BARTON	R		0	5	Y	N	N	N	N
7	ARCHER	R		13	0	Y	N	N	N	N
8	FIELDS	R		0	5	Y	N	N	N	N
9	BROOKS	D		31	75	Y	N	Y	N	Y
10	PICKLE	D		38	65	N	Y	Y	N	Y
11	EDWARDS	D		25	55	Y	N	Y	N	Y
12	GEREN	D		13	45	Y	N	Y	N	N
13	SARPALIUS	D		6	40	Y	N	N	N	N
14	LAUGHLIN	D		19	45	Y	N	N	N	Y
15	De La GARZA	D		31	70	Y	N	N	N	Y
16	COLEMAN	D		69	85	N	N	Y	N	Y
17	STENHOLM	D		0	30	Y	Y	N	N	Y
18	WASHINGTON	D		88	90	N	Y	Y	Y	Y
19	COMBEST	R		0	10	Y	N	N	N	N
20	GONZALEZ	D		63	80	N	Y	Y	N	Y
21	SMITH	R		13	20	Y	N	N	N	N
22	DeLAY	R		0	5	Y	N	N	N	N
23	BUSTAMANTE	D		31	75	N	N	Y	N	Y
24	FROST	D		56	75	Y	Y	Y	N	N
25	ANDREWS	D		38	70	Y	Y	Y	N	Y
26	ARMEY	R		0	0	Y	N	N	N	N
27	ORTIZ	D		19	60	Y	N	N	N	Y
Utah										
1	HANSEN	R		6	5	Y	N	N	N	N
2	OWENS	D		94	70	N	Y	Y	N	Y
3	ORTON	D		25	55	Y	N	N	N	Y
Vermont										
	SANDERS	I		100	95	N	N	Y	Y	Y
Virginia										
1	BATEMAN	R		6	10	Y	Y	N	N	N
2	PICKETT	D		19	35	Y	N	Y	N	N
3	BLILEY	R		0	15	Y	N	N	N	N
4	SISISKY	D		13	55	Y	N	Y	N	N
5	PAYNE	D		38	65	Y	N	Y	N	Y
6	OLIN	D		31	45	N	N	Y	Y	N
7	SLAUGHTER	R		X	X	Y	Y	N	X	X
7	ALLEN[3]	R		13	15	X	X	X	X	N
8	MORAN	D		63	80	N	Y	Y	N	Y
9	BOUCHER	D		44	90	N	N	Y	N	Y
10	WOLF	R		13	20	Y	Y	N	N	N
Washington										
1	MILLER	R		25	45	Y	Y	Y	N	Y
2	SWIFT	D		31	90	N	Y	Y	Y	Y
3	UNSOELD	D		81	90	N	N	Y	Y	Y
4	MORRISON	R		25	55	Y	Y	Y	N	Y
5	FOLEY	D		*	*	N	*	*	*	*
6	DICKS	D		44	80	N	Y	Y	N	Y

			1.	2.	3.	4.	5.	6.	7.
Washington (cont.)									
7	McDERMOTT	D	81	95	N	Y	Y	Y	Y
8	CHANDLER	R	13	20	Y	Y	Y	N	N
West Virginia									
1	MOLLOHAN	D	38	70	Y	N	N	Y	Y
2	STAGGERS	D	50	65	N	N	N	Y	Y
3	WISE	D	44	80	N	N	Y	Y	Y
4	RAHALL	D	63	70	Y	N	N	Y	Y
Wisconsin									
1	ASPIN	D	63	90	Y	Y	Y	N	Y
2	KLUG	R	50	40	Y	Y	Y	Y	Y
3	GUNDERSON	R	25	40	Y	N	Y	N	N
4	KLECZKA	D	38	80	N	Y	N	Y	Y
5	MOODY	D	81	90	N	Y	Y	Y	Y
6	PETRI	R	44	25	Y	N	N	N	Y
7	OBEY	D	73	100	N	N	Y	Y	Y
8	ROTH	R	13	15	Y	N	N	N	N
9	SENSENBRENNER	R	25	15	Y	Y	N	N	N
Wyoming									
	THOMAS	R	0	20	Y	N	N	N	N

			8.
Alabama			
1	CALLAHAN	R	Y
2	DICKINSON	R	Y
3	BROWDER	D	Y
4	BEVIL	D	Y
5	FLIPPO	D	Y
6	ERDREICH	D	Y
7	HARRIS	D	Y
Alaska			
	YOUNG	R	Y
Arizona			
1	RHODES	R	Y
2	UDALL	D	N
3	STUMP	R	Y
4	KYL	R	Y
5	KOLBE	R	N
Arkansas			
1	ALEXANDER	D	Y
2	ROBINSON	R	Y
3	HAMMERSCHMIDT	R	Y
4	ANTHONY	D	N
California			
1	BOSCO	R	N
2	HERGER	R	Y
3	MATSUI	D	N
4	FAZIO	D	N

Continued

			8.
California (cont.)			
5	PELOSI	D	N
6	BOXER	D	N
7	MILLER	D	N
8	DELLUMS	D	N
9	STARK	D	N
10	EDWARDS	D	N
11	LANTOS	D	N
12	CAMPBELL	R	Y
13	MINETA	D	N
14	SHUMWAY	R	Y
15	CONDIT	D	Y
16	PANETTA	D	N
17	PASHAYAN	R	Y
18	LEHMAN	D	N
19	LAGOMARSINO	R	Y
20	THOMAS	R	Y
21	GALLEGLY	R	Y
22	MOORHEAD	R	Y
23	BEILENSON	D	N
24	WAXMAN	D	N
25	ROYBAL	D	N
26	BERMAN	D	N
27	LEVINE	D	N
28	DIXON	D	N
29	HAWKINS	D	N
30	MARTINEZ	D	Y
31	DYMALLY	D	N
32	ANDERSON	D	N

California (cont.)

33	DREIER	R	Y
34	TORRES	D	N
35	LEWIS	R	Y
36	BROWN	D	N
37	McCANDLESS	R	Y
38	DORNAN	R	Y
39	DANNEMEYER	R	Y
40	COX	R	Y
41	LOWERY	R	Y
42	ROHRABACHER	R	Y
43	PACKARD	R	Y
44	BATES	D	N
45	HUNTER	R	Y

Colorado

1	SCHROEDER	D	N
2	SKAGGS	D	N
3	CAMPBELL	D	Y
4	BROWN	R	Y
5	HEFLEY	R	Y
6	SCHAEFER	R	Y

Connecticut

1	KENNELLY	D	N
2	GEJDENSON	D	N
3	MORRISON	D	N
4	SHAYS	R	N
5	ROWLAND	R	Y
6	JOHNSON	R	N

Delaware

	CARPER	D	N

Florida

1	HUTTO	D	Y
2	GRANT	R	Y
3	BENNETT	D	Y
4	JAMES	R	Y
5	McCOLLUM	R	Y
6	STEARNS	R	Y
7	GIBBONS	D	N
8	YOUNG	R	Y
9	BILIRAKIS	R	Y
10	IRELAND	R	Y
11	NELSON	D	Y
12	LEWIS	R	Y
13	GOSS	R	Y
14	JOHNSTON	D	N
15	SHAW	R	Y
16	SMITH	D	N
17	LEHMAN	D	N
18	ROS-LEHTINEN	R	Y
19	FASCELL	D	N

Georgia

1	THOMAS	D	Y
2	HATCHER	D	Y

Georgia (cont.)

3	RAY	D	Y
4	JONES	D	N
5	LEWIS	D	N
6	GINGRICH	R	Y
7	DARDEN	D	Y
8	ROWLAND	D	Y
9	JENKINS	D	Y
10	BARNARD	D	Y

Hawaii

1	SAIKI	R	Y
2	VACANCY		

Idaho

1	CRAIG	R	Y
2	STALLINGS	D	Y

Illinois

1	HAYES	D	N
2	SAVAGE	D	N
3	RUSSO	D	N
4	SANGMEISTER	D	Y
5	LIPINSKI	D	Y
6	HYDE	R	Y
7	COLLINS	D	N
8	ROSTENKOWSKI	D	N
9	YATES	D	N
10	PORTER	R	N
11	ANNUNZIO	D	Y
12	CRANE	R	Y
13	FAWELL	R	Y
14	HASTERT	R	Y
15	MADIGAN	R	Y
16	MARTIN	R	Y
17	EVANS	D	N
18	MICHEL	R	Y
19	BRUCE	D	N
20	DURBIN	D	N
21	COSTELLO	D	Y
22	POSHARD	D	N

Indiana

1	VISCLOSKY	D	N
2	SHARP	D	Y
3	HILER	R	Y
4	LONG	D	Y
5	JONTZ	D	N
6	BURTON	R	Y
7	MYERS	R	Y
8	McCLOSKEY	D	N
9	HAMILTON	D	N
10	JACOBS	D	Y

Iowa

1	LEACH	R	N
2	TAUKE	R	Y
3	NAGLE	D	N

Iowa (cont.)			
4	SMITH	D	N
5	LIGHTFOOT	R	Y
6	GRANDY	R	N

Kansas			
1	ROBERTS	R	Y
2	SLATTERY	D	N
3	MEYERS	R	Y
4	GLICKMAN	D	N
5	WHITTAKER	R	Y

Kentucky			
1	HUBBARD	D	Y
2	NATCHER	D	Y
3	MAZZOLI	D	Y
4	BUNNING	R	Y
5	ROGERS	R	Y
6	HOPKINS	R	Y
7	PERKINS	D	Y

Louisiana			
1	LIVINGSTON	R	Y
2	BOGGS	D	N
3	TAUZIN	D	Y
4	McCRERY	R	Y
5	HUCKABY	D	Y
6	BAKER	R	Y
7	HAYES	D	Y
8	HOLLOWAY	R	Y

Maine			
1	BRENNAN	D	N
2	SNOWE	R	Y

Maryland			
1	DYSON	D	Y
2	BENTLEY	R	Y
3	CARDIN	D	N
4	McMILLEN	D	Y
5	HOYER	D	N
6	BYRON	D	Y
7	MFUME	D	N
8	MORELLA	R	N

Massachusetts			
1	CONTE	R	N
2	NEAL	D	Y
3	EARLY	D	N
4	FRANK	D	N
5	ATKINS	D	N
6	MAVROULES	D	N
7	MARKEY	D	N
8	KENNEDY	D	N
9	MOAKLEY	D	Y
10	STUDDS	D	N
11	DONNELLY	D	Y

Michigan			
1	CONYERS	D	N
2	PURSELL	R	Y
3	WOLPE	D	N
4	UPTON	R	Y
5	HENRY	R	N
6	CARR	D	N
7	KILDEE	D	N
8	TRAYLER	D	Y
9	VANDERJAGT	R	Y
10	SCHUETTE	R	Y
11	DAVIS	R	Y
12	BONIOR	D	N
13	CROCKETT	D	N
14	HERTEL	D	N
15	FORD	D	N
16	DINGELL	D	N
17	LEVIN	D	N
18	BROOMFIELD	R	Y

Minnesota			
1	PENNY	D	N
2	WEBER	R	Y
3	FRENZEL	R	Y
4	VENTO	D	N
5	SABO	D	N
6	SIKORSKI	D	N
7	STRANGELAND	R	Y
8	OBERSTAR	D	N

Mississippi			
1	WHITTEN	D	Y
2	ESPY	D	N
3	MONTGOMERY	D	Y
4	PARKER	D	Y
5	TAYLOR	D	Y

Missouri			
1	CLAY	D	N
2	BUECHNER	R	Y
3	GEPHARDT	D	N
4	SKELTON	D	Y
5	WHEAT	D	N
6	COLEMAN	R	N
7	HANCOCK	R	Y
8	EMERSON	R	Y
9	VOLKMER	D	Y

Montana			
1	WILLIAMS	D	N
2	MARLENEE	R	Y

Nebraska			
1	BEREUTER	R	Y
2	HOAGLAND	D	N
3	SMITH	R	Y

Nevada			
1	BILBRAY	D	Y
2	VUCANOVICH	R	Y

New Hampshire			
1	SMITH	R	Y
2	DOUGLAS	R	Y

New Jersey			
1	VACANCY		
2	HUGHES	D	N
3	PALLONE	D	Y
4	SMITH	R	Y
5	ROUKEMA	R	Y
6	DWYER	D	N
7	RINALDO	R	Y
8	ROE	D	Y
9	TORRICELLI	D	N
10	PAYNE	D	N
11	GALLO	R	Y
12	COURTER	R	Y
13	SAXTON	R	Y
14	GUARINI	D	Y

New Mexico			
1	SCHIFF	R	Y
2	SKEEN	R	Y
3	RICHARDSON	D	Y

New York			
1	HOCHBRUECKNER	D	Y
2	DOWNEY	D	N
3	MRAZEK	D	N
4	LENT	R	Y
5	McGRATH	R	Y
6	FLAKE	D	N
7	ACKERMAN	D	N
8	SCHEUER	D	N
9	MANTON	D	Y
10	SCHUMER	D	N
11	TOWNS	D	N
12	OWENS	D	N
13	SOLARZ	D	N
14	MOLINARI	R	Y
15	GREEN	R	N
16	RANGEL	D	X
17	WEISS	D	N
18	SERRANO	D	N
19	ENGEL	D	N
20	LOWEY	D	N
21	FISH	R	Y
22	GILMAN	R	Y
23	McNULTY	D	Y
24	SOLOMON	R	Y
25	BOEHLERT	R	Y
26	MARTIN	R	Y
27	WALSH	R	Y
28	McHUGH	D	N

New York (cont.)			
29	HORTON	R	Y
30	SLAUGHTER	D	N
31	PAXON	R	Y
32	LaFALCE	D	N
33	NOWAK	D	N
34	HOUGHTON	R	N

North Carolina			
1	JONES	D	Y
2	VALENTINE	D	N
3	LANCASTER	D	Y
4	PRICE	D	N
5	NEAL	D	N
6	COBLE	R	Y
7	ROSE	D	N
8	HEFNER	D	Y
9	McMILLAN	R	Y
10	BALLENGER	R	Y
11	CLARKE	D	Y

North Dakota			
	DORGAN	D	Y

Ohio			
1	LUKEN	D	Y
2	GRADISON	R	Y
3	HALL	D	N
4	OXLEY	R	Y
5	GILLMOR	R	Y
6	McEWEN	R	Y
7	DeWINE	R	Y
8	LUKENS	R	Y
9	KAPTUR	D	N
10	MILLER	R	Y
11	ECKART	D	Y
12	KASICH	R	Y
13	PEASE	D	N
14	SAWYER	D	N
15	WYLIE	R	Y
16	REGULA	R	Y
17	TRAFICANT	D	Y
18	APPLEGATE	D	Y
19	FEIGHAN	D	N
20	OAKAR	D	N
21	STOKES	D	N

Oklahoma			
1	INHOFE	R	Y
2	SYNAR	D	N
3	WATKINS	D	Y
4	McCURDY	D	N
5	EDWARDS	R	Y
6	ENGLISH	D	Y

Oregon			
1	AuCOIN	D	N
2	SMITH, B.	R	Y

Oregon (cont.)

3	WYDEN	D	N
4	DeFAZIO	D	N
5	SMITH, D.	R	Y

Pennsylvania

1	FOGLIETTA	D	N
2	GRAY	D	N
3	BORSKI	D	N
4	KOLTER	D	Y
5	SCHULZE	R	Y
6	YATRON	D	Y
7	WELDON	R	Y
8	KOSTMAYER	D	N
9	SHUSTER	R	Y
10	McDADE	R	Y
11	KANJORSKI	D	Y
12	MURTHA	D	Y
13	COUGHLIN	R	Y
14	COYNE	D	N
15	RITTER	R	Y
16	WALKER	R	Y
17	GEKAS	R	Y
18	WALGREN	D	N
19	GOODLING	R	Y
20	GAYDOS	D	Y
21	RIDGE	R	Y
22	MURPHY	D	Y
23	CLINGER	R	N

Rhode Island

1	MACHTLEY	R	Y
2	SCHNEIDER	R	N

South Carolina

1	RAVENEL	R	Y
2	SPENCE	R	Y
3	DERRICK	D	Y
4	PATTERSON	D	Y
5	SPRATT	D	N
6	TALLON	D	N

South Dakota

	JOHNSON	D	Y

Tennessee

1	QUILLEN	R	Y
2	DUNCAN	R	Y
3	LLOYD	D	Y
4	COOPER	D	N
5	CLEMENT	D	Y
6	GORDON	D	N
7	SUNDQUIST	R	Y
8	TANNER	D	N
9	FORD	D	N

Texas

1	CHAPMAN	D	Y

Texas (cont.)

2	WILSON	D	Y
3	BARTLETT	R	Y
4	HALL	D	X
5	BRYANT	D	N
6	BARTON	R	Y
7	ARCHER	R	Y
8	FIELDS	R	Y
9	BROOKS	D	Y
10	PICKLE	D	N
11	LEATH	D	Y
12	GEREN	D	Y
13	SARPALIUS	D	Y
14	LAUGHLIN	D	Y
15	De La GARZA	D	Y
16	COLEMAN	D	N
17	STENHOLM	D	N
18	WASHINGTON	D	N
19	COMBEST	R	Y
20	GONZALEZ	D	N
21	SMITH	R	Y
22	DeLAY	R	Y
23	BUSTAMANTE	D	Y
24	FROST	D	N
25	ANDREWS	D	Y
26	ARMEY	R	Y
27	ORTIZ	D	Y

Utah

1	HANSEN	R	Y
2	OWENS	D	N
3	NIELSON	R	Y

Vermont

	SMITH	R	N

Virginia

1	BATEMAN	R	Y
2	PICKETT	D	Y
3	BLILEY	R	Y
4	SISISKY	D	Y
5	PAYNE	D	Y
6	OLIN	D	Y
7	SLAUGHTER	R	Y
8	PARRIS	R	Y
9	BOUCHER	D	N
10	WOLF	R	Y

Washington

1	MILLER	R	Y
2	SWIFT	D	N
3	UNSOELD	D	N
4	MORRISON	R	Y
5	FOLEY	D	N
6	DICKS	D	N
7	McDERMOTT	D	N
8	CHANDLER	R	N

West Virginia

1	MOLLOHAN	D	Y
2	STAGGERS	D	Y
3	WISE	D	Y
4	RAHALL	D	Y

Wisconsin

1	ASPIN	D	N
2	KASTENMEIER	D	N
3	GUNDERSON	R	Y
4	KLECZKA	D	N
5	MOODY	D	N
6	PETRI	R	N
7	OBEY	D	N
8	ROTH	R	Y
9	SENSENBRENNER	R	Y

Wyoming

	THOMAS	R	Y

9.

Alabama

1	CALLAHAN	R	N
2	EVERETT	R	N
3	BROWDER	D	N
4	BEVILL	D	Y
5	CRAMER	D	Y
6	BACHUS	R	N
7	HILLIARD	D	Y

Alaska

	YOUNG	R	Y

Arizona

1	COPPERSMITH	D	Y
2	PASTOR	D	Y
3	STUMP	R	N
4	KYL	R	N
5	KOLBE	R	N
6	ENGLISH	D	Y

Arkansas

1	LAMBERT	D	Y
2	THORNTON	D	Y
3	HUTCHINSON	R	N
4	DICKEY	R	N

California

1	HAMBURG	D	Y
2	HERGER	R	N
3	FAZIO	D	Y
4	DOOLITTLE	R	N
5	MATSUI	D	Y

California (cont.)

6	WOOLSEY	D	Y
7	MILLER	D	Y
8	PELOSI	D	Y
9	DELLUMS	D	Y
10	BAKER	R	N
11	POMBO	R	N
12	LANTOS	D	Y
13	STARK	D	Y
14	ESHOO	D	Y
15	MINETA	D	Y
16	EDWARDS	D	Y
17	VACANCY		X
18	CONDIT	D	Y
19	LEHMAN	D	Y
20	DOOLEY	D	Y
21	THOMAS	R	N
22	HUFFINGTON	R	Y
23	GALLEGLY	R	N
24	BEILENSON	D	Y
25	McKEON	R	N
26	BERMAN	D	Y
27	MOORHEAD	R	N
28	DREIER	R	N
29	WAXMAN	D	Y
30	BECERRA	D	Y
31	MARTINEZ	D	Y
32	DIXON	D	Y
33	ROYBAL-ALLARD	D	Y
34	TORRES	D	Y
35	WATERS	D	Y
36	HARMAN	D	Y
37	TUCKER	D	Y
38	HORN	R	Y
39	ROYCE	R	N
40	LEWIS	R	N
41	KIM	R	N
42	BROWN	D	Y
43	CALVERT	R	N
44	McCANDLESS	R	N
45	ROHRABACHER	R	N
46	DORNAN	R	N
47	COX	R	N
48	PACKARD	R	N
49	SCHENK	D	Y
50	FILNER	D	Y
51	CUNNINGHAM	R	N
52	HUNTER	R	N

Colorado

1	SCHROEDER	D	Y
2	SKAGGS	D	Y
3	McINNIS	R	N
4	ALLARD	R	N
5	HEFLEY	R	N
6	SCHAEFER	R	N

Connecticut

1	KENNELLY	D	Y
2	GEJDENSON	D	Y
3	DeLAURO	D	Y
4	SHAYS	R	Y
5	FRANKS	R	N
6	JOHNSON	R	Y

Delaware

| | CASTLE | R | Y |

Florida

1	HUTTO	D	N
2	PETERSON	D	Y
3	BROWN	D	Y
4	FOWLER	R	N
5	THURMAN	D	Y
6	STEARNS	R	N
7	MICA	R	N
8	McCOLLUM	R	N
9	BILIRAKIS	R	N
10	YOUNG	R	Y
11	GIBBONS	D	Y
12	CANADY	R	N
13	MILLER	R	N
14	GOSS	R	N
15	BACCHUS	D	Y
16	LEWIS	R	N
17	MEEK	D	Y
18	ROS-LEHTINEN	R	Y
19	JOHNSTON	D	Y
20	DEUTSCH	D	Y
21	DIAZ-BALART	R	Y
22	SHAW	R	N
23	HASTINGS	D	Y

Georgia

1	KINGSTON	R	N
2	BISHOP	D	Y
3	COLLINS	R	N
4	LINDER	R	N
5	LEWIS	D	Y
6	GINGRICH	R	N
7	DARDEN	D	N
8	ROWLAND	D	N
9	DEAL	D	N
10	JOHNSON	D	N
11	McKINNEY	D	Y

Hawaii

| 1 | ABERCROMBIE | D | Y |
| 2 | MINK | D | Y |

Idaho

| 1 | LAROCCO | D | N |
| 2 | CRAPO | R | N |

Illinois

1	RUSH	D	Y
2	REYNOLDS	D	Y
3	LIPINSKI	D	Y
4	GUTIERREZ	D	Y
5	ROSTENKOWSKI	D	Y
6	HYDE	R	Y
7	COLLINS	D	Y
8	CRANE	R	N
9	YATES	D	Y
10	PORTER	R	N
11	SANGMEISTER	D	Y
12	COSTELLO	D	Y
13	FAWELL	R	N
14	HASTERT	R	N
15	EWING	R	N
16	MANZULLO	R	N
17	EVANS	D	Y
18	MICHEL	R	N
19	POSHARD	D	Y
20	DURBIN	D	Y

Indiana

1	VISCLOSKY	D	Y
2	SHARP	D	Y
3	ROEMER	D	Y
4	LONG	D	Y
5	BUYER	R	N
6	BURTON	R	N
7	MYERS	R	N
8	McCLOSKEY	D	Y
9	HAMILTON	D	N
10	JACOBS	D	Y

Iowa

1	LEACH	R	Y
2	NUSSLE	R	N
3	LIGHTFOOT	R	N
4	SMITH	D	Y
5	GRANDY	R	N

Kansas

1	ROBERTS	R	N
2	SLATTERY	D	N
3	MEYERS	R	N
4	GLICKMAN	D	N

Kentucky

1	BARLOW	D	Y
2	NATCHER	D	Y
3	MAZZOLI	D	Y
4	BUNNING	R	N
5	ROGERS	R	N
6	BAESLER	D	Y

Louisiana

| 1 | LIVINGSTON | R | N |

Louisiana (cont.)

2	JEFFERSON	D	Y
3	TAUZIN	D	N
4	FIELDS	D	Y
5	McCRERY	R	N
6	BAKER	R	N
7	HAYES	D	N

Maine

1	ANDREWS	D	Y
2	SNOWE	R	Y

Maryland

1	GILCHRIST	R	N
2	BENTLEY	R	N
3	CARDIN	D	Y
4	WYNN	D	Y
5	HOYER	D	Y
6	BARTLETT	R	N
7	MFUME	D	Y
8	MORELLA	R	Y

Massachusetts

1	OLVER	D	Y
2	NEAL	D	Y
3	BLUTE	R	Y
4	FRANK	D	Y
5	MEEHAN	D	Y
6	TORKILDSEN	R	N
7	MARKEY	D	Y
8	KENNEDY	D	Y
9	MOAKLEY	D	Y
10	STUDDS	D	Y

Michigan

1	STUPAK	D	Y
2	HOEKSTRA	R	N
3	HENRY	R	X
4	CAMP	R	N
5	BARCIA	D	Y
6	UPTON	R	N
7	SMITH	R	N
8	CARR	D	N
9	KILDEE	D	Y
10	BONIOR	D	Y
11	KNOLLENBERG	R	N
12	LEVIN	D	Y
13	FORD	D	Y
14	CONYERS	D	Y
15	COLLINS	D	Y
16	DINGELL	D	Y

Minnesota

1	PERRY	R	N
2	MINGE	R	Y
3	RAMSTAD	D	Y
4	VENTO	R	Y

Minnesota (cont.)

5	SABO	D	Y
6	GRAMS	R	N
7	PETERSON	D	Y
8	OBERSTAR	D	Y

Mississippi

1	WHITTEN	D	Y
2	VACANCY		
3	MONTGOMERY	D	N
4	PARKER	D	N
5	TAYLOR	D	Y

Missouri

1	CLAY	D	Y
2	TALENT	R	N
3	GEPHARDT	D	Y
4	SKELTON	D	N
5	WHEAT	D	Y
6	DANNER	D	Y
7	HANCOCK	R	N
8	EMERSON	R	N
9	VOLKMER	D	Y

Montana

	WILLIAMS	D	Y

Nebraska

1	BEREUTER	R	N
2	HOAGLAND	D	Y
3	BARRETT	R	N

Nevada

1	BILBRAY	D	Y
2	VUCANOVICH	R	N

New Hampshire

1	ZELIFF	R	N
2	SWETT	D	Y

New Jersey

1	ANDREWS	D	Y
2	HUGHES	D	Y
3	SAXTON	R	Y
4	SMITH	R	Y
5	ROUKEMA	R	Y
6	PALLONE	D	Y
7	FRANKS	R	Y
8	KLEIN	D	Y
9	TORRICELLI	D	Y
10	PAYNE	D	Y
11	GALLO	R	N
12	ZIMMER	R	Y
13	MENENDEZ	D	Y

New Mexico

1	SCHIFF	R	N
2	SKEEN	R	N

New Mexico (cont.)

3	RICHARDSON	D	Y

New York

1	HOCHBRUECKNER	D	Y
2	LAZIO	R	Y
3	KING	R	N
4	LEVY	R	N
5	ACKERMAN	D	Y
6	FLAKE	D	Y
7	MANTON	D	Y
8	NADLER	D	Y
9	SCHUMER	D	Y
10	TOWNS	D	Y
11	OWENS	D	Y
12	VELAZQUEZ	D	Y
13	MOLINARI	R	Y
14	MALONEY	D	Y
15	RANGEL	D	Y
16	SERRANO	D	Y
17	ENGEL	D	Y
18	LOWEY	D	Y
19	FISH	R	Y
20	GILMAN	R	Y
21	McNULTY	D	Y
22	SOLOMON	R	Y
23	BOEHLERT	R	Y
24	McHUGH	R	Y
25	WALSH	R	Y
26	HINCHEY	D	Y
27	PAXON	R	N
28	SLAUGHTER	D	Y
29	LaFALCE	D	Y
30	QUINN	R	Y
31	HOUGHTON	R	N

North Carolina

1	CLAYTON	D	Y
2	VALENTINE	D	N
3	LANCASTER	D	N
4	PRICE	D	Y
5	NEAL	D	Y
6	COBLE	R	N
7	ROSE	D	Y
8	HEFNER	D	Y
9	McMILLAN	R	N
10	BALLENGER	R	N
11	TAYLOR	R	N
12	WATT	D	Y

North Dakota

	POMEROY	D	Y

Ohio

1	MANN	D	Y
2	VACANCY		
3	HALL	D	Y

Ohio (cont.)

4	OXLEY	R	N
5	GILLMAR	R	Y
6	STRICKLAND	D	Y
7	HOBSON	R	N
8	BOEHNER	R	N
9	KAPTUR	D	Y
10	HOKE	R	Y
11	STOKES	D	Y
12	KASICH	R	N
13	BROWN	D	Y
14	SAWYER	D	Y
15	PRYCE	R	N
16	REGULA	R	Y
17	TRAFICANT	D	Y
18	APPLEGATE	D	Y
19	FINGERHUT	D	Y

Oklahoma

1	INHOFE	R	N
2	SYNAR	D	Y
3	BREWSTER	D	N
4	McCURDY	D	Y
5	ISTOOK	R	N
6	ENGLISH	D	Y

Oregon

1	FURSE	D	N
2	SMITH	R	N
3	WYDEN	D	Y
4	DeFAZIO	D	Y
5	KOPETSKI	D	Y

Pennsylvania

1	FOGLIETTA	D	Y
2	BLACKWELL	D	Y
3	BORSKI	D	Y
4	KLINK	D	Y
5	CLINGER	R	N
6	HOLDEN	D	Y
7	WELDON	R	Y
8	GREENWOOD	R	N
9	SHUSTER	R	N
10	McDADE	R	Y
11	KANJORSKI	D	Y
12	MURTHA	D	Y
13	MARGOLIES-MEZV.	D	Y
14	COYNE	D	Y
15	McHALE	D	Y
16	WALKER	R	N
17	GEKAS	R	N
18	SANTORUM	R	N
19	GOODLING	R	N
20	MURPHY	D	Y
21	RIDGE	R	N

Rhode Island			
1	MACHTLEY	R	Y
2	REED	D	Y

South Carolina			
1	RAVENEL	R	Y
2	SPENCE	R	N
3	DERRICK	D	Y
4	INGLIS	R	N
5	SPRATT	D	Y
6	CLYBURN	D	Y

South Dakota			
	JOHNSON	D	Y

Tennessee			
1	QUILLEN	R	N
2	DUNCAN	R	N
3	LLOYD	D	Y
4	COOPER	D	Y
5	CLEMENT	D	Y
6	GORDON	D	Y
7	SUNDQUIST	R	N
8	TANNER	D	Y
9	FORD	D	X

Texas			
1	CHAPMAN	D	Y
2	WILSON	D	Y
3	JOHNSON	R	N
4	HALL	D	N
5	BRYANT	D	Y
6	BARTON	R	N
7	ARCHER	R	N
8	FIELDS	R	N
9	BROOKS	D	Y
10	PICKLE	D	Y
11	EDWARDS	D	Y
12	GEREN	D	N
13	SARPALIUS	D	N
14	LAUGHLIN	D	N
15	De la GARZA	D	Y
16	COLEMAN	D	Y
17	STENHOLM	D	N
18	WASHINGTON	D	Y
19	COMBEST	R	N
20	GONZALEZ	D	Y
21	SMITH	R	Y
22	DeLAY	R	N
23	BONILLA	R	N
24	FROST	D	Y
25	ANDREWS	D	Y
26	ARMEY	R	N
27	ORTIZ	D	Y
28	TEJEDA	D	Y
29	GREEN	D	Y

Texas (cont.)			
30	JOHNSON	D	Y

Utah			
1	HANSEN	R	N
2	SHEPHERD	D	Y
3	ORTON	D	N

Vermont			
	SANDERS	I	Y

Virginia			
1	BATEMAN	R	N
2	PICKETT	D	N
3	SCOTT	D	Y
4	SISISKY	D	N
5	PAYNE	D	N
6	GOODLATTE	R	N
7	BLILEY	R	N
8	MORAN	D	Y
9	BOUCHER	D	Y
10	WOLF	R	N
11	BYRNE	D	Y

Washington			
1	CANTWELL	D	Y
2	SWIFT	D	Y
3	UNSOELD	D	Y
4	INSLEE	D	Y
5	FOLEY	D	*
6	DICKS	D	Y
7	McDERMOTT	D	Y
8	DUNN	R	N
9	KREIDLER	D	Y

West Virginia			
1	MOLLOHAN	D	Y
2	WISE	D	Y
3	RAHALL	D	Y

Wisconsin			
1	VACANCY		
2	KLUG	R	Y
3	GUNDERSON	R	N
4	KLECZKA	D	Y
5	BARRETT	D	Y
6	PETRI	R	Y
7	OBEY	D	Y
8	ROTH	R	N
9	SENSENBRENNER	R	N

Wyoming			
	THOMAS	R	Y

		10.	11.	12.	13.	14.	15.	16.
Alabama								
HEFLIN	D	8	40	Y	N	N	N	Y
SHELBY	D	17	30	Y	N	Y	N	N
Alaska								
MURKOWSKI	R	8	25	Y	N	N	N	N
STEVENS	R	8	20	Y	N	X	N	N
Arizona								
DeCONCINI	D	17	75	N	N	Y	N	Y
McCAIN	R	8	20	Y	N	N	N	Y
Arkansas								
BUMPERS	D	50	90	N	Y	Y	N	Y
PRYOR	D	42	90	N	X	X	X	Y
California								
CRANSTON	D	83	95	N	Y	Y	Y	Y
SEYMOUR	R	25	10	Y	Y	Y	N	N
Colorado								
BROWN	R	0	20	Y	N	Y	N	N
WIRTH	D	58	60	N	Y	Y	N	Y
Connecticut								
DODD	D	83	75	N	Y	Y	N	Y
LIEBERMAN	D	100	70	Y	Y	Y	N	Y
Delaware								
BIDEN	D	67	100	N	Y	Y	N	Y
ROTH	R	42	25	Y	Y	N	N	N
Florida								
GRAHAM	D	75	75	Y	Y	Y	N	Y
MACK	R	17	10	Y	N	N	N	N
Georgia								
FOWLER	D	83	90	N	Y	Y	Y	Y
NUNN	D	67	65	N	Y	Y	N	Y
Hawaii								
AKAKA	D	92	90	N	Y	Y	Y	Y
INOUYE	D	42	65	N	Y	Y	Y	Y
Idaho								
CRAIG	R	0	0	Y	N	N	N	N
SYMMS	R	0	0	Y	N	N	N	N
Illinois								
DIXON	D	67	55	N	Y	Y	N	Y
SIMON	D	92	95	N	Y	Y	Y	Y
Indiana								
COATS	R	17	10	Y	Y	N	N	N
LUGAR	R	33	10	Y	Y	N	N	N
Iowa								
GRASSLEY	R	25	30	N	N	N	N	N
HARKIN	D	33	85	N	Y	Y	Y	Y

		10.	11.	12.	13.	14.	15.	16.
Kansas								
DOLE	R	0	5	Y	Y	N	N	N
KASSEBAUM	R	33	25	Y	Y	Y	N	N
Kentucky								
FORD	D	17	75	N	Y	N	N	Y
McCONNELL	R	17	15	Y	N	N	N	N
Louisiana								
BREAUX	D	25	60	Y	N	N	N	Y
JOHNSTON	D	25	70	Y	N	N	N	Y
Maine								
COHEN	R	67	40	Y	Y	Y	Y	N
MITCHELL	D	83	95	N	Y	Y	Y	Y
Maryland								
MIKULSKI	D	67	100	N	Y	Y	N	Y
SARBANES	D	92	100	N	Y	Y	Y	Y
Massachusetts								
KENNEDY	D	100	100	N	Y	Y	Y	Y
KERRY	D	92	100	N	Y	Y	Y	Y
Michigan								
LEVIN	D	75	100	N	Y	Y	Y	Y
RIEGLE	D	75	95	N	Y	Y	N	Y
Minnesota								
DURENBERGER	R	50	25	Y	Y	N	Y	Y
WELLSTONE	D	100	100	N	Y	Y	Y	Y
Mississippi								
COCHRAN	R	0	10	Y	N	N	N	N
LOTT	R	0	10	Y	N	N	N	N
Missouri								
BOND	R	8	25	Y	N	N	N	N
DANFORTH	R	8	25	Y	N	N	Y	N
Montana								
BAUCUS	D	58	95	N	N	Y	N	Y
BURNS	R	0	5	Y	N	N	N	N
Nebraska								
EXON	D	42	75	N	Y	N	N	Y
KERREY	D	50	90	N	Y	Y	N	Y
Nevada								
BRYAN	D	67	80	Y	Y	Y	N	Y
REID	D	67	80	Y	Y	N	N	Y
New Hampshire								
RUDMAN	R	25	15	Y	Y	N	N	N
SMITH	R	25	5	Y	N	N	N	N
New Jersey								
BRADLEY	D	83	85	N	Y	Y	N	Y

		10.	11.	12.	13.	14.	15.	16.
New Jersey (cont.)								
LAUTENBERG	D	92	100	N	Y	Y	Y	Y
New Mexico								
BINGAMAN	D	58	75	N	Y	Y	N	Y
DOMENICI	R	0	15	Y	Y	N	N	N
New York								
D'AMATO	R	58	30	Y	Y	N	N	N
MOYNIHAN	D	67	100	N	Y	Y	Y	Y
North Carolina								
HELMS	R	0	5	Y	N	N	N	N
SANFORD	D	67	75	N	Y	Y	N	Y
North Dakota								
BURDICK	D	0	85	N	Y	Y	Y	Y
CONRAD	D	17	90	N	Y	Y	N	Y
Ohio								
GLENN	D	75	80	N	Y	Y	Y	Y
METZENBAUM	D	100	90	N	Y	Y	Y	X
Oklahoma								
BOREN	D	42	60	N	Y	N	N	Y
NICKLES	R	0	0	Y	N	N	N	N
Oregon								
HATFIELD	R	42	70	N	Y	N	Y	N
PACKWOOD	R	25	60	Y	Y	Y	N	N
Pennsylvania								
SPECTER	R	50	65	Y	N	Y	N	N
WOFFORD[4]	D	67	100	Y	Y	Y	N	Y
Rhode Island								
CHAFEE	R	67	40	Y	Y	Y	Y	N
PELL	D	83	80	N	Y	Y	Y	Y
South Carolina								
HOLLINGS	D	42	35	N	N	Y	N	N
THURMOND	R	0	10	Y	Y	N	N	N
South Dakota								
DASCHLE	D	58	95	N	Y	Y	N	Y
PRESSLER	R	8	20	Y	N	N	N	N
Tennessee								
GORE	D	58	60	Y	Y	Y	N	Y
SASSER	D	50	95	N	Y	Y	N	Y
Texas								
BENTSEN	D	50	80	N	Y	Y	N	Y
GRAMM	R	0	0	Y	N	N	N	N
Utah								
GARN	R	0	5	Y	N	N	X	N
HATCH	R	0	5	Y	N	N	N	N

		10.	11.	12.	13.	14.	15.	16.
Vermont								
JEFFORDS	R	75	65	Y	Y	Y	N	Y
LEAHY	D	100	100	N	N	Y	Y	Y
Virginia								
ROBB	D	67	60	Y	Y	Y	N	Y
WARNER	R	8	20	Y	Y	N	N	N
Washington								
ADAMS	D	92	100	N	Y	Y	N	Y
GORTON	R	17	25	Y	Y	Y	N	N
West Virginia								
BYRD	D	42	100	N	Y	Y	N	Y
ROCKEFELLER	D	75	100	N	Y	Y	N	Y
Wisconsin								
KASTEN	R	58	20	Y	Y	N	N	N
KOHL	D	83	95	N	Y	Y	Y	Y
Wyoming								
SIMPSON	R	0	15	Y	N	N	N	N
WALLOP	R	0	10	Y	N	N	N	N

		17.
Alabama		
HEFLIN	D	Y
SHELBY	D	Y
Alaska		
MURKOWSKI	R	Y
STEVENS	R	Y
Arizona		
DeCONCINI	D	Y
McCAIN	R	Y
Arkansas		
BUMPERS	D	N
PRYOR	D	N
California		
CRANSTON	D	N
WILSON	R	Y
Colorado		
WIRTH	D	N
ARMSTRONG	R	Y
Connecticut		
DODD	D	N
LIEBERMAN	D	N
Delaware		
BIDEN	D	N

Continued

		17.
Delaware (cont.)		
ROTH	R	Y
Florida		
GRAHAM	D	Y
MACK	R	Y
Georgia		
FOWLER	D	Y
NUNN	D	Y
Hawaii		
INOUYE	D	N
AKAKA	D	N
Idaho		
McCLURE	R	Y
SYMMS	R	Y
Illinois		
DIXON	D	Y
SIMON	D	N
Indiana		
COATS	R	Y
LUGAR	R	Y
Iowa		
HARKIN	D	N
GRASSLEY	R	Y

Kansas		
DOLE	R	Y
KASSEBAUM	R	Y

Kentucky		
FORD	D	Y
McCONNELL	R	Y

Louisiana		
BREAUX	D	Y
JOHNSTON	D	Y

Maine		
MITCHELL	D	N
COHEN	R	Y

Maryland		
MIKULSKI	D	N
SARBANES	D	N

Massachusetts		
KENNEDY	D	N
KERRY	D	N

Michigan		
LEVIN	D	N
RIEGLE	D	N

Minnesota		
BOSCHWITZ	R	Y
DURENBERGER	R	N

Mississippi		
COCHRAN	R	Y
LOTT	R	Y

Missouri		
BOND	R	Y
DANFORTH	R	N

Montana		
BAUCUS	D	Y
BURNS	R	Y

Nebraska		
EXON	D	Y
KERREY	D	N

Nevada		
BRYAN	D	Y
REID	D	Y

New Hampshire		
HUMPHREY	R	N
RUDMAN	R	N

New Jersey		
BRADLEY	D	N
LAUTENBERG	D	N

New Mexico		
BINGAMAN	D	N
DOMENICI	R	Y

New York		
MOYNIHAN	D	N
D'AMATO	R	Y

North Carolina		
SANFORD	D	N
HELMS	R	Y

North Dakota		
BURDICK	D	Y
CONRAD	D	Y

Ohio		
GLENN	D	N
METZENBAUM	D	N

Oklahoma		
BOREN	D	N
NICKLES	R	Y

Oregon		
HATFIELD	R	Y
PACKWOOD	R	N

Pennsylvania		
HEINZ	R	Y
SPECTER	R	Y

Rhode Island		
PELL	D	N
CHAFEE	R	N

South Carolina		
HOLLINGS	D	Y
THURMOND	R	Y

South Dakota		
DASCHLE	D	N
PRESSLER	R	Y

Tennessee		
GORE	D	N
SASSER	D	N

Texas		
BENTSEN	D	Y
GRAMM	R	Y

Utah		
GARN	R	Y
HATCH	R	Y

Vermont		
LEAHY	D	N
JEFFORDS	R	N

Virginia		
ROBB	D	N
WARNER	R	Y

Washington		
ADAMS	D	N
GORTON	R	Y

West Virginia		
BYRD	D	Y
ROCKEFELLER	D	Y

Wisconsin		
KOHL	D	N
KASTEN	R	Y

Wyoming		
SIMPSON	R	Y
WALLOP	R	Y

Alabama		
HEFLIN	D	N
SHELBY	D	Y

Alaska		
MURKOWSKI	R	Y
STEVENS	R	Y

Arizona		
DeCONCINI	D	Y
McCAIN	R	Y

Arkansas		
BUMPERS	D	Y
PRYOR	D	Y

California		
BOXER	D	Y
FEINSTEIN	D	Y

Colorado		
CAMPBELL	D	Y
BROWN	R	N

Connecticut		
DODD	D	Y
LIEBERMAN	D	Y

Delaware		
BIDEN	D	Y
ROTH	R	Y

Florida		
GRAHAM	D	Y
MACK	R	N

Georgia		
NUNN	D	Y
COVERDELL	R	N

Hawaii		
AKAKA	D	Y
INOUYE	D	Y

Idaho		
CRAIG	R	N
KEMPTHORNE	R	N

Illinois		
MOSELEY-BRAUN	D	Y
SIMON	D	Y

Indiana		
COATS	R	Y
LUGAR	R	N

Iowa		
HARKIN	D	Y
GRASSLEY	R	N

Kansas		
DOLE	R	N
KASSEBAUM	R	N

Kentucky		
FORD	D	Y
McCONNELL	R	N

Louisiana		
BREAUX	D	Y
JOHNSTON	D	Y

Maine		
MITCHELL	D	Y
COHEN	R	Y

Maryland		
MIKULSKI	D	Y
SARBANES	D	Y

Massachusetts		
KENNEDY	D	Y
KERRY	D	Y

Michigan		
LEVIN	D	Y
RIEGLE	D	Y

Minnesota		
DURENBERGER	R	Y
WELLSTONE	D	Y

Mississippi		
COCHRAN	R	N
LOTT	R	N

Missouri		
BOND	R	Y
DANFORTH	R	Y

Montana		
BAUCUS	D	Y
BURNS	R	Y

Nebraska		
EXON	D	Y
KERREY	D	Y

Nevada		
BRYAN	D	Y
REID	D	Y

New Hampshire		
GREGG	R	N
SMITH	R	N

New Jersey		
BRADLEY	D	Y
LAUTENBERG	D	Y

New Mexico		
BINGAMAN	D	Y
DOMENICI	R	N

New York		
MOYNIHAN	D	Y
D'AMATO	R	Y

North Carolina		
FAIRCLOTH	R	N
HELMS	R	N

North Dakota		
CONRAD	D	Y
DORGAN	D	Y

Ohio		
GLENN	D	Y
METZENBAUM	D	Y

Oklahoma		
BOREN	D	Y
NICKLES	R	N

Oregon		
HATFIELD	R	Y
PACKWOOD	R	Y

Pennsylvania		
WOFFORD	D	Y
SPECTER	R	Y

Rhode Island		
PELL	D	Y
CHAFEE	R	Y

South Carolina		
HOLLINGS	D	N
THURMOND	R	X

South Dakota		
DASCHLE	D	Y
PRESSLER	R	N

Tennessee		
GORE	D	Y
SASSER	D	Y

Texas		
KRUEGER	D	Y
GRAMM	R	N

Utah		
BENNETT	R	N
HATCH	R	N

Vermont		
LEAHY	D	Y
JEFFORDS	R	Y

Virginia		
ROBB	D	Y
WARNER	R	N

Washington		
MURRAY	D	Y
GORTON	R	N

West Virginia		
BYRD	D	Y
ROCKEFELLER	D	Y

Wisconsin		
FEINGOLD	D	Y
KOHL	D	N

Wyoming		
SIMPSON	R	N
WALLOP	R	N

Acknowledgments

In producing this atlas, I was fortunate in having the advice of several knowledgeable people. For commenting on certain sections I wish to thank Herbert E. Alexander of Citizens' Research Foundation, Munroe Eagles of the State University of New York at Buffalo, and Roderick J. Harrison of the U.S. Bureau of the Census. Heather E. Hudson of the University of San Francisco, Calvin Beale of the U.S. Department of Agriculture, Howard Hayghe of the U.S. Bureau of Labor Statistics, Jacqueline V. Lerner of Michigan State University, Roy Bryce-Laporte of Colgate University, and Susan Lapham of the U.S. Bureau of the Census have been most helpful in answering my many questions on various aspects of the subjects in this book. I also wish to thank the following for providing key information: Marie Pees, Jean M. Dee, Diana DeAre, and Martin O'Connel of the U.S. Bureau of the Census; James R. Hansen of Goddard Institute for Space Studies; Joseph P. Fuhr, Jr. of Widener University; Amy Fabian of the U.S. Telephone Association; D.L. Elliott of the Pacific Northwest Laboratory, Batelle Memorial Institute; Ernest Woodson, curator of the map library at SUNY-Buffalo; Robin Kane of the National Gay and Lesbian Task Force; Tallmadge Doyle, of Eugene, Oregon, for artistic consulting; and Fred Derf, Esq. of Buffalo, for legal services.

Tom Bresnahan and his coworkers at Golden Software of Golden, Colorado, have been extraordinarily patient in guiding me through the ins and outs of computer mapmaking. I am particularly indebted to Lee Smith of the State University of New York at Buffalo and formerly of the *Buffalo News* for his sage comments on extensive portions of the manuscript. I am grateful to my wife, Doris Doyle, whose advice at every stage contributed greatly to improving this book. Finally, my heartfelt thanks to Norma Jean Lipanski, who produced many of the maps in the book.

I wish to thank the following for permission to reproduce copyright material: Southern Illinois University Press, for permission to reproduce a map from *Vocabulary Change: A Study of Variation in Regional Words in Eight of the Southern States* by Gordon R. Wood, p. 358 (Figure 2-49); Glenmary Research Center, for permission to adapt the following maps based on their 1990 survey of churches: "Major Denominational Families," "Percent of Population Unclaimed," "Liberal Protestant," "Moderate Protestant," "Conservative Protestant," and "Jewish" (Figures 2-43 to 2-46); James E. Hansen, for permission to adapt from his map "Scenario B," July 2000, Plate 6, p. 9354, in "Global Climate Change as Forecast by Goddard Institute for Space Studies, Three-Dimensional Model," by J. Hansen et al., *Journal of Geophysical Research*, 93 (1988):9341-9364 (Figure 3-2); Yale University Press, for permission to reproduce two maps from an article by Margaret B. Davis and Catherine Zabinski, "Changes in Geographical Range Resulting from Greenhouse Warming: Effects on Biodiversity in Forests," pp. 300-301 (sugar maple and beech), in *Global Warming and Biological Diversity*, Robert L. Peters and Thomas E. Lovejoy, eds. (Figure 3-3).

Also, H. E. Dregne of Texas Tech University, for permission to reproduce his map showing estimated desertification (Figure 3-8); Dennis L. Elliot and Pacific Northwest Laboratories, Battelle Memorial Institute, for permission to reproduce map, "Proportion of U.S. Electricity Needs That Could Be Generated by Wind," from *An Assessment of the Available Windy Land Area and Wind Energy Potential in the Contiguous United States*, prepared for the U.S. Department of Energy by Pacific Northwest Laboratory (Figure 3-11); American Geographical Society, for permission to reprint map, "Annual Physioclimatic Stress Zones in the United States," by Werner F. Terjung, *Geographical Review*, 57 (1967):225-240 (Figure 3-14); League of Conservation Voters, for permission to use its data on ratings of senators and representatives from *1992 National Environmental Scoreboard* as the basis for two maps (Figures 3-17, 3-18); permission of Renew America to use data from *The State of the States, 1989*, by Renew America to create a map (Figure 3-16); *The Atlantic*, for permission to use information from *Guide to America's Museums, 1990-1991* to construct a map (Figure 3-20); Urban Land Institute, for permission to use data from *Tall Office Buildings in the United States* by James W. Pygman and

Richard Kateley, pp. 85-114, to create a chart (Figure 3-15).

Also, *Congressional Quarterly*, for permission to use certain data from *Vital Statistics on Congress, 1991-1992* by Norman J. Ornstein et al., pp. 48 and 156, in two charts (Figures 4-4, 4-9); Americans for Democratic Action, for permission to use its analysis of the 1992 congressional voting record as the basis for constructing four maps and a chart (Figures 4-10 to 4-14); the U.S. Conference of Mayors, for permission to use its tabulations for constructing a map (Figure 4-15); Robert S. McIntyre and Citizens for Tax Justice, for permission to use data from *A Far Cry From Fair* by Robert S. McIntyre et al. to construct a map (Figure 5-6); the National Association of Realtors, for permission to use data from *Home Sales*, 6:1(January 1993), to create a map (Figure 5-7); Grant Thornton, for permission to use data from *Tenth Annual Manufacturing Climates Study* to create a map (Figure 5-10); *Financial World*, for permission to use data from "Rating America's Large Cities" by Katherine Barrett and Richard Greene, March 2, 1993 and "Fifty Report Cards" by Geoffrey N. Smith, May 11, 1993, to create two maps (Figures 5-13 and 5-14).

Also, *American Journal of Epidemiology*, for permission to use a map from article by Wayne B. Davis et al., "Geographic Variation in Declining Ischemic Heart Disease Mortality in the United States, 1968-1978,"p. 662 (Figure 6-3); Steve Wing and the American Heart Association, for permission to use map from article by Steve Wing et al., "Stroke Mortality Maps," *Stroke*, 19:12(1988), p. 1509 (Figure 6-4); Susan P. Baker and Williams & Wilkins, for permission to use map from article by Susan P. Baker et al., "County Mapping of Injury Mortality," *Journal of Trauma*, 28(1988):741-745 (Figure 6-15); Arnold S. Linsky and *Journal of Studies on Alcohol*, for permission to use "Alcohol Prescriptive Norm Index," in "Drinking Norms and Alcohol-Related Problems in the United States" by Arnold S. Linsky et al., 47(1986):384-93, as the basis for a map (Figure 6-17); American Medical Association, for permission to use data from Gene Roback et al., *Physician Characteristics and Distribution in the U.S.* (Chicago: American Medical Association, 1990) as the basis for a map (Figure 6-19); NARAL Foundation, for permission to create a map based on data from *A State-by-State Review of Abortion Rights, Fourth Edition, 1993* (Figure 7-2); NOW Legal Defense and Education Fund, for permission to use information from *Legal Resource Kit, 1988* (Figure 7-4).

Also, Thomas C. Castellano, for permission to use data on rate of drug-related arrests by city as tabulated in the 1990 *Sourcebook of Criminal Justice Statistics*, pp. 453-455, by Thomas C. Castellano and James L. Lebeau, Center for the Study of Crime, Delinquency, and Corrections (Figure 7-12); Anti-Defamation League of B'nai B'rith, for permission to use information from *Audit of Anti-Semitic Incidents* annuals, showing data for 1988, 1989, 1990, and 1991, as the basis for a map (Figure 7-17); and to use information from *Hate Groups in America*, 1988, as the basis for a map (Figure 7-18); National Gay and Lesbian Task Force, for permission to use information from its listing of states and municipalities, "Lesbian and Gay Civil Rights in America," press release of December 1991, as the basis for a map (Figure 7-20) and to reprint its map in *Privacy Project Fact Sheet* (Figure 7-19); People For the American Way, for permission to use data from *Attacks On the Freedom to Learn*, editions of 1986-87, 1987-88, 1988-89, 1989-90, and 1990-91, as the basis for a map (Figure 7-21); Robert Ellis Smith and *Privacy Journal*, for permission to use data from (1) *Compilation of State and Federal Privacy Laws*, (2) *1989 Supplement to Compilation of State and Federal Privacy Laws, 1988 Edition*, and (3) *1991 Supplement to Compilation of State and Federal Privacy Laws, 1989 Edition* as the basis for a series of maps (Figures 7-23 to 7-30); U.S. English, for permission to use map in *U.S. English*, 1:2, p. 3, "Status of Official English in the States" (Figure 7-31); American Bar Association, for permission to use data from *Supplement to the Lawyer Statistical Report: The Legal Profession in 1988*, by Barbara A. Curran and Clara N. Carson as the basis for a map (Figure 7-32).

Sources for Maps and Charts

CHAPTER 1: DEMOGRAPHIC PATTERNS

The source for all maps in this chapter is a special tabulation of 1990 U.S. Census data. The source for all charts is the *Statistical Abstract of the United States*, 1991 edition, except for: the chart in Figure 1-3, which is from Diana Peare, *Geographical Mobility, March 1990 to March 1991* (Washington, D.C.: Bureau of the Census, 1992); and the chart in Figure 1-15, which is from Phillip Kaufman et al., *Dropout Rates in the United States, 1991* (Washington, D.C.: National Center for Education Statistics, 1992).

CHAPTER 2: ETHNIC, LINGUISTIC, AND RELIGIOUS DIVISIONS

2-1 to 2–42; 2–47;

2-48. Special tabulations of 1990 U.S. Census data.

2-43. Adapted from a map produced by the Glenmary Institute, Atlanta, Ga.: "Percent of Population Unclaimed, by Counties of the United States, 1990."

2-44. Adapted from "Major Denominational Families by Counties of the United States, 1990," a map produced by the Glenmary Institute, Atlanta, Ga., 1992.

2-45. Adapted from three maps produced by the Glenmary Institute, Atlanta, Ga., 1992: "Liberal Protestant, Percent of Adherents, 1990"; "Moderate Protestant, Percent of Adherents, 1990": and "Conservative Protestant, 1990." Liberal Protestants consist of the Episcopal Church, the Presbyterian Church (USA), the United Church of Christ, and the National Association of Congregational Christian Churches. Moderate Protestants include all Lutheran denominations, Reformed denominations, the Christian Church (Disciples of Christ), the United Methodist Church, and several smaller denominations. Conservative Protestants include the Southern Baptist Convention, the Assemblies of God, the Seventh-Day Adventists, the Christian Churches and the Church of Christ, the several denominations of the Church of God, and more than a score of smaller denominations. The Mormons, who are not included in the Glenmary maps, are shown in Figure 2-47 as a conservative religious organization.

2-46. Adapted from a map produced by the Glenmary Institute, Atlanta, Ga.: "Jewish, Percent of Adherents, 1990."

2-49. Gordon R. Wood, *Vocabulary Change: A Study of Variation in Regional Words in Eight of the Southern States* (Carbondale: Southern Illinois University Press, 1972), 358.

CHAPTER 3: THE ENVIRONMENT

3-1. *National Air Quality and Emissions Trends Report, 1990.* (Research Triangle Park, N.C.: Environmental Protection Agency, annual).

3-2. James E. Hansen et al., "Global Climate Changes as Forecast by Goddard Institute of Space Studies—Three-Dimensional Model," *Journal of Geophysical Research* 93(1988):9354.

3-3. Margaret B. Davis and Catherine Zabinski, "Changes in Geographical Range Resulting from Greenhouse Warming: Effects on Biodiversity in Forests," in *Global Warming and Biological Diversity*, Robert L. Peters and Thomas E. Lovejoy, eds. (New Haven: Yale University Press, 1992), 300.

3-4. *National Acid Precipitation Program: 1990 Integrated Assessment Report* (Washington, D.C.: NAPAP Office of the Director, 1991), 182.

3-5. Jeffrey L. Phillips, *A Cumulative Examination of the State/EPA Radon Survey* (Washington, D.C.: U.S. Environmental Protection Agency, undated). See also: *Statewide Scientific Study of Radon* (Trenton: New Jersey Department of Environmental Protection, 1989); *Indoor Radon in New York State* (Albany: State of New York Department of Health, 1990); S.W. Fong, Department of Environment, Health, and Natural Resources, Division of Radiation Protection, Raleigh, N.C., undated tabulation; Douglas A. Sprinkel and Barry J. Solomon, *Radon Hazards in Utah* (Salt Lake City: Department of Environmental Quality, 1990); *New Hampshire Radon Survey, 1987-1989* (Concord: New Hampshire Division of Public Health Services, 1989); *Florida Statewide Radiation Study* (Bartow: Florida Institute of Phosphate Research, 1989).

3-6. "National Priorities List Sites" (Washington, D.C.: Environmental Protection Agency, issued periodically).

3-7. *Summary Report, 1987, National Resources Inventory* (Washington, D.C.: Department of Agriculture, 1989).

3-8. Harold Dregne, Texas Tech University, Lubbock, Texas, 1992.

3-9. Special tabulation, 1990 U.S. Census data.

3-10. David J. Trickett and Ken Bossong, *Nuclear Lemons: An Assessment of America's Worst Commercial Nuclear Power Plants* (Washington, D.C.: Public Citizen, 1991), 93-94.

3-11. D.L. Elliot, L.L. Wendell, and G.L. Gower, *An Assessment of the Available Windy Land Area and Wind Energy Potential in the Contiguous United States* (Richland, Wash.: Pacific Northwest Laboratory, Battelle Memorial Institute, 1991), 55.

3-12. *Tornado Safety* (Rockville, Md.: National Oceanic and Atmospheric Administration, 1982).

3-13. Adapted from map in "Seismic Risk Maps," by David M. Perkins, *Earthquake Information Bulletin*, 6:6(November-December 1974).

3-14. Werner H. Terjung, "Annual Physioclimatic Stresses in the United States," *Geographical Review*, 57(1967): 225-40.

3-15. James W. Pygman and Richard Kateley, *Tall Office Buildings in the United States* (Washington: Urban Land Institute, 1985). The 1992 data for Manhattan are from the Real Estate Board of New York.

3-16. *The State of the States* (Washington, D.C.: Renew America, issued periodically).

3-17. *The National Environmental Scoreboard, 1991* (Washington, D.C.: League of Conservation Voters, 1992).

3-18. ibid.

3-19. Musical institutions shown on the map were selected on the basis of their funding, length of season, and general reputation from lists of companies in *Symphony* (Jan.-Feb. 1993), issued by the American Symphony Orchestra League, Washington, D.C.; *Profile 1991* (annual publication of Opera America, Washington, D.C.); and a list prepared by Dance America, Washington, D.C. The selection is solely that of the author.

3-20. *Guide to America's Museums* (New York: Atlantic Monthly Co. and Brant Publications, annual). Several additions have been made at the suggestion of Tallmadge Doyle, M.F.A., of Eugene, Oregon, and Margaret Prentice, of the University of Oregon in Eugene.

3-21. Association of American Universities. List of members issued March 1992.

CHAPTER 4: POLITICS

4-1. Calculated from data on congressional spending supplied by Federal Election Commission.

4-2. ibid.

4-3. Federal Election Commission, Washington, D.C.

4-4. Calculated from tabulation provided by Clerk of the House of Representatives. (Washington: issued following each general election.) Supplemental chart based on data from Norman J. Ornstein, Thomas E. Mann, and Michael J. Malbin, *Vital Statistics on Congress* (Washington, D.C.: Congressional Quarterly, annual).

4-5. Memorandum, Gerry F. Cohen, North Carolina General Assembly, Raleigh, January 23, 1992.

4-6. Map, Texas Legislative Council, Austin, August 24, 1991.

4-7. Map, State Board of Elections, State of Illinois, Springfield, 1991.

4-8. *1990 Census, Population and Housing Profile: Congressional districts of the 103rd Congress* (Washington, D.C.: Bureau of the Census, undated).

4-9. Pages of public bills from *Vital Statistics on Congress*. Number of journalists from *Congressional Directory* (Washington, D.C.: U.S. Government Printing Office, annual). Number of PACs from Federal Election Commission.

4-10. Americans for Democratic Action, Washington, D.C. Press release, issued annually.

4-11. ibid.

4-12. ibid.

4-13. ibid.

4-14. ibid.

4-15. U.S. Conference of Mayors (Washington: listing issued annually).

4-16. Clerk of the House of Representatives.

4-17. ibid.

4-18. ibid.

4-19. Congressional Record, various issues.

4-20. ibid.

CHAPTER 5: THE ECONOMY

5-1. Special tabulation of 1990 U.S. Census data.

5-2. ibid.

5-3. United States Department of Commerce, "Census Bureau Releases 1990 Decennial Counts for Persons Enumerated in Emergency Shelters and Observed on Streets," press release (Washington, D.C., April 12, 1991).

5-4. Annual average salary is from U.S. Department of Labor, Bureau of Labor Statistics press release, "Average Annual Pay Levels in Metropolitan Areas, 1990" (Washington, D.C.: annual). The data were adjusted for differences in cost of living by metropolitan area using a formula based on the value of homes as reported in a special tabulation of 1990 U.S. Census data. The formula, which relates cost of housing to total cost of living, provides only a rough approximation of adjusted pay in each area. However, the map is valid as an indicator of broad regional differences in the purchasing power of the average salary.

5-5. Special tabulation of 1990 U.S. Census data.

5-6. Unpublished tabulation supplied by Robert S. McIntyre of Citizens for Tax Justice.

5-7. Calculations of minimum family income needed to buy an existing median-priced home based on prices of houses shown in National Association of

Realtors, *Home Sales* January 1993 (Washington, D.C.: annual).

5-8. Special tabulation of 1990 U.S. Census data.

5-9. *International Science and Technology Data Update, 1991* (Washington, D.C.: National Science Foundation, annual). See also *Science and Engineering Indicators, 1991* (Washington, D.C.: National Science Board, annual).

5-10. Grant/Thornton, Chicago, Ill. *Manufacturing Climates Study*, (annual, as reported in *Statistical Abstract*).

5-11. Bureau of Economic Analysis, Department of Commerce, "BEA Economic Area Projections of Income, Employment and Population to the Year 2000," *Survey of Current Business* (November 1990), 39-41.

5-12. Special tabulation of 1990 U.S. Census data. Katherine Barrett and Richard Greene, "Tales of 30 Cities," *Financial World* (February 18, 1992), 28-47.

5-13. *Financial World*. Report on city management by Katherine Barrett and Richard Greene, issued annually.

5-14. *Financial World*. Report on state management by Katherine Barrett and Richard Greene, issued annually.

5-15. McDonald Corporation and Pepsico.

CHAPTER 6: HEALTH

6-1. Unpublished data provided by Centers for Disease Control, Hyattsville, Maryland.

6-2. ibid.

6-3. W.B. Davis et al., "Geographic Variation in Declining Ischemic Heart Disease Mortality in the United States, 1968-1978," *American Journal Epidemiology*, 122(1985): 657.

6-4. Steve Wing, Michelle Casper, Wayne Davis, et al., "Stroke Mortality Maps: United States Whites Aged 35-74 Years, 1962-1982, *Stroke 19* 1509(1988): Figure 3.

6-5. National Cancer Institute, *Atlas of U.S. Cancer Mortality Among Whites, 1950-1980* (Washington, D.C.: U.S. Department of Health and Human Services, 1987). Areas on the map with "above average" and "below average" rates are those that are outside the 95 percent confidence limits of the average U.S. rate. The trend data are from National Cancer Institute Monograph 59, *Cancer Mortality in the United States, 1950-1977* (Washington, D.C.: U.S. Department of Health and Human Services, 1982). See also National Cancer Institute, *Cancer Statistics Review* (Washington, D.C.: U.S. Department of Health and Human Services, annual).

6-6. ibid.

6-7. ibid.

6-8. ibid.

6-9. ibid.

6-10. ibid.

6-11. National Cancer Institute, *Atlas of U.S. Cancer Mortality Among Nonwhites, 1950-1980* (Washington, D.C.: U.S.Department of Health and Human Services, 1991). Areas on the map with "above average" and "below average" rates are those that are outside the 95 percent confidence limits of the average U.S. rate. The trend data are from National Cancer Institute Monograph 59, *Cancer Mortality in the United States, 1950-1977* (Washington, D.C.: U.S. Department of Health and Human Services, 1982). See also National Cancer Institute's *Cancer Statistics Review*, annual.

6-12. *HIV/AIDS Surveillance* (Atlanta: Centers for Disease Control, issued quarterly); also, unpublished data from Centers for Disease Control.

6-13. *Sexually Transmitted Disease Statistics* (Atlanta: Centers for Disease Control, annual); also, unpublished data from the Centers for Disease Control.

6-14. ibid.

6-15. Susan P. Baker, R.A. Whitfield, and Brian O'Neill, "County Mapping of Injury Mortality," *Journal of Trauma*, 28(1988): 741-745. See also J.A. Weed, "Suicide in the United States," in *Mental Health, United States, 1985* (Rockville, Md.: National Institute of Mental Health, 1985), 135-155.

6-16. *Monthly Vital Statistics Report* (Centers for Disease Control).

6-17. Arnold S. Linsky, John P. Colby, Jr., and Murray A. Straus, "Drinking Norms and Alcohol-Related Problems in the United States." *Journal Studies on Alcohol*, 47(1986): 384-93.

6-18. Unpublished data, Office on Smoking and Health, Centers for Disease Control, Rockville, Md.

6-19. Gene Roback, Lillian Randolph, and Bradley Seidman, *Physician Characteristics and Distribution in the U.S.* (Chicago: American Medical Association, 1990).

6-20. *Fluoridation Census, 1985* (Atlanta: Public Health Service, 1988).

CHAPTER 7: CONTENTIOUS ISSUES

7-1. *Morbidity and Mortality Weekly Report; Abortion Surveillance—United States* (Atlanta: Centers for Disease Control; reports on abortion are issued annually).

7-2. *Who Decides?: A State-by-State Review of Abortion Rights*, third edition (Washington, D.C.: NARAL Foundation/NARAL, annual).

7-3. *Facts at a Glance* (Washington, D.C.: Child Trends, Inc., annual).

7-4. Legal Resource Kit, Equal Rights Amendment (New York: NOW Legal Defense Fund, 1988).

7-5. *Job Patterns for Minorities and Women in Private Industry* (Washington, D.C.: Equal Employment Opportunity Commission, annual).

7-6. ibid.

7-7. ibid.

7-8. Roderick J. Harrison and Daniel H. Weinberg, "Racial and Ethnic Residential Segregation in 1990," paper prepared for the meeting of the Population Association of America, Denver, May 1992.

7-9. ibid.

7-10. ibid.

7-11. ibid.

7-12. *Sourcebook of Criminal Justice Statistics*, 453-455.

7-13. *Uniform Crime Reports, 1990* (Washington, D.C.: Federal Bureau of Investigation, 1991). See also *Sourcebook of Criminal Justice Statistics, 1990* (Washington, D.C.: U.S. Bureau of Justice Statistics, 1991).

7-14. ibid.

7-15. Federal Bureau of Investigation, special tabulation.

7-16. "Death Row, U.S.A.," tabulation (New York: NAACP Legal Defense Fund, spring 1992) quarterly.

7-17. *Audit of Anti-Semitic Incidents* (New York: Anti-Defamation League of B'nai B'rith, annual).

7-18. *Hate Groups in America*, new revised edition (New York: Anti-Defamation League of B'nai B'rith, 1988).

7-19. Adapted from map produced by the National Gay & Lesbian Task Force, Washington, D.C. Map is undated but shows the status of state laws in April 1992.

7-20. National Gay & Lesbian Task Force, "Lesbian and Gay Civil Rights in the U.S.," tabulation (Washington, D.C.: issued periodically).

7-21. *Attacks on the Freedom to Learn* (Washington, D.C.: People for the American Way, annual)

7-22. Data on teachers' salaries from *Estimates of School Statistics, 1989-90* (Washington, D.C.: National Education Association). Average pay from Bureau of Labor Statistics, press release, "Average Annual Pay by State and Industry, 1990," August 8, 1991.

7-23. Robert Ellis Smith, *Compilation of State and Federal Privacy Laws* (Washington, D.C.: Privacy Journal, 1988); see also *1989 Supplement to Compilation of State and Federal Privacy Laws; 1991 Supplement to Compilation of State and Federal Privacy Laws*. Privacy Journal is now located in Providence, Rhode Island.

7-24. ibid.

7-25. ibid.

7-26. ibid.

7-27. ibid.

7-28. ibid.

7-29. ibid.

7-30. ibid.

7-31. U.S. English, "Text of Laws Designating English as States' Official Language" (Washington, D.C.: undated tabulation).

7-32. Barbara A. Curran and Clara N. Carson, *Supplement to the Lawyer Statistical Report: The U.S. Legal Profession in 1988* (Chicago: American Bar Foundation, 1991).

7-33 to
7-46. Congressional Record, various issues.

7-47. Adapted from *Atlas of United States Foreign Relations* (Washington, D.C.: United States Department of State, 1985, 90).

7-48. *World Military Expenditures and Arms Transfers, 1990* (Washington, D.C.: U.S. Arms Control and Disarmament Agency, annual).

7-49. Leonard S. Spector, with Jacqueline R. Smith, *Nuclear Ambitions: The Spread of Nuclear Weapons, 1989-1990* (Boulder, Colo.: Westview Press, 1990); see also, Center for Defense Information, *The Defense Monitor*, 21:3 (1992).

7-50. John Prados, *Presidents' Secret Wars* (New York: William Morrow, 1986). See also Gregory F. Treverton, *Covert Action: The Limits of Intervention in the Postwar World* (New York: Basic Books, 1987); L. Fletcher Prouty, *The Secret Team* (New York: Ballantine Books, 1974); *New York Times*, August 2, 1974, "U.S. Said to Order CIA to Curtail Role in Greece"; *Newsweek*, August 12, 1974, 36. The following is a brief description of the covert operations shown on the map. *Guatemala*: CIA managed successful coup against government of Jacobo Arbenz in 1954. CIA helped suppress insurrection against government of Miguel Ydigoras Fuentes by nationalist officers in 1960. U.S. provided support to Guatemalan government for suppression of rebel movements from 1962 to 1980s. *Nicaragua*: CIA trained and funded "contras," covertly in early 1980s and thereafter overtly. *Cuba*: CIA organized armed invasion at Bay of Pigs in 1961. Several aborted attempts by CIA to assassinate Fidel Castro from 1961 to 1963. Several attempts by CIA to sabotage Cuban economy in the 1960s. *Chile*: CIA and other U.S. government agencies destabilized Chile economically and politically. President Allende was killed in 1973 military coup in which U.S. military forces allegedly participated. CIA subsidized Christian Democratic Party and other non-leftist parties, 1964-73. *Greece*: CIA gave King Constantine covert funds used to unseat George Papandreou government in 1965. CIA supported George Papadopoulos, who headed a successful coup, establishing the colonel's junta in 1967. CIA subsidized military and political figures from 1948 to 1972. *Chad*: CIA recruited ex-Libyan soldiers to conduct guerrilla operations against Libya in 1980s. *Angola*: U.S. supported UNITA and FNLA insurrections with military aid and training in 1975-76. From 1985 to 1991 overt aid was supplied to UNITA, headed by Jonas Savimbi. *Iraq*: U.S. and Iran gave military supplies to insurgent Kurdish minority in Iraq. When the shah reached a *modus vivendi* with Iraq, he cut all Iranian aid and stopped the passage of U.S. aid to the Kurds. The U.S. then abandoned the Kurds. *Iran*: CIA helped support successful coup against government of Mohammed Mossadegh in 1953. *Afghanistan*: CIA sent military supplies to insurgents, covertly in the early 1980s, overtly thereafter. *Laos*: CIA created secret army of 30,000 to wage war against communist Pathet Lao, 1962-1973. *Cambodia*: U.S. supported forces opposed to government of Prince Norodom Sihanouk from 1958 to 1970. Sihanouk was overthrown, allegedly with assistance of CIA, in 1970. Cambodian territory covertly bombed by American B-52s in 1969-70. *Indonesia*: CIA gave military assistance and supplies to insurgents opposing President Achmed Sukarno in 1957-58. U.S. aided in the overthrow of Sukarno in 1965.

Bibliography

Chapter 1: Demographic Patterns

Cherlin, Andrew. "The Polls—A Review: The Strange Case of the "Harvard-Yale Study," *Public Opinion Quarterly* 54:(1990), 117-124.

Fosler, R. Scott, William Alonso, Jack A. Meyer, and Rosemary Kern. *Demographic Change and the American Future.* Pittsburgh: University of Pittsburgh Press, 1990.

Gill, Robert T., Nathan Glazer, and Stephan A. Thernstrom. *Our Changing Population.* Englewood Cliffs, N.J.: Prentice-Hall, 1992.

Glenn, Norval D. "The Recent Trend in Marital Success in the United States," *Journal of Marriage and the Family,* 53(May 1991), 261-270.

Greeley, Andrew. "The Declining Morale of Women," *Sociology and Social Research,* 73(1989), 53-58.

Greeley, Andrew, Robert T. Michael, and Tom W. Smith. "Americans and Their Sexual Partners," *Society* 21(July-August, 1990), 36-42.

Phillips, Roderick. *Putting Asunder: A History of Divorce in Western Society.* Cambridge: Cambridge University Press, 1988.

Popenoe, David. *Disturbing the Nest.* New York: Aldine de Gruyter, 1988.

Riley, Glenda. *Divorce: An American Tradition.* New York: Oxford University Press, 1991.

Van Tassel, David, and Peter N. Stearns, eds. *Old Age in a Bureaucratic Society.* New York: Greenwood Press, 1986.

Whyte, Martin King. *Dating, Mating, and Marriage.* New York: Aldine de Gruyter, 1990.

Chapter 2: Ethnic, Linguistic, and Religious Divisions

Aculna, Rodolpho. *Occupied America: A History of Chicanos,* 2nd. ed. New York: Harper & Row, 1981.

Ahlstrom, Sidney E. *A Religious History of the American People.* New Haven: Yale University Press, 1972.

Alba, Richard D. *Italian Americans.* Englewood Cliffs, N.J.: Prentice-Hall, 1985.

Archdeacon, Thomas J. *Becoming American: An Ethnic History.* New York: Free Press, 1983.

Ashton, Elwyn T. *The Welsh in the United States.* Hove, Sussex: Caldra House, 1984.

Bailyn, Bernard. *The Peopling of British North America: An Introduction.* New York: Alfred A. Knopf, 1986.

———. *Voyagers to the West: A Passage in the Peopling of America on the Eve of the Revolution.* New York: Alfred A. Knopf, 1986.

Battistella, Graziano, ed. *Italian Americans in the 80s: A Sociodemographic Profile.* Staten Island, N.Y.: Center for Migration Studies, 1989.

Berthoff, R.T. *British Immigrants in Industrial America, 1790-1950.* Cambridge: Harvard University Press, 1953.

Bradley, Martin B., Norman M. Green, Jr., Dale E. Jones, Mac Lynn, and Lou McNeil. *Churches and Church Membership in the United States, 1990.* Atlanta: Glenmary Research Center, 1992.

Carver, Craig M. *American Regional Dialects.* Ann Arbor: University of Michigan Press, 1987.

Conrad, G.R., ed. *The Cajuns: Essays on Their History and Culture.* Lafayette: Center for Louisiana Studies, University of Southwestern Louisiana, 1983.

Crispino, James A. *The Assimilation of Ethnic Groups: The Italian Case.* Staten Island, N.Y.: Center for Migration Studies, 1980.

Cuddy, D.L., ed. *Contemporary American Immigration: Interpretive Essays.* Boston: Twayne, 1982.

Desbarats, J. "Indochinese Resettlement in the United States." *Annals of the Association of American Geographers,* 75:4(1985), 522-538.

Donaldson, G. *The Scots Overseas.* London: Robert Hale, 1966.

Dunn, Charles W. *Religion in American Politics.* Washington, D.C.: *Congressional Quarterly Press,* 1989.

Fermi, Laura. *Illustrious Immigrants: The Intellectual Immigration from Europe, 1930-41,* 2nd ed. Chicago: University of Chicago Press, 1971.

Finke, Roger, and Rodney Stark. *The Churching of America, 1776-1990.* New Brunswick, N.J.: Rutgers University Press.

Fischer, David Hackett. *Albion's Seed: Four British Folkways in America.* New York: Oxford University Press, 1989.

Gallup, George, Jr., and Jim Castelli. *The People's Religion: American Faith in the 90s.* New York: Macmillan, 1989.

Glazer, Nathan, and Daniel Patrick Moynihan. *Beyond the Melting Pot: The Negroes, Puerto Ricans, Jews, Italians, and Irish of New York City.* Cambridge: M.I.T. Press, 1963.

Greeley, Andrew M. *Religious Change in America.* Cambridge: Harvard University Press, 1989.

———. *That Most Distressful Nation: The Taming of the American Irish.* Chicago: Quadrangle Books, 1972.

Greeley, Andrew M., William C. McCready, and Gary Theisen. *Ethnic Drinking Subcultures.* New York: Praeger, 1980.

Greenberg, Joseph H., and Merritt Ruhlen. "Linguistic Origins of Native Americans," *Scientific American* (November 1992), 94-99.

Haines, David W. *Refugees as Immigrants: Cambodians, Laotians, and Vietnamese in America.* Totowa, N.J.: Rowman & Littlefield, 1989.

Hartmann, E. *Americans from Wales.* Boston: Christopher, 1967.

Hertzberg, Arthur. *The Jews in America: Four Centuries of an Uneasy Encounter.* New York: Simon and Schuster, 1989.

Jacquet, Constant H., Jr. *Yearbook of American and Canadian Churches, 1990.* Nashville: Abingdon Press, 1990.

Katsup, A. *The Swedish Heritage in America.* Minneapolis: Swedish Council of America, 1975.

Kirschbaum, Erik. *The Eradication of German Culture in the United States, 1917-1918.* Stuttgart: H.-D. Heinz, 1988.

Leyburn, James G. *The Scotch-Irish: A Social History.* Chapel Hill: University of North Carolina Press, 1962.

Lopez, Enrique Hank. *Eros and Ethos: A Comparative Study of Catholic, Jewish, and Protestant Sex Behavior.* Englewood Cliffs, N.J.: Prentice-Hall, 1979.

Luebke, Frederick C. *Germans in the New World: Essays in the History of Immigration.* Urbana: University of Illinois Press, 1990.

McKee, J.O., ed. *Ethnicity in Contemporary America: A Geographical Appraisal.* Dubuque, Iowa: Kendall/Hunt, 1985.

Mead, Frank S., and Samuel S. Hill. *Handbook of Denominations in the United States,* 9th ed. Nashville: Abingdon Press.

Meinig, D.W. "The Mormon Culture Region: Strategies and Patterns in the Geography of the American West, 1847-1964," *Annals of the Association of American Geographers,* 55:2(1965), 191-220.

Nelli, Humbert S. *From Immigrants to Ethnics: The Italian Americans.* New York: Oxford University Press, 1983.

Polenberg, Richard. *One Nation Divisible: Class, Race, and Ethnicity in the United States Since 1938.* New York: Penguin, 1980.

Pozzetta, George E., ed. American Immigration and Diversity, a 20-volume series of previously published articles. New York: Garland, 1991.

Samora, Julian, and Patricia Vandel Simon. *A History of the Mexican-American People.* South Bend, Ind.: University of Notre Dame Press, 1977.

Smith, T.W. "Ethnic Measurement and Identification," *Ethnicity,* 7:1(1980), 78-95.

Sowell, Thomas. *Ethnic America: A History.* New York: Basic Books, 1981.

Sowell, Thomas, ed. *Essays and Data on American Ethnic Groups.* Washington, D.C.: Urban Institute, 1978.

Steinberg, Stephen. *The Ethnic Myth: Race, Ethnicity, and Class in America.* New York: Atheneum, 1981.

Thernstrom, Stephan A., ed. *Harvard Encyclopedia of American Ethnic Groups.* Cambridge: Harvard University Press, 1980.

Thornton, Russell. *American Indian Holocaust and Survival: A Population History Since 1492.* Norman: University of Oklahoma Press, 1987.

Wood, Gordon R. *Vocabulary Change: A Study of Variation in Regional Words in Eight of the Southern States.* Carbondale: Southern Illinois University Press, 1971.

CHAPTER 3: THE ENVIRONMENT

Batie, Sandra S. *Soil Erosion.* Washington, D.C.: Conservation Foundation, 1983.

Conway, Donald J. *Human Response to Tall Buildings.* Stroudsburg, Pa.: Dowden, Hutchinson & Ross, 1977.

Council on Environmental Quality. *Environmental Quality.* Washington, D.C.: Council on Environmental Quality, annual.

Dunn, Edgar S., Jr. *The Development of the U.S. Urban System,* volume I. Baltimore: Johns Hopkins, 1980.

Frick, Dieter, ed. *The Quality of Life.* New York: Aldine de Gruyter, 1986.

Fund for Renewable Energy and the Environment. *The State of the States, 1988.* Washington, D.C.: Fund for Renewable Energy and the Environment, 1988.

Gimlin, Hoyt, eds. *Earth's Threatened Resources.* Washington, D.C.: Congressional Quarterly, 1986.

Gould, Jay M. *Quality of Life in American Neighborhoods.* Boulder, Colo.: Westview Press, 1986.

Halacy, D.S., Jr. *Earthquakes.* Indianapolis: Bobbs-Merrill, 1974.

Idso, Sherwood B. "Carbon Dioxide—An Alternative View," *New Scientist,* November 12, 1981, 444.

League of Conservation Voters. *The National Environmental Scoreboard.* Washington, D.C.: League of Conservation Voters, annual.

Mohnen, Volker A. "The Challenge of Acid Rain," *Scientific American,* August 1988, 30-38.

National Academy of Sciences, National Academy of Engineering, and Institute of Medicine. *Policy Implications of Greenhouse Warming.* Washington, D.C.: National Academy Press, 1991.

National Acid Precipitation Study, 1990 Integrated Assessment Report. Washington: National Acid Precipitation Assessment Program, 1991.

Peters, Robert L., and Thomas E. Lovejoy, eds. *Global Warming and Biological Diversity.* New Haven: Yale University Press, 1992.

Pygman, James W., and Richard Kateley. *Tall Office Buildings in the United States.* Washington, D.C.: Urban Land Institute, 1985.

Schneider, Stephen H. "Climate Modelling," *Scientific American,* May 1987, 72-80.

———. "Fact and Fancy on Greenhouse Earth," *Wall Street Journal,* August 30, 1988, 22.

Singer, S. Fred. "Ozone Scare Generates Much Heat, Little

Light," *Wall Street Journal*, April 16, 1987, 20.

Snow, John T. "The Tornado," *Scientific American,* April 1984, 86-96.

Upton, Arthur C., Roy E. Shore, and Naomi Harley. "Health Effects of Low-level Ionizing Radiation," *Annual Review of Public Health*, 13(1992), 127-150.

CHAPTER 4: POLITICS

Alexander, Herbert E., and Monica Bauer. *Financing the 1988 Election.* Boulder, Colo.: Lexington Books, 1991.

Ceaser, James W. *Reforming the Reforms: A Critical Analysis of the Presidential Selection Process.* Cambridge, Mass.: Ballinger, 1982.

Drew, Elizabeth. *Election Journal: Political Events of 1987-1988.* New York: William Morrow, 1989.

———. *Politics and Money.* New York: Macmillan, 1983.

Epstein, Leon D. *Political Parties in the American Mold.* Madison: University of Wisconsin Press, 1986.

Keeter, Scott, and Cliff Zukin. *Uninformed Choice: The Failure of the New Presidential Nominating System.* New York: Praeger, 1983.

Maddox, William S., and Stuart A. Lilie. *Beyond Liberal and Conservative.* Washington, D.C.: Cato Institute, 1984.

Neuman, W. Russell. *The Paradox of Mass Politics.* Cambridge: Harvard University Press, 1986.

Ornstein, Norman J., Thomas E. Mann, and Michael J. Malbin. *Vital Statistics on Congress.* Washington: Congressional Quarterly, annual.

Reichley, A. James, ed. *Elections American Style.* Washington, D.C.: Brookings Institution, 1987.

Shienbaum, Kim Ezra. *Beyond the Electoral Connection.* Philadelphia: University of Pennsylvania Press, 1984.

Smith, Hedrick. *The Power Game.* New York: Random House, 1988.

Teixeira, Ruy A. *Why Americans Don't Vote.* New York: Greenwood Press, 1987.

CHAPTER 5: THE ECONOMY

Balk, Alfred. *The Myth of American Eclipse.* New Brunswick, N.J.: Transaction, 1990.

Central Intelligence Agency. *Handbook of Economic Statistics.* Washington, D.C.: Central Intelligence Agency, annual.

Clark, Gordon L. *Unions and Communities Under Siege: American Communities and the Crisis of Organized Labor.* Cambridge: Cambridge University Press, 1989.

Denison, Edward F. *Trends in American Economic Growth, 1929-1982.* Washington: Brookings Institution, 1985.

Epstein, Jason. "The Tragical History of New York," *New York Review of Books*, April 9, 1992, 45-52.

Fantasia, Rick. *Cultures of Solidarity: Consciousness, Action, and Contemporary American Workers.* Berkeley: University of California Press, 1988.

Gall, Gilbert J. *The Politics of Right To Work: The Labor*

Federations as Special Interests, 1943-1979. New York: Greenwood Press, 1988.

Grenier, Guillermo J. *Inhuman Relationships.* Philadelphia: Temple University Press, 1988.

Heilbroner, Robert, and Peter Bernstein. *The Debt and the Deficit: False Alarms/Real Possibilities.* New York: W.W. Norton, 1989.

Huang, Wei-Chiao, ed. *Organized Labor at the Crossroads.* Kalamazoo, Mich.: W.E. Upjohn Institute for Employment Research, 1989.

McIntyre, Robert S., Douglas P. Kelly, Michael P. Ettlinger, and Elizabeth A. Fray. *A Far Cry From Fair: CTJ's Guide to State Tax Reform.* Washington, D.C.: Citizens for Tax Justice, 1991.

Nossiter, Bernard D. *Fat Years and Lean: The American Economy Since Roosevelt.* New York: Harper & Row, 1990.

CHAPTER 6: HEALTH

American Heart Association. *Heart and Stroke Facts.* Dallas: American Heart Association, annual.

Arnold, Lauren S. et al. "Lessons From the Past: A Historical Account of Infant Mortality in the United States Useful for Judging Current Initiatives," *MCN* 14(March/April 1989), 75-82.

Baker, Susan P., R.A. Whitefield, and Brian O'Neill. "County Mapping of Injury Mortality," *Journal of Trauma*, 28(1988), 741-745.

Bibel, Jan Debra. "Santayana's Warning Unheeded: The Parallels of Syphilis and Acquired Immune Deficiency Syndrome (AIDS)," *Sexually Transmitted Diseases*, 16(1989), 201-209.

Boone, Margaret S. *Capital Crime: Black Infant Mortality in America.* Newbury Park, Calif.: Sage Publications, 1989.

Brandt, Allan M. *No Magic Bullet.* New York: Oxford University Press, 1985.

———. "The Syphilis Epidemic and Its Relation to AIDS," *Science*, 239(1988), 375-380.

Brecht, Mary C. "The Tragedy of Infant Mortality," *Nursing Outlook*, 37:1(1989), 18-22.

Brunelle, J.A., and J.P. Carlos. "Recent Trends in Dental Caries in U.S. Children and the Effect of Water Fluoridation," *Journal Dental Research*, 69(1990), 723-27.

Carpenter, Myra A., and John Ewing. "The Outbreeding of Alcoholism," *American Journal of Drug and Alcohol Abuse*, 15(1989), 93-99.

Chin, James, and Jonathan M. Mann. "HIV Infections and AIDS in the 1990s," *Annual Review of Public Health*, 11(1990), 127-142.

Dardis, Tom. *The Thirsty Muse.* New York: Ticknor and Fields, 1989.

Davis, Wayne B. et al., "Geographic Variation in Declining Ischemic Heart Disease Mortality in the United States, 1968-1978," *American Journal Epidemiology*, 122(1985), 657-672.

Easley, Michael W. "The Status of Community Water

Fluoridation in the United States," *Public Health Reports*, 105(1990), 348-53.

Escobedo, Luis G., et al. "Sociodemographic Characteristics of Cigarette Smoking Initiation in the United States," *Journal of the American Medical Association*, 264(1990), 1550-55.

Frank, Deborah A., and Steven H. Zeisel. "Failure to Thrive," *Pediatric Clinics of North America*, 35:6(1988), 1187-1206.

Fraser, Gary E. *Preventive Cardiology*. New York: Oxford University Press, 1986.

Goodwin, Donald W. *Alcohol and the Writer*. Kansas City, Mo.: Andrews and McMeel, 1988.

Harsch, Harold H., and Robert E. Holt. "Use of Antidepressants in Attempted Suicide," *Hospital and Community Psychiatry*, 39(1988), 990-992.

Hilton, Michael E. "The Demographic Distribution of Drinking Patterns in 1984," *Drug and Alcohol Dependence*, 22(1988), 37-47.

———. "Trends in Drinking Problems and Attitudes in the United States: 1979-1984," *British Journal of Addiction*, 83(1988), 124-127.

Horowitz, H.S. "The Future of Water Fluoridation and Other Systemic Fluorides," *Dental Research*, 69(special issue, 1990), 760-64.

Jaffe, Harold W. "AIDS: Epidemiologic Features," *Journal American Academy of Dermatology*, 22(1990), 1167-1171.

Johnson, Diane, and John F. Murray. "AIDS Without End," *New York Review of Books*, August 18, 1988, 57-63.

Johnston, William B., and Kevin R. Hopkins. *The Catastrophe Ahead: AIDS and the Case for a New Public Policy*. New York: Praeger, 1990.

Kaslow, Richard A., and Donald P. Francis, eds. *The Epidemiology of AIDS: Expression, Occurrence, and Control of Human Immunodeficiency Virus Type 1 Infection*. New York: Oxford University Press, 1989.

Kushner, Howard I. *Self-Destruction in the Promised Land: A Psychocultural Biology of American Suicide*. New Brunswick, N.J.: Rutgers University Press, 1989.

Lester, David. "The Suicide Rate by Drowning and the Presence of Oceans." *Perceptual and Motor Skills*, 69(1989), 338.

———. "Suicide Rates by Region of Death and Place of Birth," *Perceptual and Motor Skills*, 67(1988), 942.

Linsky, Arnold S., John P. Colby, Jr., and Murray A. Straus. "Drinking Norms and Alcohol-Related Problems in the United States," *Journal of Studies on Alcohol*, 47(1986), 384-393.

Marshall, Eliot. "The Fluoride Debate: One More Time," *Science*, 247(1990), 276-277.

Monk, Mary. "Epidemiology of Suicide," *Epidemiologic Reviews*, 9(1987), 51-69.

Ostfield, Adrian M. "A Review of Stroke Epidemiology," *Epidemiology Reviews*, 2(1980), 136-152.

Pastorek, Joseph G., II, ed. "Sexually Transmitted Diseases," *Obstetrics and Gynecology Clinics of North America*, 16:3(1989).

Pendrys, D.G., and J. W. Stamm. "Relationship of Total Fluoride Intake to Beneficial Effects and Enamel Fluorosis," *Journal Dental Research* 69(special issue, 1990), 529-38.

Rolfs, Robert T., and Allyn K. Nakashima. "Epidemiology of Primary and Secondary Syphilis in the United States," *Journal American Medical Association*, 264(1990), 1432-1437.

Rinear, Charles E. *The Sexually Transmitted Diseases*. Jefferson, N.C.: McFarland, 1986.

"Scientific Update on Fluoride and the Public Health," *Journal of Dental Research*, 60(1990), 1343-44.

Siomopoulos, V. "When Patients Consider Suicide," *Postgraduate Medicine*, 88:3(1990), 205-213.

Starr, Paul. *The Social Transformation of American Medicine*. New York: Basic Books, 1982.

Summer, Laura. *Limited Access: Health Care for the Rural Poor*. Washington, D.C.: Center For Budget and Policy Priorities, 1991.

Surgeon General of the United States. *Reducing the Health Consequences of Smoking: A Report of the Surgeon General*. Rockville, Md.: U.S. Department of Health and Human Services, 1989.

———. *Smoking and Health: A Report of the Surgeon General*. Rockville, Md.: U.S. Department of Health, Education, and Welfare, 1979.

Watkins, James D. *Report of the Presidential Commission on the Human Immunodeficiency Virus Epidemic*. Washington, D.C.: Government Printing Office, 1988.

Wei, Stephen H. Y. "The Worldwide Smoking Epidemic: Tobacco Trade, Use, and Control," *Journal of the American Medical Association*, 263(1990), 3312-18.

CHAPTER 7: CONTENTIOUS ISSUES

Baron, Denis. *The English-Only Question*. New Haven: Yale University Press, 1990.

Berkin, Carol Ruth, and Mary Beth Norton. *Women of America: A History*. Boston: Houghton Mifflin, 1979.

Bosmajian, Haig A., ed. *The Freedom to Read*. New York: Neal-Schuman, 1987.

Bryson, Joseph E., and Elizabeth W. Detty. *Censorship of Public School Library and Instructional Material*. Charlottesville, Va.: Miche Company, 1982.

Burnham, David. *The Rise of the Computer State*. New York: Random House, 1983.

Clarke, Ronald V., and David Lester. *Suicide: Closing the Exits*. New York: Springer Verlag, 1989.

Cott, Nancy F. and Elizabeth H. Pleck, eds. *A Heritage of Her Own: Toward a Social History of American Women*. New York: Simon and Schuster, 1979.

Davis, Sally. "Pregnancy in Adolescents," *Pediatric Clinics of North America*, 36(1989), 665-680.

Dobkowski, Michael N. "A Historical Survey of Anti-Semitism in America," in *Persistent Prejudice: Perspectives on Anti-Semitism*, ed. Herbert Hirsch and Jack D. Spiro. Faifax, Va: George Mason University Press, 1988; 63-81.

Editors of the Harvard Law Review. *Sexual Orientation and the Law*. Cambridge: Harvard University Press, 1990.

Faux, Marian. *Crusaders: Voices From the Abortion Front*. New York: Birch Lane Press, 1990.

Frager, Bernadette. "Teenage Childbearing," *Journal of Pediatric Nursing*, 6(1991), 131-133, 202-205.

Graham, Hugh Davis. *The Civil Rights Era: Origins and Development of a National Policy, 1960-1972*. New York: Oxford University Press, 1990.

Greene, Kathanne W. *Affirmative Action and Principles of Justice*. New York: Greenwood Press, 1989.

Gross, Samuel R., and Robert Mauro. *Death and Discrimination: Racial Disparities in Capital Sentencing*. Boston: Northeastern University Press, 1989.

Haas, Kenneth C., and James Inciardi, eds. *Challenging Capital Punishment: Legal and Social Science Approaches*. Newbury Park, Calif.: Sage Publications, 1988.

Harrison, Cynthia. *On Account of Sex: The Politics of Women's Issues, 1945-1968*. Berkeley: University of California Press, 1988.

Hate Groups in America: A Record of Bigotry and Violence, rev. ed. New York: Anti-Defamation League of B'nai B'rith, 1988.

Hayes, Cheryl D., ed. *Risking the Future: Adolescent Sexuality, Pregnancy, and Childbearing*, volume 1. Washington, D.C.: National Academy Press, 1987.

Hixson, Richard F. *Privacy in a Public Society: Human Rights in Conflict*. New York: Oxford University Press, 1987.

Hoff-Wilson, Joan, ed. *Rights of Passage: The Past and Future of Affirmative Action*. New York: Scribner's, 1991.

Hood, Roger. *The Death Penalty: A World-Wide Perspective*. Oxford: Clarendon Press, 1989.

Hook, Donald D., and Lothar Kahn. *Death in the Balance*. Lexington, Mass.: Lexington Books, 1989.

Lerner, Gerda. *The Majority Finds Its Past*. New York: Oxford University Press, 1979.

Luker, Kristin. *Abortion and the Politics of Motherhood*. Berkeley: University of California Press, 1984.

Mansbridge, Jane J. *Why We Lost the ERA*. Chicago: University of Chicago Press, 1986.

Mathews, Donald G., and Jane Sherron De Hart. *Sex, Gender, and the Politics of ERA: A State and the Nation*. New York: Oxford University Press, 1990.

Mohr, James C. *Abortion in America: The Origins and Evolution of National Policy, 1800-1900*. New York: Oxford University Press, 1978.

National Gay and Lesbian Task Force. *Anti-Gay Violence, Victimization, & Defamation*. Washington, D.C.: National Gay and Lesbian Task Force, annual.

Nisbet, Lee. *The Gun Control Debate: You Decide*. Buffalo, N.Y.: Prometheus Books, 1990.

Noble, William. *Bookbanning in America: Who Bans Books?—and Why?* Middlebury, Vt.: Paul S. Eriksson, 1990.

Paige, Connie. *The Right to Lifers: Who They Are, How They Operate, Where They Get Their Money*. New York: Summit Books, 1983.

Pepinsky, Harold E., and Paul Jesilow. *Myths That Cause Crime*. Cabin John, Md.: Seven Locks Press, 1984.

Piatt, Bill. *Only English?: Law and Language in the United States*. Albuquerque: University of New Mexico Press, 1990.

Privacy Journal. Monthly newsletter published in Providence, Rhode Island.

Provenzo, Eugene F., Jr. *Religious Fundamentalism and Public Behavior: The Battle for the Public Schools*. Albany: State University of New York, 1990.

Rickel, Annette U. *Teen Pregnancy and Parenting*. New York: Hemisphere, 1989.

Rodman, Hyman, Betty Sarvis, and Joy Walker Bonar. *The Abortion Question*. New York: Columbia University Press, 1987.

Rosenfeld, Michel. *Affirmative Action and Justice: A Philosophical and Constitutional Inquiry*. New Haven: Yale University Press, 1991.

Saney, Parviz. *Crime and Culture in America: A Comparative Perspective*. Westport, Conn.: Greenwood Press, 1986.

Schwartz, Bernard. *Behind Bakke: Affirmative Action and the Supreme Court*. New York: New York University Press, 1988.

Sheeran, Patrick J. *Women, Society, the State, and Abortion: A Structuralist Analysis*. New York: Praeger, 1987.

Singerman, Robert. "The Jew as Racial Alien: The Genetic Component of American Anti-Semitism," in *Anti-Semitism in American History*, ed. David A. Gerber. Urbana: University of Illinois Press, 1986; pp.103-128.

Smith, Page. *Daughters of the Promised Land: Women in American History*. Boston: Little, Brown, 1970.

Smith, Robert Ellis. *Privacy: How to Protect What's Left of It*. Garden City, N.Y.: Anchor Press/Doubleday, 1979.

Stone, Geoffrey R. "Flag Burning and the Constitution," *Iowa Law Review*, 75(1989), 111-120.

Urofsky, Melvin I. *A Conflict of Rights: The Supreme Court and Affirmative Action*. New York: Scribners's, 1991.

Voydanoff, Patricia, and Brenda W. Donnelly. *Adolescent Sexuality and Pregnancy*. Newbury Park, Calif.: Sage Publications, 1990.

Wright, James D., Peter H. Rossi, and Kathleen Daly. *Under the Gun: Weapons, Crime, and Violence in America*. New York: Aldine de Gruyter, 1983.

Wright, Kevin N. *The Great American Crime Myth*. Westport, Conn.: Greenwood Press, 1985.

Zimring, Franklin E. "Firearms, Violence and Public Policy," *Scientific American*, 265(November 1991), 48-54.

Zimring, Franklin E., and Gordon Hawkins. *The Citizen's Guide to Gun Control*. New York: Macmillan, 1987.

Index

Maps indicated by m following page number; graphs by g; notes by n

clergy
  confidentiality right 179
  influence on congressional
    candidates 104
Cleveland (Ohio)
  African-Americans 98–99m
  city management 133m
  employment 132
  homeless 122m
  housing segregation 162m
  metropolitan area 10m
  minority mayors 113m
  sex orientation bias ban 174m
client-lawyer confidentiality
    179m
climatic stress 93m
Clinton, Bill 105, 114m
coal-burning power plants 83
cocaine 146, 165
Cold War 10, 190
college graduates 24, 26gm
Colombia 67
colon cancer 8, 142–143m
Colonels' Junta (Greece) 194
Colorado see also specific topics
    (e.g., elections)
  anti-Semitic crimes 171m
  city management 133m
  cultural institutions 99m
  employment 130
  equal rights legislation 159
  homeless 122m
  housing segregation
    162–163m
  language statute 180m
  lung cancer 142
  minority mayors 113m
  population 9m
  privacy right statutes
    178–179m
  sex orientation bias ban 174m
  uranium miners 84
  water fluoridation 153
Colorado Springs (Colorado)
  cultural institutions 99m
  homeless 122m
  housing segregation 163m
Columbia (Missouri) 152m
Columbus (Ohio)
  city management 133m
  cultural institutions 98–99m
  homeless 122m
  metropolitan area 10m
Commerce, U.S. Department of
    130gm
Commonwealth of Independent
    States (CIS)
  nuclear weapons 192
  U.S. policy toward 190
communism
  censorship of 175
  water fluoridation as
    conspiracy 154
competition 128g
Compton (California) 76m

confidentiality see privacy rights
Congregationalists 34
Congress, U.S.
  Black Caucus 112
  British-Americans 34
  and campaign finance 102,
    104g, 108g
  challengers 102–103m
  committees 104
  environmental ratings
    96–97m
  ideological classification
    109–111m, 112g,
    116–117m
  incumbents 102
  media exposure 108g
  minority candidates 106
  minority districts 107m
  new districts 106–107m
  noncompetitive races 102–103
  organization change 104
  and PACs 108g
  pay raises 182
  votes on contentious issues
    182–189m
  vote tabulations 200–224
  workload 108g
Congressional Record 10
Connecticut see also specific
    topics (e.g., elections)
  anti-Semitic crimes 171m
  cultural institutions 99m
  equal rights legislation 159
  housing segregation
    162–163m
  Italian-Americans 48
  and personnel files 179
  privacy right statutes
    178–179m
  sex orientation bias ban 174m
Conservative Judaism 75
conservatives 109–111m, 112,
    116–117m
Constitution, U.S.
  Eighth Amendment 169
  English-only Amendment 180
  Equal Rights Amendment 159
  First Amendment 180
  Fourteenth Amendment 169
Cook, Captain James 70
Cook County (Illinois) 174m
Corinth (Greece) 92
coronary heart disease (CHD)
    138gm, 151
Corpus Christi (Texas)
  Hispanics 76m
  homeless 122m
  minority mayors 113m
Costa Rica 67
cost of living (COL) 120–121,
    123
counties see also specific county
    name (e.g., Queens County)
  demographic patterns 9,
    12–27m

environmental standards 80m
  ethnic divisions 30–71m
  heating fuel 88m
  linguistic divisions 76–78m
  poverty and wealth
    120–121m, 124m
  religious divisions 72–75m
  suicide 148m
  telephones 127m
covert operations, U.S. 10,
    193–194m
Crane, Hart 150
creationism 176
Creole (language) 68–69
crime 8, 165–167gm see also
    specific crime (e.g., murder)
Cuba
  American cultural penetration
    134
  arms imports 191m
  immigration to U.S. 66
  revolution 66
  U.S. covert operations 193m,
    194
  U.S. naval base 190m
Cuban-Americans 30n, 66m
culture and cultural institutions
    98–99m see also specific topic
    (e.g., language); institutions
    (e.g., museums)
  American penetration 134m
  back country 31
Cupertino (California) 174m
Custer, George Armstrong 71
Cuyahoga County (Ohio) 174m
Czech-Americans 51–52m
Czechoslovakia 52, 84

D

Dallas (Texas)
  city management 133m
  cultural institutions 98–99m
  employment 130
  metropolitan area 10m
dance companies 98m
Dane County (Wisconsin) 174m
Danish-Americans 45m
Danville (Virginia) 18, 162m
Darwinian theory 176
data sources 9–10
Davis (California) 174m
Davis, Margaret B. 82
Dayton (Ohio)
  housing segregation 162m
  metropolitan area 10m
  sex orientation bias ban 174m
death penalty see capital
    punishment
death rates 10, 25, 136–137gm
Decatur (Georgia) 163m
Delaware see also specific topics
    (e.g., elections)
  African-Americans 76m
  British-American migration 31

cultural institutions 99m
  nuclear plant safety 89m
  privacy right statutes
    178–179m
  singles 23
Delaware River 41, 43
Delaware Valley 31
Delray Beach (Florida) 162m
Democrats
  congressional votes
    109–111m
  election losses 102–103
  environmental votes 96
  ideological classification
    109–111m, 112g
  southern 117
demography 11–27m see also
    specific demographic patterns
    (e.g., mobility); subjects (e.g.,
    families)
denominational families 73–74m
dental caries 153–154
Denton (Texas) 163m
Denver (Colorado)
  city management 133m
  cultural institutions 99m
  employment 130
  homeless 122m
  housing segregation 163m
  lung cancer 142
  metropolitan area 10m
  minority mayors 113m
  sex orientation bias ban 174m
desertification 87m
Detroit (Michigan)
  African-Americans 76m
  city management 133m
  cultural institutions 98–99m
  employment 130
  homeless 122m
  housing segregation 162m
  manufacturing jobs 131–132
  metropolitan area 10m
  sex orientation bias ban 174m
  venereal disease 147m
Dewey, Thomas 109
diabetes 138
dialects 78m
Diary of Anne Frank, The 176
Diego Garcia 190m
diet 142–143
discrimination
  against gays 174
  in jobs 8, 160
disease 134 see also specific type
    (e.g., lung cancer)
Disney World 134
District of Columbia see
    Washington, D.C.
divorce and separation 20gm
  church membership 20
  and families headed by women
    17
  and population mobility 14
  singles shortage 22

foreign intervention 193–194m
Fort Lauderdale (Florida)
    AIDS 145m
    cultural institutions 99m
    housing segregation 162m
    metropolitan area 10m
Fort Meyers (Florida) 162m
Fort Nassau (New York) 41
Fort Ross (California) 54
Fort Smith (Arkansas) 163m
Fort Walton Beach (Florida)
    162m
Fort Wayne (Indiana) 162m
Fort Worth (Texas)
    city management 133m
    cultural institutions 99m
    homeless 122m
    metropolitan area 10m
    minority mayors 113m
fossil fuels 81
Fourteenth Amendment to the
    U.S. Constitution (due process
    guarantee) 169
France
    American culture 134
    arms exports 191
    colonies 39
    emigration to U.S. 39
    and nuclear weapons 192
    U.S. trade 128n
Franck, Michael 181
fraud *see* property crime
freedom of information
    arrest records 178–179m
    bank records 179
    employee drug testing 178m
    library records 178m
    medical records 179
    personnel files 179m
Freethinkers 52
French (language) 77
    of Acadians 40
    of Cajuns 40
    of Haitians 69
French-Americans 39–40m, 45
French-Canadians 39–40
French Revolution 39
Fresno (California) 10m, 122m
Frisians 41
Frost, Robert 150n
fuel 88m
fundamentalists
    Baptists 73
    ethnic profile 9
    and schoolbook censorship
        175–176
Furman v. Georgia (1972) 169

G

Gainesville (Florida) 152m, 162m
Gaithersburg (Maryland) 174m
Galicia
    Polish-Americans from 50
    Ukrainian-Americans from 55

Gallic culture 134
Galveston (Texas) 10m
Gambia 58
Ganges region (India) 62
García Márquez, Gabriel 176
Gary (Indiana)
    African-Americans 76m
    housing segregation 162m,
        164
    metropolitan area 10m
    minority mayors 113m
gas *see* natural gas
gay rights *see* homosexuality and
    gay rights
geography
    of one-party rule 102–103m
    sugar maple trees 82m
Georgia (state) *see also specific
    topics (e.g., elections)*
    African-Americans 76m
    anti-Semitic crimes 171m
    anti-sodomy statute 173
    capital punishment statute
        169
    cultural institutions 98–99m
    homeless 122m
    housing segregation
        162–163m
    Italian-Americans 48
    language statute 180m
    lung cancer 140–142
    minority mayors 113m
    oral cancer 143
    physicians 152m
    population 9m
    privacy right statutes
        178–179m
    sex orientation bias ban 174m
    two-parent families 16
    venereal disease 146m
German (language) 37–38, 77
    of Austrians 38
    of Jews 75
    of Swiss 38
German-Americans 8, 37–38m
    after World War I 180
    ancestry 34n
    assimilation 48
    compared with British-
        Americans 34–34n
    compared with Irish-
        Americans 36
    religion 73–74
Germany
    arms exports 191
    Catholics from 73
    nuclear technology 192
    Polish-Americans from 50
    Reform Judaism in 75
    religion in 72
    U.S. policy toward 190n
    U.S. trade 128n
Ghana 58
Glenmary Research Center 9–10
global warming 81–82m, 96

Goddard Space Institute (New
    York) 81–82
Goldwater, Barry 102
gonorrhea 147gm
GOP *see* Republicans
government intervention 117
Grand Rapids (Michigan)
    cultural institutions 99m
    metropolitan area 10m
    water fluoridation 153
Great Britain *see* United Kingdom
Great Depression 148
Greece
    earthquake 92
    immigration to U.S. 49
    U.S covert actions 193m, 194
Greek-Americans 49m
Greek Orthodox Church 49
Green Bay (Wisconsin) 163m
greenhouse effect 81
Greensboro (North Carolina)
    10m, 113m
Greenville (South Carolina) 10m
Gregg v. Georgia (1976) 169
Grenada 193m
ground water protection 95
growth retardation 151
Guam 190m
Guantanamo (Cuba) 190m
Guatemala 193m, 194
Gujarat (India) 62
gun control
    congressional ratings 109
    congressional votes 182,
        185m
guns
    in crimes 166
    in murders 168gm
    in suicides 148

H

Haiti
    occupied by U.S. 69
    revolution of 1791-1803 69
    West-Indian Americans from
        68
Hammett, Dashiell 150
Hammond (Indiana) 162m, 164
handguns *see* guns
Hansen, James 81–81n, 82
Hapsburg Empire
    Czechs from 51
    Slovaks from 52
Hardwick, Michael 173
Harrisburg (Pennsylvania) 162m,
    174m
Harrison, Roderick 162, 164n
Hartford (Connecticut)
    cultural institutions 99m
    housing segregation 162m
    minority mayors 113n
    sex orientation bias ban 174m
Hasidim 75
hate groups 8, 172m

Hawaii *see also specific topics
    (e.g., elections)*
    American annexation 70
    Asian population 76m
    Chinese-Americans 59
    equal rights legislation 159
    Filipino-Americans 60
    Hilo earthquake of 1946 92
    homeless 122m
    housing affordability 126m
    Japanese-Americans 61
    Korean-Americans 63
    language statute 180m
    naval base 190m
    Portuguese-Americans 47
    privacy right statutes 178m
    sex orientation bias ban 174m
Hawaiian (language) 70
Hawaiian-Americans 70m
Hayakawa, S.I. 180
Haywood (California) 174m
hazardous-waste management 95
health and health care
    136–154gm *see also specific
    health issue (e.g., AIDS); care
    providers (e.g., physicians)*
    future of 194
    homeless and 122
    insurance 117
    medical record access 179
    poverty and 121
    quality of 137
Health Statistics, National Center
    for 10
heart disease 138gm
    and cigarettes 151
    and death rate 136, 138gm
    and stroke 139
    and water fluoridation 154
Hemingway, Ernest 150
hemlock trees 82
herbicides 86
heterosexual sodomy 174
Hialeah (Florida) 76m, 113m
Hickory (North Carolina) 162m
high blood pressure
    (hypertension)
    and coronary heart disease
        138
    and stroke 139
high schools *see* schools
Hillsborough County (Florida)
    174m
Hilo (Hawaii) 92
Hindus 62
Hispanic-Americans 65–67m
    AIDS 145g
    ancestry 30n, 67m
    census undercount 9
    cities with majority of 76m
    college graduates 26
    congressional redistricting
        106–107
    divorce 20
    and English-only Amendment

180
  executions of 170
  families headed by women 17
  homeless 122
  housing segregation 162m,
    164
  poverty 121g
  school dropouts 27
  telephone 127
  as top racial group 30
  two-parent families 16
HIV (human immunodeficiency
  virus) 145–146
hoboes 122
Hollywood (Florida) 113m
Holmes County (Ohio) 27
homeless, the 9, 122m
homes see housing
homosexuality and gay rights
  173–174m
  among never-marrieds 24
  and gonorrhea 147
  harassment 174
  school censorship 175
  state laws 173m
  and syphilis 146
Honolulu (Hawaii)
  Asian-Americans 76m
  homeless 122m
  housing affordability 126m
  metropolitan area 10m
  sex orientation bias ban 174m
Hooker Chemical Company 85
hospitals 152
House of Representatives, U.S.
  see Congress, U.S.
housing
  affordability 8, 126m
  discrimination 164
  heating fuel 88m
  mobility 14m
  mortgage requirements 26
  segregation 8, 162–164m, 194
  telephones 127m
Houston (Texas)
  city management 133m
  coronary heart disease 138
  cultural institutions 98–99m
  employment 130
  metropolitan area 10m
  sex orientation bias ban 174m
Howard County (Maryland)
  174m
Hudson River 41
Huguenots 39
human immunodeficiency virus
  see HIV
Hungarian-Americans 56m
Hungary
  religious composition 56
  Ukrainian-Americans from 55
  1956 uprising in 56
Huntington Beach (California)
  113m
hypertension see high blood

pressure (hypertension)

I

Icelandic-Americans 45
Idaho see also specific topics (e.g.,
  elections)
  fertility 19
  housing segregation 162m
  Japanese-Americans 61
  population 9m
  privacy right statutes 179m
  singles 23
Idso, Sherwood P. 82
illegal aliens 9, 65
Illinois see also specific topics
  (e.g., elections)
  abortion 156
  anti-Semitic crimes 171m
  city management 133m
  congressional redistricting
    106m
  cultural institutions 98–99m
  Czech-Americans 51
  divorce 20
  earthquake 92
  employment 130
  equal rights legislation 159
  heart disease 138
  homeless 122m
  housing segregation
    162–163m
  manufacturing jobs 132
  minority mayors 113m
  never-marrieds 24
  nuclear plant safety 89m
  physicians 152m
  population 9m
  privacy right statutes
    178–179m
  sex orientation bias ban 174m
  skyscrapers 94
  Swedish population 43
  tornadoes 91
immigration
  Canadian 39–40
  Catholic 35
  Dutch 41
  Hispanic 67
  illegal 9, 65
  laws and legislation 58–63
  Protestant 35
Immigration Law of 1924 61
incomes
  of the affluent 124gm
  privacy rights 179m
India
  arms imports 191m
  emigration 62
  languages spoken in 77
  nuclear weapons 192
  U.S. policy toward 190n
Indiana see also specific topics
  (e.g., elections)
  African-Americans 76m

  city management 133m
  cultural institutions 98–99m
  homeless 122m
  housing segregation 164
  language statute 180m
  lung cancer 142
  manufacturing jobs 132
  minority mayors 113m
  population 9m
  privacy right statutes 178m
  tornadoes 91
Indianapolis (Indiana)
  city management 133m
  cultural institutions 98–99m
  homeless 122m
  housing segregation 162m
  lung cancer 142
  manufacturing jobs 132
  metropolitan area 10m
Indian Territory 71
Indonesia 193m, 194
infant mortality 149gm, 151, 158
influenza epidemic (1918-1919)
  136
Ingham (Michigan) 174m
Inglewood (California) 76m,
  113m
insurance 117
interracial marriages 8
intravenous drug users 145
Introduction to Thematic
  Cartography (Tyner) 10
Iowa see also specific topics (e.g.,
  elections)
  cultural institutions 99m
  housing segregation
    162–163m
  nuclear plant safety 89m
  physicians 152m
  population 9m
  population loss 13
  privacy right statutes
    178–179m
  sex orientation bias ban 174m
Iowa City (Iowa)
  housing segregation 162m
  physicians 152m
  sex orientation bias bar 174m
IQ (intelligence quotient) 158
Iran
  American cultural penetration
    134
  arms imports 191m
  nuclear weapons 192
  U.S. covert actions 193–194
Iraq
  Arab-Americans from 57
  arms imports 191m
  nuclear weapons 192
  U.S. covert actions 194
  U.S. war with 193m
Ireland (Eire) 35, 72
Irish-Americans 35–36m
  assimilation 48
  compared with Polish-

Americans 50
drinking 150
Protestants 9, 35
religion 9, 73
working class 48
isopleth map design 8
Israel
  arms imports 191m
  nuclear weapons 192
  U.S. policy toward 190
Italian (language) 8, 48m, 77
Italian-Americans
  compared with Polish-
    Americans 50
  drinking 150
  religion 73
Italy 48, 72
Ithaca (New York) 174m

J

Jackson (Michigan) 152m
Jackson (Mississippi) 76m
Jacksonville (Florida)
  city management 133m
  homeless 122m
  housing segregation 162m
  lung cancer 142
  metropolitan area 10m
Jacksonville (North Carolina)
  152m, 162m
Jamaica 68
Jamestown (Virginia) 50, 58
Jane Eyre (Charlotte Brontë) 176
Jansenist sect 43
Japan
  earthquake of 1923 92
  infant mortality 149
  products in U.S. 131
  U.S. strategic position toward
    190n
  U.S. trade 128n
Japanese-Americans 30n, 61m,
  143
Jersey City (New Jersey) 174m
  AIDS 145m
  homeless 122m
  sex orientation bias ban 174m
Jews 75m
  assimilation tendency 48
  Austrian 38
  compared with Polish-
    Americans 50
  crimes against 171m
  and drinking 150
  French 39
  German 37
  hatred of 172
  Hungarian 56
  Russian 55
jobs and jobless see employment
  and unemployment
Johnson, Lyndon B. 102
Jones Act of 1917 66
Joplin (Missouri) 163m

Jordan 57, 191m
journalists 108g
Judaism *see* Jews
Justice Statistics, U.S. Bureau of 167

K

Kansas *see also specific topics (e.g., elections)*
  cultural institutions 99m
  homeless 122m
  housing segregation 162–163m
Kansas City (Missouri)
  cultural institutions 99m
  homeless 122m
  metropolitan area 10m
  minority mayors 113m
Kennedy, John F. 34
Kentucky *see also specific topics (e.g., elections)*
  cultural institutions 99m
  homeless 122m
  housing segregation 162m
  language statute 180m
  minority mayors 113m
  physicians 152m
  population 9m
  privacy right statutes 179m
kerosene 88m
Key West (Florida) 174m
kidney disease
  and cancer 151
  and water fluoridation 154
Killeen (Texas) 162m
King County (Washington) 174m
King Jr., Martin Luther 178
Kings County *see* Brooklyn (New York)
KKK *see* Ku Klux Klan
Knoxville (Tennessee) 10m
Korea *see* North Korea; South Korea
Korean-Americans 63m
Ku Klux Klan (KKK) 172m

L

labor unions 104, 129m
La Crosse (Wisconsin) 152m, 163m
Lafayette (Indiana) 162–163m
Laguna Beach (California) 174m
Lake County (Illinois) 162m
Lakewood (Colorado) 113m
Lancaster (Pennsylvania) 162m, 174m
Landrum-Griffin Act (1959) 129
language and linguistics 77–78m
  see also specific language or dialect (e.g., Creole)
  English as official language 180m
  Native-American 71

spoken at home 77m
Laos 193m, 194
Lardner, Ring 150
Laredo (Texas)
  Mexican-Americans 76m
  minority mayors 113m
  physicians 152m
larynx cancer 143, 151
Las Vegas (Nevada)
  employment 130
  homeless 122m
  housing segregation 163m
  metropolitan area 10m
  minority mayors 113m
Latinos 65
Latter-Day Saints, Church of Jesus Christ of *see* Mormons
Lawrence (Kansas) 162–163m
laws
  on capital punishment 169–170m
  in congress 182–189m
  for equal rights 159m
  on immigration 58–63
  against labor unions 129
  for 'official' English 180m
  on privacy 178–179m
  against sex orientation bias 174m
  against sodomy 173m
  in states 8, 173–174m
Lawton (Oklahoma) 152m, 162–163m
lawyers 181m
League of Conservation Voters 96
Lebanon
  Arabs from 57
  U.S. occupation of 193m
legislation *see* laws
leisure ethic 31
lesbians *see* homosexuality and gay rights
leukemia 143
Lewis, Sinclair 150
Lexington (Kentucky)
  homeless 122m
  minority mayors 113m
  physicians 152m
Lexington (North Carolina) 18
liberals 109–111m, 112–112n, 116–117m
libertarians 116–117, 154
library records 178m
Libya
  arms imports 191m
  nuclear weapons 192
  U.S. bombing 193
  U.S. covert actions 193m, 194
life expectancy 136
life imprisonment 187m
Lilie, Stuart A. 117
linguistics *see* language and linguistics
lipoproteins 138

Lithuanian-Americans 53m
Little Rock (Arkansas) 10m, 113m
Little Russians 55
livestock *see* cattle
Llano County (Texas) 15
Llocano (language) 60
London, Jack 150
Long Beach (California)
  homeless 122m
  naval base 190m
  sex orientation bias ban 174m
Lorain (Ohio) 10m, 162m
Los Alamos County (New Mexico) 26
Los Angeles (California)
  breast cancer 143
  Chinese-Americans 59
  city management 133m
  cultural institutions 98–99m
  employment 130
  homeless 122m
  housing affordability 126m
  housing segregation 162–163m
  metropolitan area 10m
  racial composition 76m
  sex orientation bias ban 174m
  water fluoridation 154
Louisiana *see also specific topics (e.g., elections)*
  Acadians 40
  African-Americans 58, 76m
  Cajuns 40, 140
  cancer 140
  Catholics 73
  city management 133m
  cultural institutions 99m
  and David Duke 172
  dialects 78
  Hispanics 67
  homeless 122m
  housing segregation 162–163m
  minority mayors 113m
  population 9m
  privacy right statutes 178–179m
  sex orientation bias ban 174m
  singles 23
  Spanish acquisition 40
  venereal disease 146–147m
Louisville (Kentucky) 10m, 122m
Love, William T. 85
Love Canal (New York) 85
Loving County (Texas) 17
low-birthweight babies
  and cigarettes 151
  mortality rate for 149
  and teenage pregnancy 158
Lowell, Robert 150
lung cancer 140–142m
  and cigarettes 151
  and radon 84
Lutherans 73m

Austrian 38
as Christian denomination 73–74
Finnish-Americans 46
German 37
in North Central states 72
Norwegian-Americans 45
Slovak 52
and smoking 142
Swedish 43
Lynchburg (West Virginia) 162m
Lynwood (California) 76m

M

Macao 47
Macon (Georgia) 76m
Maddox, William S. 117
Madeira 47
Madison (Wisconsin)
  cultural institutions 99m
  housing segregation 163m
  physicians 152m
  sex orientation bias ban 174m
Madison County (Idaho) 19
Maine *see also specific topics (e.g., elections)*
  French-speaking settlers 40
  population 9m
  1992 presidential election 114
  privacy right statutes 178–179m
Malamud, Bernard 176
Malden (Massachusetts) 174m
male dominance 31
males *see* men
management
  of cities/states 133m
  jobs held by women/minorities 8, 160g–161m
Manhattan
  never-marrieds 24
  population density 12
  settlement of 41
  skyscrapers 94
manufacturing 131–132m
  labor unions 129
  working mothers in 18
Maritime Provinces (Canada) 40
Marquesas Islands 70
marriage
  interracial 8
  never-marrieds 24–25gm
  poverty level 120g, 121
  of priests 55
  35 and over 24–25gm
  two-parent families with children 16gm
Marshall (Minnesota) 174m
Maryland *see also specific topics (e.g., elections)*
  affluent families 124
  African-Americans 58m, 76m
  anti-Semitic crimes 171m
  Arab-Americans 57m

Dutch 41
German immigration 37
handgun murders 168
Hispanics 66–67
homeless 122m
housing segregation
162–163m
lung cancer 142
minority mayors 113m
Mormons 74
never-marrieds 24
Norwegians 43
nuclear plant safety 89m
population 9m
1992 presidential election 114
privacy right statutes
178–179m
sex orientation bias ban 174m
singles 23
telephones 127
toxic waste dumps 85
venereal disease 147m
water fluoridation 153
Niagara Falls (New York) 85
Nicaragua
arms imports 191m
U.S. military intervention
193m–194
Nicholas I, Czar 50
Nigeria 58
nitrate deposition 83m
nitric acid 83
nitrogen dioxide 80
nitrous oxide
in acid rain 83
and global warming 81
Nobel Prize for Literature 150
nonsmokers 84
nonwhites *see also specific ethnic*
group (e.g., African-Americans)
abortion 156
cancer 143–144m
congressional redistricting
106–107m
coronary heart disease 138
hatred of 172
stroke 139
suicide 148
Norco (Louisiana) 163m
Norfolk (Virginia)
homeless 122m
housing segregation 162m
lung cancer 142
metropolitan area 10m
naval base 190m
venereal disease 147m
North, the *see also specific region*
(e.g., Northeast); state name
(e.g., Maine)
African-Americans 58
lung cancer 142
regional dialects 78
voter participation 105
North American Free Trade
Agreement (NAFTA) 182

Northampton County
(Pennsylvania) 174m
North Atlantic region 96
North Atlantic Treaty
Organization (NATO) 190
North Carolina *see also specific*
topics (e.g., elections)
African-Americans 58
congressional redistricting
106m
cultural institutions 99m
homeless 122m
housing segregation
162–163m
language statute 180m
minority mayors 113m
nuclear plant safety 89m
physicians 152m
population 9m
privacy right statutes
178–179m
sex orientation bias ban 174m
working mothers 18
North Central states
Lutherans 72
never-marrieds 25
regional dialects 78
North Dakota *see also specific*
topics (e.g., elections)
language statute 180m
population 9m
population loss 13
privacy right statutes
178–179m
school dropouts 27
singles 23
wind-powered electricity 90
Northeast *see also state name*
(e.g., Connecticut)
breast cancer 140, 142–143
Catholics 73
college graduates 26
cost of living 121
Greek-Americans 49
housing affordability 126
Lithuanian-Americans 53
manufacturing jobs 131
oil dependence 88
poverty 121
regional dialects 78
violent crime 166
Northern Ireland (Ulster) 31, 35
North Korea
arms imports 191m
nuclear weapons 192
U.S. war with 193
North Vietnam 193
Norwegian-Americans 8, 43–45m
NOW *see* National Organization
for Women
nuclear plants 8, 89m
nuclear proliferation 192m
Nuclear Regulatory Commission
(NRC) 89
nuclear weapons 192

O
Oakland (California)
cultural institutions 99m
homeless 122m
metropolitan area 10m
minority mayors 113m
sex orientation bias ban 174m
Oak Park (Illinois) 174m
Ocala (Florida) 152m, 162m
Occidental Chemical Company
85
Occupational Health and Safety
Act of 1970 179
Of Mice and Men (John
Steinbeck) 176
Ohio *see also specific topics (e.g.,*
elections)
anti-Semitic crimes 171m
cancer 143
city management 133m
cultural institutions 98–99m
divorce 20
homeless 122m
housing segregation 163m
manufacturing 132
minority mayors 113m
population 9m
privacy right statutes 179m
school dropouts 27
sex orientation bias ban 174m
singles 23
oil *see* petroleum
Oklahoma *see also specific topics*
(e.g., elections)
cultural institutions 99m
homeless 122m
housing segregation
162–163m
minority mayors 113m
Native Americans 71
never-marrieds 25
physicians 152m
population 113
privacy right statutes
178–179m
West-Indian-Americans 69
Oklahoma City (Oklahoma)
city management 133m
cultural institutions 99m
homeless 122m
housing segregation 163m
metropolitan area 10m
Old Northwest *see* North-Central
states
old people *see* elderly
Olympia (Washington)
162–163m, 174m
Omaha (Nebraska) 10m, 122m
One Hundred Years of Solitude
(Gabriel García Márquez) 176
O'Neill, Eugene 150
one-party rule 102–103m
Ontario (Canada) 84
opera companies 98m

oral cancer 143
orchestras 98m
Oregon *see also specific topics*
(e.g., elections)
city management 133m
cultural institutions 99m
homeless 122m
housing segregation
162–163m
minority mayors 113m
nuclear plant safety 89m
population 9m
privacy right statutes
178–179m
sex orientation bias ban 174m
water fluoridation 154
Organization of American States
(OAS) 194
Orlando (Florida)
cultural institutions 99m
metropolitan area 10m
minority mayors 113m
Orthodox Judaism 75
ovarian cancer 143
Oxnard (California)
African-Americans 76m
housing segregation
162–163m
miniority mayors 113m
ozone 80

P
Pacific states *see* West Coast
pacifism 31
PACs *see* political action
committees
Pakistan 191m, 192
Palo Alto (California) 174m
Panama 193m
pancreatic cancer 143, 151
paper industry 142
Parker, Dorothy 150
particulates 80
party bosses 104
Passaic County (New Jersey)
162m
pasteurization 136
patents 128m
patient-physician confidentiality
179
Pearl Harbor (Hawaii) 61, 190m
penicillin 147
Pennsylvania *see also specific*
topics (e.g., elections)
anti-Semitic crimes 171m
cancer 143
city management 133m
cultural institutions 98–99m
employment 130
equal rights legislation 159
German immigration 37
Haitian-Americans 69
homeless 122m
housing segregation

162–163m
manufacturing jobs 132
minority mayors 113m
naval base 190m
nuclear plant safety 89m
population 9m
privacy right statutes
178–179m
sex orientation bias ban 174m
Swiss 38
Pentacostalists 34
Pentagon 190–190n
People for the American Way
175–176
Pepsi-Cola 134
peptic ulcers 151
peripheral vascular disease 151
Perot, Ross 114–115m
Persian Gulf
1991 congressional war vote
182, 184m
1987 U.S. intervention 193m
U.S. policy in 190
personal income 126
personnel files 179m
Peru 191m
petroleum
field workers 25
as home heating fuel 88m
imported 90
industrial lung cancer rate
142
for power plants 83
Philadelphia (Pennsylvania)
city management 133m
cultural institutions 98–99m
employment 130
Haitian-Americans 69
homeless 122m
housing segregation 162m
manufacturing jobs 132
metropolitan area 10m
naval base 190m
sex orientation bias ban 174m
Philippines 60
Phoenix (Arizona)
city management 133m
cultural institutions 99m
homeless 122m
housing segregation 163m
sex orientation bias ban 174m
physicians
patient confidentiality 179
scarcity/surplus 152m
Pilgrims 92
Pinochet Ugarte, Augusto 194
Pittsburgh (Pennsylvania)
cultural institutions 98–99m
employment 132
homeless 122m
metropolitan area 10m
minority mayors 113m
sex orientation bias ban 174m
Plains states see also specific
region (e.g., Upper Plain states);

state name (e.g., Iowa)
chemical exposure 142
elderly 15
lung cancer 142
radiation 142
regional dialects 78
young people 15
polar bears 82
Polish-Americans 50m
compared with Czech-
Americans 51
compared with Scandinavian-
Americans 45
and farming 51
language 77
religion of 73
Polish Catholics 73
political action committees (PACs)
104, 108g
political corruption 8
political parties 116–117m
campaign spending
102–104m
differences 112g
ideology 109–11m
politics 102–117m
pollution see environment and
pollution
polychlorinated biphenols 85
Polynesians 70
Pomona (California) 76m
poor people see poverty
popular culture 134
population 12–27m
centers of 13
change 13gm
college graduates 26gm
density 12m
divorce rate 20gm
English-American 34
families headed by women
17gm
fertility rate 19gm
limitation 96
mobility 14gm
Native-American 71
never-marrieds 24–25gm
school dropouts 27m
singles 22–23m
by state 9m
two-parent families 16gm
widows and widowers 21gm
working mothers 18gm
young and old 15gm
populism 116–117
in Congress 116–117m
and Democrats 109
Portland (Oregon) 163m
city management 133m
cultural institutions 99m
homeless 122m
metropolitan area 10m
sex orientation bias ban 174m
water fluoridation 154
Portsmouth (Virginia) 113m

Portugal 75
Portuguese-Americans 47m
potato famine 35
Poughkeepsie (New York) 163m
Pound, Ezra 150n
poverty 120–121gm, 127
and crime 166
in families headed by women
17, 120g
future of 194
and taxes 125
and telephones 127
and working mothers 18
power plants 83, 89m–90m
pregnancy, teenage 158gm
Presbyterian Church (USA) 74
Presbyterians
British-American 34
Korean-American 63
Scottish 31
presidential election (1964) 102
presidential election (1992)
electoral/popular vote
114–115m
voter participation 105m
prison
blacks in 25
life sentences 187m
Privacy Act of 1974, U.S. 178
privacy rights 173–174, 178–179
arrest records 178–179m
bank records 179
constitutional 173
consultations with clergy
179m
consultations with
psychologists 179
employee drug testing 178m
future of 194
legislation 178–179m
library records 178m
medical records 179
Professional Air Traffic
Controllers Organization
(PATCO) 129
property crime 166–167gm
prostate cancer 143
prostitution 146
Protestant churches 74m
Protestants 74
British-American 34
Czech-American 51–52
drinking 150
Dutch 41
fundamentalist 159
Hungarian 56
immigrants 35
Irish 9, 35
Portuguese-American 47
Scotch-Irish 35
in Southwest 73
Providence (Rhode Island) 10m,
162m
Provo (Utah) 162m
Prussia 53

and Poland 50
and Schleswig 45
psychologists 179
Public Citizen 89
public schools see schools
Puerto Rican-Americans 66m
Puerto Rico 166, 190m
Pullman (Washington) 174m
purchasing power
of average worker 123m
of teachers 177m
Puritans
dialect 78
immigration 31
religion 74

Q

Quakers
dialect 78
migration 31
Quayle, Dan 181
Quebec (Canada) 40
Queens County (New York) 12

R

Rabat (Morocco) 190m
racial groups 9, 30m
Radelet, Michael L. 170
radiation 142
radon 84m
railroad towns 59
rainfall 81
Raleigh (North Carolina)
cultural institutions 99m
homeless 122m
metropolitan area 10m
physicians 152m
sex orientation bias ban 174m
random drug testing 178m
ratings
congressional environmental
programs 96–97m
state environmental programs
195m
Reading (Pennsylvania) 162m
Reagan, Ronald W. 129
reapportionment, congressional
107
rectal cancer 143
red blood cells 139
Redding (California) 162m, 164
reelections 105
Reformed Church 37
Reformed Church of Hungary 56
Reform Judaism 75
regional dialects see dialects
religion 72–75m
of British-Americans 34
Christian denominations 73m
church membership 72m
data on 9
dissidents 38
and divorce 20

56–60m, 62–64m, 68m
Russian-Americans 54m
sex orientation bias ban 174m
skyscrapers 94
venereal disease 146–147m
West Indian-Americans 68m
Washington (state) *see also*
specific topics (*e.g.,* elections)
housing segregation
162–163m
waste recycling 95
water
fluoridation 153–154m
management 96
purification 136
Watergate scandal 103–104
Watertown (New York) 174m
Wausau (Wisconsin) 163m
Weinberg, Daniel J. 162, 164n
welfare *see* poverty
Welsh-Americans 31, 33m, 34
Wesley, John 74
West, the *see also specific region*
(*e.g.,* Midwest); *state name*
(*e.g.,* Wyoming)
English ancestry 3
population mobility 14
regional dialects 78
West-Central states
regional dialects 78
telephones 127
working mothers 18
West Coast *see also state name*
(*e.g.,* California)
affluent families 124
Chinese-Americans 59
college graduates 26
cost of living 121
divorce 20
employment 129
illegal drugs 165
Japanese-Americans 61
lung cancer 142
never-marrieds 24
poverty 121
purchasing power and average
salary 123
regional dialects 78
singles 22
Western Europe 190–190n
Western states *see* West, the

West Germany *see* Germany
West Hollywood (California)
174m
West-Indian Americans 68–69m
West Palm Beach (Florida)
AIDS 145m
cultural institutions 99m
housing segregation 162m
metropolitan area 10m
sex orientation bias ban 174m
West Virginia *see also specific*
topics (*e.g.,* elections)
cigarettes 151
population 9m
population loss 13
privacy right statutes 178m
Wharton, Edith 150n
White, Byron 173
white men *see also* men
cancer 140–143m
coronary heart disease 138gm
mayors 113
stroke 139m
syphilis 146
whites
AIDS 145g
cancer 140–144m
census data 8–9
college graduates 26
and crime 167
Cuban-Americans as 66
death rates 136gm
drinking 150
executions 170
gonorrhea 147
homeless 122
infant mortality 149g
men *see* white men
against Native-Americans 71
never-marrieds 24
poverty 121g, 127
Puerto Rican classification 66
school dropouts 27
stroke 139m
suicide 148
telephones 127
as top racial group 30
women *see* white women
white women *see also* women
cancer 140–144m
fertility 19g

head of families 17
job equality 160m
syphilis 146
Wichita (Kansas) 10m, 122m
widows and widowers 21gm
as family heads 17
singles shortage 22
Willkie, Wendell 109
Wilmington (Delaware) 76m,
99m
metropolitan area 10m
windmills 90
wind-powered electricity 90m
Winston-Salem (North Carolina)
113m
Wisconsin 46 *see also specific*
topics (*e.g.,* elections)
cultural institutions 98–99m
homeless 122m
housing segregation
162–163m
minority mayors 113m
physicians 152m
population 9m
privacy right statutes
178–179m
sex orientation bias ban 174m
"woman's right to choose" 182
women *see also* white women
abortion 156–157, 182
cancer 142–144m
census undercount 9
cigarettes 142, 151
college graduates 26
coronary heart disease 138
drinking 150
families headed by 17gm
farm wives 18
fertility 19gm
homeless 122
in-two parent families 16
job equality 160g, 161m
management jobs 8
mayors 113m
poverty 120g
privacy rights 178
public office 194
rights movement 175
stroke 139
suicide 148
syphilis 146

textile industry 18
as widows 21
as working mothers 18gm
wood 88m
Wood, Gordon R. 78
Worcester (Massachusetts) 162m,
174m
work ethic 18, 31
working class 48
working mothers 8, 18gm
World War I
African-American migration
58
anti-German hysteria 37
Worth County (Missouri) 21
Wright, Richard 176
Wyoming *see also specific topics*
(*e.g.,* elections)
Chinese-Americans 59
Greek-Americans 49
housing segregation 162m
Mexican-Americans 65
population 9m
population loss 13
privacy right statutes
178–179m
singles 23
size 10

Y

yellow birch trees 82
Yellow Springs (Ohio) 174m
Yemen 191m
Yiddish (language) 75
Yokasuka (Japan) 190m
York (Pennsylvania) 174m
Youngstown (Pennsylvania)
162m
youth *see* teenagers
Yuba City (California) 162–163m
Yuma (Arizona) 163m

Z

Zabinskie, Catherine 82
Zimring, Franklin E. 168
zinc 142